ALGERIA CUTS

Cultural Memory
in
the
Present

Mieke Bal and Hent de Vries, Editors

ALGERIA CUTS

Women and Representation, 1830 to the Present

Ranjana Khanna

STANFORD UNIVERSITY PRESS
STANFORD, CALIFORNIA

Stanford University Press
Stanford, California
© 2008 by the Board of Trustees of the Leland Stanford Junior University.
All rights reserved.
No part of this book may be reproduced or transmitted in any form or by any means, electronic or mechanical, including photocopying and recording, or in any information storage or retrieval system without the prior written permission of Stanford University Press.
Printed in the United States of America on acid-free, archival-quality paper

Library of Congress Cataloging-in-Publication Data
Khanna, Ranjana, 1966-
  Algeria cuts : women and representation, 1830 to the present / Ranjana Khanna.
    p. cm.--(Cultural memory in the present)
  Includes bibliographical references and index.
  ISBN 978-0-8047-5261-9 (cloth : alk. paper)--ISBN 978-0-8047-5262-6 (pbk. : alk. paper)
    1. Women--Algeria--Political activity. 2. Women--Algeria--Social conditions. 3. Women's rights--Algeria--History. I. Title.

HQ1791.5.K43 2007
305.48'892765--dc22   2007026788

Typeset by Bruce Lundquist in 11/13.5 Adobe Garamond

For Mona,
"My sister, if you are not asleep, I beg you, before the sun rises,
to tell me one of your charming stories."

Contents

List of Figures xi
Preface xiii
Acknowledgments xix

Introduction: The Living Dead 1

PART I. THEORIZING JUSTICE

1. Frames, Contexts, Community, Justice 31
2. The Experience of Evidence:
   Language, the Law, and the Mockery of Justice 68

PART II. MELANCHOLIC REMAINDERS

3. *The Battle of Algiers* and *The Nouba of the Women*:
   From Third to Fourth Cinema 103
4. *Women of Algiers in Their Apartment*:
   Trauma, Melancholia, and Nationalism 139

PART III. ALGERIA BEYOND ITSELF

5. Latent Ghosts and the Manifesto:
   Baya, Breton, and Reading for the Future 173
6. "Araby" (*Dubliners*) and *A Sister to Scheherazade*:
   Women's Time and the Time of the Nation 211

Afterword 237

Notes 245
Index 295

Figures

I.1	Makam Al-Shahid, Algiers (The Martyrs' Monument)	19
I.2	Cimetière arabe	23
1.1	Photograph of Jacques Derrida, age three	32
1.2	Zineb Sedira, "Don't do to her what you did to me!," still from video installation	63
1.3	Zineb Sedira, "Don't do to her what you did to me!," still from video installation	64
1.4	Zineb Sedira, "Don't do to her what you did to me!," still from video installation	64
1.5	Zineb Sedira, "Quatre générations de femmes," installation	66
1.6	Zineb Sedira, "Quatre générations de femmes," installation detail	67
1.7	Zineb Sedira, "Quatre générations de femmes," installation detail	67
3.1	Still from Gillo Pontecorvo, *The Battle of Algiers*	115
3.2	Still from Gillo Pontecorvo, *The Battle of Algiers*	119
3.3	Still from Gillo Pontecorvo, *The Battle of Algiers*	119
3.4	Still from Assia Djebar, *La Nouba des Femmes du Mont Chenoua*	127
4.1	Eugène Delacroix, *Femmes d'Alger dans leur appartement* (1834)	141
4.2	Eugène Delacroix, *Femmes d'Alger dans leur appartement* (1849)	141

4.3	Pablo Picasso, *Femmes d'Alger dans leur appartement* (December 29, 1954)	156
4.4	Pablo Picasso, *Femmes d'Alger dans leur appartement* (January 1, 1955)	156
4.5	Pablo Picasso, *Femmes d'Alger dans leur appartement* (January 24, 1955)	157
4.6	Pablo Picasso, *Femmes d'Alger dans leur appartement* (February 14, 1955)	157
4.7	Pablo Picasso, *Femmes d'Alger dans leur appartement* (December 13, 1954)	158
4.8	Houria Niati, *No to the Torture*, mixed media installation (1983–1996)	167
5.1	Baya Mahieddine, *Mère au bouquet* (1945)	174
5.2	Baya Mahieddine, *Femme bleue à l'oiseau* (1945)	178
5.3	Hélène Smith, *Text no. 18* (October 10, 1897) in Théodore Flournoy, *From India to the Planet Mars*	185
5.4	Hélène Smith, "Martian Landscape," in Théodore Flournoy, *From India to the Planet Mars*	189
5.5	"Plate 32: So That the Angle of the Head Can Be Varied," in André Breton, *Nadja* (1960)	193
5.6	"Plate 29: The Lovers," in André Breton, *Nadja* (1960)	195
5.7	Baya Mahieddine, *Au bord de la rivière* (1945)	197
5.8	Baya Mahieddine, *Femme et oiseau en cage* (1946)	197
5.9	Baya Mahieddine, *Deux femmes jouant de la musique* (1974)	208
5.10	Baya Mahieddine, *Femmes pourtant des coupes* (1966)	208

Preface

The immediate provocation for writing this book came from my sense of horror at the recent war against civilians in Algeria, and at how women have been affected by what some have referred to as a particularly "virile war."[1] Systematic collective rape, kidnapping, and murder of women are common in all wars, of course; the current war in Algeria is no exception. Such incidents are rarely reported, however, or given adequate attention in the media, either within Algeria or outside. The work of a few feminist reporters—notably Salima Tlemçani, Salima Ghezali, and Ghania Mouffok in Algeria—has been exceptional in this regard.[2] What is also striking in Algeria is the way in which feminists, and others who correctly or incorrectly have been viewed as "westernized," have been singled out for persecution in the war against civilians that has been waged since 1992. In the 1960s and even into the 1970s, Algeria set itself up as the avant-garde third-world nation that had effectively rid itself of the imperial machine and was working on an Islamic socialist model to build the state in a manner that would value the work done by men and women alike during the war of independence. It was only in the early 1980s that women's access to public space began to be severely curtailed, with the institution of the 1984 Family Code, which clearly made women legally into citizens of a different class who would have to seek permission from men in the family to do things previously considered to be part of everyday life. The Family Code was significantly amended, but not abrogated, by President Abdelaziz Bouteflika in February 2005.

My commitment to a transnational—or perhaps more appropriately, a new internationalist—feminism demanded that I consider what had gone so wrong in Algeria, and also what structures of violence have shaped women's lives in the colonial and postcolonial period in Algeria. Focusing on both the colonial relationship between France and Algeria and the neocolonial situation of Algeria in the era of globalization, my research on Algeria has encountered ethical and scholarly problems arising from the corrupt colonial history of protofeminism in cross-border analyses. But a commitment to the idea that justice cannot be sought unless done so on an international scale caused me to start writing about Algeria in spite of claims of limitations that could (with some justification) be leveled against me from a nativist angle. My focus on Algeria derived from an interest in a kind of feminism that could reach across borders—indeed, from a feminism that would not deserve that name unless it had some global reach.

In recent years, much research has been conducted on colonialism and how its historical narrative has to be revised in the light of postcolonial societies. Competing historical accounts suggest alternative positions on women in nationalist histories. *Algeria Cuts* assesses the ways in which figures of woman have critically cut into the construction of these nationalist stories of the past, thus demonstrating, in the interstices, an engendering of the pursuit of justice, both material and imagined. By analyzing how national cohesion is simultaneously sustained and broken down through conceiving a shared history, an inassimilable ethical remainder can be perceived. The concept of "shared history" involves more than the power of institutional molding of groups. It also involves psychical investment in the idea of ethical responsibility to the group. *Algeria Cuts* provides a way of understanding how the shift away from group identification toward critical identification paradoxically engenders the pursuit of justice. The critical apparatus I have employed involves resistance to the idea that identity is formed through empathetic relation to others within a group, particularly when empathy involves projective identification. The book instead looks to and develops the idea of *critical identification* and the *refusal of identification*. I argue that it is this breakdown of assimilative identification that provides a critical agency in pursuit of justice.

Each of the chapters considers, through different media, what it means to write as a response to injustice performed on others and in the interest of achieving justice for others. Each also addresses forms of responsibility appropriate to feminism as it acts across borders to try to listen to the damage done by persons, events, or manifestations at and beyond those borders. The philosophical, literary, fine art, filmic, legal, and policy examples that make up the book provoke questions about representational politics and about the forms of women's political reasoning that cause damage to the masculinist frames currently dominating world politics. More pointedly, it considers how the figure of woman cuts into the masculinist frame of the Franco-Algerian relationship and manifests itself in the works discussed.

Algeria Cuts represents an interest in three periods of Algerian history: the period of French colonialism (1830–1962), the Algerian Revolutionary War of Independence (1954–1962) and the intriguing role women played in it, and contemporary Algeria and the feminist issues that have arisen there, where feminists, once strong and respected figures, have recently been singled out for persecution by both religious fundamentalists and the state (1962 to the present). The manner in which the imagined construct of the nation and the figure of woman that emerges alongside it has material consequences is a core concept of the book.

Given the cultural forms employed to elaborate the argument of this book, I propose a model of national history as developed through culture. Rather than construct a national history out of cultural enunciation, or indeed reduce culture to politics, economics, and history, my aim is to understand cultural artifacts as an "acting out" of national identities in their complex relationship to context.[3] My concern is to elaborate how individuated histories are imagined in the force field of the nation and in the context of colonial conceptions of the past through cultural artifacts. It is also to understand how the national force field creates supplements and how those supplements manifest themselves, and damage, or *cut through*, the frame.

I have studied a variety of cultural artifacts to demonstrate the three phases of this complex relationship between France and Algeria. For the first phase, which spans the early years of French colonial rule, I include Delacroix's *Femmes d'Alger dans leur appartement* (1834 and 1849) and early French colonial documents on assimilation. The second phase of colonial history I address is the 1930s to the 1960s, that is, from modernism to the early years of Algerian independence, when Algeria attempted to conceive itself as an entity separate from France, and France struggled with separation. The artifacts from this period include surrealist and neorealist work ranging from Breton's *Manifeste des 121* (1960), which protested the treatment of Algerians by the French during the war, and the *First Surrealist Manifesto* (1924), both of which blur the distinction between cultural artifacts and *realpolitik*. Also included are analyses of the paintings of Baya and Picasso's *Femmes d'Alger dans leur appartement*, and narratives of torture by Algerian women, including legal testimony, mock trials, and Pontecorvo's film *The Battle of Algiers*, which, in keeping with a neorealist style, presents us with a fictionalized documentary. For the third and final phase, the period following independence, in which the nation-states were separate yet struggled with the politics of separation and the deferred effects of hybridity, I consider the books and films of well-known Algerian Francophone writer, filmmaker, and historian Assia Djebar and other contemporary films on and from Algeria, and mock and real trials. Interspersed throughout the book is a reading of the current work of "French" or "Franco-Maghrebi" scholars working through their *nostalgérie* while Algeria has been split apart in civil war.

The book is divided into three sections. "Theorizing Justice" dwells on the ways in which a theoretical notion of justice emerges in the Franco-Maghrebi context. This includes chapters on Derridean notions of justice, and on mock and real trials in Algeria. The second section, "Melancholic Remainders," explores the legacy of Pontecorvo's *Battle of Algiers* and Delacroix's *Women of Algiers in Their Apartment* to reveal how the figure of woman challenges notions of representational politics and restitution. The final section, "Algeria Beyond Itself," is organized around the paintings of Baya and the writings of Assia Djebar in a comparative frame that questions comparison by thinking through mutual constitution. These two final chapters of the book take the questions raised by the figure of woman in the Franco-Algerian context beyond that site of mutual constitution and conflict in order to parochialize surrealism and modernism respectively, but also to provide a means of understanding modernist ideas of the international from the global periphery, as a cut into its dominant framework. The final section questions the space of the nation as an exclusively determining framework.

Algeria Cuts conceives of the relationship between individualized imagining and group formation in terms of history and memory, and in terms of conceptions of the past that seek to understand how the passing of a historical moment, framed as it is through global and local politics and economics, is introduced into the cultural imagination of the citizens or subjects of an artificial group such as the nation-state. One way of imagining the relationship to the past, the function of which is to sustain a cohesive group into the future, has been through the concepts of mourning and melancholia. I argue that early models of the French nation-state required that the national subject be in a mournful relationship to the history of the state. In such a relationship, a series of events are worked through and remembered as forgotten, as Ernest Renan would formulate it, and successfully introjected into the national self. These *cuts* through Algerian history on my part focus on the inassimilable, the barely incorporated, and the melancholic traces that in turn cause damage to the force field of mournful national history that fails to introject them. In my readings, a focus on the figure of woman allows for a different political reason to emerge, one that cuts through the force fields that allow for injustice, looks to the future, and allows for the emergence and pursuit of justice. The conceptual weight of the *cut, couper,* or *coupure* is primarily Anglophone and Francophone in this project. Given the politics of language in Algeria, I hope the book will be cut through with the Arabic قطع or قص, or the Tamazight *anegzum* or *gzem*, or with the appropriate words in Kabyle, Chaoui, Chenoua, Hassaniya, or other languages whenever necessary.

With this focus on justice, Algeria ultimately becomes more and perhaps less than its history because it ultimately cannot be seen in this book only as an ontology. Algeria becomes the occasion for thinking about different forms of knowledge production, and my intellectual investment in Algeria also becomes philosophical. How metropolitan *epistemes* were written out of their relationship to colonies emerges as one of the foci of the project, particularly how conceptions of alterity (in abstract as well as in political categorizations of the foreign and the female) were theorized coterminous with, but in silence about, coloniality. Questioning the frames within which philosophical questions were posed clarifies the implications of understanding some "French theories" as *Franco-Maghrebi* theories shaped through the complicated history of decolonization from France faced by the countries of the Maghreb region. To some extent, this questioning foregrounded the shortcomings of accounts that neglected the context, pretext, subtext, and discipline of colonialism and decolonization in recent intellectual developments. But what also emerged was the necessity of a theory of the inadequacy of causality, biography, and foundationalism as ways of accounting for the production of certain forms of knowledge. The introduction and first chapter of the book lay out, and subsequent chapters expand on, how deconstructive reading techniques produced through the years of Algerian decolonization are particularly pertinent in the work of pursuing justice internationally, and are accountable to the history of decolonization, its psychical as well as its historical impact, and its reshaping of the world's subjects.

Acknowledgments

There are many people to thank for their assistance in the research for this book, and for their intellectual engagement and friendship. I spent a semester as a Rockefeller fellow at the University of Rochester's Susan B. Anthony Center for Women's Studies, where I started researching Algerian film. I thank everyone who was part of my brief stay in Rochester for their hospitality and comments. Sarah Apple, Lisa Cartwright, Douglas Crimp, Elizabeth Ezra, Brian Goldfarb, John Michael, Tom DePiero, and Sharon Willis made my stay there particularly memorable. A year at Cornell's Society for the Humanities saw a chapter on torture come to fruition. At Cornell I would particularly like to thank Anne Berger and Jim Siegel for their kindness and generosity, and for thinking I had something important to say about Algeria. Anne Berger was kind enough to invite me to present at two conferences about Algeria, from which I learned a great deal. Cornell's particularly intense intellectual environment was added to by conversations with Brett de Bary, Assia Djebar, Salah Hassan, Dominick LaCapra, Tim Murray, and Hortense Spillers. Satya Mohanty's skeptical questions were particularly useful. My time there was greatly enriched for me by dear friends, interlocutors, and colleagues Mieke Bal, Natalie Melas, Ramez Elias, Mitchell Greenberg, Marie-Claire Vallois, and Eleanor Kaufman. At Duke, thanks go to many sustaining friends and colleagues, including David Aers, Ian Baucom, Tina Campt, Alberto Moreiras, Negar Mottahedeh, Diane Nelson, Fredric Jameson, Charlie Piot, Teresa Vilaros, Priscilla Wald, Robyn Wiegman, and Susan Willis. My writing partner Carol Mavor has given me immense help and has read many drafts of the manuscript.

Many have helped with specific chapters of the book, including Joyce Goggin and Michael Burke at the Amsterdam School of Cultural Analysis. Thanks also go to the image librarians at the Louvre; to Monsieur

Bouchouchi at the Centre Culturel Algérien in Paris; to the staff at the Musée des Beaux Arts in Algiers; to Martine Delacombre, Mme Fleuri, and the other helpful staff at I.N.A. in Paris; and to Tamara Fernando, for her research on the concept of the mock trial. Deborah Cherry gave very helpful comments on art history questions, particularly for the chapter on Baya. My research assistant in the final stages of this book, Sarah Lincoln, has been incredibly helpful and organized. I am very grateful to Hussein Elkhafaifi and Lisa White for allowing me to attend their Arabic classes. I am also grateful for the time I spent in the seminars of the Franco-Maghrebi intellectuals Hélène Cixous and Jacques Derrida when I was the recipient of an Erasmus scholarship in Paris. Parts of this book have been presented at the University of California Los Angeles, the University of Virginia, Boston College, Cornell University, the University of Rochester, the University of Utah, the University of Washington, Duke University, the Amsterdam School for Cultural Analysis, and the Nordic Summer School. Versions of some of the chapters have been published elsewhere.[1]

The generous support of Rob Sikorski and the Center for International Studies, and of Ebrahim Moosa and the Center for Muslim Networks, both at Duke University, made it possible for this book to include so many beautiful images. I am extremely grateful that they understood how much the book needed the images—indeed, how it would be impossible for it to exist without them.

My father, Shyam Khanna, as well as Mona, Sunil, Aditya, Shefali, Dorai, Srimathi, Seetu, Krishna, and Aditi, continue to maintain a sense of calm in my life, partly because of their very different approaches to it. Many thanks to Srinivas Aravamudan for his continued enthusiasm, sparkle, incisiveness, clarity about the important things in life, sense of humor, and patience.

ALGERIA CUTS

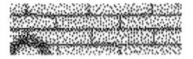

Introduction:
The Living Dead

> No justice is exercised, no justice is rendered, no justice becomes effective nor does it determine itself in the form of law, without a decision that cuts and divides (*une decision qui tranche*). This decision of justice does not simply consist in its final form—for example, a penal sanction, equitable or not, in the order of proportional or distributive justice. It begins, it ought to begin, by right (*en droit*) or in principle, in the initiative that amounts to learning, reading, understanding, interpreting the rule, and even calculating. For if calculation is calculation, the *decision to calculate* is not of the order of the calculable, and it must not be so (*et ne doit pas l'être*).
>
> JACQUES DERRIDA, "Force of Law: The Mystical Foundation of Authority"

In 2001, Mohamed Garne, a caretaker in a French department store, was awarded compensation for a form of violence played out on him during the Algerian war of independence (1954–1962). In 2001, he was thirty-one years old. In other words, he was two years old when Algeria won its independence from France in 1962. In a landmark case hailed as the first of its kind, a French appeals court awarded him damages in the form of disability benefits and a partial military pension for three years.[1] The court acknowledged the physical and psychological trauma suffered by Garne. His mother, Kheira, had been systematically gang-raped over several months by thirty to forty French soldiers in an internment (or concentration) camp in Theniet el-Had, southwest of Algiers, in 1959, that is, in the fifth year of Algeria's eight-year war of independence. She was fourteen or fifteen at the time. When she became pregnant, the soldiers beat her repeatedly with electrical wires to try to make her abort. She did not, however, miscarry, and Mohamed was placed in an Algerian orphanage soon after he was born, scrawny and sick. Once he was separated from his mother, he did not encounter her again until a search initiated in 1988 yielded results.[2]

In 1989, when Mohamed was still living in Algeria, he found his mother. The story goes that she was living, like a ghost, in a cemetery in a district know as La Cité Cellier. In a small space between two graves, she had constructed a place to live with a tarpaulin and a door. An appropriate scene for a ghost perhaps, but for various spiritual and economic reasons, graveyard dwelling is not unusual in this era of slums within colonial cities, or indeed within the overpopulated cities of late capitalism.[3] Mohamed approached her against the advice of others in the area, including the other living dead—the other living inhabitants of the graveyard—who told him that she was mad. They referred to her as *la louve*—the she-wolf or wolf woman—alternately evoking the mother of Romulus and Remus and a prostitute (frequently referred to as *la louve*). Also suggested is the savage in a warring state of nature—*femina homini lupus*—as if that is where war could be located, as if the battle between the sexes was indeed the original battle and developed in a vacuum rather than through the instruments of coloniality's legacy of virile war.[4] The naming of Kheira as *la louve* both marks her as feminine and cuts her off from her own sex, castrated, as it were, within this narrative framework of patrilineal descent in which reproductive labor is made invisible.[5]

Kheira appeared with a hatchet, and when Mohamed pleaded that he was her son, she told him that if that were true he should take the risk of being cut and lay his head on her shoulder, which he did. The invitation to enter all that is undecideable in understanding the constituents of justice in the postcolonial state of culture occurred in that moment when she opened the possibility of understanding justice as a cut that was more than what is immediately calculable or possible to provide for in terms of compensation.

Kheira provided her son with a narrative of patrilineal descent, telling him that his father was an Algerian who died in the war. She also told him that the family would not acknowledge paternity, even though it seems no one disputed that Kheira had been married to a freedom fighter,

Bengoucha. To cut a long story short, Mohamed, like his alleged paternal family, eventually began to doubt that he knew everything about his mother's story. In 1994, against the wishes of his mother, he took the man he thought to be his paternal uncle to court in Algeria to determine his right to the family name and property. In this struggle over patrimony and patrilinearity, the "uncle," Mohamed, and the judge demanded the truth of his conception, and Kheira was subpoenaed. It was here that Kheira told the story, and according to the *Irish Times* she fainted after blurting out the truth when the judge threatened to throw her in jail if she did not reveal all. The Irish narrativization suggests that at the moment of testifying in court she lost consciousness, effectively cutting herself out of the court at the moment of telling what she had endured and witnessed. Garne's book, however, perhaps significantly, interprets a different affective response, one of Kheira's rage at the whole process to which she was being exposed.[6]

A combination of factors angered her: being forced into court against her will; being raped; being forced to confront her brother-in-law, who had denied her money owed to her as a widow and aimed to take her as a wife after the death of his brother; and being forced into a marriage with a much older man after having been effectively sold off by her own brother. That her husband had been good to her did not change her response to this fraternal betrayal. She had ultimately also been betrayed by her son, who insisted on going to court to seek a calculable finality where there was none. Finally, she had been humiliated by a legal system that had never protected her. Being itself seemed to overwhelm her.

In the courtroom, Kheira narrated her story of being discovered hiding in a tree during a bombardment. The soldiers apparently then took her to the camp in the mountains, tortured her with electricity and water, and raped her. The soldiers could not, of course, be tried, as a result of amnesty laws related to the war in Algeria that were passed as part of the Evian Accords of 1962, which stated the conditions for the end of French rule in Algeria. In 1966, 1968, and 1974, further amnesty laws protected veterans of the war on both sides, placing them in an uncomfortable complicity and preventing a great deal of research and investigation into misconduct and criminality.[7]

Mohamed Garne demanded compensation, and a war victim's pension, for what he described as his ruined life, plagued as he had been by physical and mental disabilities. The courts initially denied him this, acknowledging that his mother may have been raped but declaring that he was not a direct victim. The appeals court, however, was convinced, thanks partly to the expert testimony of a professor and army psychiatrist, Louis Crouq. Garne, he said, had suffered three forms of direct violence: as a fetus, when his mother was beaten during pregnancy; as an infant abandoned by his mother; and as a man of thirty being told by his mother that he was the product of war rape. Garne's lawyer in the case was Jean-Yves Halimi, son of the celebrated Tunisian lawyer Gisèle Halimi, with whom Garne was advised not to work.[8] She had been an outspoken critic of the activities of the French in Algeria, and indeed of U.S. involvement in Vietnam. She had represented, at the time of the Algerian war, Djamila Boupacha, an Algerian woman accused of terrorism who was tortured during the Algerian war by the French military, but charges against her were eventually dropped because of amnesty laws.[9]

Jean-Yves Halimi, on hearing the decision in the Mohamed Garne case, said, "That terrible war ended without anyone being found guilty.... (N)ow we know that it left behind at least one victim."[10] Recognizing the singularity of Mohamed's victimhood, Halimi neglected his mother's labor through his own labor for Garne and through the exclusion of maternal labor from the case. Nothing in his language acknowledged that Mohamed could be a victim by virtue of the violence done to his mother. She was not portrayed as even a secondary victim. Even though it was implicitly acknowledged that Kheira was violated, she was acknowledged only because of her son's trauma, and because, unlike Mohamed, she had no claim to French citizenship, she had no rights to a case such as her son's. The case demonstrates how the shadow figures of the war are violently cut from this pathbreaking legal finding in which the father nation, France, belatedly acknowledges its bastard son—by skipping a generation of women silenced through amnesty or madness. In the awarding of reparation from father to son, Kheira herself became incidental, the instrument of the violent reproduction of the masculinist state. In many ways, by association even the figures of more celebrated woman martyrs of the war become recognizable as cuts within the forms of legal representation described here: Djamila Boupacha (represented by Gisèle Halimi) or Djamila Bouhired (represented by and then married to the controversial though quite brilliant lawyer Jacques Vergès). These familial dramas are indeed testimony to the ways in which women become supplements—ancillary terms designating an originary lack. Even when they seem to be the focal point of representational frameworks or force fields, they frequently cut through these frameworks because they are incommensurable with them.

If, in cinematic terms, to *cut* is to splice together two shots from different time and space configurations, the cut itself is the edge that belongs neither to one frame nor to the other. Depending on how seamless the cut is, it presents either a smooth transition from one time and space frame to another, or it pierces both, indeed damages both frames, because it demonstrates its own liminality and therefore the representational structure of the frame itself. Kheira, in many ways, could be understood as the "jump cut" who disturbs, on the one hand, the representational force field of amnesty laws designed to protect perpetrators of violence on both sides of a war, and on the other, the narrative of patrilineal success that can be announced by Mohamed Garne and Jean-Yves Halimi. As a figure of the living dead, her insistent materiality foregrounds an absence in the moments of closure hailed in amnesty and reparation. Her poverty, her madness, and the fact that she is a woman make her effectively disposable within the time and space frames she splices together. She becomes the editorial matter that allows for a narrative of patrilineal trauma from which she, and women's labor, are made absent. The cut pierces the time and space configurations. It is simultaneously made absent by what is made present, and is therefore bound to its particular form of exclusion. But it is also quite singular in its difference from the framework of those particularities and its irreducibility to them. In a sense the cut involves a moment of stasis (when the hatchet hovers, if you will) within the time and space configuration of the frame, within, in fact, a patrilineal unfolding of time. This is a question explored more fully in the final chapter of the book.

Algeria Cuts analyzes such forms of cutting, interruption, impurity, and incommensurability that I see surfacing around questions about representation and women in the relationship between France and Algeria from 1830—the year the French arrived in Algiers—to the present. Roland Barthes, in his more structural phase, analyzed the mythology that, for the French, the love of a glass of red wine is a marker of virility, conviviality, and national identity. Barthes claims that the status of wine is instead "the product of an expropriation"—simply a commodity of the appropriation of land in Algeria, and the product of exploitation of the land (which could have been used for crops) and the people (who could have benefited from those crops rather than producing something that they, for the most part, would not drink).[11] Barthes' practice as a mythologist meant that his analysis would demystify and expose the alibis performed in the artificiality of denotative signs like the *ballon de rouge*, whose associations (or connotations, as he would put it) allowed for the covering up of a story of violence and expropriation. But it was in theorizations about photography and his dead mother that he highlighted the concept of cutting or piercing in the *punctum*—an experience that feels like a bruising and cutting that exists only in a subjective response to an incidental detail.[12] The work of his earlier years as mythologist confined him to what he would later call the *studium*, or an analysis of the codes, threads, or voices that combine to constitute the text. The *punctum*, on the other hand, cuts, pierces, or bruises in a way that touches more personally, providing subjective and experiential understanding that cannot be confined to the codes. Barthes did not, of course, use the language of *studium* and *punctum* until *Camera Lucida*. In this more poststructuralist phase, and in the moment of mourning his mother, Barthes was concerned precisely with what could not be represented or named exactly, even if it could be hailed. Rather like the cutting supplement, the *punctum* tells another story. Jacques Derrida, in turn, frequently returns to the question of his Algerian background by referring to his mother in particular and to the figure of the mother in general, and to contemplations of his mother's death or indeed partial death, whether in *Glas*, *Circumfessions*, or *Monolingualism of the Other*. In a variety of texts emerging from the Franco-Maghrebi philosophical tradition, a cutting incommensurability is gestured toward in relation to the dead or dying mother as a site of castration of a phallic form of representation—legal, religious, philosophical, artistic, cultural, or political. And while the cut is on one level a metaphorical cut, it nonetheless has a material quality that brings together the forms of life and death that are admissible and inadmissible within sovereign discourse.

Algeria Cuts does not reduce *woman* to *mother*, or indeed limit the term *mother* to signifying reproduction. But it questions the manner in which the new nations of colonial and postcolonial France and Algeria have come to reproduce themselves through gendered violation that continues to haunt and cut through the time and space representational frameworks in which women appear and disappear. The feminist analysis in this study, then, insists on looking at the cuts through representation, sometimes sewing them together and other times acknowledging the pertinence of the gape in such a way as to give the possibility of hope through acknowledging that very impossibility.[13] In *Algeria Cuts*, women are shown to elude and confound the dominant structures of colonial and postcolonial representation presented in art, film, literature, politics, and law—even when, and perhaps especially when, the figure of woman seems most present. In its inquiry into gendered representation, identification, and justice around objects conventionally belonging to specific disciplines—paintings, trials, novels, and manifestos—the book implicitly explores how certain questions are foreclosed by disciplinary division (in art history, law, literature, or political science) even as responsibility to those disciplines seems necessary.

In an attempt to find avenues for the pursuit of justice, *Algeria Cuts* challenges some of the ways in which disciplines have shaped themselves around configurations of time and place, that is, in their immediate context, period, and nation. So, for example, some chapters analyze different slices of history next to each other, not simply to suggest or claim historical continuity or essentialist notions of woman over time and space so much as to show how structures of marginalization function. Similarly, even as the book is unquestionably concerned with the Franco-Algerian relationship, it also looks at moments of interruption in women's narrative temporality in other colonial sites while acknowledging the spatio-temporal gap.

In turning to the question of hope for justice, my labor in this project has been to seek out, precisely in texts in which the figure of woman haunts, cuts through, and indeed exposes what Theodor Adorno called "the damaged life," moments of justice even as they seem to be elided by the mechanisms of law and language that are present and that seek compensation and closure.[14] The book does not focus on the law and the mechanisms of legal representation; indeed it attends to the distinctions between *vertreten* and *darstellen*—between representation as "acting on behalf of" and representation as "standing in for"—importantly highlighted by Karl Marx in the *Eighteenth Brumaire of Louis Bonaparte*. These distinctions are crucial in the configuration of a distinction between legal and political representation on the one hand and forms of cultural, artistic, and linguistic representation on the other. Rather, the book attempts to find those cuts that both highlight violation and present a future justice through readings of philosophical, cultural, and politico-legal texts.

8   *Introduction*

In searching out these cuts of justice in the French and Algerian relationship, I show, on the one hand, as Barthes did economically in his essay on wine, how the history of France and things French is cut through with the relation to Algeria, but on the other hand, how inadequate this analysis is to address the vicissitudes of violence in the colonial situation. This does not mean that I reject a materialist reading practice. On the contrary, my study involves both analysis of the very particularity of the Algerian situation in its materiality in terms of the forms of exception, marginalization, erasure, and amnesia that characterize it, and the moments of singularity that cannot be reduced to or indeed assimilated into any such representational framework.

Developing a feminist reading practice that dwells on these moments of interruptive cuts allows for an understanding of the processes through which women's labor is elided. It also reveals the manner in which this elision enables (sometimes through reinforcement) a structure of sexual difference that is invested in both colonial and capitalist interests. In this regard, my analysis assumes already the validity and fundamental importance of arguments by such figures as Rosa Luxemburg and Messali Hadj, both crucial thinkers on the question of capital's relation to colonialism and imperialism. My analysis also, however, seeks to traverse the terrain mapped out by them to develop, ultimately, an alternative reading practice.

So, for example, I am entirely convinced by Rosa Luxemburg's claim in *The Accumulation of Capital* that in spite of the huge upheavals in French mainland politics from 1830–1870, and in spite of the language of civilization employed as the French decried the existence of Ottoman-influenced forms of familial structure, slavery, and land ownership, the French had one purpose in mind: "[France] pursued a single aim from beginning to end; at the fringe of the African desert, it demonstrated plainly that all the political revolutions in nineteenth-century France centered in a single basic interest: the rule of a capitalist bourgeoisie and its institutions of ownership."[15] As she goes on to explain the global mechanisms of capital, Luxemburg reminds us of the practices that were being put in place worldwide. Capitalism demanded, according to her, that on a global level the bourgeoisie maintain their status only by developing the following goals: "(1) To gain immediate possession of important sources of productive forces such as land, game in primeval forests, minerals, precious stones and ores, products of exotic flora such as rubber, etc. (2) To 'liberate' labour power and to coerce it into service. (3) To introduce a commodity economy. (4) To separate trade and agriculture."[16]

My invocation of Rosa Luxemburg indicates my own desire, in this book, to understand how an analysis of imperialism such as that in Algeria's history may shed light on the possibilities of Marxist internationalism and permanent revolution. But to achieve this my readings here are designed to highlight the distinct forms of marginality that were established. While revolution must always think of the formal mechanisms of overthrow, it limits itself if it is suspicious of all content in its analysis, and the singularities that attend the established narratives of violent exclusion that continue to exist in the aftermath of revolution.

A fundamental Algerian example of this would be the exceptional laws of the infamous *Code de l'indigénat* that were in place more or less from 1870 to World War II. These laws reflected a distinct form of marginality that would come to characterize an eventual suspicion of any possibility of a just politics. They included thirty-three infractions that were not illegal under the French civil code but were illegal in Algeria when carried out by Muslims—for example, speaking disrespectfully to French officials, defaming the French Republic, traveling without a permit, begging outside of one's commune, or shooting into the air for celebrations. These laws were enforced by either the justice of the peace or the civil administrators, depending on the zone, which itself made the code distinct from that which could be enforced only by officers of the law. The Code de l'Indigénat and the forms of marginalization and division put in place at that point can be seen as echoed in the 1984 institution of the Family Code, which in principle was designed to replace colonial law (the 1916 Code Morand and the 1959 Marriage Ordinance). The Family Code instituted some forms of Shar'ia law and produced laws for women that violated family-related elements of the 1976 revised Algerian Constitution, as Marnia Lazreg has persuasively shown.[17] Similarly, Said Chikhi has argued that the unemployed and youth are social outcasts in Algeria and have become socially and culturally marginalized in the larger framework of political marginalization that is part of the civil society brought about through the deeply hierarchical structures of governance that have been in place from the early 1980s.[18] Ghania Mouffok also has suggested that this field of marginalization in which exceptional laws are created by the state is also responsible for the marginalized position of the Berbers of

Kabylia.[19] Communist Messali Hadj, secretary general of the Etoile Nord-Africaine, described this form of institutionalized marginalization, which would eventually land him in jail, in a 1928 speech:

In order to prevent us from crying out "Thief! Assassin!" imperialism gags us with the Code de l'Indigénat, a vestige of the darkest barbarism. By virtue of this code, all the violence carried out on the natives by the colonists is legitimated in advance. Theft, torture, and murder are openly encouraged, and the guilty assured of impunity.

No political rights, no freedom to assemble or to speak.

Though 98 years separate us from the conquest, we remain the hostages of the war of 1830, and the freedom to travel is parsimoniously granted us. Even under the feudal regime—which imperialism claims to have abolished—this iniquity didn't exist.

All of this under the hypocritical mask of civilization.[20]

In the Algerian context, the marginalized are rarely called the enemy or enemy-combatant. Rather, they are criminalized by these exceptional laws and structures of marginalization.[21]

*

After World War II, the exceptional status of Algerians was made clear once again. Some had thought that the promise of reform announced by De Gaulle in Constantine in 1944, which changed possibilities concerning French citizenship and ended the Code de l'indigénat, was indication of a more equal possibility for inhabitants of the three departments of France collectively known as Algeria. Others rejected De Gaulle's reforms and were less sanguine concerning what they promised. In 1945, when crowds marched in the streets demanding the release of Messali Hadj under what would become the Algerian flag on VE (Victory in Europe) Day, the army attacked, and between fifteen thousand and forty-five thousand were killed at Sétif. Many consider this to have been the spark that ignited the Algerian war of independence.[22]

During the war of independence, similarly vague figures were produced depending on the sources: 500,000 to 1,500,000 Algerians killed, 50,000 to 150,000 French killed. Amnesty laws, as I have said, prevented combatants from being tried. Amnesty laws are themselves structurally exceptional laws in that they are retroactive; result from parliamentary votes, referenda, or decrees; and are designed to prevent or stop legal action, erase sentences, and stop the pursuit of knowledge around a particular incident after a war has ended. More often than not, amnesty laws are invoked following civil wars, and indeed, because Algeria was a constitutive part of France, we can think of the war of independence as a civil war even if it was not acknowledged as such by the French. In the context of French, or Franco-Algerian, amnesty laws, referenda are usually performed to demonstrate support. Although no case can be brought against anyone, there are provisions that are rarely pursued, for third-party claims, as if justice can be performed through the exchange of money, where the calculation of money can stand in, in direct equivalence, for affect.

Nicole Loraux, in her brilliant book *The Divided City*, writes of how amnesty—the root of which is *amnestia*, or forgetting—was crucial in the formation of a notion of the political in Athens in 403 B.C. "Renouncing vengeance," she writes, "citizens call for—if not invent—amnesty . . . and this must be interpreted as constitutive of, if not a threat to, politics and political life. Divided from within and against itself, the city is formed by that which it refuses."[23] Taking this idea from Loraux, I am consistently struck in the Algerian context by that which is politically elided and cut from politics but plays itself out in the political unit of the city, occasionally writ large as the nation—in workers' rights and unemployment, in poverty, in the memorialization of martyrs of the war, and in cultural production. Loraux discusses too how the terms *stasis*—or conflict and division—and *diaphora*—or voting—provide new ways of understanding politics as conflict, and sometimes the erasure of conflict and the imperative to forget. The referendum for amnesty on the war of independence and indeed the referendum concerning the Algerian civil war introduced in Algeria on September 29, 2005, and approved by the government in February 2006 serve in many ways to force an erasure of difference, and to force mourning and reconciliation. Once again, figures of the living dead, the liminal figures who fit neither the time-and-space frame of war nor the time-and-space frame of reconciliation start to haunt and cut through these frames, revealing what was concealed or erased in the process of the reproduction of the nation-state.

In "Force of Law," Derrida points toward lawyer Jacques Vergès, who "defends the most unsustainable causes by practicing what he calls the 'strategy of rupture,' that is, the radical contestation of the given order of the law (*loi*), of judicial authority, and ultimately of the legitimate authority of the state that summons his clients to appear before the law (*loi*)."[24] Vergès cut his teeth, as it were, during the Algerian war when he defended Djamila Bouhired. When he defended his most controversial client, Klaus Barbie, he referenced the contradictions in French law to confirm its imperial hypocrisy. If the French could put Barbie on trial for atrocities committed in the 1940s, then why would they not speak to their own violations in Algeria and Indochina in the 1950s and 1960s? The case of Algeria was explicitly used by Vergès to topple France's overt relation to justice by revealing this cut or rupture that showed the remainders of the judicial system. It is within the affect initiated by this remainder that one could perhaps find a specter calling for justice. These melancholic specters, available to us only through listening to the often unspoken demands of a text, point the way toward a different future and are profoundly material.

I have leaped through these moments of exceptionality, marginality, and amnesty in order to signal telegraphically a particular Franco-Algerian form of erasure and amnesia within which I seek cuts. I am not writing of the need to narrativize that which has been forgotten or erased from history. Such a task falls to historians, and many have been doing this work in the Algerian context for some time—most notably Benjamin Stora, who has written on many aspects of history, memory, war, and women's writing in Algeria from a historian's perspective and whose work has informed much of what follows.[25] The plethora of works that have emerged in the last fifteen years, as though they were letters that had lost their way in the mail from the past, have done much to remedy the diagnosis of silence in narrative and representation.[26] Also, much material, by both French and Algerians, and by men and women, that has been produced on the trauma of and torture within the Algerian war of independence, has presented a narrative of recognition within the terms of embattled or achieved justification, reconciliation, and reparation.[27]

In *Algeria Cuts* I seek to understand how such instruments of simultaneous marginalization and exploitation occurred by analyzing how mechanisms of representation—in its broadest connotations—were played out on the figure of woman. I have begun with Kheira in order to highlight how the contemporary story of Franco-Algerian relations is cut through with questions of feminine labor, the puzzle of kinship, the relationship between the state and the family, and a patrilineal repetition of violence, elision, and amnesia that is inscribed within the law and its practices of justice distribution. Kheira, if we can ask her to carry such a burden, becomes, with her hatchet in hand, a reminder and a remainder of these repetitions of violence. And it is perhaps in the cuts through which her figure emerges that a different notion of the political could be elaborated.

But I would not want simply to make an example of Kheira, or to suggest that she is merely an example of the larger mechanisms of virile capitalism and colonialism in play. I would not, in other words, want to do what Hegel did with poor Antigone, who, like Kheira, returned to the earth, or to a tomb, refusing the familial mechanisms that may have brought her into a patrilineal existence even as she acted on behalf of the newly illegitimate son of the state.[28] But it would be equally problematic to mistake Kheira for Khora—simply, a state of liminality. Plato inscribed Khora as a feminized receptacle, a mother or a nurse who is nonetheless a nonspaced spatiality. Julia Kristeva, in *Revolution in Poetic Language*, associated the Platonic *Khora* with the pre-Oedipal and preverbal semiotic space that could nonetheless interrupt the symbolic—for example, through rhythm in poetry: "the *chora*, as rupture and articulations (rhythm), precedes evidence, verisimilitude, spatiality and temporality. . . . Neither model nor copy, the *chora* precedes and underlies figuration and thus specularization, and is analogous only to vocal or kinetic rhythm."[29] The *khora*, for Kristeva, is shaped by the symbolic but can in no way be reduced to its workings, and it becomes the site of possibility within the maternal receptacle. Luce Irigaray, in *Speculum of the Other Woman*, criticizes the way in which Plato, among others, represses the metaphorics and rhythms of women's labor, citing, for example, the *Hystera* or the cave-womb of Plato's *Republic*. The devalued and debased space of transition between the mythical and the sensible and between representation and reality is, for Irigaray, rejected because of its feminine metaphorics. If Kristeva theorized this maternal instability in ontological terms, Irigaray, seeing the cave as the metaphor for the origins of knowledge, aims to think more in terms of the epistemological loss of footing that comes from the active suppression of the feminine.

To understand Kheira's agency, it seems, would involve such epistemological cutting away of the ground on which any ontology would be based. Rather than seeing *khora* as dwelling in the maternal, as Kristeva does, Irigaray acknowledges the spatiality of Plato's original formulation of the term even as she sees it as inscribed with feminine and maternal features, even though, as Derrida reminds us, it is a third *genos* that is more than model or copy. Kheira is therefore not simply the cutting space on the margin, but attention to her allows for an understanding of the mechanisms through which representative force fields shape the *chora* as the mother, nurse, receptacle, and imprint-bearer. The labor of feminist work, then, becomes to understand how inscriptions of the feminine challenge the whole structure of being as a temporal and spatial cut within it, as well as to acknowledge the materiality of women's relation to this. Kheira is a particular woman, of course, and she also marks a place in which the figure and the essence of woman come into question. A task of feminism would then be to seek out the cuts within which the figure of woman is structured, and acknowledge a name that is not tied to patrilineal descent: Kheira Khora. Derrida writes, "The bold stroke consists here in going back behind and below the origin. . . . This necessity (*khora* is its surname) seems so virginal that it does not even have the figure of a virgin any longer. . . ."[30] The cuts within the temporal, spatial, and gendered analogies given to figurations of Khora become the site within which justice could be shown to be an impossibility within the current structures, but nonetheless a necessity.

Amnesia and the City

The apparent exemplarity of the Algeria case in understanding coloniality, postcoloniality, sovereignty, and neo-imperialism has implicitly been recently confirmed. When *The Battle of Algiers* was screened at the Pentagon in 2003, many journalists commented on how the film had been required viewing for those on the left in the late 1960s.[31] This requirement was especially true for those interested in the mechanisms of what Sartre, using Maoist terminology in the Russell War Tribunals on the war in Vietnam, called "a people's war"—a war fought on the ground by those faced with the possibility of total annihilation. According to Sartre, in the face of a much greater military force, the people inevitably resorted to a new form of war, usually including "terrorism" and "torture."[32] The forty or so Pentagon officers and civilian experts were invited, on the flier advertising the screening, to consider "how to win a battle against terrorism and lose the war of ideas. Children shoot soldiers at point blank range. Women plant bombs in cafes. Soon the entire Arab population builds to a mad fervor. Sound familiar? The French have a plan. It succeeds tactically but fails strategically. To understand why, come to a rare showing of the film."[33] Organized by a civilian-led group, the message suggested that while in Iraq today it may be tempting to use tactics similar to those used by the French forty-five years earlier, there are positives and negatives to be discerned. In the 1957 battle depicted by filmmaker Gillo Pontecorvo, of course, Algerians were fighting for independence and sovereignty in the face of a France reluctant to let go despite the length and bloodiness of the war and the loss of around one hundred thousand French lives. And the war front (unlike in Iraq today, where military camps define the front, those who fight are considered "radical insurgents" rather than combatants, and fighting beyond this front is perceived as terrorism) was particularly intimate; it was fought in the city of Algiers as a battle between the old Arab casbah and the modern French city.

It is well-known that Pontecorvo was a reader of Frantz Fanon and based much of his understanding of the women of Algiers, as depicted in the film, on Fanon's famous essay, "Algeria Unveiled."[34] It is a film, as we shall see, that has everything to do with the agency of the cut, whether cutting hair or a cut in the filmic sense. The film depicts a stark division between the settler, or European, section of the city and the casbah as described in Fanon's posthumous *The Wretched of the Earth*. The apparent exemplarity of the film and, I will suggest, of Algeria in the understanding of postcoloniality, necessitates a drawing out of many different aspects of the "return" in this film in belated fashion. What returns in the film is an excess of historical teleology that could not find rest in the political trajectory suggested in neorealist style or be unthought through comparison. The analogy drawn between Algeria and other sites of troubled civil war does not simply suggest a historical continuity among the forms of colonial or neocolonial rule that were in place. In this book I analyze the case of Algeria, and more specifically Algiers, with its legendary borrowed theorist of decolonization, Frantz Fanon, because it becomes exemplary as a site in which a certain form of sovereignty was played out and systematically engendered a melancholic remainder.

Fanon almost certainly had Algiers in mind when he wrote the following concerning colonial spatiality:

The settlers' town is a strongly built town, all made of stone and steel. It is a brightly lit town; the streets are paved with asphalt, and the garbage cans swallow all the leavings, unseen, unknown, and hardly thought about. The settler's feet are never visible, except perhaps in the sea, but there you're never close enough to see them. His feet are protected by strong shoes although the streets of his town are clean and even, with no holes or stones. The settler's town is a well-fed town, an easygoing town, its belly is always full of good things. The settler's town is a town of white people, of foreigners.

The town belonging to the colonized people, or at least the native town, the Negro village, the medina, the reservation, is a place of ill fame, peopled by men of evil repute. They are born there, it matters little where or how; they die there, it matters not where or how. It is a world without spaciousness, men live there on top of each other. The native town is a hungry town, starved of bread, of meat, of shoes, of coal, of light. The native town is a crouching village, a town on its knees, a town wallowing in the mire. It is a ton of niggers and dirty Arabs.[35]

Not having a clear architectural plan for the city or for the future, Fanon famously already bemoaned the almost inevitable failure of national culture in newly independent nation-states. Even within the context of the hopeful internationalist communism evident in the title of his book (*The Wretched of the Earth* comes from "L'Internationale," the song of the first and second communist internationals), Fanon found it difficult to imagine how a postcolonial national bourgeoisie, with its history of hunger and bad digestion, would be able to create a national culture. In spite of this hopeful investment in communist internationalism, he would of course have to acknowledge that the PCF (the French communist party), even though it had been critical of the French army's tactics in Algeria and had supported strikes resisting participation in the army, was ultimately against Algerian decolonization.

Generalizing from what he had observed in Algeria, Fanon wrote that middle-class background in poverty and hunger, the very stuff of indigestible ideological assimilation, and the squalor of years of colonial sovereignty created a situation in which it hardly mattered, and would hardly matter, where, how, and whether the colonized lived or died. The colonized people, in Fanon's reading, are utterly disposable for the settlers and the French at home. He saw them as crouching and wallowing in mire, ready, like all leavings of colonialism, to be swallowed up by the garbage cans of empire. For Fanon, the very structure of the divisive colonial city shaped the temporality of colonial and postcolonial life. It was difficult for him to find any prospect of hope, and that is precisely why this late style manifesto of decolonization is full of remainders of colonial life that beg the question of how a future could be imagined out of the degradation of contemporary colonial existence. It is most often the explicit Marxist, sometimes Sartrian, dialectical vein that is drawn out of Fanon's text, yet there is a dissonance on every level of the prose that is suggestive of the ways in which remainders will insist upon the future, and will call any already theorized form of politics into question if justice cannot be fulfilled.

The contrast between Fanon's vision of the late 1950s and early 1960s, on the one hand, and that of the classic modernist architect Le Corbusier, on the other, has rightly been remarked upon by Zeynep Çelik. Le Corbusier had extraordinary and numerous never-realized plans for Algiers. In writings spanning the years from 1930 to 1950, he depicted the city as part of a radiant block for "our machine-age civilization" in which Paris, Barcelona, Rome, and Algiers would constitute a "unit extending north to south along a meridian" and in which Algiers (though presumably still under French rule) would "cease to be a colonial city," becoming instead "the head of the African continent, a capital city."[36] Addressing the mayor as he proposed plans for the city, Le Corbusier imagined "witnesses," writing, "The 'barbarians' speak." He described the beauty and poetry of the "barbarian" Arab areas of the city and the hospitality of the domestic architecture in contrast to what he saw as the pitiable shoddiness of the modern city where Europeans live "like rats in holes":[37]

Seen from the sea, European Algiers is nothing but crumbling walls and devastated nature, the whole is a sullied block. . . . Europeans did not exploit the fortune offered to them.

The casbah of Algiers made the site: it gave the name of White Algiers to this glittering entity, that welcomes, at dawn, the boats that arrive at the harbor. Inscribed in the site, it is irrefutable. It is in consonance with nature, because from every house, from the terrace—and these terraces add on to each other like a magic and gigantic staircase descending to the sea—one sees the space, the sea.[38]

Bodies that to Fanon, who saw them in the streets and in the hospital, seem disposable and ready to be swallowed up by the French are to Le Corbusier, who sees them from the sea, resident barbarians, deeply connected to nature, able to command the space of the city as well as the Mediterranean, and willing hospitably to draw in guests. The architecture of the city suggests that, far from disposable, bodies too are irrefutable, even if they cannot be mapped.

It has been famously asserted by Benedict Anderson that print capitalism and its culture of novels, newspapers, censuses, and maps, and institutions such as museums, participate in the formation of the modern nation-state. Each of these institutions shapes people's notion of temporality and, therefore, according to Anderson, their idea of an "imagined community."[39] Drawing on Walter Benjamin's notion of "homogeneous, empty time" that is structured by the existence of the calendar and clock and that disenables us to experience a messianic sense of absolute simultaneity between past, present, and future events, Anderson suggested that the products of print capitalism allow instead for a synchronic relationality among people who exist and feel commonality with anonymous others who are reading and otherwise experiencing the same materials. Drawing on Ernest Renan's notion that a nation-state exists as a function of will, these institutions constitute the parameters within which the "daily plebiscite" of national belonging is performed. For Anderson, they create a notion of imagined community that allows one to forget the impossibility of commonality among sometimes sworn enemies. Buried in the past, these institutions can be commemorated as something remembered as forgotten, and mourned, swallowed as it were into the garbage bin of national history in favor of the new relations coming into existence. And the citizen comes into being and into human subjectivity as the author of his belonging, confident in the idea that the sovereignty of the state honors his existence. Nowhere is this more vividly felt, according to Anderson, than at memorials, or monuments to the dead and the ceremonies that surround them.[40] The monument performs the work of mourning, and hence the assimilation of the dead object into the national body, swallowed as if by a garbage can. It also celebrates a cause, demonstrating the power of the sovereign nation-state to honor its martyrs, and thereby validating the cause for which they died. While Fanon proposed that the settler colony creates divisions that will potentially be perpetuated into the future and that cannot be forgotten but will always insist that they are the remainder demanding justice, Anderson asks us to focus on how the monument becomes a single location through which to channel a process of mourning, loss, and victory. The injustices strewn throughout the city's architecture become occluded in the new focus on the palliative of the monument.

In 1982, in the period of Chadli Benjedid's unpopular presidency, when the economy of Algeria was beginning to shift from its socialist model; when concessions were given to Islamists on such important subjects as women's rights for private and public sovereignty; when corruption in the ruling party, the National Liberation Front (FLN), was at its height;

and when Berber demands were greatly suppressed, Makam al-Shahid, or the Martyr's Monument, was constructed in Algiers to celebrate, and to commemorate, twenty years of Algerian independence (see Figure I.1). The monument, with its three flamelike sides, each protected in federalist style by a massive statue of three different faces and dressed in the attire of soldiers of the revolution, dominates the landscape of Algiers. It is visible from all quarters of the city and is popularly and disparagingly known as "the banana," to which it bears a vague resemblance. In the basement of the monument is a museum of Algeria's war of independence. A tension between celebration and commemoration is evident in this monument, as is the way in which the sovereign nation-state came to elide the difference between those two functions and effectively rendered the 800 thousand to 1.5 million dead, disposable "martyrs."[41]

In 1982, many of the more progressive forms of politics theorized during and in the aftermath of the struggle for independence were being erased from collective memory, and the monument serves to commemorate the hope associated with independence as much as to commemorate the

FIGURE I.1 Makam Al-Shahid, Algiers (The Martyrs' Monument). Christine Osborne Pictures, www.copix.co.uk.

dead soldiers. The *work of mourning* materialized in the monument simulates the past in the service of political myths that serve the state. However, the boundaries of the *work*, I would suggest, are *irrefutably* unstable. Assia Djebar's book *Algerian White* mourns individuals, yet shows the generalized architecture of Algeria (invoked in the title) put to the work of mourning and death.[42] Mourning is therefore not singularly locatable in one structure, and therefore not confined to one identifiable and delimited historical event, as in Makam al-Shahid. There is a melancholic and parergonal—that is, subordinate and supplementary—excess of monumentality in reading the leavings, the uncounted, the utterly disposable as the affective expression of disidentification and critical politics in late sovereignty. Once again, the case of Algeria seems to ask why modern nation-states in general, and other emerging late sovereignties, celebrate their treatment of disposable bodies while occluding their more generalized existence within state sovereignty. Modernity's injunction to mourn is exemplified in the monument, as if to construct a palliative in which disposability can be located once and for all and buried. A melancholic reading affectively resists this injunction. It exposes that disposability as generalized to the whole populace in late sovereignty. It is located not only in Makam al-Shahid but also throughout the white of Algeria, described in the modern period from Le Corbusier to Assia Djebar. Modern divisions, whether Fanonian or of Le Corbusier, become, in postcolonial Algeria, divisions among the sovereigns and the disposable, rendered in a constant state of war.

Again, then, we arrive at *femina homini lupus*—a state of war as the state of culture rather than the state of nature. Kheira too paid tribute to the dead, but her memorial seems quite different. As the living dead, Kheira could not pay tribute with an acknowledgment of buried beings who died for the existence of Algeria. Her tribute to that past has to be read in a different light, one that refuses the romance of ontological mourning by building something that gives face to the dead or that inscribes them with a cause and a meaning. If we were going to give a counterimage of Kheira's witnessing of Algerian war and mourning and its figuration of woman, perhaps unlike Makam al-Shahid, it would have to be with a transitory object that bears the traces of state violence, familial intimacy, and the dwelling of the living dead—maybe a postcard from the past. We could imagine that it has been lost in the mail for a hundred years or so and has arrived as if addressed to someone who no longer exists or who no longer can be sure what was corresponded or communicated, so exchange has broken down. The postcard would be, of course, so much more transitional and disposable than the monument.

The Franco-Algerian postcard has been written about extensively by Malek Alloula in *The Colonial Harem*, a book dedicated to the memory of Roland Barthes, in which the author wishes to "return this immense postcard to its sender" in a gesture of postcolonial defiance.[43] The returned gaze is, for Alloula, an exorcism of sorts because, in a gesture of identification, he believes himself stared at, documented, and objectified in a relation of *scopophilia*, in which the harem becomes, in his view, a violent phantasmatic obsession and a representative of a right of viewing arrogated to the colonizer. The veil, the cut of cloth, in this scenario becomes a tantalizing marker of refusal of his gaze. Already, for Alloula, the returned glare of the photographed women becomes, indexically, defiant. Retrospectively, then, the women are called on to witness the scopophilia of the colonizer, allowing for a broader analysis of colonial eroticism.

In a somewhat different vein, the extraordinary photographs of Marc Garanger call on the photograph to bear witness of some sort. Indeed, Isaac Julien's documentary about Frantz Fanon makes use of one of Garanger's portraits as if to bear witness to the multiple violations in play in relation to Fanon's revolutionary struggle and his sexual politics. During his military service in Algeria in 1960, Garanger was asked to photograph indigenous peoples so they could be issued identity cards to restrict their movements and to monitor their collectivities. Interestingly, it was the postmaster who assisted Garanger in his task, calling up the women to lift their veils and be photographed. Garanger took about ten photographs every day over two hundred days, producing some two thousand images. It was as if the obsessive photography of Gaëtan de Clérambault, who during World War I also took thousands of images of North African veiled men and women wrapped in reams of cloth, was inverted here. If the human form was unclear in the excess of cloth presented in de Clérambault's images, Garanger's photographs, taken as they were to present an identity through a face, were called on to be read as revealing rather than obfuscating, as framed rather than exuding movement.[44]

Ultimately, Garanger wrote, he was the first to witness the protest apparent on the women's faces. He hoped that the photographs themselves bore witness to the multiple violations the women had had to bear, including being photographed, and to their defiance of legibility. It is as if they break out of the constraints of the frame offered to them by the official photographic genre and provide something that could never be predicted by the formal element of the repetitive task in which the photograph represents identity. Instead, the face, by the slightest indication of individuation, marks its own parameters of being as potential defiance. The photograph is, however, the constitution of the subject and being; it is as if prior to the moment Garanger took the photograph, the face, attached to individuated identity such as that revealed in the production of identity cards, did not exist.[45]

The postcard, however, tells another story that we could perhaps link to Kheira, who builds her home, and indeed her own monument, in the nonspace of the graveyard and refuses, in fact, the hospitality of her son. Because Alloula dedicated his book to Barthes and his *Camera Lucida*, it is perhaps worth remembering that Barthes could not reproduce the image of *The Wintergarden* he held so dear. It would perhaps be like rendering his own dead mother as if all the loss and affect around her could be depicted. The postcard, as Jacques Derrida has explored, is a very particular object. There is always a back and a front to a postcard, or a recto and verso, which sometimes makes one wonder which is the front and which the back. It is always also clearly marked by its passage—the date, the place, the signature, and the addressee seem to be publicly announced, as is its official status as it moves from one site to another. In spite of its addressee, it is open to being read by one and all, so its destination is never final. Etymologically, it carries the weight of the card, paper, or papyrus on which it is written, and a *carta*, or map, and a charter. It carries a stamp that marks its passage through the state and its debt to taxation, "the duty to be paid on natural language and on the voice."[46] But the figure on this postcard in some ways indicates to us which side is the front by presenting us with a back (see Figure 1.2). The postcard proposes its own back as the back of the figure on it, as that figure whose face is denied us. The figure looks toward a monument in the graveyard, and a cut of cloth falls over it as if it were a shelter, a wrap, or indeed a veil that contrasts with flags wrapped around the coffins of state mourning. Placed next to the memorial, what we see here is junk life, the leavings and remainders of state sovereignty, disposable housing, and the wrapped memorial made into a home for the living dead.[47]

Introduction 23

FIGURE I.2 Cimetière arabe

Yet the desire to turn over the postcard is also the desire to see the face of the person looking at the wrapped gravestone. This is, however, something refused to us—we see the back (*le dos*) and no more. Kheira, the wolf-woman, after all, knew how she was inscribed but seemed also to refuse the terms of inscription, of legacy, of dowry (*la dot*).[48] The back of the postcard and the back of a person can both be designated by the French words *le dos*, but the term also designates the blunt edge of a knife, as if to suggest that the front may be precisely not the face of sujectivation but the sharp edge of the hatchet or knife poised to cut through the legacy and teleology of masculinist justice.

Sovereignty's Late Style

In a recent essay, Achille Mbembe has formulated the concept of *necropolitics*, which underscores the profoundly cynical nature of the form of politics enunciated in disposability. Sovereignty, according to Mbembe, is generally understood rather romantically as the subject being "master and the controlling author of his or her own meaning."[49] In Mbembe's rendering, sovereignty is always associated with Hobbes' distinction between life and death, and the sovereign's power to decide on either for his population. Mbembe insists that though we may think of the notion of sovereignty as one that draws on Greek notions of the *demos* (the people or commons), in fact it has many varied and particularly modern roots. Drawing on Giorgio Agamben, and registering his own departure from Foucault, Mbembe asks us to think of politics as a form of war which since Hobbes has been associated with the state of nature.[50] Michel Foucault, at the end of his *History of Sexuality*, describes the turning of politics into *biopolitics*: the moment in which life, or natural life, becomes the terrain on which the state's power is played out. Foucault writes, "For millennia, man remained what he was for Aristotle: a living animal with the additional capacity for human existence; modern man," he adds, "is an animal whose politics calls his existence as a living thing into question."[51] Considering the disciplinary control of what have become, through state enforcement, docile bodies to be manipulated, Foucault implores us to understand the genealogy of the mechanisms of biopower. In *Society Must Be Defended*, he stresses that modern state racism is an instantiation of other, earlier racisms and their relation to sovereignty. From Foucault we must understand that the system of biopower threatens all of us, not only those who are singled out. Contrary to Hobbes, who thought that the state of nature was one of war that would be overcome by the state of culture, Foucault proposes that this narrative is a palliative. It forces an ahistorical understanding of sovereign power that stops us from seeing the forms of violence directed toward all of us. It causes us to counter biopower with biopolitical critique, itself symptomatic of sovereign power. For Foucault, the state of modern culture in which we find ourselves is a state of permanent war, and politics has to be put into the service of defending society against the forces of modern sovereignty.[52]

Taking this notion a step further, Agamben considers it in relation to sovereignty and the state of exception, formulating a notion of bare life that he sees coming into existence in the Nazi camps—"the place in which the most absolute *conditio inhumana* ever to appear on earth was realized."[53] Whereas the state of exception is abstractly understood as a temporal aberration, in the camps it acquired a permanent spatial organization and established itself within this area as the norm, that is, as the primary mode in which sovereignty operated. Sovereignty thus becomes associated with the sovereign's absolute right to kill or keep alive, for no representative purpose other than to demonstrate and enforce power. Sovereignty, for both Agamben and Mbembe, becomes a discourse of death.

Mbembe, without disputing the particularity and the horror of the camp, departs from Agamben's Eurocentric focus on the Holocaust, and his inability to acknowledge the importance of the category of slavery in spite of the fact that the historical genealogy he traces is from Roman law. It appears, in fact, that Agamben can make his totalizing distinction between *bios* and *zoe* precisely because he does not account for slavery or colonialism.[54] Mbembe not only cites various historians who contend that slavery and some colonialisms have to be understood as similarly forming a systematization through which biopolitics becomes irrelevant because all bodies are deemed disposable. Through this contention, he persuades us that the state of exception is not a spatial category at all. Rather, he says, rejecting the adequacy of Foucault's biopolitical argument, "to exercise sovereignty is to exercise control over mortality and to define life as the deployment and manifestation of power."[55] In this sense, politics is no longer "the exercise of reason in the public sphere"[56] but rather a form of war. Politics, argues Mbembe through Bataille, is not a dialectical movement toward a Hegelian becoming human but rather the movement of beings that pushes the limits of life, death, and all forms of taboo. Mbembe asks, "What place is given to life, death, and the human body (in particular the wounded or slain body)? How are they inscribed in the order of power?"[57] Politics, for Mbembe, is the decision to let die rather than the Schmittian-Derridean formulation of the sovereign's power to decide when to decide and when to suspend the rule of law in the state of exception—the state in which the sovereign arrogates to itself the right to suspend democratic procedures and to legislate by decree.[58]

As Derrida formulated his notions of sovereignty, he wrote in the context of the suspension of elections, supposedly in the name of democracy, in Algeria in 1992. The power to decide when to grant the state of exception in the name of democracy is also the moment, he writes, when the *demos* becomes secondary to the *kratos* (-cracy), that is, the taking of power, rule, and authority in the moment of demonstrating the might of the sovereign.[59] Here the emphasis shifts toward the moment of decision and away from the particulars of whether the sovereign decides to "live or let die." This shifts the relationship of the sovereign to death, and makes sovereignty apparent at the moment of a demonstration of the power to decide. This can always be instrumentalized in so-called democratic states, or states being "brought into" the state of democratic sovereignty, whether cynically, through the apparent violent imposition of democracy by an alien occupying force, or through the increasingly dismal struggle of a frequently thwarted people.

Although I would not underestimate the importance of Derrida's Algerian background (and indeed Chapter 1 explores this topic) or his writing with the knowledge of illness that may lead us to understand *Rogues* as a late work, it is not merely biographical reasons that caused Derrida to turn to the example of Algeria in his discussion of sovereignty. Algeria seems like a test case for him, full of all the contradictions of a form of democracy that will cancel elections in its name. For him, the cancellation of elections in 1991–92, a strategy used by the FLN and backed by the French to stop the Islamic Salvation Front (FIS) from coming to power, exemplifies how the state of exception becomes normalized within the system of late sovereignty.[60] On the one hand, the state of exception appears to have been isolated in a particular moment of Algerian politics: the opening up of elections to a full multiparty system in 1988 and the removal of socialism from the constitution. While some would argue that this led to the subsequent success of the FIS in provincial elections in 1990, I propose that, understood *melancholically*, it was perhaps merely an extension of the general state of Algerian politics that came to a head thirty years after independence in 1962.

The story of sovereignty and citizenship witnessed a shift during the Algerian war of independence that exposed the systematic disposability of bodies in struggles for sovereignty. Restoring any kind of voice attempting to apologize, to reinstate order, to rectify, or to trace a story of the exceptionality of violence is an alibi when circumstances show that it had become the norm. And if the revolutionary desire for national sovereignty ends with exceptional violence as the norm, how is it possible to think of the postcolonial project as anything other than a lost cause in which a military-backed state of exception can be declared at any time and without much need for rationalization? How is it possible to conceive of hope when those categories of democracy and sovereignty that have become in enlightenment thought the framework within which justice has been conceived seem adulterated at their foundation? How to maintain hope when state politics seems to have been reduced to war, with the total war of nuclear power threatening absolute annihilation, and a strong economy being the rationalization for a form of constant war through which states can maintain their imperial power? How also to maintain hope when, as Mbembe would put it, the attempt at sovereignty in, for example, the Palestinian situation has been reduced to an overt mechanism of death in the figure of the suicide bomber?[61]

Algeria's erection of the huge memorial that dominates the melancholic landscape is in a sense also the burial of the idea of sovereignty as self-determination of the people. In its place, and in this combination of commemoration and celebration, it is the very disposability of bodies that is celebrated. The extraordinarily different accounts of how many died—between 800 thousand and 1.5 million—registers indeed that bodies do not count, that they are born and die with no account or census to mark the nationalist agenda. The structure, more than a massive flame burning in respect to the unknown soldier, resembles a chimney in which they burn. The dominance of the structure over the city, in which it has become a landmark now combining the separate parts of the once divided city, makes it a navigation point in this city without maps.[62] The museum to the martyrs in the cavernous basement, attempting to bury the dead, also attempts to bury the cause of sovereignty as self-determination. The organizing principle of the new nation-state by the time of the erection of the monument was all that Fanon feared for the postcolony. But while the monument tells a tale of necropolitics, a critical melancholia remains in which the leavings of an ideal leave an irrefutable mark—what Freud calls a "narcissistic scar" over an "open wound."[63] No map, census, print, or museum can be entirely successful at presenting the exterior nation seamlessly. While the work of mourning may relegate swallowed disposable bodies to the garbage can of modern nationalism, the work of melancholia, critically attesting to the fact of the lie that is intrinsic to modern notions of sovereignty, is the only hope for the future. To sustain a people existing in the sovereign state of necropolitics and lost causes, critical melancholia, formulated through the ghosts with ideals, is the only answer for democracy to come.[64] Critical melancholia neither offers no palliatives nor thinks that justice has been fulfilled. Sovereignty's late style can be mined for the cutting antinomies of postcolonial life to find demands for justice, and therefore hope for the future.

I close this introduction, then, by gesturing toward the sound of Kheira, the spectral mother wolf-woman who seems to demand a different form of representational logic than that understood through exchange or reparation. Her figure demands a form of justice, if you will, that allows a critical agency, an acknowledgment of damaged life within which the force of colonial and postcolonial modernity confine us. If France can acknowledge its bastard son through patrilineal descent, it will wed justice to reparation and calculation without questioning the forms of cutting critical agency that are the promise of the future. Each chapter of this book is an example of the cutting technique I have derived through notions of mourning and melancholia, inassimilable remainders, and a Franco-Maghrebi deconstruction so as to read for justice through these cuts of the living dead. It is these cuts that mark the violations of amnesia that I seek out in *Algeria Cuts*.

PART I

THEORIZING JUSTICE

1

Frames, Contexts, Community, Justice

There is a photograph of Jacques Derrida, about age three, in a toy car at his childhood home in Algiers (see Figure 1.1). It is not an unusual photograph. In fact, its typicality is striking; it is the kind of photograph one could find in most family albums. The little boy is often found in the toy car, just as the little girl is frequently holding a doll, or dancing.[1] The codes of a family album transposed to an academic album highlight the manner in which typicality itself tells a story of framing, of gendered gestures, of senses of belonging, of familial legend making, and of intellectual genealogy.[2] Such codes also provide a frame for a general contextual understanding of the photograph, and therefore for what Barthes calls its *studium*.[3] But as Barthes remarked in his *Camera Lucida*, a book about photography and about his dead mother, there is frequently something else in a photograph that he refers to as the *punctum*. It wounds a viewer, and remains in the viewer's memory when he or she looks away from the photograph. It is a singular relationality and, for the mourning Barthes, encloses the possibility of a hopeful reciprocity. Beyond the gendered coding of this photograph is, however, for me, not the promise of a reciprocity but a demand made by something unknowable that exists potentially beyond the frame of the photograph. For me it is the rectangular void that appears to be the back window of the large car opening onto an unknown. The opening itself is a wounding of the frame.

The photograph includes multiple frames in the sense that a doubling occurs, with one frame in the foreground, in which Derrida sits in his toy car, and the other frame in the background, containing a real car. The

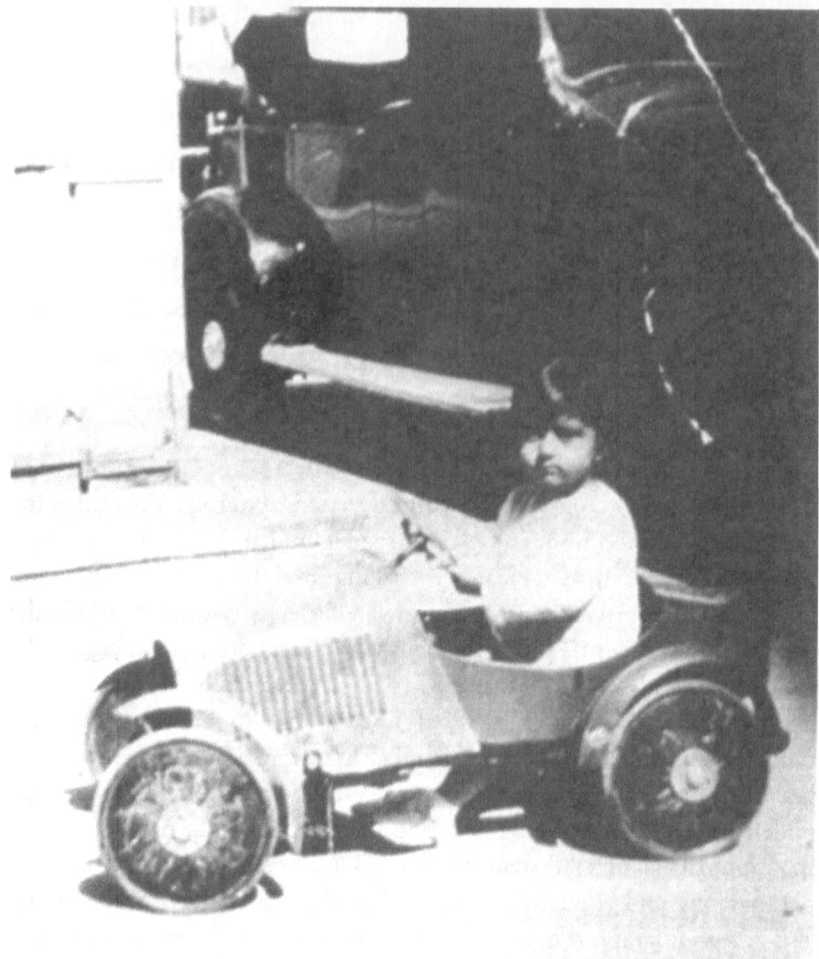

FIGURE 1.1 Photograph of Jacques Derrida, age three. Courtesy of Madame Marguerite Derrida.

child in his car is enclosed in this scene by perpendicular lines, as if framing him in a safe world. The real car is separated from the scene of the toy car by these lines, as if in a square of its own. And through the rear window of the real car there is another enclosure, a rectangular opening, that alerts the viewer to an infinite regression of frames, each enclosing its own image and its own universe, each thematizing the mobility that suggests it could move beyond its immediate frame. But this superimposition of a toy car onto an adult scene of mobility not only alerts the viewer to the thematic exploration of infinite generational migration and immigration; it also presents us with a visual doubling and echoing, suggesting the excess that always exceeds the frame. The frame may appear to exist on its own terms, permitting or excluding hospitality to its hostile excess, yet what persists in this photograph is the permeability of the frame, and its necessary acknowledgment of the other at its border, which both frames and unframes.

A frame both determines and supplements meaning. It is both host to meaning and simultaneously hostile to its narrow condition. This rendition of the frame visualizes both its enclosed protective nature as host and its permeability to the outside, to a potentially hostile supplement. Derrida's thinking has explored the concepts of framing and hospitality in a manner that has often called attention to, and yet not engaged with, women as a sometimes hostile supplement. The concept of hospitality, whether political, academic, domestic, or psychical, has allowed for, however, a consideration of something that supplements this thinking, and indeed this boyhood photograph of potential mobility: the various frames in which Algerian women have been situated, and their different relation to gesture, mobility, and symbolization in the modern period. This chapter engages with Derrida's work on framing and hospitality in order to reach its supplement, allowing for a more succinct consideration of the political stakes of doing feminist work across borders. The stakes of the philosophical apparatus that seem pertinent to the ethical work of postcolonial feminism are permeated with questions of framing and hospitality. Academic hospitality means both openness to one's subject matter and openness to those who want, in some way, to take a stand for Algeria in the current climate of civil war and internal conflict, or to analyze the region's cultural, political, or economic history.[4] This chapter addresses the importance of academic hospitality through a reading of Derrida's concepts of frame, hospitality, and supplement. It argues for what Gayatri Chakravorty Spivak has called a "setting to work of deconstruction."[5] This putting to work of deconstruction would have to be accountable to a feminism engaged with and open to the challenges of crossing borders, and open to the risk of damage to itself, and even of desubjectivation, in this encounter.[6] I put deconstruction to work here ultimately to propose a feminist internationalism, departing from the Marxist internationals of another moment. But in order to reach this supplement of woman, the challenges of framing, of auto- and bionarrative, and the antinomy represented through framing need to be addressed. If the subtext of this chapter is to develop a form of academic hospitality that allows for a sense of solidarity with and openness to imagining a very different future, Derrida's *nostalgérie* becomes a pretext for thinking about coloniality, and about structures of thought that constitute the supplement of foreigner.

The framing of politics, disciplines, and nation-states has become permeable for some and effectively less permeable for others for whom a new form of selective hospitality is in place. The very notion of *selective* hospitality of course goes against the idea of hospitality, introducing limits into it, through codes and laws, whether it be the law of hospitality overseen by Zeus (whose most important epithet, *Xenios*, means "the protector of strangers")[7] or the commercial context of a hospitality suite.

What follows is a consideration of the four types of supplementation, or *parergons*—subordinate or accessory materials that nonetheless are necessary for the work—that constitute the framework of this chapter: Parergon One: Frame; Parergon Two: Example; Parergon Three: Foreigner; and Parergon Four: Woman—and an ethics of openness to them. The supplements together form a kind of "poetics of the parergon." This phrase suggests the deconstructive methodologies addressed here and put to work to formulate a theory for feminism. This chapter and these parergons address why deconstructive methodologies and their trace of coloniality are useful in understanding the complex history of the colonial and postcolonial relationship between France and Algeria. It also addresses why deconstruction is useful in thinking about the hostile supplement of woman, and how to think about how frames and borders are traversed in the pursuit of justice.

Derrida himself has gestured toward the importance of analyzing the relationship between his native Algeria and France, although he has for the most part not set his reading in a geographical context.

If I had the time, and if it were appropriate to give a slightly autobiographical note to my remarks, I would have liked to study the recent history of Algeria from this point of view (the hostage structure). Its impacts upon the present life of two countries, Algeria and France, are still acute, and in fact still to come. In what had been, under French law, not a protectorate but a group of French departments, the history of the foreigner, so to speak, the history of citizenship, the future of borders separating complete citizens from second-zone or non-citizens, from 1830 until today, has a complexity, a mobility, an entanglement that are unparalleled, as far as I know, in the world, and in the course of the history of humanity.[8]

Derrida's Algerian origins are obscurely referenced here, although it remains unclear how they relate to this unparalleled entanglement. The idea of an origin, and specifically the status of an autobiographical example, have for the most part been handled with suspicion in deconstructive circles because of the identitarian narrative teleology of identification with community that such writing often prefaces. Simultaneously, there can paradoxically be both dismissal of singularity and the exceptionalization of a life that often accompanies autobiography and biographical contextualization of a life. Hélène Cixous's comments on looking through her family album are instructive in this regard. She elaborates on her identification with both her mother's Ashkenazi German Jewish background and her father's Sephardic Algerian Jewish background. Tracing a "genealogy of graves" in distant lands, she can relate to her past beyond the framework of the self and of familial ties to a "sort of world-wide resonance . . . the echoes always came from the whole earth. From all the survivors."[9] The example of Derrida's Algerian origin helps to discern the postcolonial politics of deconstruction, the question of what frames and supplements have to do with coloniality, and how the supplement as foreigner carries conceptually the trace of coloniality. The teleology of this thinking will not lead to a foundationalist claim about the Algerian origins of Derridean deconstruction (although there is clearly one to be made if foundationalism were adequate here). Thinking about the supplemented frame through the example of the foreigner allows for the theorization of a postcolonial anticommunitarian and anti-identitarian responsibility that is open to others. It also presents a notion of postcolonial justice outside of and beyond an ontological framework. This chapter, then, theorizes justice through the notion of the frame and the cut. It follows a trajectory that is deeply committed to both an abstract and an antipositivist notion of justice and of attention to the materiality of the historical specificities and textures of the Derridean Algerian text. Attention to the fine line between the two frames—that is, the cut or fugue—allows for the emergence of Algeria as philosophy and not only as knowable entity embodying its own ontology. What may at first seem a detour through some of the intricacies of Derrida's thought, then, will ultimately be shown to assist in a formulation of an Algerian philosophy of justice and internationalist feminism.

Parergon One: Frame

Derrida provides this parenthetical (and parergonal) quotation from his *Glas* in *The Truth in Painting*:

> Imagine the damage caused by a theft which robbed you only of your frames, or rather of their joints, and of any possibility of reframing your valuables or your art objects.[10]

The loss of the frame, and particularly of its binding joints, is damage, and a loss of protection. This could be loss of a conceptual framework when reading or writing, loss of a frame around a painting or collage that may cause it to disintegrate, loss of national protection if the joints of borders are compromised, or loss of police integrity if evidence is seen to be compromised, revealing a case as a frame-up. But this passive mood employed to explicate Derrida's idea substitutes "the loss of" for Derrida's "a theft," in which causality is clearly presented—"damage caused by a theft." Fear of theft is not fear of losing that which is protected by frames—your "valuables," for example, or "art objects," mementoes, loved ones, or things of monetary or sentimental value. The damage is done by theft of a protective enclosure. This means losing the frame but perhaps not losing the painting, the house, or the home, only the possibility of protecting them; losing the skeleton, and perhaps therefore the core of the life; or losing the laws that govern and create borders, and the ability to make new ones, but perhaps maintaining the safety of those they apparently protect. What is projected in Derrida's musing is the loss not of those valuables (although there is a logical possibility that they too would be lost at some point) but the protective and restrictive structures enclosing them, leaving things usually considered "off-frame" (to use the language of cinema) in order to move into this permeable frame, opening it up to risk. That this would feel like an affront is presented in the language of "damage"—the damage of being robbed of protection (even if one is safe.) The function of the frame, and the sense of what constitutes the frame at any given moment, would be deferred, so the valuables would be "out of joint."[11]

This notion of the *parergon* of the frame discerns the implications of threatened borders, their antinomies, and the opening up of oneself to potential risk and damage by the supplement or trace that is threatening the border. But this "opening up of oneself to" cannot entail a complete embrace of a principle of hospitality, because materiality always intervenes to erect frames and delimit access. It is this "nondialectizable antinomy"[12] that marks the importance of and contamination by the "prosthesis of origin," as well as the originary trace, and distinguishes it from the always corruptible violence of metaphysics.[13]

This somewhat threatening idea of "damage" on a conceptual level begs the question of how damage to a frame functions within a particular context. In *Framing the Sign*, Jonathan Culler has suggested that framing our arguments or our histories reveals where we are coming from conceptually.[14] If context appears transparently as a backdrop for an argument, we elide the fact that retrieval of this background molds it and that it is inevitably back-formation, in which origin is created with some element of inevitable falsification as it creates a notion of the prior within the terms of the present or the future. The past is proffered as an appendage carried into the present and the future when in reality it functions more as a prosthesis, an additional support added for strength, often to take the place of something irretrievably lost, and that makes its presence felt as a haunting intervention in the current force field. A context is created both to elucidate the past (sometimes in the terms of the present, sometimes as a way of giving a history of the present) and to offer up that past as some kind of explanation, whether causally related to the thing explored or not. Without a frame, context appears as empiricism without interpretation. This gives at best very little, and at worst, a divisive selective presentation of naturalized facts through the frame of transparency. The etymology of "frame" also references this idea of an established order or a plan, and the methodology of its construction. The notions of advantage, benefit, and profit are also associated with the word. So the activity of framing has advantages, because it supplies us with a frame of reference from which to work. It makes explicit the frame of mind of the person doing this construction of the argument.[15]

Culler also writes of negative framing: the police frame-up or manufacturing of evidence. The frame-up compromises the legal system, leading to wrongful accusation and condemnation of an innocent person. The compromise is negatively viewed because the accused may subsequently be condemned on "wrongful grounds." Here the theft is of the legal framework, and the frame itself (whether it protects or not) has become the thing of value. On occasions when the frame-up is discovered (usually through some supplementary information that exceeds the frame-up), legal structures are validated and sanctified. There is little provision for assessing the frame itself—the claims it makes and its ability to adapt to damage caused by the supplement's challenging of its norms. The discovery of a frame-up leads to a liberal response—to save the frame—even if those it apparently protects are not protected by it. But this would always leave the supplement outside of the frame, and the frame would remain unresponsive to its own corruptibility and exclusionary nature.

In social psychology and in the symbolic interactionist school of sociology, Erving Goffman analyzed forms of self-presentation and the framing of an image of another person using the language of film analysis. Following Gregory Bateson's notion of framing, or the organizing principles of social situations, Goffman discussed how "strips" (like filmstrips) are understood differently depending on the context within which the viewer views, that is, the location of filming or of projection.[16] For Goffman, a strip refers to "any arbitrary slice or cut from the stream of ongoing activity . . . not . . . a natural division. . . ."[17] The context allows the framing of interactions with someone, and what precedes the strip influences the interpretation of the person and the event witnessed, and thus the assessment of behavior appropriate to the interaction. Multiple frames must be both socially and temporally analyzed if they are not to put each other at risk, threatening the borders of another frame. The easiest example of these numerous frames is a game. If I walk into a room and hear someone say, "X is dead," I may very well presume that X is indeed dead. I would therefore adopt an appropriate mode of behavior and would probably consider the laughter of another in the room to be tactless or an improper breaking out of the frame.[18] However, if I then understand that a game of *Murder* is being played, I am less likely to make such an error. The frame of the utterance determines how the utterance is expected to be read, and what the appropriate response would be. To some extent, one could add that all understanding takes place "out of context," because everything that is said will be understood in the context of one's own (mis)understanding. One can never really know the full context of any utterance, whether another person's or one's own. So while a frame determines a meaning, it is also a supplement that throws it into undecidability.

*

The cinematic frame, from which Goffman draws his terminology, as well as the photographic frame capture a moment of a more extended event leading to a "cut," or an interruption of the frame by a supplement outside. The supplement can be understood not simply as an interruption by an alternative framework or force field, however. It is also the cut of nonknowledge, of something that opens the possibility of knowledge but is not simply reducible to any currently existing knowledge formation or paradigm. It is a nonknowledge that threatens borders. It is also a nonknowledge that gestures toward what Theodor Adorno calls the "damaged life," which questions ontology and metaphysics in favor of epistemology—a damaged violent epistemology that cuts through the normativity of being.[19] While the frame is therefore all about stasis, capturing a moment or holding a particular instance hostage, it also exceeds itself, through what happens "off-frame," through the sound or voice complicating an image, or through the *punctum*, an apparently insignificant signifier piercing or wounding the viewer, as analyzed by Barthes.[20] This piercing, for Barthes, is at first unlocatable, as if it responds to memories or nostalgia etched onto the body of the viewer, thus causing an interruption in the force field of the *studium*. This also introduces a different time frame, and a spectral presence that indicates being out-of-joint.[21] Photographs in particular capture something irretrievably lost, allowing for the grasp of a real past in the present. Nostalgia grows to encompass the remnant. (Given the negative connotations of nostalgia, we could remind ourselves of its original meaning and Greek root: the pain or longing to return home. The *Oxford English Dictionary* defines nostalgia as an illness. It is "a form of melancholia caused by prolonged absence from one's home or country; severe home-sickness." Uncannily, nostalgia is given a more critical edge than its contemporary form, *sentimental longing*, suggests. It is a wound rather than simply a romanticization. Perhaps, then, examples of nostalgia could include an encrypted critical relation to that home for which the nostalgic person longs.)[22]

Derrida has analyzed the frame in painting through Kant as an example of parergon—a supplement to the work itself, even though it may interrupt the work, the *ergon*, and question its boundaries, its "truth," or its "meaning." The parergon also includes other supplements, such as the example. In his reading of Kant's *Critique of Judgment*, Derrida explores whether the supplements (frames, examples, parenthetical notations) implicate the apparent meaning theorized within the main frame assaulting the borders of its enclosed frame of reference. In a section on the notion of beauty in Kant, Derrida explains that the "cut" caused by something outside the force field of the work contains the unknown. The "cut" does not simply engender an already formulated alternative. It opens up the work to the possibility of a different intervention or response as yet unknown and is stripped of recognizable utility. This, in effect, is why it is beautiful, and as yet unclassifiable. "It is finality-without-end which is *said to be* beautiful. . . . So it is the *without* that counts for beauty; neither the finality nor the end, neither the lacking goal nor the lack of a goal but the edging in *sans* of the pure cut . . . the *sans* of the finality-*sans*-end."[23] The aesthetics of the parergon is especially concerned with this "cut" or interruption. It is a nonknowledge intervening into the force field of the work enclosed within a frame. Not without agency, the supplement is nonetheless without intentionality at the moment it cuts through the border. Unencumbered by content or interest, the supplement is a threat to the borders even as it accomplishes the undoing of the stasis of the border.

An early use of the word *frame* explicitly references this idea of threatened borders. *Hymns to the Virgin and Christ*, published in 1430, uses an obscure, now obsolete definition of frame: *Þhe deuelis gadriden Þer greet frame, And heelden Þer perlament in Þhe myst*. ("The devils gathered their great army, and held their meeting in the mist").[24] *Frame*, in this instance, is a warlike array or a host. The devils gather it around them so they can hold their meeting and protect their borders from a race engendered by Jesus, who is himself of doubtful paternity. With the introduction of the idea of the host, hospitality and hostility are associated with the border that can accept or reject the "foreigner"—the figure who wants to cross over the warlike array to another side. In this instance, the paternity and presence of the foreign child, Jesus, is under discussion. The devils are threatened by his presence and resolve to defend their place. *Ordeyne we us wiÞ al oure gere / For hidir he ÞinkiÞ to make a race / Arise we alle Þat ben bounden heere / And foond we to defende oure place.*[25] ("Prepare ourselves with all our things / For he thinks of making a race here / All of us who are bound in the place, arise! / And prepare to defend our place.")

The warlike array exists solely by virtue of the potential permeability of the border it in fact constitutes. It functions like any army that apparently protects the people who "belong" within the borders, who are deemed worthy of protection by the army, and who have entered into some kind of agreement or social contract (as citizens or, in rare cases, as refugees or "asylum seekers") with the state or with the host country. The contract includes abiding by the laws of that country and defending its borders in exchange for protection and political representation. The protective frame is a force field. Often those who are protected by the same frame (in other words, those who are included in the civil society that political society apparently protects) are understood to be a community with shared values, and those outside of it are foreigners (sometimes subalterns). At worst, these foreigners are aggressors; at best, they are guests. They may be perceived negatively, as parasites, or positively, as incidental beneficiaries in a symbiotic relationship.[26] More often than not they are perceived as wanting to gain something from their relationship with the host, even in instances when the host needs the guest (to supplement the labor force as a "reserve army of labor" or, for example, as "guest workers," "mothers," "resident aliens," or indeed, "illegal aliens").[27] The earlier example from *Hymns to the Virgin and Christ* also includes the possibility that the political society is constituted by devils rather than by a host of heavenly creatures or gods. Frames may create lack of clarity concerning who is being protected for what ends, or indeed whether any form of protection is being exerted at all. It is possible that a guest, as much as a host, would be held hostage by the devils, gods, soldiers, police, enforcers, aggressors, or strangers. They may indeed end up being *hostia*, or sacrificial victims (human or animal).

The term *host* carries its double as its inverse. In the example of the Middle English "frame" cited earlier, there is an armed company of devils, but a host may equally be heavenly. A host lodges someone in his or her (broadly conceived) "home," but the term *host* is also used for the corollary—the guest. (This is more apparent in the French *hôte* than in the English *host*, but it holds true in both languages. The Latin *hostis* means a foreigner, a stranger, the enemy, in fact, of the state.)[28] So the host is someone who opens up frames or borders. Rather like a parergon, the host-guest is a supplement to that which is protected within the frame. And the host community, like the ergon, is challenged by the arrival or presence of a supplement at its borders. Equally, the permeability of the borders challenges their function. (What do they protect other than themselves? And what damage does theft of them cause?)

The opening afforded by the host has origins in its etymology. The Latin *ostio* is a door with a frame, a starting gate, the entrance into the underworld (rather like the "frame" of the devils), or a mouth or river mouth. The orality of the host body (politic) suggests the ability to take into one's midst physically (or perhaps psychically, given the oral metaphorics of engaging with otherness that we see in psychoanalysis, the eating of the host in communion, or the swallowing of the talisman in Islam), and suggests communicability—the mouth offers a possibility of interaction, rather in the way that a host computer in a mainframe allows (depending on where you live, of course) for the potential communicative coming together of numerous inlets and outlets. It presents the possibility of communication (or perhaps—and this perhaps is important, of course—even of community) beyond the frame or border.

The double-edged nature of the term *host*, like the double-edged nature of the term *frame* (protector, excluder; host, guest; communication, failure of communication; naturalized, formulated; internal structure, outer rim) indicates how hospitality and hostility vie against each other, because the "law" of unlimited hospitality conflicts with its actualized laws. Derrida suggests that there is

> an insoluble antinomy, a non-dialectizable antinomy between, on the one hand, *The* law of unlimited hospitality (to give the new arrival all of one's home and oneself, to give him or her one's own, our own, without asking a name, or compensation, or the fulfillment of even the smallest condition) and, on the other hand, the *laws* (in the plural), those rights and duties that are always conditioned and conditional, as they are defined by the Greco-Roman tradition and even the Judeo-Christian one, by all of law and all philosophy of law up to Kant and Hegel in particular, across the family, civil society, and the state.[29]

The protective mechanisms of borders, like those of frames, introduce antinomy into the picture because of potential damage. When someone or a group resists the presence of the foreigner into their home, it is because they entertain the idea that they may cause damage, hold them hostage, rob them, or leave them "out of joint." Their collectivity is indeed threatened. What Derrida suggests as a mental exercise is the following:

> Let us say yes *to who or what turns up*, before any determination, before any anticipation, before any *identification*, whether or not it has to do with a foreigner, an immigrant, an invited guest, or an unexpected visitor, whether or not the new

arrival is the citizen of another country, a human, [an] animal, or [a] divine creature, a living or dead thing, male or female.[30]

Acceptance without identification, and before risk is conceived, is for Derrida the law of hospitality. This is a law without empathy, without the empathetic identification on which community, communion, democracy, and indeed the market are based. It is the welcoming of potential damage prior to its conception. It is not a greater or more capacious empathy that includes more types of strangers. It is before *identification* and, importantly, before kinship. It is as if the host and the event of hospitality are an opening, a door frame or threshold, a mouth, an invagination, between a Freudian *fort und da*—a shuttling back and forth in an attempt to control presence and absence—rather than an enclosure. And the feminine gesture at the border may well be different from the back and forth of the *fort und da*, enacting a different kind of relationship between presence and absence, and a different kind of playfulness and shape than one driven by enclosure.[31] It is the parergon not as extraneous to but as a part of and as a substitutable part of that may challenge the meaning of that which is enclosed or protected by the parergon.

Parergon Two: Example

In *The Coming Community*, Giorgio Agamben positions the form of antinomy that emerges in doubling as the antinomy between the universal and the particular. If examples are called on to explain in particular terms things that have general implications, the singularity of the examples poses questions about the universal and puts universal and particular at odds with each other.

One concept that escapes the antinomy of the universal and the particular has long been familiar to us: the example. In any context where it exerts its force, the example is characterized by the fact that it holds for all cases of the same type, and, at the same time, it is included among these. It is one singularity among others, which, however, stands for each of them and serves for all. On one hand, every example is treated in effect as a real particular case; but on the other, it remains understood that it cannot serve in its particularity. Neither particular nor universal, the example is a singular object that presents itself as such, that shows its singularity. . . . These pure singularities communicate only in the empty space of the example, without being tied to any common property, by any identity.[32]

The parergon of the example *exemplifies* further the relationship between frame and context, and puts further pressure on the concept of community. By distinguishing between ethical singularity (or the "idiomatic," singular, and untranslatable in Derrida's *Monolingualism of the Other*)[33] and political particularity (the translatable and paradigmatic, for Derrida), the example's supplements demonstrate the ethical damage performed by the guest. The *singular* and the *particular* are parallel but not interchangeable terms. The singular stands in relation to the ideal; the particular, in relation to the universal. Universal claims can often be challenged politically and conceptually with reference to particular instances and examples. The singular is a unique instance that cannot be explained solely in terms of a context or a framework and is irreducible to it. In that sense, it carries the trace of the ideal. (This is to say not that idealism is free of universal claims but that it does not have to be reduced to universalism. Of course no instance of the singular in the world can be understood separately from its particular instantiation.) It is between these two analytical distinctions that responsible acts have to take place, and through which the nondialectizable antinomy functions.

The example that will help elaborate this idea of frames, borders, and hospitality is the photograph of Jacques Derrida with which the chapter began. In the photo, Derrida is about three years old and is in a toy car on the Rue Saint Augustin in Algiers. The photo is provided as an example of autobiography and automobility.[34] It appears in *Jacques Derrida* by Geoff Bennington and Derrida, in which Bennington summarizes the central ideas of Derrida's work in pedagogical fashion in a "Derridabase," and Derrida writes the parergonal hypertext—the footnotes that are partly a commentary on Bennington's pedagogical exercise, partly a nostalgic reflection on an Algerian upbringing, partly a preemptive lament for his dying mother, and partly an analysis of Saint Monica, Saint Augustine's mother, seen through the eyes of that North African saint. Saint Augustine becomes the point of departure for Derrida—the photo is on the Rue Saint Augustin—and through circuitous routes he returns to the theme of the burial of mothers in foreign lands. "Circumfession," as his section is called, tells the story of the slow and protracted death and burial of mothers. The circumfession (a Jewish North-African confession—a circumcised or "cut" confession—that also departs from Saint Augustine's *Confessions*) is partly about what it means to belong. The photograph also leads off from Saint Augustine, this time by way of the road named after him on which the boy Derrida lived. With Saint Augustine as his point of departure, Derrida is clearly on the move. As we are told in the notes beneath the photograph, the theme of the racing car comes up repeatedly in Derrida's writing. "The racing of a car is filmed or photographed, always on the verge of an accident, from one end of J. D.'s work to the other."[35]

The photograph's Augustinian roots foreshadow other routes potentially taken. The photo is also a cutting into the time of autobiography and automobility. "Delay" is built into the photograph. The image of the car is always a reminder of a kind of doubling. For Derrida, the car is rather like a photo that is "over-printed with the negative of a photograph already taken with a 'delay' mechanism."[36] It captures the moment of motion but holds it in a form of stasis. While this photo does not appear to have been overprinted in this way, it does involve a kind of doubling. It has a double frame: the large car in the frame at the back of the photo is overtaken by the secondary frame, introducing temporality into the image, and nomadism. It is no longer possible simply to say, here is Derrida, age three or so, by the looks of it, sitting in a toy car in Algeria, the place of his origin. The double frame introduces a wound, and punctuation, to this photo, and the frame, or back window of the large car in the background, takes the story back even further to a questionable origin.[37] In the "Circumfessions," a frame is given to us over a knowable context that can give a foundational grasp of Derrida's *Algerian singularity* or be an intact referent for the photograph. This is not simply a rejection of a vulgar empiricism but a wound opened about the burial of context. The seventh section of the "Circumfessions" (written without periods, denoting moments of completion of a concept) relates this repetitive doubling to the representability of life:

I wonder if those reading me from up there see my tears, today, those of the child about whom people used to say "he cries for nothing," . . . compulsion to overtake each second . . . the memory of what survived me to be present at my disappearance, interprets or runs the film again. . . .[38]

The moment of a life past, therefore inevitably lost forever and, in Derrida's terms, buried, will always be cited out of context and placed within a frame. To build a picture of a past and an origin, as a prosthetist would, will always be an artificial exercise, regardless of how closely it approximates the life, because it will always rebuild a context to explain a singular life. Context appears like a foundation when it is actually a back-formation or a prefix, like an additional letter or syllable excluded from or appended to a word for emphasis, or like a prosthetic limb, replacing the function of something damaged.[39] This "cut" into autobiography and automobility is where the particular and the singular come together. What Derrida calls the "prosthesis of origin" in *The Monolingualism of the Other* is an exemplary moment of the coming together of the singular and the particular. It is not the reduction of a singular life to its particular contextual origin.

In an interview with *Le Nouvel Observateur*, Derrida speaks of how the trace of Algeria is present in everything he does, says, and writes. That is not to say that everything is reducible to his particular history in Algeria. It does not suggest the possibility of rationalizing everything he writes in terms of his Sephardic Algerian-Jewish background so much as it suggests learning something from the fact that his family fled the Spanish Inquisition and that his grandfather became a French citizen in the 1870s with the signing of the Crémieux decrees. Crémieux, a French general, was Jewish and granted Jews French citizenship. Very few Jews in Algeria had French citizenship prior to these decrees. Interestingly, Hélène Cixous, whose primary heritage through the matriline is German Jewish, discusses discovering the mixed roots of her father as Spanish, Berber, and Arab. But in 1867—that is, before the Crémieux decrees—her paternal family requested French citizenship along with another 144 Jews in Algeria.

I have a copy of this certificate by which a certain Jonas Cixous, native of Gibraltar and interpreter for the French army, was made and unmade "French," a certificate signed by Napoleon III. This is how some Jews had a despotic emperor as godfather for their historic baptism. People on the left never forgave them for this upstage entrance. Gambetta, whom I liked, did not like us. . . ."[40]

Jews in Algeria were stripped of their citizenship during World War II, thrown out of schools, and made unable to continue with their professions (though some midwives, as Cixous tells us, remembering her mother's profession, were able to continue their reproductive labor).[41] This disenfranchisement led to many Jews having increased sympathy for the anticolonial movements in Algeria. But rather than draw on the historical mistrust and trust of Jews because of their complex citizenship background, Derrida chooses to propose that although the traces of Algeria remain in him, they do not, however, explain him. What is idiomatic in his language, and what remains as a singular form of responsibility toward Algeria, emerges not in a style, but in

> an intersection of singularities, of manners of living, voices, writing, of what you carry with you, what you can never leave behind. What I write resembles, by my account, a dotted outline—"the *old-new language*," the most archaic and the newest, unheard of and thereby presently unreadable."[42]

Extending the example of Derrida's photograph and deconstruction's Algerian origins poses the question of what is afforded by the notion of a prosthesis of origin. Does the language of prosthetics elucidate the function of knowing and problematizing foundationalist "origins," and does it help to understand the "frame" and giving hospitality to whomever arrives at one's gate? Does it demonstrate what framing and borders have to do with coloniality, and how to understand the "foreigner" as a trace of coloniality? How does a face (through *prosopopeia*), a signature (through *hypographiern*), and a proper name (here through the word *foreigner* and the proper name *Jacques Derrida*) emerge in writing in a manner that inscribes singularity? Derrida claims that a signature emerges as a counterpart to a context, or a prosthesis of origin. Origin and context themselves do not constitute a reliable foundation, which is created out of an identitarian teleology. It is this signature of the singular and untranslatable that stands with and against community. Derrida's acknowledgment of the material force of an Algerian Jewish community is presented as a result of being marked by the complex history of Jewish citizenship, but he has no desire to claim community as authentically his or as the paradigm through which autobiography is to be imagined. Similarly, he has no desire to posit a framed community as the possibility for the future, and in this way is quite distinct from Giorgio Agamben, with whom I began this section. Even though Agamben acknowledges that a future radical community would be one in which singularities communicate and in which common property or identity are irrelevant factors, he nonetheless proposes a community to come as the source of revolutionary political change, after the day of judgment, when naked life, albeit somewhat Christianized in Agamben's rendition, will be all that is left. For Derrida, however, the future and hope are not marked by community, which will always be deconstructible and exclusionary even when it aspires to be otherwise, but rather by justice, and by the promise that is uttered as an appeal to come, gathering difference, as the simultaneous possibility and impossibility of all speech, unrealizable but crucial to the pursuit of justice.[43]

If an explanatory foundationalist claim for an origin from an identitarian community—a Jewish Algerian community—is inadequate, then why and how should deconstruction be linked to decolonization? Does the example bring together philosophical and historical discourse in a way that provides an instance of the singular? And does this parergon complicate the idea of these universal-particular oppositions?

Parergon Three: Foreigner

Derrida has often approached the subject of foreigners obliquely, sometimes returning to former examinations to draw out a neglected element that has haunted him and that demands attention previously deemed unwarranted. In a parenthetical quotation from *Monolingualism of the Other*, Derrida looks back to *Glas*, in which the philosophical conundrum set up by Antigone and her brothers exemplifies how community is developed out of its own dissolution and through antinomy. The brothers Polyneices and Eteocles die as singular and opposing entities, and the community is maintained through this death of community. The quotation looks forward to *Of Hospitality*, in which Oedipus's arrival at Colonus is the exemplary arrival of the foreigner:

One day it will be necessary to devote another colloquium to language, nationality, and cultural belonging, by death this time around, by sepulture, and to begin with the secret of Oedipus at Colonus: all the power that this "alien" holds over "aliens" in the innermost secret place of the secret of his last resting place, a secret that he guards, or confides to the guardianship of Theseus in exchange for the salvation of the city and generations to come, a secret that, nevertheless, he refuses to his daughters, while depriving them of even their tears, and a just "work of mourning."[44]

Derrida speaks here of the secret burial place of Oedipus, who held his host, Theseus, hostage to the secret of his burial place. In return, Theseus' kingdom will be peaceful. Antigone and her sister Ismene would be prevented from mourning their father, condemned, says Derrida, to mourn mourning, as that which is lost is totally inaccessible. From the mourning of Santa Monica to the preemptive mourning of his own mother who will be buried in a foreign land (France), we arrive at a secret burial for a foreigner buried in a foreign land. While *Oedipus at Colonus* is in many ways the *urtext* of the mourning of foreigners, the play acts out a gender inversion of the deaths that otherwise preoccupy Derrida. Derrida and Saint Augustine mourn their mothers patrilineally, tracing a history of deaths in foreign lands and the work of mourning; and Antigone fails to mourn her father. In Hélène Cixous' "My Algeriance," dedicated to her dead father, she reads her Algerian origins, her paradoxical relationship to French citizenship, the trace of Algeria that remains with her, and its particular feminine instantiation. It is an instance of what Gayatri Spivak would call the epistemic violence of coloniality. The violent particularity of the father's Sephardic origins, and her mother's Ashkenazi origins with their history of Northern military graves, presents to Cixous a climate of violence in which peoples were "gathered together in hostility by hostility."[45] And as if experiencing the cutting off of familial lines, she laments, "I see a sort of genealogy of graves. When I was little, it seemed to me that the grave of my father came out of that grave of the North. My father's grave is also a lost grave. It is in Algeria. No one ever goes there any more or will ever go."[46]

While Derrida, in *Glas*, concentrates on Hegel's reading of *Antigone*, in *Of Hospitality* he turns to Sophocles. Interestingly, he turns to Sophocles' late play, *Oedipus at Colonus* (*Antigone* was performed first in 441 B.C., *Oedipus Tyrannus* in 430 B.C., and *Oedipus Coloneus* in 406 B.C.). The status of the secret turns the play into something quite distinct from the tragic actions of the two earlier plays, and is a turn toward the poetics of tragic thought.

The beginning of the play foregrounds debate as to the relative guilt and innocence of Oedipus. He arrives in a foreign land with his daughter Antigone, and first a citizen and then the chorus, provisionally but with some apprehension, allows him to enter into sacred land. It appears at first as if we are going to find here a somewhat less than satisfactory version of justice in the form of a debate such as we find in Aeschylus' *Eumenidies*, in which the ghost of Clytamnestra remains ignored and the nonhumanoid Eumenides is paid off with a new wardrobe of fine clothes. But this is not what we are given. That *urtext* of mourning follows the establishment of laws of the state. In *Oedipus at Colonus*, by contrast, the laws established are more about the protection of the foreigner. Theseus does not entertain the question of Oedipus' culpability. He invites Oedipus to tell his story, as if inviting him to inhabit a language he can carry with him. (Similarly, in *Of Hospitality*, Derrida is invited to speak by Anne Dufourmantelle in a long invitation). For Derrida, language appears as the vehicle of automobility. It is internal, not like the prosthetics of communicative mobility—the cell phone or the fax machine. But language, Derrida says, "only works from me."[47] It makes sense only when it leaves you, even if you think you carry it with you as you travel. Oedipus imparts to Theseus an obligation to maintain the secret of his burial place. The host becomes obliged to his dead guest and held hostage to the secret. Theseus explains his decision to welcome Oedipus in terms of his own birth in a foreign land. His move is not, however, identificatory. The guest is substitutable and demands an obligation, a taking in, and a form of sacrifice on the part of the host (the sacrificial victim, the mouth, the source of a protective frame). And in taking the host hostage, the guest is instrumental in creating laws of hospitality.

Derrida remarks on the gendering of such laws, calling feminine sacrifice an instance of mourning mourning. For example, Antigone's status as the daughter of the foreigner takes away her own agency as a foreigner with knowable origins and burial mounds. Or the story of Lot's protection of his guests from the Sodomites by making *hostiae*, or sacrificial victims, of his daughters. (We could add that women's access to physical mobility in most cultural contexts makes travel more difficult and more limited than it is for men, and that women often achieve the status of foreigner or citizen through relation to males, complicating further the proper name *foreigner*, placing it at one remove.) Similarly, Antigone's feminine sacrifice leads to a distancing and removal—an instance of mourning mourning.

Mourning mourning, however, rather than mourning something known to be lost, seems more like a form of melancholia—an emotion at one remove that has lost the ability to know what is lost. Derrida has written extensively of the distinction between *mourning* and *melancholia*, and between *introjection* and *incorporation*. Taking his lead from Nicolas Abraham and Maria Torok, he writes that introjection is the full assimilation of a lost object into oneself, and that incorporation is like swallowing whole a lost and inassimilable object. The incorporated object results in something similar to Freud's melancholia, an autocriticism that is actually a criticism of that which is unidentifiable in the body of the melancholic. It manifests itself in phantasms encrypted in language, or in *demetaphorization*—the taking literally of something that makes sense only figuratively. Even though he finds the analytical distinctions useful, Derrida has rejected the distinction between mourning and melancholia, and introjection and incorporation, in favor of a concept of *mid-mourning*. The only way to mourn ethically is not to mourn successfully, because full introjection would assume the possibility of assimilation of the other. The other's otherness would thus be lost. For Derrida, such an assimilation is not possible because of the important radical alterity of the other, and the responsibility toward that alterity.

But something is lost in the elision of the distinction. The mourner, after all, has some sense of what has been lost, even if there is an inassimilable, radically other, unknowable part that remains inaccessible. The melancholic does not have that sense.[48] The daughter of the foreigner, Antigone, is more of a melancholic. She does not know what secret Theseus holds and she is condemned to carry the phantom of that secret within her language. Antigone's complicated filiations and affiliations are singular. Yet she is *like* all women who function within a patrilineal society. Filiation is mutable, and a relationship to the representative teleologies of group or state affiliation is tenuous.

Judith Butler, in an extensive reading of *Antigone* through Hegel and Lacan, has suggested that Antigone's melancholia is dramatized in catachrestical language of antistate and antikinship protest. Its source lies in the establishment of kinship patterns that exclude a form of the feminine seen in Antigone.[49] In her overt mourning of Polyneices and Eteocles, Antigone hardly knows what she mourns. Her melancholia originates in the failure to mourn the father before the brothers; or indeed, buried even further, is the failure to mourn her incestuous mother-grandmother.

Although Butler's reading is compelling, partly because it presents the melancholic protest of the foreign daughter as a source of something like what Gayatri Spivak (taking Greek tragedy and comedy as well as Paul de Man as her source) would call "a permanent parabasis"—the breaking out of a frame in order to make direct (and nonrepresentative) political commentary—there is a problem in both Derrida's and Butler's (and indeed Hegel's, Lacan's, Steiner's, Loraux's, Irigaray's, Patočka's, and so on) use of the example.[50, 51]

Butler is right to draw on melancholia; and one could claim another foreigner, Derrida, as a melancholic who similarly disidentifies, or rejects identification, with the laws of kinship and the laws of the state. But to defer back (from the brothers to the father to the mother, Jocasta) maintains a framework in which the prosthesis of origin is a human in a Greek tragedy. It is not just that no document of the birth of kinship, community, statehood, and justice can be more canonically exemplary. Rather, the question arises, Why this prosthesis of origin rather than any other? Why not take one's example from other (nonwestern, nonhuman, foreign) canons of origin? The example, the "cut," the "frame," or the moment of exemplarity is, after all, singular *and* particular. It is not a particular that stands in for a universal. The example of this foreigner's daughter (who is, after all, the daughter of an exiled king) does not demonstrate radical nonidentification and nonhumanism. When Butler writes that Antigone is nonhuman because she is outside the realm of kinship, her dehumanization and her repression are effectively confused with her status as a human. (Dehumanization is not the same as being nonhuman).[52]

If hospitality is the welcoming of (and the possibility of being held hostage by) another's language, with all its secrets, phantoms, specters, and prehistories, then it should allow for the welcoming and incorporation of other prostheses of origin, and phantoms and specters of death, even though they may hold one hostage. For example, noncatachrestic, nonhuman(oid) prostheses, whether literal (as in the wonderful work done by Lisa Cartwright and Brian Goldfarb on the issue of prosthetic limbs that are more practical than human copies but less acceptable because they appear nonhuman)[53] or metaphorical, as in the Pterodactyl that haunts Mahasweta Devi's story of that title, would introduce into the frame a different notion of the human and nonhuman than the examples of dehumanized figures.[54] It is only by considering such nonhuman strangers that the possibility of nonidentificatory and nonempathetic community emerges. The politics of the frame (understanding hospitality through the arrival of the foreign melancholic Derrida or Antigone—the foreign daughter-melancholic rather than the "foreigner's daughter" of whom Derrida speaks) speaks only to the antinomy of some laws with *the* law of hospitality. As Gayatri Spivak has argued, in a reading of *Pterodactyl*—Mahasweta Devi's story about funeral rites, the lie of community, and the radical corporeality of the specter—the manner in which frames and examples rely on the prostheses of certain examples—will always leave some figures outside of a frame (unprotected, anomalous, foreign, subaltern).[55] To acknowledge this is to foreground the ethicopolitical constraints of any framing, the opening of justice, the establishment of communities even where the gesture of *unworking* is being made.

Robert Young's essay "Deconstruction and the Postcolonial" is a defense of postcolonial theory's use of deconstruction by those who claim that theories so deeply embedded in western philosophical discourse should at best be suspect analyses of nonwestern contexts. Young's essay elegantly begins with a reflection on sending to Derrida his book *White Mythologies* (whose title he takes from Derrida's essay on metaphor), and ends (with a consideration of Derrida's writing on Algeria) in a second-person address to Derrida as if in postcards framing a more conventionally argued section. He suggests that "Derrida, a colonized subject bearing the effects and affects of the complex recent history of French colonial Algeria, was immediately placed in a marginal position to the still imperial social and cultural politics of metropolitan France." Reading Derrida's critique of metropolitan structuralist and particularly Lévi-Straussian anthropology in terms of marginalized origins, Young concludes that there is a sort of "cultural and intellectual decolonization" that demonstrates both the differential logics of nonwestern societies elided by structuralism, and the conversion of western mythologies into universalisms.[56]

Mustapha Marrouchi has posed the question of how "to make visible the historical bases of intellectual signatures." He suggests that "all poststructuralist rejections of origin myths are, in fact, alibis for a-historical and a-political posturing. . . ."[57] Marrouchi does not want the reader to reject the idea that there is too much humanist fantasizing in the search for origins that are at best messy. But in the interests of "geo-politically aware protocols of vigilance," he wants to understand what connects Derrida and Algeria, and how the connection between the two "calls the relationship from its absolute singularity."[58] In other words, he wants to understand how the singular, in any given instance or in any example, will also relate out of its singularity to a context, and in fact manifest itself in a kind of a trace or remainder. Marrouchi is critical of Derrida because he feels that Derrida evades responsibility toward Algeria and encrypts Algerian signatures. He criticizes Derrida for speaking out on apartheid as the exemplary form of racism while remaining relatively quiet about Algeria's traumatic relationship with France, and indeed about the particular forms of trauma undergone by Jewish Algerians who were stripped by the French of French citizenship during World War II without being prompted to do so by the Nazis behind the Vichy regime. Since Marrouchi's article, and in fact just preceding its appearance, Derrida has indeed been more directly vocal about his Algerian background, about the problems that have been afflicting the country for the last ten to fifteen years, about the racist immigration laws that have been put in place by Pasqua in France, and about the exploitative status of the *sans papiers* workers in France. But Marrouchi's initial question nonetheless remains: What does it mean to consider Derrida's relationship to Algeria given that origin is a prosthesis and a substitute for that which is lost? What is the relationship between the singular as opposed to the particular (context) or the communal (another form of foundational thought)? And what are the political implications of understanding origin as a hopelessly reductive presentation of a particularity?

Marrouchi argues that poststructuralist critiques of origins are a-political alibis leading to outright hostility. One could also argue that the political disempowerment of colonized peoples in Algeria, or Jewish-Algerian Franco-Maghrebians "like" Derrida, leads to the development of a secondary form of analysis that acts out a politics without engaging with it directly. But Derrida gives us a way of understanding what is problematic about such gestures in his claim to exemplarity and singularity made in *The Monolingualism of the Other, or The Prosthesis of Origin*. Taking the "case" of Derrida and Algeria as an example to elaborate an idea about frames, borders, and foreigners allows for an examination of how autobiography and automobility have been central to community, framing, and context. The example, as we know from the earlier citation by Giorgio Agamben, is singular even though it acts as if it were a particular case history that can exemplify a more general and perhaps universal argument.

> If I have indeed revealed the sentiment of being the only Franco-Maghrebian here or there, that does not authorize me to speak in the name of anyone, especially not about some Franco-Maghrebian entity whose identity remains in question. . . . To be a Franco-Maghrebian, one "like myself," is not, not particularly, and particularly not, a surfeit or richness of identities, attributes, or names. In the first place, it would rather betray a *disorder of identity*.[59]

On the one hand, Derrida explains this disorder in terms of "community"—one that suffered the ablation, or removal, of citizenship. On the other hand, however, he describes a "community" that goes against any notion of coming together through commonality. It is "disintegrated," and exists only retrospectively through the experience of disintegration.[60] Derrida describes the lack of identification in a community that relies on the memory of something that did not take place. This relational configuration constitutes the essence of nostalgia and, in the cut we have taken here, of what Derrida would call his *nostalgérie*. The nostalgic photograph of the young boy Derrida is thus framed through the Rue Saint Augustin as if the context we are given foreshadowed a circonfession, mobility, and the necessity of arriving elsewhere from an irretrievable route.

To translate the memory of what, precisely, did not take place, of what, having been forbidden, ought, nevertheless, to have left a trace, a specter, the phantomatic body, the phantom member—palpable, painful, but hardly legible—of traces, marks, and scars. As if it were a matter of producing truth of what never took place by avowing it. . . . Invented for the genealogy of what did not happen and whose event will have been absent. . . ."[61]

There is no past that is accessible through which to identify, other than a reconstructed past presented as true rather than prosthetic. For Derrida, given the lack of a knowable past, there lies only a form of futurity within which that past may inscribe itself: "As if there were only arrivals (*arrivés*), and therefore only events without arrival. From these sole "arrivals," and from these arrivals alone, desire springs forth. . . ."[62] These arrivals, in the French, suggest both occurrences—events—and the arrival of people. These examples of arrivals, which make up a new language of singularities, carry a trace, a mark, or a scar. The trace is also present in Cixous' theorization:

To depart not to arrive from Algeria is also, incalculably, a way of not having broken with Algeria. I have always rejoiced at having been spared all "arrival." I wanted *arrivance*, movement, unfinishing in my life. It is also out of departing that I write. I like the phrase *j'arrive* (I'm coming, I manage, I arrive . . .) its interminable and subtle and triumphant messianicity. The word *messiance* comes to me from Algeria.[63]

Unlike Agamben, who sees the singularities coming together as a nonidentificatory community-to-come, "these pure singularities communicate only in the empty space of the example, without being tied to any common property, by any identity"; the arrivals, for Derrida, carry a secret and melancholic something with them.[64] For Cixous, they carry an affective messianicity. The singular, apparent in exemplarity, does not stand in relation to the revolutionary ideal (in a similar relation to the particular and the universal) for Derrida as it seems to for Agamben. Those who arrive and that which arrives exemplify the antinomy between the laws of history and the law of singularity. And the arrival-as-guest, whether the young Derrida arriving in France from Algeria or something else with which we cannot identify, exemplifies the antinomy between *the* law of hospitality, and the laws of hospitality. The example of the foreigner reveals how the example cannot stand for the general. The example of the proper name—*foreigner*—will always be the counterexample who—or which—breaks the law of exemplarity, and who also demonstrates the imagining of damage to the frame.

Parergon Four: Woman

> This civil war is for the most part a war of men. In many ways not limited to Algeria, this *civil* war is also a *virile* war. It is thus also, laterally, in an unspoken repression, a mute war against women. It excludes women from the political field. I believe that today, not solely in Algeria, but there more sharply, more urgently than ever, reason and life, political reason, the life of reason and the reason to live are best carried by women; they are within the reach of Algerian women: in the houses and in the streets, in the workplaces and in all institutions.[65]

One hardly needs Jacques Derrida to make such an insight about women in Algeria, or indeed in almost any war zone. His emphasis, however, on the life of political reason poses the question of what that might be in the context of consistent political exclusion. The virility of war, after all, extends to the virility of the "community" in whose name the war is fought. Practically speaking, that community includes women (hence the designation *Algerian women*, and also the assumption that the noun or proper name *Algerians* includes the women of that nation-state). However, the virile community often speaks in the name of women but fails to represent women's interests. A *critical melancholia* emerges from these representations of women. It is in the attempt to listen to this melancholia that a critical politics can be perceived. It emerges from marginalization, repression, and exclusion from community. Such a situation cannot simply be resolved through liberalism—through inclusion, representation, centralization, or released repression. If one exists at the margins of community, it is as a frame that causes damage to the interior. If community is revealed as virile, then it is damaged by the supplement of woman, and other forms of political coming together need to be examined. The identitarian logic of community, whether anticolonial, anticapitalist, or feminist, does not allow for the "cut" in autobiography. While a prosthesis for this melancholia can be identified, it is a self-critical one that emerges from the failure of community. It also, however, reveals the necessity for a nonsolipsistic form of political protest without identification among protestors; for a *just* work of melancholia, a *messiance* of sorts, but not one that can simply be proposed as the solution for a future. It would have to be an undoing and unworking rather than a utopian leap of faith.

How do we move from the philosophical category of woman and the feminine to "women"? Or indeed from the supplement of "foreigner" to foreigners? It is here that the category of the subaltern is most useful in understanding the social implications of philosophical speculation on the parergon. Lifting the category of liminality—the feminine—into the political and critical arena of women should not, however, make them synonymous. Not all women occupy liminal positions, and the feminine is not exclusively or inevitably characterized in women. And clearly not all women are subalterns, even if it is the condition of femininity that marks them as subalterns. The subaltern is a category used by Antonio Gramsci in *The Prison Notebooks* to describe a class of people who are not members of civil society and therefore have no representation within it and no protection from the political society that governs it. This class of people does not, however, exactly constitute a class because they have no coherent or recognizable class consciousness. They are not unified politically and they are not visible to political or civil society. When they are recognizable, they have probably ceased to exist *as subalterns* and have begun to emerge in civil society, perhaps in the form of what Gramsci calls an *organic intellectual*, who works to constitute a counterhegemony. Subalterns manifest themselves, however, in moments of spontaneous insurgency. They are disruptive to political society precisely because they cannot be identified as a specific group with coherent demands. They cannot therefore simply give their consent to the hegemonic structure. If civil society is maintained by political society through consent to domination, it is through the work of traditional intellectuals. However, if the subaltern group cannot be identified, they exist as a remainder to this group, a supplement or parergon to the force field maintained in the frame: civil society. If the feminine subaltern has been inassimilable to civil society, it is largely because of the apparently invisible modes of feminine production internationally.

In *Beyond the Frame*, Deborah Cherry discusses the idea of framing through pictorialization. Drawing from Derrida's *Truth in Painting* and from Gayatri Chakravorty Spivak's concept of *worlding*, Cherry discusses the travels of British militant feminists to Algeria in the nineteenth century, and their role in *textualizing* Algeria. For Cherry, the concept of worlding refers to a process through which colonies—presented as blank territories—were inscribed and pictorialized through an imperial lens. Analyzing the writings and paintings of Barbara Leigh Smith (Bodichon), she explains how Smith's largely orientalist (though perhaps protofeminist) work functioned to introduce Algeria into the discourse on European landscape art by showing how it had been beyond the frame of reference. Derrida contends that the frame is a field of force, violently imposed and restricting. Cherry understands this as an instance of *worlding*—colonial epistemic violence. She argues that the land was enclosed through the techniques of (imperial) European landscape art, and that the violence and trauma of the act was denied within the process.

The process is double-edged, of course. If the parergon of the frame is both protector and the condition of possibility for permeability, Cherry reminds us of Derrida's suggestion that a "gesture of framing, by introducing the *bord*, does violence to the inside of the system and twists its proper articulations out of shape...."[66] Once Algeria is pictorialized into the frame of landscape painting, damage is done to that frame, and its permeability and supplementarity are made apparent. Its function as a force field has been interrupted. In the case of Barbara Leigh Smith, doing feminist work and putting women onto the agenda allows viewers paradoxically to see interruptions to the force field created in the process of pictorializing Algeria. Smith's painting itself interrupts the frame of European colonialist presence in Algeria through her femininity. It also involves creating a new force field through the pictorialization of the landscape. So, while there damage has been done to a largely masculinist world of painting, another force field has been established, with another potential guest waiting at the gate.

To some extent this chapter has suggested that nonsubstitutable and nonequivalent supplements of all forms are based in a variety of contexts. But at the same time it is worth being alert to what Saïd Chikhi has called a field of marginality that seems distinctly Algerian. Not all forms of marginality are equivalent, nor is degree the most important consideration in understanding marginality. The Sephardic-Jewish Algerian Derrida theorizes marginality, and the Ashkenazi Algerian Cixous theorizes her *algeriance* as a trace that draws her to Algerian women in France.[67] For Algerian Jews, the ablation of citizenship during World War II underlined the tenuousness of their 130 years of French belonging. For other Algerians, the very complicated laws around citizenship, rights, and assimilation were responsible for the peculiar mixture of hegemony and domination. Azzedine Haddour, in his book *Colonial Myths: History and Narrative*, has described this paradoxical relation very persuasively, in terms of the co-optation of the *évolués* and the expropriation of the masses.[68] He sees in colonial and postcolonial Algeria a melancholia emerging from the policies of assimilation and the actuality of expropriation.

The inassimilable other, or the remainder of assimilation, manifests itself as melancholia and is the site of the subaltern. Unable to achieve representation in the language of the state, it nonetheless interrupts through insurgency, through representational breakdown, through a critical agency always in search of justice.

This critical agency is melancholia. Freud developed the idea of melancholia in relation to mourning. In his 1917 essay "Mourning and Melancholia," he presented a form of unsuccessful mourning as melancholia. The concept was associated with loss. In the early stages, the melancholic and the mourner seem quite similar. Both are withdrawn from the world, both feel incapable of love, both feel horribly dejected. These feelings extend over a long period—a couple of years of severe symptoms of this sort are not uncommon after a loss. The mourner gradually "succeeds" in mourning by slowly detaching herself from the lost object, assimilating, or introjecting, parts of it into her and freeing herself to love something or someone else.

The melancholic, however does not mourn successfully. This is not least because, unlike the mourner, the melancholic cannot identify the lost object because her loss is at least partly unconscious. I say at least partly because it is possible that the melancholic knows, for example, that her lover has died and that she is therefore in mourning. But she may not know that she has feelings of hatred towards the lover that remain not only unresolved but unconscious. The loss may also be entirely unconscious, with no conscious association at all with its cause.

Freud briefly describes the symptoms of melancholia as feelings of worthlessness, characterized particularly by self-criticism. This may well lead the analyst to feel astonished at the patient's shrewd powers of self-perception, until it becomes clear that the patient is criticizing characteristics of the loved one and not the self. Drawing on a theory of narcissism, in which the melancholic's lost object must be narcissistically conceived as constituting a part of the self (and not someone or something conceivable as an absolute other distinct from the self), he suggests that the self is at war with the lost object, now a part of the self. This civil war, as it were, occurs because it is too difficult to stop mourning and therefore release the lost object: this civil war is melancholia.

The "critical agency" identified as characteristic of the melancholic becomes very important for Freud. It constitutes the basis for his concept of the superego, which he theorized in his 1923 essay "The Ego and the Id." In that essay he describes the way in which conflict becomes internalized. In fact, lost figures, like grandparents, are internalized in order to ward off conflict or absolute loss. Through this internalization, the lost objects constitute a part of the self. They become, in fact, the controlling moral fiber of the self that Freud theorized as the superego. The lost object, or person, has become assimilated to the extent that the principles associated with the grandparents or parents have been internalized. The child, once scolded by the grandparents, now censors her own behavior. This critical agency is not, however, melancholic, even though Freud has taken his idea of critical agency from his work on melancholia. The "lost object" has effectively been assimilated even as it often works in opposition to the subject's other desires.

Melancholia's manifestation as *colonial melancholy* emerges in Europe's colonies as a critical resistance to imperial rule and to state nationalism.[69] Colonial melancholy is a term I adapted first from Antoine Porot, a colonial psychiatrist from the School of Algiers who identified something called "pseudo-melancholy" among Algerian men. In European psychiatry, melancholia was identified with introspection and moral growth. By contrast, Porot saw Algerian Muslims' melancholy as violent and gave a diagnosis of physical difference. His understanding of melancholia among Algerian Muslims is characterized by a "constellation of revolt" without the narcissistic regression that characterizes the European "crushed state of melancholia."[70] Colonial psychiatry was clearly an instrument of oppression and control, and it demonstrated almost entire misunderstanding of native peoples. It also, however, documented the manner in which colonialism and nationalism molded selfhood, health, and pathology as well as ideas about them.

Melancholia, then, is the loss of an ideal of the right of subjecthood that the French in Algeria ostensibly endorsed. Melancholia manifests itself in subaltern interruptions, as guests at the doors of nation-states that cause damage to the exclusionary force field within. It is through Derridean concepts of hospitality and through psychoanalytic notions of melancholia that we see how foreign women potentially damage those force fields. The damage leaves an open wound that the force field itself would try to heal as a narcissistic scar. The language employed here derives from psychoanalytic theory. The remainder of an inassimilable "other," whether an object, affect, person, or ideal, can manifest itself only as a "narcissistic scar," says Freud, because there is no room for it to be pleasure in the adult, assimilated as she is into "civilization." The *open wound* is a term used by Freud for melancholia. It cannot be healed through the curative hospitality of the hospital. The difference of the lost other would be betrayed in such a process, leaving at best a narcissistic wound. For the melancholic, the lost other remains an ambivalent presence, damaged and damaging.[71]

Clearly *woman* and *foreigner* are not the same in terms of particularity or singularity, as the example of the foreigner's daughter testifies. The foreigner's daughter is not simply doubly supplemented, and it is insufficient to add *gender* onto *foreign* as a category of analysis. The logic of the supplement itself disallows such additive progression.

Additive progression and prioritization have historically not allowed for engagement with the supplement or for hospitality because of the potential damage it causes to the frame. A supplement to a supplement is by definition marginalized by the force field of the first supplement. This suggests a prioritization of the center rather than attention to the undoing of the center performed by the supplement. If we think of a movement toward national independence that, for example, excludes the rights of an ethnic sector or that considers feminism—or even something as basic as women's rights—as lower priority, then sustaining a new hegemony clearly has become more important than the undoing of injustice. Out of what seemed like political necessity, the ethical exclusion of Berbers and feminist issues from Algerian national politics has been a case in point. The idea of substitution is important here. The supplement is not interchangeable. When Derrida speaks of the substitutability of the guest, it is not in the sense of the interchangeable. The French words *supplément* and *suppléer* are somewhat untranslatable. As Ellen Armour has noted, the *supplément* means not only something added on but also something that exceeds. And *suppléer* suggests supplanting or replacing or substituting as well as supplementing. There will always be a supplement, and it will always supplant that which has been included in the force field of the frame. One supplement will substitute for another only in the sense that each, in its singularity, will do damage to the frame, and having done damage, will inevitably be subsequently damaged itself by another supplement.[72] Derrida says this not to create the nihilistic or the endlessly deferrable. Rather, he asks us to do the work of not accepting closure, not simply including the marginalized, and not recentralizing. Such gestures do not take into account the betrayal of difference made in such a gesture, and do not allow for the damage done to an unjust frame.

The field of marginality that exists within Algeria is constituted by the force field of the state. The forms of marginality that emerged revealed the problems of that force field, even as it changed to adjust to different global economic demands. Whereas the concepts of counterhegemony and hegemony emphasize alternative modes of new power structures, the concept of hospitality returns one to the openness to damage caused by the arrival of the supplement, and to undoing rather than building an alternative of recentralized force fields. Less about building hegemony or community, hospitality listens for fractures so as to understand how a force of criticism functions in the supplement, politically and ethically. The notion of international responsibility for the pursuit of justice, rather than the call for rights or for inclusion in a community of those who have been marginalised by it, motivates this listening. It involves learning the lesson of damage to the force field that it has constituted.

*

A video installation by Zineb Sedira, a French-Algerian conceptual artist living in London, captures this lesson. The installation's title is a pedagogical imperative: "Don't Do to Her What You Did to Me!" The video works from the idea of the talisman—something written on a piece of paper by an Imam that should be kept on the body of the person to whom it is given as a form of protection and well-wishing. Some people swallow the talisman to keep it within them. In Sedira's video, a woman's hands are shown writing repeatedly, "Don't do to her what you did to me!" (see Figure 1.2). The command is clearly also an accusation of alleged damage done to the "me," and imparts a sense of protection toward the "her." It also involves a third person to whom the imperative is addressed.

The hands are then shown tearing the paper into small pieces and placing it in a glass of water (see Figure 1.3). As the paper is placed in the water, the ink runs, and for a moment we are presented with a screen of black tails swirling together as if in reference to Arabic script (see Figure 1.4). This is the most aesthetic and aestheticized section of the video, as if to draw on the familiar association of script and to inscribe the talismanic reference. The sound of the film is minimal and yet striking. We hear the tearing of paper, and then the sound of a metal spoon stirring against glass. The torn paper is being mixed as if it could fully dissolve like an effervescent medicine or a digestive. The camera closes in on the words swirling around in the glass. We see now that the talisman has been written in English and in French. Although the sound of the stirring is insistent, and although the papers are mixed rapidly, they do not appear to dissolve. The stirring ceases, the hand stops. The spoon is removed, and the glass

FIGURE 1.2 Zineb Sedira, "Don't do to her what you did to me!" Still from video installation. Video projection duration: eight minutes (1998/2001). Funded by Arts Council of England and Africa in Venice. Courtesy of the artist.

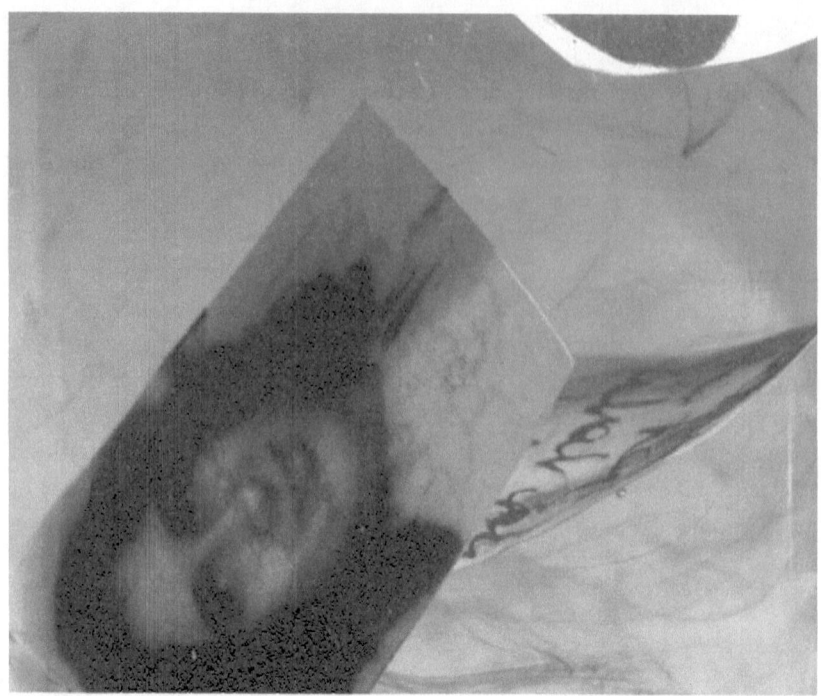

FIGURE 1.3 Zineb Sedira, "Don't do to her what you did to me!" Still from video installation. Video projection duration: eight minutes (1998/2001). Funded by Arts Council of England and Africa in Venice. Courtesy of the artist.

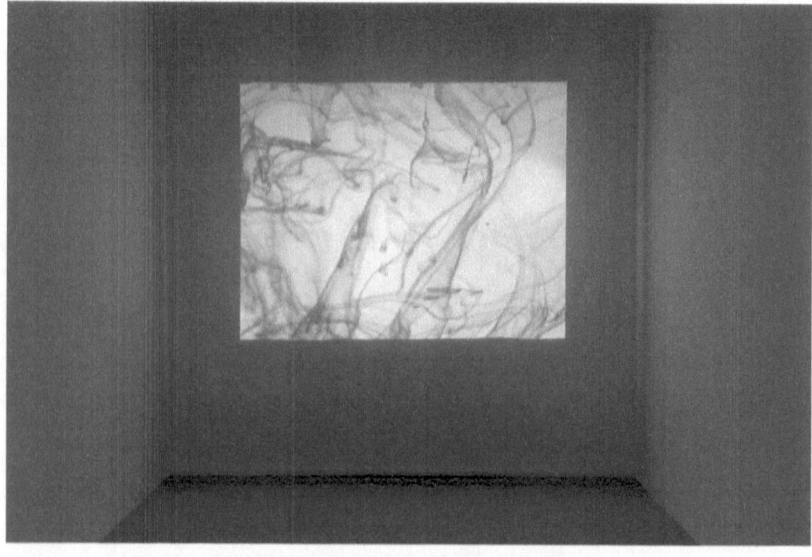

FIGURE 1.4 Zineb Sedira, "Don't do to her what you did to me!" Still from video installation. Video projection duration: eight minutes (1998/2001). Funded by Arts Council of England and Africa in Venice. Courtesy of the artist.

is picked up. We assume that its contents are drunk (although given the quantity of paper in the glass some effort would be involved in the swallowing) because an empty glass is then placed on the table. The ritual has taken eight minutes of real time. Although there are at least three figures involved in the plot (the addressee, the "me" and the "her"), we have witnessed one person only: the writer, the mixer, and now the drinker are the same person. And the insistence of the feminine gesture—the simple sound, the repetitive writing, the real-time rendition—causes a variety of conjectures. What did the person do to receive such a reprimand? Do the hands we see in the film belong to the addressee? Or is it the "me" writing and drinking out of despair, as if overdosing on the lesson to be taught? Or is this the "her," attempting to swallow a difficult and inassimilable lesson of betrayal so as to warn against all damage done to "hers"? Is this a lesson that could be digested, or has it been swallowed whole? Whoever the hands belong to, they communicate that repetition of the same, or working within the same convention, has brought despair. The lesson attempts to do damage to the framework of convention, so that what was done to "me" would not continue to be done to "her." And the visual, linguistic, and aesthetic appeal is made in at least three languages—those of the three figures involved: English, French, and the Islamic talismanic ritual that is damaged and performed in the feminine.

Other works by Sedira depict an encrypted feminine that does damage to both Islamic art forms and Western stereotypical conceptions of these forms. What appears to be an almost overly conventional geometrically patterning panel of tile work in *Quatre générations de femmes* (*Four Generations of Women*) is more complex up close (see Figure 1.5). The geometric patterns conventionally held extremely complex mathematical and cosmological arrangements and were built on an intricate philosophical system. It was conventionally a purely masculine art form and often included Arabic calligraphy (see Figure 1.6). Sedira breaks through these conventions by producing them herself, by depicting computer-generated images of her grandmother, her mother, her daughter, and her own eyes, thus defying through the digital image the Islamic prohibition against figurative images (see Figure 1.7). The complex geometrical designs include writing in French, telling a story of geographical rather than cosmological immigration—one generation to France and herself to Britain.

Sedira's point is not simply to identify herself as a London *beurette* but to work into the material of convention an encrypted story of reproductive labor—the hidden work of women behind the art form. Playing with this idea of the hidden and the figurative, she photographs herself in a series, "Don't Do to Her What You Did to Me II!" putting on a head scarf. The photographs depict various stages of the ritual. But rather than the plain white or sometimes black *hijab* common in Algeria, Sedira's head scarf is covered in passport images of a woman. They speak of the complexity of border crossings and invisibility, working through pictorialization with the idea of a visual pun that causes damage to the force field of what are understood to be conventional visual practices. There is an ironic iconoclastic twist here, as the veil—a barrier to seeing women's faces in the Islamic context and a Western stereotype of Islam's oppression of women—becomes imprinted with the visual marker of singularity: the face. These lessons of damage are not simply assimilable into the fields that generated them. They do damage to those force fields. Read in terms of the various frameworks that inform dominant paradigms of discipline formation, as well as in terms of the cultural, political, and historical frames that sustain a work, that damage can be perceived and the call for the undoing of injustice can be heard.

FIGURE 1.5 Zineb Sedira, "Quatre générations de femmes." Installation. Computer-generated designs silk-screened onto ceramic tiles/interior installation (1997). Commissioned by the Gallery of Modern Art, Glasgow Museum, Manchester. Courtesy of the artist.

FIGURE 1.6 Zineb Sedira, "Quatre générations de femmes." Installation detail. Computer-generated designs silk-screened onto ceramic tiles/interior installation (1997). Commissioned by the Gallery of Modern Art, Glasgow Museum, Manchester. Courtesy of the artist.

FIGURE 1.7 Zineb Sedira, "Quatre générations de femmes." Installation detail. Computer-generated designs silk-screened onto ceramic tiles/interior installation (1997). Commissioned by the Gallery of Modern Art, Glasgow Museum, Manchester. Courtesy of the artist.

2

The Experience of Evidence:
Language, the Law, and the Mockery of Justice

> Given that all experience is the experience of a singularity and thus is the desire to keep this singularity as such, the "as such" of the singularity, that is, what permits one to keep it as what it is, is what effaces it right away. And this wound or this pain of the effacing in memory itself, in the gathering up of memory, is wounding, it is a pain reawakened in itself. . . .
>
> JACQUES DERRIDA, "Passages—from Traumatism to Promise"[1]

> Since they have dared, I too will dare. I will tell the truth, for I have promised to tell it, if the courts, once regularly appealed to, did not bring it out fully or entirely. It is my duty to speak; I will not be an accomplice. My nights would be haunted by the specter of the innocent. . . .
>
> ÉMILE ZOLA, "J'accuse"[2]

On March 8, 1995—International Women's Day—a mock trial took place in La Salle Ibn Khaldoun in Algiers, near the offices of the prime minister. Although none of the accused was present, Algerian women (for the most part members of the Algerian Union of Democratic Women, or RAFD, run by Leila Asslaoui), along with some women from the international feminist community, staged a trial of Abassi Madani and Ali Belhadj, leaders of the outlawed FIS (Islamic Salvation Front); Anwar Haddam and Rabah Kebir, two exiled FIS leaders; the Armed Islamic Group (GIA), a branch of the FIS that has been responsible for the extraordinary level of real and symbolic violence against civilians; and former president of Algeria Chadli Benjedid.[3] All were on trial for "crimes against humanity," and Chadli was also charged with "killing democracy" by legalizing the FIS in 1989. The presiding judge was Leila Asslaoui, a former spokesperson for the government, a judge, and minister of national solidarity and the family; her husband, who was a dentist, had been brutally killed two days after she resigned. The trial differed from earlier trials: Madani and Belhadj were already serving official twelve-year sentences for "acts against the state." This mock trial was championed around the country at rallies calling for women's "right to life" (a phrase not associated with abortion rights but rather with the human right to survive).[4]

What was the purpose of the mock trial symbolically held on International Women's Day? What was the purpose of women symbolically performing and anonymously taking the bench to pass judgment on these political figures? "Witnesses" gave their testimony on videotape or their testimony was dramatized, with actors dressed up as ghosts returning to haunt the halls of justice.[5] These were women who had themselves been violated, or who had been widowed or lost children, and frequently those whose loved ones had been "disappeared." Such disappearance affects the ability of the body to be represented.[6] In one sequence, women witnesses were dressed in white (the most common color of the Algerian veil) and splattered with blood, their faces made up to look pallid. They spoke primarily in French and stood up to condemn the torturers on trial, who defended themselves in Arabic. The torturers too wore white, but as if they were actors in a diabolical simulation of humanity, they had executioners' masks over their faces. The ghostly and pallid women in mourning were figured as witnesses and as signs—gaps in language haunted by their desire to be represented and their traumatic relationship to the language and judicial system that had failed to represent them. These were women who had returned from the dead to bear witness to their own deaths for the sake of the living. Conscience could not be erased, so it continued to manifest itself as a ghost, as a spirit that both has returned from the recent past and carries with it associations with the war of independence. In that war, perhaps overoptimistically called a "revolution," the homogenization of the people of Algeria by the nationalists failed to take into account the inadequacies of the oppositional revolutionary discourse, which neglected the nation's heterogeneity. The ghost of that revolution hovered over the performance. Two important issues were at stake in the mock trial: first, the use of a French legal model and the French language (the discussion that followed the mock trial was in French); and second, the use of symbolism and performance in the face of violence.

To conduct the trial in both French and Arabic in a country whose judiciary has functioned in Arabic at least since the mid-1980s was to respond to an imposition of Arabic with an act recalling an earlier oppressive cultural, political, and legal regime. Education in classical Arabic and instruction in Modern Standard Arabic rather than in the local popular Arabic that has always been spoken in Algeria, in Tamazight, in other Berber languages, or in French, which was seen as the language imposed by a foreign power and its legal system, has produced generational differences in relationship to language even as the anticolonial force of pan-Arabism lay behind it.[7] For some, the French language, and even the use of the French courtroom model, harks back to the tyranny of colonial rule, which spoke the language of the citizen's rights while at the same time imposing on Algeria, an integral part of France from 1848–1962, the most complicated history of citizenship in the world, and therefore denying access to the very rights the French had proclaimed to be a basic human need.

The violence in the recent civil war from 1992 on, during which approximately two hundred thousand people have been murdered, is characterized by its spectacular nature. In the symbolism of the trial itself, this spectacular violence is countered with performativity. There have been an extraordinary number of murders and rapes, particularly of intellectuals, journalists, and foreigners, women as well as men: throats have been slit inside mosques; decapitations and mutilations, rapes, and murders have been carried out deliberately in front of families, including children. Decapitated heads have been thrown into the street through windows after being severed from already-dead bodies; alternatively, they have been placed inside bodies that have been sliced open.[8] Such incidents may bring to mind a *people's war* (in which the lack of arms against a much greater military force leads people to resort to a form of "terrorism" and "torture"), but in this case they are considered by the Islamists in Algeria to be acts of a *jihad* that began during the war of independence and has continued since then.[9] Following the logic of torture, in which the threat of potential suffering constitutes the deed, rather than the logic of war, which kills without drawing attention to suffering, the viciousness of recent crimes against humanity has instituted a reign of terror. The GIA has set itself up as a combination of a mystical and a military organization that acts on *fetwate*, which call, for example, for the murder of unveiled women or those who speak French.[10] An important case in point is the murder of a seventeen-year-old girl, Katya Bengana, who had wished to attend college and was posthumously awarded an annual anti-Islamist award by the RAFD.[11]

The FIS, which has publicly condemned all terrorist activities, whether conducted by the GIA or by the state, has nonetheless called for control of women's activities along lines they associate with Islam.[12] It is, however, by no means the only party or political group that has called for a curtailment of women's rights.[13] Indeed, between 1978 and 1984 the Family Code was debated and finally passed by the National Liberation Front (FLN), the group that had fought most actively for independence and that ruled Algeria officially until 1992, then unofficially and under new guises following the change to a multiparty system in 1988. The FLN's Family Code reinforced what was constructed as *traditional* Islamic law, and was concerned in particular with women's status and access to public space.[14] However, it is in the GIA's bulletin, *El Ançate*, which details the *fetwate*, that we find the murdering of women encouraged, and assurances that the "terrorists," as they are called in Algeria, will "dine at the table of the prophet." The average life expectancy of one of these self-proclaimed militants is, by some accounts, between five and six months.

The economic, social, and political reasons for the rise of fundamentalism in Algeria are beyond the scope of this chapter, as is an explanation for the popularity of the FIS among the younger generation and the radical nationalism it once encouraged much to the horror of the United States and Western Europe. It does have to be said, however, that when the FIS won the local elections in 1990 and the first round of national elections in 1991, it did so within a corrupt system, which led to a very low turnout for the elections. By contrast, when General Zéroual was elected president in November 1995, the turnout was more than 80 percent. The voice of protest against the FIS, then, has been loud and clear, even under the threat of violence. That voice, however, has appealed to a repertoire of images drawn from the struggle for independence—ghosts, in fact, that enunciate the failure of representation, political and linguistic. Zora Flici, who works for the Association for Victims of Terrorism, has spoken of this all-too-familiar pain inflicted by "terror": "We understand this pain, because we've already been through it once, and I think we understand it better than others."[15] But these ghosts are not simply repetitions of the past. As Benjamin Stora has written,

> The recurrence of war in Algeria and the repetition of words of war in France do not provoke the historian to look for hypothetical "beginnings." The quest of correspondences allows us to see discontinuities, fresh appearances, and discordances. . . . Behind the frequency of vocabulary and old habits still in use, it is necessary to recognize singular silhouettes of new and different practices.[16]

Hence, although it is true that the current discourse of politics and the media in both Algeria and France draws on the vocabulary of religious war and on that of the war of independence, the political scene cannot be understood without some sense of history, and particularly the history of colonial rule in the area—the Ottoman Empire, of course, but even more, the peculiar model of French colonial rule, which made Algeria into three *départements* (or administrative units) of France from 1848 to 1962.

Without a doubt, comparisons can be drawn between the oppressive political system of the French bureaucracy and that of the FLN after colonialism. Some believe that following the rousing statement in the 1964 Algeria Charter that disavowed the colonial administration the colonial bureaucrats were simply replaced by Algerian ones. Thus the current struggle of the FIS is viewed as similar to that of the FLN during the war years. At the end of that war, when Arabic was proclaimed the national language—which at that point seemed to be a positive devaluation of the gallicization of Algeria under colonial rule and part of the pan-Arab movement—Algerian nationalism looked like a more resistant secular nationalism, even though this socialist country had proclaimed Islam the national religion. Socialism and Islam were in fact bound together in the constitution as complimentary means for modernizing Algeria. Parallels have also been drawn between the violence of the French and that of the FIS—in this scenario it is again national independence that is seen to be at risk. Similarly, condemnation of the form of violent fundamentalism we see in the GIA, which has now been loud from the FIS, and of what some claim is the peculiarly Islamic nature of the violence is seen as an attack on Islam in general, something once more associated with France and with the neocolonialism of the United States.[17] And the use of French is considered to be a further devaluation of the many languages currently in use in Algeria.

This relationship to the language in which many Algerians are most proficient raises interesting questions regarding the manner in which testimony can be given, whether legal testimony in a court of law or some other kind of performance, without any intention on the part of the listener to produce evidence and based on the possibility of communication of what actually happened. The court of law is one place where we call on language to act as if pure referentiality were possible, where information conveyed through language is supposed to be least ambiguous, and where, as a result of this transparency of language, firm evidence can be given and justice can be served.

Interestingly, in two "cases" where women organized a collective protest against state torture—in the mock trial I have described and in Gisèle Halimi and Simone de Beauvoir's committee for Djamila Boupacha, which called for a fair trial on behalf of a victim of torture—the relationship of legal language to referentiality is foregrounded in a manner that reflects a changing attitude both toward the legal system and toward the French and Arabic languages predominating in Algeria.[18] These cases represent a shift in the concept of the relationship between referentiality and justice, and in the relationship between referentiality and politics. This shift could not have happened without three historical occurrences: the revolution, when a call for independence, glorified since in national memory, intentionally ignored the nuances of the "Algerians" it claimed to represent; the war against civilians in Algeria from 1993 to the present, which has often worked to destroy memories of political violence; and the changes in international feminism during the period of decolonization.[19]

This chapter has three central concerns in its broad theorization of justice. First, how can transnational feminism be practiced effectively at this time, given the thorny colonial politics during the war and at present? Although decolonization and cultural loyalty have frequently led to a rejection in the colonies of international intervention or commentary (as Boupacha herself did, though she may have been manipulated by the FLN),[20] more recently some feminists in Algeria have called for feminist activism both in the Arab world (thereby avoiding some of the significant problems of modern colonialist interactions with the First World) and outside of it.[21] This means considering some of the work that seems to have been effective, at least in bourgeois circles, perhaps the only arena where women can take advantage of what the law has to offer while simultaneously questioning its very ability to provide justice.[22] Second, what is the relationship between language, justice, and the law, and in what way might the mock trial constitute a recourse to justice? This involves analyzing the differences and similarities between designation and arbitration—terms that are often used interchangeably within the context of representation. And third, how does the politics of language in contemporary Algeria intersect these other two concerns? The first two questions appear to lead in opposite directions: the practice of transnational feminism is a pragmatic problem, the relationship among language, justice, and the law is, in my analysis, a philosophical question that contains within itself a tension between a messianic and a pragmatic understanding of justice. In making the claim that French is at this point (and possibly only at this point) the only language in which there is a possible recourse to justice, I do not want to reify any of the languages at issue. Obviously, on one level the pragmatic and pertinent appeals, such as Hélie-Lucas has made to other feminists in the Arab world, presumably in Arabic, may pose a vehement challenge, and with some justification. At a pragmatic level, justice sometimes seems to be served—the guilty are sometimes convicted and the innocent acquitted—and this may occur in principle in any language, whether or not one is against the politics associated with that language. Similarly, as Amilcar Cabral has argued, on the borders of political centers, resistant cultures may emerge that embody cultural counterhegemonies.[23] In making this bold claim about the status of French in the mock trial, I do not want to suggest that any language can rid itself of its colonial history, though it may become quite a different language in another context. I also do not want to posit *justice* as something pure and accessible within the French language. Rather, in my analysis, access to justice is *virtual* and is enunciated in a language *haunted by the specters of colonialism*. The notion of *virtual justice* that I want to formulate describes simultaneously the possibility of justice and the mockery of that very concept.

To use the terms of my analysis of Simone de Beauvoir, my argument functions metonymically to represent this moment of transnational feminism, and inasmuch as it takes the law and justice as its theme, it establishes transnational connections along fairly bourgeois lines. Like Djamila Boupacha, who went on to become a spokesperson for women's causes in Algeria, the women who participated in the mock trial were not subalterns, but they nonetheless performed the very problem of women's representation (and perhaps, by extension, of representation more generally, which happens to be foregrounded in discussions about transnational feminism).[24] The political work performed by the mock trial, and understood through the concept of a haunted virtual justice, causes a rupture in the conventional notion of public space, which we may associate with justice and the law, and places the concept of repression at its very heart.[25]

Language and the Law

A brief consideration of the changes in the politics of language and the legal system in Algeria will allow us to understand how these linguistic ghosts now manifest themselves, and how ghosts may paradoxically be the only recourse available to what we are calling *virtual justice*. Since the first constitution of Algeria came into effect in 1963, language as a nationalist issue has been at the forefront of juridical consciousness in that country. At that time, Arabic was supposed to supplant French as the language of the nation, even though government work continued to be conducted largely in French, and for all practical purposes Algerian elites (the politicians, the upper class, and the intelligentsia) remained bilingual. Which Arabic? And what of the languages other than French and colloquial Arabic that circulated in the Algerian state? What of Tamazight and other languages of the Berbers, which are spoken by a large portion of the population? The power of language was recognized not only as a force of potential national cohesion, but also as a force of law, and alternative control. The language named in the 1963 constitution was classical Arabic, and no mention was made of Tamazight or of any Maghrebi dialects. As part of Ben Bella's promise of "education for all," modern standard Arabic was the language of school instruction, echoing the broader desires of unification in the more leftist utopian elements of pan-Arabism. Although some efforts were made to employ teachers to assist in the transition, these were rather weak. After a lull in the enforcement of Arabization in the 1970s, the mid-1980s saw a massive resurgence, and the judiciary system was Arabized in 1986.[26] From that moment on, and particularly since December 1990, what had been an unenforced, and unsuccessful, statute of the constitution became an occasion for violent civil unrest.[27] Not only has freedom of speech been effectively obliterated in Algeria, with the murder of tens of thousands of civilians, a large number of whom were from elite or bourgeois backgrounds, writers, journalists, and feminist activists who often worked and spoke in French. In addition, Arabic is also achieving the status that French once had in the region; it is becoming the language of power designed to obliterate local cultures, often for corrupt political ends. The recent institutionalization of English as Algeria's second language is further testament to the attempt to demote French, ending its literary, political, and legal hold over the Algerian imaginary. As John Entelis remarked as early as 1981, "The government's official policy of Arabization, Algerianization and Islamization gives additional expressive and symbolic meaning to Arabic language used by all concerned."[28]

The idea that occasioned the change of national language may be too obvious to repeat here. The politics of language had become an urgent issue in Algeria with the institution of a language policy in colonial education. Under French colonialism, the rationale for teaching French was articulated quite differently than the rationale for teaching English under British colonialism. The British in India, for example, did not demonstrate any particular desire to assimilate the natives of India, either culturally or linguistically, and seemed content to enforce power without hegemony. Famously, Thomas Macaulay's 1835 Minute on Education in British Parliament called for the education, in the most British manner, of an elite who could mediate between the British ruling class and the people, with their various local cultures and languages. In that way, British economic and political goals could be more effectively achieved.[29]

In the case of Algeria, however, the policy of assimilation dictated that, in principle, the French language be taught to all inhabitants of Algeria, which after 1848 became three departments of France.[30] According to some, however, what occurred was the gradual destruction of literacy in any language for Algerians.[31] At the time of independence, an astonishing 80 to 90 percent of Algerians were illiterate, as a result, some say, of the systematic eradication of local schools teaching Arabic during the first forty years of French rule (1830–1870). Gradually the difficulties of establishing a French colonial education system were reflected in a lack of infrastructure in the country to effectively teach French—a lack of infrastructure, one could say, that betrayed any pretension to enact the *mission civilisatrice*, regardless of how spurious that mission was in its initial overt intentions. From 1870 to World War I, France established and consolidated its schools and its economic and political hold. That hold would be vigorously challenged in the postwar period with the reestablishment of local schools.

The drive to educate that came with the early colonial policy of assimilation was justified by French scientific studies of the region that had developed from the same roots as those policies. The need to educate in the French system was articulated as early as 1831 by the Institut National de France, and Pierre Genty de Bussy quickly established three schools in his first months as chief governmental representative in Algiers, even though they were for Europeans. Discouraged by France in his effort to establish a French school in a mosque in Algiers, he established Arab-French schools, which were initially bilingual in instruction. The number of schools, however, diminished drastically after 1870. Thus, although integration seemed a possibility at one point, this effort quickly foundered for lack of funding, and because the policy demands of an apparently secularized education were interpreted to mean that French instruction should be established in the schools. Far fewer women than men were educated in the colonial system. The colonial endeavor did not merely reinforce differential education for boys and girls, it actively refashioned it, and placed new pressures on social gender dynamics. Without the resource of colonial education or of indigenous schooling, women became increasingly deskilled. And the French colonizers frequently attributed this deskilling to "Islamic tradition" rather than to the particular dynamics of the political context. Although pockets of cultural resistance still formed, they were largely invisible to the French in Paris, and thus were only partially effective in offering a challenge to it.[32]

The status of the spoken language, then, was of course inextricably bound up with the status of the colonial regime, and its political, military, and juridical power and abuse of power. Indeed, even some religious practices, despite the status of scriptural language, were recast in Catholic French. This was a result of both the education system and the legal system. Both British and French colonial law had to deal with local legal systems in their colonies, the legacy of which continues today. In some instances—for example, in India—separate local courts dealt with family law, whereas criminal law was administered by the state.[33] The *Shari'a*, even in its varied oral local renditions, put particular pressures on colonial juridical systems. In Algeria, some efforts were initially made to maintain the local legal system with its accompanying law schools (which were in the mosques) to avoid disturbing the system and thereby giving rise to insurgency. Even though the schools were initially maintained, however, the status of the law changed considerably. Local variations of Islamic law were subsumed under a more centralized system that began to resemble the system more familiar in France. Some have even called the system a "romanized . . . qadi justice."[34] The *Shari'a* became a highly codified written law associated not only with the state but also with divine law. The peculiarity of the relationship to codified French law actually led to the replacement of a two-tiered concept of law (the *Shari'a* and divine law) with another two-tiered concept (Islamic law and French law) that effectively forged a stronger relationship between the *Shari'a* and divine law, blurring the distinction between the two, which has had serious consequences for contemporary Algeria. In addition to recourses to the newly codified *Shari'a*, appeals could always be made to the "higher court"—the French court. Thus, not only did the nature of local law change, sometimes in ways that secularized it and sometimes in ways that did the opposite; but the law was also formalized and subordinated to French law. In the 1880s, an effort was made to remove the local courts entirely and put both French law and Muslim law in the hands of French judges, but this met with great resistance and the French were obliged to back down. After 1919, in rare cases when an Algerian was eligible for citizenship, he had to renounce the *Shari'a*.

The clash between the two legal codes had many consequences, including, for women, impoverishment. For example, they were no longer awarded alimony by the Muslim court in cases of divorce; and in the nineteenth century, changes in the land tenure system often meant that property negotiations with the colonial masters were conducted by the head of the family, to the detriment of women's interests.

Although in retrospect it is possible to identify a history of resistance and insurgency against the French language and the civil code, the power of those codes persists in postindependence Algeria. The status of French during the colonial period had become sufficiently normalized, that is, sufficiently hegemonized, to make it a desirable acquisition, even though for many people it did not seem to be their own language. That is, it was not a mother tongue.[35] For our purposes, a mother tongue is one in which we believe we can represent ourselves linguistically, and even psychologically, politically, religiously, and legally.

Djamila Boupacha

It is exactly these complications in representability that arose in Halimi and de Beauvoir's committee for Djamila Boupacha.[36] In 1960, Gisèle Halimi asked Simone de Beauvoir to assist her in publicizing in France the case of Djamila Boupacha, a young woman who had been tortured by French police officers in Algiers to extract information (that is, testimony) from her about those involved in "terrorist" activities during the war of independence (1954–1962). Halimi (Djamila's lawyer, a woman of Tunisian descent) and de Beauvoir had a central aim: to achieve full legal representation for Djamila in a court of law in the French metropolis. Despite the fact that it was the law that had brutally tortured this woman—and rationalized it in the name of justice (as information retrieval necessary to counteract "terrorist" activities planned by the FLN and ALN)—these women embraced the law as an instrument of adjudication.

In 1961, de Beauvoir and Halimi decided to compile a book about Djamila, then a political prisoner. The bulk of the book was written by Halimi, who described her encounters with Djamila and recounted in narrative form her first contact with the case and the trajectory it took. Halimi's text is unfinished, but it takes us up to Djamila's hearing. The remainder of the book consists of an introduction by de Beauvoir, her article from *Le Monde*, testimony by Djamila's father regarding the events leading up to Djamila's arrest and his own, and their subsequent torture at the hands of the French military forces. It also includes Djamila's civil indictment, various "testimonies"—articles written by French intellectuals about torture in Algeria by French forces, drawings of Djamila by Pablo Picasso and Robert Lapoujade, and a painting by Roberto Matta.

The book was compiled by Halimi and de Beauvoir as a document for the Djamila Boupacha committee, which was headed by de Beauvoir at Halimi's request and formed to bring Djamila's torture, her private suffering, into Parisian public discourse. Although the function of the committee was ostensibly to bring the case to a court in the French metropolis, the torturers were ultimately granted amnesty through the extensive amnesty laws discussed in this book's introduction.[37] The English translation of the book begins with a statement that might have been obvious to French readers but came into effect after the publication of the book in France:

> Since this book was completed, the Evian agreement has come into force. It was signed on the 18th March, 1962, and on the 20th an amnesty was declared for all Moslem political prisoners, to take effect between 18th March and 8th April.
>
> Djamila's family were consequently released in early April, and Djamila herself on 21st April, but under the terms of the amnesty her torturers also gain immunity. No further action will be taken against her for her activities in support of the FLN, but she will be unable to proceed with her case against General Ailleret or the Minister of War. Nor will she be able to take further steps to bring her torturers to justice.[38]

In a sense, then, the book announced itself as the only recourse to justice given the impossibility of legal redress. The book granted justice *virtually*, as a record that haunts the manipulation of the language of law and as a text that moved beyond the apparent referentiality of language. This pressure of the virtual foregrounds both the *force of circumstance* and the very impossibility of succumbing to that force when considering justice. Against the impossibility of law we see justice maintained as an impossible yet perceivable ethics.

De Beauvoir agreed to head the committee and to have her name appear on the book, primarily so that she would share responsibility with Halimi were there to be any legal repercussions. Although the book was her idea, she refrained from contributing very much, and we are obliged to turn to *Force of Circumstance*, the third volume of her autobiography, and to her letters to Nelson Algren to get her impressions of the event.[39] The purpose of the project was to appeal to metropolitan French citizens to save themselves from the disease of apathy, and from the normalization of a corrupt and "infected" legal and governmental system. The call for a fair trial was, in a way, a medical call—to heal a psychological illness of the French people and of a sick legal system that failed to represent Algerians (both in the sense of allowing them to speak and be heard, and as a way of giving them legal representation).

For de Beauvoir, the work for the Boupacha committee satisfied another need. She had to find a way of doing something for the Algerian cause that was quite different from what Jean-Paul Sartre was doing. She writes:

I wanted to stop being an accomplice in this war, but how? I could talk in meetings or write articles; but I would only have been saying the same things as Sartre less well than he was saying them. I would have felt ridiculous following him like a shadow. . . .[40]

She also wanted to continue her work on women, to demonstrate that there was such a thing as gendered violence, the repercussions of which for women were often less visible. She was in this regard taking a double stand against Albert Camus, who had not only disappointed her in his war efforts but had also trivialized her feminist work. He had dismissed *The Second Sex*, she tells us, "in a few morose sentences," accusing her "of making the French male look ridiculous. . . ."[41]

Camus, of course, was equally disparaging of Sartre's efforts during the Algerian war, accusing him of adopting a naive attitude, as if a simple condemnation of colonialism in grand terms could address the particular difficulties of any nation going through decolonization.[42] Camus's unwillingness to condemn his fellow French *colons* came from a sense that it was the mainland French rather than the relatively less wealthy *colons* who had always stood to gain most from the colonial enterprise in Algeria. It was easy, in his estimation, for someone like Sartre to condemn the *colons* and the colonial army's actions in Algeria, and indeed Camus also condemned the violence on both sides. But perhaps Camus saw in Sartre and de Beauvoir two people making up for their lack of sustained activity in the French Resistance during World War II. And Camus too was (wrongfully) accused of inaction during the Algerian war.

De Beauvoir's language actively works to resist any connection made by the French to World War II and the Vichy period, condemning those who rationalized torture as a disease. When de Beauvoir, Germaine Tillion, and other members of the Boupacha committee requested that Djamila's case be tried in France, Edmond Michelet, the Minister of Justice, spoke of the army in Algeria in metaphors of disease, an interesting analogy given that many of the perpetrators of violence were doctors, who were, on the one hand, there to keep patients alive and, on the other, to administer torture:[43]

It's terrible, this gangrene the Nazis have bequeathed to us. It infects everything, it rots everything, we simply aren't able to root it out. Roughing up is one thing—

you can't have a police force without it; but torture! . . . I try to make them understand; the line must be drawn somewhere. . . . It's a gangrene. . . . Fortunately it will all be over soon.[44]

Similarly, Maurice Patin, head of the Committee of Public Safety, speaks of "a canker in our midst," adding with relief that Djamila was raped vaginally with a bottle and not penetrated "per anum" as was the practice of torture in Indochina.[45]

De Beauvoir, however, does not allow this "disease" to serve as an excuse, as if there were no agency involved in enacting violence and as if this were something distant, a Nazi tropical frenzy, in which those in the Hexagon (France) had no complicity. She brings the sickness back home, expressing her disgust at her compatriots, and even at herself, speaking of a "tetanus of the imagination" that she feels looking again at the documented descriptions of torture. At the time (in 1957) she said she wished simply to push the vivid description aside in disgust.[46]

By the time de Beauvoir wrote the article for *Le Monde* in 1960, however, her style had changed. Reproaching the French public for their complacency, she transferred the "gangrenous," torturous mentality inherited from the Nazis back onto the inhabitants of metropolitan France, to show that the "tetanus of the imagination" was also inherited and had persisted since the time of the Nazi occupation. The sickness of complacency became iconic—a threatening metaphor of the memories of occupied Paris rather than a rationalizing displacement. She now framed it as a scandalous abdication of responsibility.

In his introduction to Henri Alleg's *La Question*, Sartre speaks of the "annihilation of the colonized." He continues, "We have wiped out their civilization while refusing them our own. . . . For most Europeans in Algeria there are two complimentary and inseparable truths: the colonists are backed by divine right, the natives are subhuman."[47] This internalized divine right that, according to Sartre's logic, leads to a lack of humane treatment on the part of the French, can also be seen in the report of the Committee of Public Safety. De Beauvoir cites her article from *Le Monde* in *Force of Circumstance*: "Acts which in other times and in normal circumstances might appear exorbitant are perfectly legal in Algeria."[48] She remarks with horror that "this narrative—[of] hangings, beatings, torture—[related in the case against Ben Saddock] was read out in stony silence; not one gasp of surprise or disgust: everyone knew already. My heart froze inside me as I once again faced the truth: everyone knew and didn't give a damn, or else approved."[49]

It is this shocking complacency that de Beauvoir sought to address in her article in *Le Monde* on June 3, 1960. It began, "The most scandalous aspect of any scandal is that one gets used to it," and concluded, "such an abdication of responsibility would be a betrayal of France as a whole, of you, of me, of each and every one of us.[50] She painted a picture of a France that had already lost control of its army in Algiers, and reported that Djamila herself had appealed while being tortured, that de Gaulle had outlawed torture. In response to Djamila's plea the army officer responded, "De Gaulle can call the odds back home but we are masters here."[51]

Between this threatening vision of an army run amok and a French people indifferent to the tortures being meted out in its name, there is a vivid description, taken from the text of Djamila's civil indictment, of the tortures perpetrated on her body: she was illegally imprisoned in a detention center, where she should not have been held; was kicked in the chest by a group of soldiers and had a rib permanently displaced; had electrodes affixed with transparent tape to her nipples, legs, face, anus, and vagina and was given electrical shocks; was burned with cigarettes; and was "deflowered" with a beer bottle. De Beauvoir includes the voice of the victim and assailants at this point, as if her own words cannot do justice to the horror:

Several days later the men interrogating her said: "You won't be raped, you might enjoy it." Djamila Boupacha herself states what in fact took place: "I was given the most appalling torture of all, the so-called 'bottle treatment.' First they tied me up in a special posture, and then they rammed the neck of a bottle into my belly. I screamed and fainted. I was unconscious, to the best of my knowledge, for two days. . . ."

De Beauvoir wrote in parentheses, "(She was a virgin)."[52]

De Beauvoir leaves out one of the tortures described by Djamila: "the bath treatment," where the victim was "trussed up and hung over a bath on a stick, and submerged until (she) nearly choke(d)."[53] At the request of Robert Gauthier from *Le Monde*, de Beauvoir reluctantly replaced the word *vagina* with *belly* (a euphemism, to be sure, but connoting the belly of the virgin Mary) but would not omit the phrase stating Djamila's virginity.[54] De Beauvoir alluded to, but does not describe, the tortures experienced by Djamila's father and brother-in-law. Halimi, in her narration of the case and of her experiences as Djamila's lawyer, speaks extensively of the water-hose torture, in which the victim is filled with water by placing a hosepipe in the mouth and then jumped on so that water is expelled through the orifices.

Vivid depictions of torture abound in the book prepared by de Beauvoir and Halimi, and the exactness of the legal language, which entails a precise description of the instrument of torture, becomes a necessary means of representing pain, as if, in fact, the instruments of torture conveyed the pain. The internal pain and humiliation of the rape is the only torture represented by speechlessness—by a literal loss of consciousness, which points to an epistemic and cultural gap whereby a particular type of gendered sexual violence cannot be articulated in a description of the instrument of torture. Language describing pain will always be inadequate because pain is characterized by its irreducibility to language. In a courtroom the victim is asked to recognize instruments of torture. Household items such as bottles or water hoses, or more specifically engineered instruments, are introduced as evidence. If the victim recognizes their function, they become indexes of her pain. It is language that is undone by pain, as Elaine Scarry has pointed out.[55] Articulating pain in the language of the courtroom gives it shape or structure. It fails, however, to acknowledge the undoing caused by pain. The instruments of torture become indexical references to the torture, and "the decisive test" for the torture victim is to recognize the instrument of torture. For the reader, the decisive test is a commitment to language and the law at the very moment of their undoing. The conflation among language, the law, and recognition ignores the undoing of meaning by establishing a clear and unambiguous path of action. Perhaps the demand for this is necessitated because the form of war has changed since World War II, when absolute genocide became more conceivable than ever with the ability of industrial powers to create atomic fission: this was genocide without index, and the inverse of what Sartre called the "people's war" being waged in Algeria.

The possibility of complete annihilation and the failure of political and legal representation, or indeed the failure to recognize that Algeria and France were at war, produced in Algeria the "people's war," a new form of war that emerged in the colonies following World War II. It was in some ways a civil war—or to use a term employed for the current unrest in Algeria, *a war against civilians*—and the only strategies that could be used, given the lack of arms, were "terrorism, ambushes and harassing the enemy."[56] The forms of justice then employed—torture as trial—assumed that a war was not taking place. (That the French also employed terrorist tactics against civilians is a point, of course, not without its contradictions. But state terrorism is rarely considered among acts of terrorism.)

In her article in *Le Monde*, de Beauvoir depicts Djamila's case as unexceptional in itself. She was arrested, along with her father and brother-in-law, in her home in Algiers. It is alleged that she had planted a bomb in a university canteen, which was defused before it exploded. Boupacha admitted that she was a militant FLN activist but did not admit planting the bomb until she was illegally detained and cruelly tortured, at which point she confessed. When she did so, however, she also confessed to crimes for which other people had already been imprisoned and executed. In this gesture of confession she recognized herself as a symbol for the humiliated French military—a woman who had fooled them in order to further the independence struggle through whatever means necessary, an Algerian to whom they could attribute military action. For the French army in Algiers, then, she became a metonymy for "terrorist" activity—a substitutable signifier of the threat to the French public; whether she committed the crime or not, she admitted to being a militant FLN member, which means she might commit a crime of this sort and could therefore, by association, be condemned on suspicion.

What betrayed her, then, was less the "information" she agreed to give under torture than her symbolic and rhetorical positioning. It is true that the demand for information, like that of testimony, points to a referential use of language. For the type of information requested and delivered in court (or in police chambers) is supposed to establish facts to produce and support material evidence, not to refer one back to something as allegedly suspect as "experience." Yet confession, in this case, is obviously proof of nothing other than the pain inflicted through torture.

In *The Body in Pain: The Making and Unmaking of the World*, Elaine Scarry speaks of the language of the body being tortured and enduring war. She refers to the separate spheres that the sufferer and witness occupy, suggesting that "to have great pain is to have certainty; to hear that another is in pain is to have doubt."[57] The imprecision of the language of pain, the difficulty of articulating the intensity and mechanisms of pain, causes the sufferer and the witness to resort quickly to analogy—"it feels like"—and in the case of torture, the victim often describes the instruments and the physical marks of torture as a means not only to describe the pain but also to externalize it. For the witness to that pain, or for the jury that hears the account of that pain as testimony, the mechanism works quite differently. For the legal discourse of the courtroom, where proof is the central concern, the mechanism of suffering indeed has to be testified to through external signifiers. Halimi wrote in her narrative that she was anxious for Djamila's case to be tried before the electrode burns had faded from her skin. Similarly, the officials who verified the evidence needed to be sure that Djamila recognized the *gégène*, one of the instruments of torture. They insisted that she identify the instrument, the sight of which caused her terror, as if she were identifying the perpetrator of the violence, as if, indeed, the instrument itself had agency. The witness, then, always doubts the accuser, precisely because the pain itself cannot be communicated.

In Scarry's terms, the externalization of pain through language can be a mode of human making that documents the process of unmaking (the infliction of pain), and it can also be a means by which an analogy is produced for the benefit of the witness. For Edmond Michelet, who speaks of a gangrene overtaking the army in Algiers, the metaphor of physical incapacitation is displaced from Djamila to the army, through an invocation of Nazi-occupied Paris. Camus, who in 1955 had proposed a "civil truce" in response to the despair he felt at the slaughter of the French in his homeland of Algeria, called for attacks on civilians on both sides to be outlawed.[58] In war, then, according to Camus, civilians on either side of the conflict can be substituted for one another. Sartre, of course, would take issue with this idea: a people's war leads to certain kinds of combat that become necessary in the face of the threat of genocide. To focus on civilians is to suggest their lack of agency in a violent war. Each victim, then, is generalized: the immediate conflict is set aside and the victim becomes a synecdoche for all "innocent" victims of war. Camus's own sense of the horror of occupied countries, so vividly described in *La Peste*, on this occasion leads him to see an equivalence between the two sides of this war, a view that separated him from de Beauvoir's and Sartre's circle of intellectuals, who were adamant that the FLN be supported in their struggle for independence. In spite of his support of the FLN, Sartre recognized the complex and shocking human rights issues confronting the French at this time, while also acknowledging the importance of supporting the victims.

Appalled, the French are discovering this terrible truth: that if nothing can protect a nation against itself, neither its traditions nor its loyalties nor its laws, . . . then its behavior is no more than a matter of opportunity and occasion. Anybody, at any time, may equally find himself victim or executioner.[59]

This crisis of humanism is taken up quite differently in de Beauvoir's work. All French people, according to de Beauvoir, are guilty of complacency unless they speak out about the torture of Algerians. All French people are guilty if they fail to acknowledge that, for Algerians such as Djamila, her father, and her brother-in-law, speaking out against their torture is practically impossible unless they have the *public* support of a Parisian lawyer. Djamila refused to speak when her lawyer was not present, perhaps realizing that the eloquence of her silence would protect her more than words ever could, or perhaps because she had little access to her own pain, a possibility that seems to be compounded by her loss of consciousness for an astonishing two days.[60] The loss of consciousness enacts a traumatic and illocutionary breakdown of the access to pain at the moment it occurred, and for as long as the trauma remains traumatic. "She would stay mute," Halimi informs us.[61] But the refusal to speak also suggests something else, which may undo Scarry's opposition between the victim's and the witness's access to pain. Although Scarry quite pragmatically advocates a linguistic code for measuring the immeasurable—that is, for expressing the types and degrees of pain—she assumes that victims always have access to their own pain and fully understand it. Work in trauma studies, whether it draws on psychoanalysis or on the psychological works of Pierre Janet, has taught us something quite different, however. Pain, especially when it is traumatic, cannot always be expressed, is not always known, and is likely to produce faulty memory and testimony that differ from what we may discover actually occurred.[62] This is certainly difficult to account for in the courtroom, which is why de Beauvoir insists that all French people are guilty if they fail to recognize how the French military and governing bodies in Algeria make the political representation of Algerians very difficult. Halimi, for example, was on many occasions denied the proper visas that would allow her to stay in Algiers so she could gather information, prepare her case, and represent Djamila. Djamila's words betrayed her—in torture she confessed. In other words, the mechanisms of war—acts of violence that, according to Scarry, rely on injury but deny the rhetoric of injury in favor of the rhetoric of strategy and politics, generally understood to exist in the realm of public discourse—force us to understand the torture of Algerians simply as a part of that rhetoric of "information gathering" that is so important to war strategy. For Algerians, however, torture, although occurring in the public context of war, is confined through the enforcement of silence and the threat of more torture to a private sphere of suffering; this is the psychological consequence of a "people's war." Instruments of torture and marks on bodies cannot bring about the articulation and externalization necessary for the public discourse of law on a victim's private pain and suffering. As Simone de Beauvoir says, "The exceptional thing about the Boupacha case is not the nature of the facts involved, but their publication."[63] Indeed, exactly for this reason, Halimi's narrative of Djamila's torture and her own experiences as Djamila's legal representative slips between the registers of the discourse of personal exchange and the register of information extraction for the purpose of public testimony. The personal trauma of the young Muslim girl who lost her virginity (described by Halimi through analogy as "a kind of amputation") indeed intrudes into Halimi's narrative.[64] Yet there is no room for personal trauma in the public discourse of the courtroom. For the French, however, the personal humiliation they feel because Djamila has dressed in a coquettish fashion, like an *évoluée* who wears European clothes, does have a place within public discourse. Their humiliation is in itself attributed to an act of violation on her part.[65]

For Djamila Boupacha, speaking of the signifiers of torture—its instruments and its marks on her body—becomes a means to externalize her own pain and to transmit the private discourse of torture as the public discourse of war, through her lawyer, Gisèle Halimi. Without Halimi, and without her legal know-how in the specific context of the discourses circulating about the Algerian War, Djamila's creation of terms to designate her pain—her description of her "unmaking"—would remain within the realm of the private. For Djamila, torture became a metaphor for her existence; she externalized what was specifically internal—pain—through the instruments that threatened to unmake her again if her speech were found by the French military to be inappropriate. For her, torture became icon. Halimi's narrative of Djamila's case demonstrates the means to measure silences. For her, the language of torture has to gain credence within the public realm of the courtroom. As Scarry says, "Under the pressure of this requirement, the lawyer, too, becomes an inventor of language, one who speaks on behalf of another person (the plaintiff) and attempts to communicate the reality of that person's physical pain to people who are not themselves in pain (the jurors)."[66] Halimi's testimony had to demonstrate the deliberate and systematic attempt to silence the whole affair, by showing the mechanisms of corruption. In that sense, the instruments of pain, and indeed Djamila, had to become, in the courtroom, metonymies (indexes) for the system of corruption. They were therefore brought into the public discourse of a corrupt war—a war in which even militants had their agency stolen from them by torture and the discourses surrounding it.

*

To make her feminist intervention (though it is not articulated as such), de Beauvoir has to use a different form of influence, which makes her use of metonymy and metaphor quite different from that used by Halimi, Boupacha, and indeed Michelet, Patin, Camus, and Sartre. To cure the French public of this "tetanus of the imagination," she must make Djamila an unexceptional figure—a metonymy for the suffering of Algerians. "The most scandalous aspect of any scandal is that one gets used to it."[67] Here is yet another case of torture. De Beauvoir must also appeal to France's humanity: "Such an abdication of responsibility would be a betrayal of France as a whole, of you, of me, of each and every one of us."[68] Djamila's case here becomes a metaphor for the "unmaking" of France. It also draws on another unmaking—the memory of a previous "unmaking" of Paris under the occupation. It draws, in fact, on that iconic anxiety, the gangrenous violence inherited from the Germans to which Michelet refers. De Beauvoir also individualizes Boupacha, citing her testimony—giving her a voice—but not leaving her with an impossible task of speaking alone. She thus recognizes the impossibility of both legal and linguistic representation. The worst torture for Djamila was her "deflowering" with the bottle. The pain externalized through the description and cited in de Beauvoir's article is characterized as an outrage. The private horror of pain lives through de Beauvoir's article, which places the private discourse of torture at the very heart of the public discourse of war. Her work stands in sharp contrast to Sartre's on torture during this period, for what we see there is a highly virilized discourse of combat: "The torturer pits himself against the tortured for his 'manhood' and the duel is fought as if it were not possible for both sides to belong to the human race."[69] He pays very little attention to the silences, to the unspoken and perhaps unspeakable trauma and pain of the victim, which de Beauvoir carefully describes in a manner that is empathetic but also very conscious of the function of her own writing and of Boupacha's political commitment. This approach enables the generally tough-minded Boupacha to emerge as something more than a victim, but as traumatized nonetheless. What we begin to hear in Boupacha's language, and in the manner in which it is represented by de Beauvoir, is the emergence of phantoms that foreground the unspeakable and that acknowledge that, although the pragmatic language of the courtroom (or indeed of the code that Scarry calls for) may be necessary, it also performs a demetaphorization of language. The language of law assumes that justice can be fully done, that the phantoms emerging from one's own repression and those that remain in one's language from the generations of colonial violence could be laid to rest by a verdict, or that the work of healing can always begin after judgment. Abraham and Torok theorize such haunting as the moment when the inability to assimilate begins to manifest itself. "The fantasy of incorporation reveals a gap within the psyche; it points to something that is missing just where introjection should have occurred."[70] The emergence of the phantom is then the unidentifiable trace of melancholia—an undoing rather than an ontology.

The Djamila Boupacha committee, whose most vocal members were women, allowed de Beauvoir to make a transnational feminist gesture, which demonstrated the importance of a discourse using both the indexical as well as the iconical, and the necessity of understanding the performative context of discourse. This gesture had a specifically pedagogical aim: to save the French from themselves. The performativity of both legal and journalistic writing, under the guise of absolute transparency and with a belief in that transparency, makes possible a strong political gesture in the face of a crisis. De Beauvoir is also attentive to the particular problems of aggressive and violent sexual behavior that accompany a military conflict, behavior that is, at worst, exacerbated and, at best, ignored, by a conception of torture as a battle for masculinity.[71]

In spite of de Beauvoir's commitment to the Algerian cause, there is little evidence in the text of her overall view of Algeria. She confines her remarks to the case at hand, the horror of a war crime performed in France's name. Her aim is to "prevent the crime of silence," to cite the title of another attempt at virtual justice, the reports of the Russell War Crimes Tribunal for Vietnam (in which Sartre, de Beauvoir, and Halimi played an active part).[72] She also aims to acknowledge and be sensitive to the form of that silence and the failure of language, which in the legal context is understood to be merely referential. The particular problems of making the courtroom a viable place for Algerians seeking justice (problems that have been recently documented in Jean-Marc Théolleyre's collection *Juger en Algérie 1944–1962*) require that the ghosts from World War II that de Beauvoir invokes be included, and indeed that they bear witness.[73] These ghosts challenge the language of justice and empowerment and establish the inability to represent.

People's War

Speaking of the need for justice, for a condemnation of terrorist and other violent activities in Algeria during the war, and for a civil truce, Camus criticized those who reproached the French nation by "endlessly going back to the errors of the past." "It is dangerous," he wrote, "to expect that a nation will confess that it alone is guilty and condemn it to perpetual penance. . . . Problems must be seen in relation to the future. . . ."[74] Of course we will never know what would have happened without the violent revolutionary uprising in Algeria. We will never know whether the French would have continued to hold on to a colony that was not financially lucrative, and Camus to some extent acknowledged this. His "Appeal for a Civilian Truce" offered concrete plans for a future that would acknowledge that the age of colonialism had passed. His inability to consider that the two sides were unequal placed him firmly, as he says himself, on an ethical ground that is not political and cannot really take into account the political situation. His ethical quandary transcends but also falls short of the task of dealing with the political context. In fact, his language transcends the referential. Consider Camus's comments on the relationship among ethics, politics, and justice:

Such a spirit of equity, to be sure, seems alien to the reality of our history, in which relationships of force outline another sort of justice; in our international society there is no good ethical system except a *nuclear ethics*. Then the only guilty one is the vanquished. It is understandable that many intellectuals have consequently come to the conclusion that *values and words derive their meaning altogether from force*. Hence some people progress without transition from the *fait accompli* or the cruelest party. I continue, however, to believe with regard to Algeria and to everything else that such aberrations, both on the Right and on the Left, merely define the nihilism of our epoch. If it is true that in history, at least, values—whether those of the nation or those of humanity—do not survive unless they have been fought for, the fight is not enough to justify them. The fight itself must rather be justified, and elucidated, by those values. When fighting for your truth, you must take care not to kill it with the very arms you are using to defend it—*only under such a double condition do words resume their living meaning*. Knowing that, the intellectual has the role of distinguishing in each camp the respective limits of force and justice. The role is to clarify definitions in order to disintoxicate minds and to calm fanaticisms, even when this is against the current tendency [emphasis added].[75]

A purely referential language, stripped bare of any *living meaning*, is a language that responds to the loss of meaning—nuclear holocaust—by undoing its very potential. Through total annihilation, language's referential function is of course destroyed. But countering this with a kind of absolute referentiality, a language stripped bare, is another form of annihilation that makes of language a law of absolute referentiality. The *nuclear death* of language as meaning is thus countered by another form of killing, making it exist in a very limited sense, as if direct communication were possible, as if, in effect, language could be transparent and, in a demetaphorized manner, could simply denote. Justice, understood as only *virtually* available, is possible only with a living language that produces meaning because it is haunted but is not simply referential. If we contrast this with Sartre's comments on the "people's war" (taken from his essay "On Genocide," which was presented at the Russell War Tribunal but works well as a commentary on Algeria), we find that for him the people's war is the flip side of a nuclear ethics in which meaning is lost. "Terrorism, ambushes and harassing the enemy" is in a way justified politically in Sartre's argument.[76] Camus, however, believes that language can live again only through an ethical position that he believes "can spare useless bloodshed . . . in the solutions that guarantee the future of a land whose suffering [he shares] too much to be able to indulge in speech making about it."[77] And what does it mean for language to live? It means language recovers the "simple reason" that allows us to move into the future, without the ghosts of injustice hanging over us. Nevertheless, we know that "simple reason," language, and the law, have betrayed and alienated. If we are to give life to language, we would surely have to hear the ghosts that language bears within it, to see, in other words, what exceeds (but does not preclude) both its referentiality and its reason. The language of pain, or rather the unmaking of language in pain, has already forced us to consider this, and the pain we have encountered is not abstract but the concrete pain of a people's war.

To be fair to Sartre, it is worth acknowledging that in 1948 when he published both *What Is Literature?* and *Black Orpheus*, he made an exception to the argument that literature should be politically referential and that poetry should be rejected in favor of prose, which draws less attention to the performativity of its own language.[78, 79] In *Black Orpheus* he calls on black (male) poets to rise up "spermatically" and create something new from a language that has alienated them. He thus argues that refashioning language and allowing it to perform is itself a political act. But at the moment of revolution he might consider such work inappropriate, and he might be right. Even if, at one level, he were realistic in his sense of political efficacy, would that mean that a sense of being alienated from a language and a legal structure would be beside the point? Would it mean that one had to assume that the only form of justice is one dictated by *nuclear ethics*, as Camus argued? And what sort of ghosts would that erasure of meaning and performativity, which transcends the revolutionary moment, produce? Although Camus may have been blinded by a colonialist ideology when he spoke of a "reestablishment of the necessary justice" (*establishment* would have been the more appropriate term), *justice* is a necessary ideal to hold on to.[80] And in this situation justice must entertain the possibility that a performance of language exceeds referentiality, but that in its performativity language inevitably maintains an attenuated relationship with the political context, which leaves behind its ghosts or, we could say, its phantoms that remain incorporated but not introjected.[81]

Sartre, in the Russell War Tribunal, recognized the problems of making judgments about war crimes from a particular political position. No government sanctioned the tribunal. Unlike the Nuremberg trials that took place after the war when the victors could identify the war crimes of the vanquished, the tribunal, according to Sartre, could function free from political pressure precisely because it could not pass judgment, and could not therefore enforce its findings. To some extent, this is the case with any international war tribunal, because in spite of the Geneva Convention it is clearly difficult to enforce international law. In that sense, the tribunal was a kind of *mock trial*—a performance of justice that can exist only outside the political realm.

De Beauvoir invoked ghosts of inactivity during World War II to force Algeria into French consciousness; she forced the French to remember what may have been haunting them. And for the future of Algeria, which is now Algeria's present, we see another haunting, a sense of a war repeating itself. It is that haunting that occasioned a mock trial in which political opposition took the form of a lament. It might be more appropriate to call that trial, which took place on March 8, 1995, International Women's Day, a mock tribunal.

The Mock Trial: Virtual Justice

What the trial mocks is the availability of recourse to justice through the law, and through the language of the law, which demands referentiality in evidence.[82] In doing so, however, the mock trial performs a kind of justice in the face of the inadequacy of the law. Justice exceeds the structure of law, and the performance of ghosts—signs that haunt language as much as politics—demonstrates the very nature of justice as *impossibility*, as an ethics that haunts the law. The use of the French language in the trial made possible a performance of that haunting. French was now demoted from its status as the language of law to a language that potentially performs the very difficulty of claiming and enforcing a national language. The use of French, in fact, highlights the complex way in which all the languages of Algeria have become haunted by a politics that expresses the very difficulty of representation in the postnuclear, postcolonial period. This is foregrounded in the fact that even the FIS, while calling for Arabization, wrote its manifesto in French.

Intellectuals from Algeria, such as Assia Djebar and Benamar Mediene, as well as intellectuals from France who grew up in Algeria—Jewish Franco-Algerians such as Benjamin Stora, Jacques Derrida, and Hélène Cixous—speak of their memories of the tyranny of the French language—and not just any French language, but that of Parisian intellectuals, the Académie Française, and a French spoken *without an accent*. In other words, not only is this the French associated with the law through the Declaration of the Rights of Man, but it is also a French that is reconstructed as Law, in relation to which one can only be other. The unrelenting attempt to reproduce and be attuned to the cadences, rhythms, and intonations of the language has left some of these authors with such an uncompromising, and perhaps pathological, sense of the *purity* of the language as they surrender to the law of the Other that the result is a handicapped memory of anything beyond monolingualism. Although this is certainly a symptom of the repressive nature of politically enforcing the use of French, it has led to a radical change in the status of the language. Although the FIS appeals to its authority when it writes its manifesto in French, the very act of writing a call for a *jihad* in French places law and culture in a strange relationship. After all, Arabic is also inextricably associated with the law, bound to both divine and civil law since the years of French colonial rule; and it is that language that is now taking over as the uncompromising and absolute law, as the Other. The consequences of speaking any other language but Arabic are violent, which makes the French language, paradoxically, not only the language of an elite but also a language of protest.

Why then has French been adopted by some of the very people who have recently been the focus of the violence of political Islam? It is surely not from a naive notion of democracy, which views French, and the legal system associated with it, simply and unproblematically. Memories, although handicapped, are not that short. But French paradoxically becomes the language of protest even as it carries with it the ghosts of the past. Perhaps the uncanniness of the language—its paradoxical status as the language of the Other and, simultaneously, as an elusive mother language that provided opportunities—has become the only viable alternative, however haunted it may be by its own colonial specters. Language as Law, once associated with French, has undergone a displacement to Arabic. If in precolonial times the distinction between divine law and civil law was clear, and if in the colonial period that distinction began to erode because of the preeminent status of French law, in the last few years civil law has become more closely associated with divine law. This happened first because of concessions the FLN made to Islamic traditionalists and second because of the confusion about who the perpetrators of violence were, and about to whom those acts are attributed. In a sense French has become decolonized, creating a *virtual lingua franca* in which the hauntedness of that language is revealed itself at the very moment of its performance, which is an alternative to the attempt to institutionalize a highly politicized and centralized Islamic Law.

In the mock trial, as in much Franco-Algerian intellectual writing, French has paradoxically lost its taboo and has become the language of the performative possibilities for the future—a language in which protest is performed in a manner that exceeds the law, as a way to find a form of justice that dramatizes the very impossibility of its full realization in language, but nonetheless the centrality of its impetus. The repetitions of and associations with an earlier moment have produced a kind of mockery of the power once associated with French at a time when that power and a violent reign of terror are now in the domain of Arabic. The association of both languages with the law forces French to reveal its own ghosts, just when, tragically, Arabic is becoming associated with absolute power. *If justice can be performed, it is only virtual.* The trace of French linguistic and legal injustice is present in a form both material and immaterial. The specters of the dead are present in this trace and demand that justice be done. They therefore put pressure on the present. The pressure on language from the postnuclear people's war calls for a recognition of both the impurity of all linguistic performance and the shortcomings of ignoring language's extrareferentiality, its ghosts. The performativity of these women in pain, who have little recourse to representation of any kind, becomes in effect the sign of singular traumas that are not dated but that carry the wounds of war and give life to language. Legal speech, which bears the traces of trauma, is ultimately speech without a legal end, and this may be why it performs some recourse to justice in the very impossibility of justice. The illocutionary failure that is foregrounded in the women's laments articulates both justice as impossibility and the difficulty of inhabiting the language of law and sovereignty when it is the state and religion that make the recourse to justice impossible. The phantom that appears in virtual justice negotiates between the material and historical on the one hand and the mystical on the other.

Virtual justice includes a simulation of justice that is not simply a false justice (though it may be that as well) but a justice that actually enacts the failure of the law to do justice, understood as an ideal form, as something pure. Justice cannot be served, though it may perhaps be bequeathed. Although the law fails to do justice (even when it may seem that justice has been served—remember that many of the accused had already been condemned in courts of law), justice requires that the law exist to maintain the possibility of its bequest. Although the law may fail to do justice because it is inevitably tied to the immediacy of the political dynamics (to the state-machine), justice must rely on the law to lodge the possibility of its existence. It cannot simply float freely, as if it bore no relation to the law, or as if it were not bound by the history of legal discourse. Hence law may be a *simulation* of justice, and therefore a false or diabolical version of the truth, but it also sustains justice. Justice, however, is not free from the snares of the law machine. And virtual justice is not simply a simulacrum of justice—as opposed to the simulation of law—that is, an imitation of justice somehow purified by virtue of its departure from the law, freed from referentiality and legal or political responsibility. Such a notion of justice would give it very little traction, and probably remove it completely from the realm of the material.

Virtual justice is haunted by specters of traumas impossible to introject. Haunting is a constitutive part of virtual justice, not just to the extent that the performance of a simulacrum—or indeed a repetition or citation—is haunted by the fact of its displacement.[83] Rather, language itself bears the traces of particular phantoms, particular historical events, and particular traumas. Therefore, although in the case of the mock trial the women assume roles, the words bear within them not simply a displacement from one mode—the traumatic—to another—the performance of something traumatic. The continuity between the law court and the hotel theater and between the law court and other forms of cultural production allows the mock trial to be something more than simple mimicry. That is why justice may be bequeathed but not served.

The concept of the bequest of trauma as it emerges in the haunting of specters raises a set of questions within the context of colonialism, because it is hardly possible to assume a first or last term, the ultimate cause of trauma, in a single historical event. To bring the concept of trauma into the study of colonialism also requires a particular concept of forgetting and remembering—at times a repression, and at other times a new and conscious fabulation, or testimony. One could say, for example, that the Truth and Reconciliation Commission in South Africa performed justice through narrativizing trauma. This was done in the service of national cohesion. It is as if national cohesion could be achieved only by "remembering to forget," allowing trauma to be articulated in the service, ultimately, of what Ernest Renan said was necessary: for all nations to will themselves each day as a daily plebiscite through remembering to forget.[84] It is unclear whether this is in the service of hegemony or counterhegemony. And in the context of coloniality, Amilcar Cabral has spoken of the work of culture that emerges in resistance in spite of an apparent hegemony.[85] But this kind of performance is slightly different, at least potentially, from the kind I am considering, because of a difference in the mode of testimony. It is not simply that, in the case of South Africa, the testimony is in the service of the state and could be subject to the same criticisms that Sartre made of the Nuremberg trials; in addition, the commission functions precisely as a recourse to justice through the narration of a traumatic history. Although it is possible that such testimonies could still be haunted by what cannot be thematized or articulated, by what is not bound by referentiality, or by the bequest from a previous generation, it is likely that such hauntings will be ignored in favor of choosing to forget what is already conscious, or what has been identified as the chosen trauma of a people.

Trauma brings a notion of temporality into justice, which challenges our understanding of the latter term as a simple reparation or restitution for events in the past. It makes possible the thematization in language of specific acts of cultural repression, which emerge at particular and contingent moments. The traumatic events of colonialism, or indeed of slavery, are quite different from those of the Holocaust, for example, because different notions of historical event and traumatic event are at issue. In the first place, although certain events under colonialism may produce traumatic responses, which we may acknowledge to be horrifying—a massacre, the death of a significant person or loved one, torture—we cannot speak so easily of a single defining traumatic incident. (The same might be said about the Holocaust, however. Although it is considered an event, it obviously lasted for years, and the buildup to the actual Holocaust included a number of anti-Semitic, antigay, and anti-Gypsy occurrences.) With colonialism, or slavery, it becomes far more difficult to think of them as events, perhaps because it is the very structure of the modern that was built on colonialism. In contrast, we could say that the *event* of the Holocaust brought about the destruction not only of a people but also of the very structure of the modern, which posited the knowability of the event. How one responds to an event—that is, whether it becomes traumatic—depends on a completely different set of relations and variables. The thing is not traumatic in itself; it becomes traumatic when we fail to introject it into the (national) ego. In that sense, the historical event is not the same as the traumatic event, which can continue throughout a lifetime and could manifest itself in our language across generations without our even being aware of the repression that has taken place. I would suggest that this form of melancholic repression, which manifests itself as critical agency, haunts language as a kind of disjuncture, particularly when the history of the language has been so fraught with political and cultural aspirations, disappointments, and suppression and repression. The accumulation of incidents that are not introjected but that leave an incorporated trace haunts the language, and at particular moments and for particular reasons cause a phantom to appear. This form of haunting as a bequest from one generation to the next, which seems so apt for the analysis of colonialism, is not simply a postmodern questioning of master narratives, nor is it restricted to the postcolonial era. This counternarrative bears the weight of history even as it questions that history's temporal structure. It has coexisted with the discourses of European modernism, not as a response to it but as a constituent part of it, or we might say, as a shadow, a phantom, or a *virtual modern*.

PART II

MELANCHOLIC REMAINDERS

3

The Battle of Algiers and *The Nouba of the Women*: From Third to Fourth Cinema

> The unveiled body seems to escape, to dissolve. She has an impression of being improperly dressed, even of being naked. She experiences a sense of incompleteness with great intensity. She has the feeling that something is unfinished, and along with this a frightful sensation of disintegrating. The absence of the veil distorts the Algerian woman's corporal pattern. She quickly has to invent new dimensions for her body, new means of muscular control. . . . The Algerian woman who walks stark naked into the European city relearns her body, re-establishes it in a totally revolutionary fashion.
>
> FRANTZ FANON, "Algeria Unveiled"[1]

> In sound, and in the consciousness termed *hearing*, there is in fact a break with the self-complete world of vision. . . . In its entirety, sound is a ringing, clanging scandal. Whereas, in vision, form is wedded to content in such a way as to appease it, in sound the perceptible quality overflows so that form can no longer contain its content. A real rent is produced, through which the world that is here prolongs a dimension that cannot be converted into vision.
>
> EMMANUEL LEVINAS, "The Transcendence of Words"[2]

Frantz Fanon's essay "Algeria Unveiled" is famously one of the sites in which he gives his most sympathetic reading of the status of women under colonialism. It is, however, a strange and messy essay in many ways, drawing as it does from the various traditions of phenomenology and moral psychology to discuss and to a certain extent participate in the instrumentalization of women in the colonial sphere, and to examine what it has meant visually to discover and rediscover how the figure of woman functions both as fetish object and as weapon. Fanon is most deeply invested in the meaning of the symbolic venture of defending against the unveiling of Algeria. A negotiation takes place around the meaning of the veil as variously confinement and oppression on the one hand and camouflage and defiance on the other. In spite of the persistent masculinism of Fanon's own vision, and indeed his political, moral, and emotional identification with Algerian men, in the essay women are shown to be overburdened with meanings in which they become akin to coverings, camouflage, and screens, and part of the machinery of the psychic, of the visual, and of war itself. The veiling and unveiling of the body highlights the body as machinery, and indeed as a technology of both war and the everyday. The revolution in Fanon's text is bodily for women, and yet the body of woman is always a screen, albeit one with projected feeling.

In the second epigraph to this chapter, Levinas withdraws from an emphasis on the visual, understanding it as too powerfully present to itself, in a way that hides its insistence on internal self-sameness. Denied within the visual is the formal mechanism of mimesis, which binds together and preserves a total sense of reality as it simultaneously resists the mimetic element of representation itself. Brought into conversation with Fanon's text, a reading emerges that suggests that the screen of visuality we observe in film is to be understood in terms of both what is seen and what is unseen on the scene of representation. As Peter Brunette and David Wills put it succinctly in the context of the filmic image, "The 'origin' is thus always mimetic, and the imaging process is always already at work in the very conception of the reality whose wholeness mimesis is asked to preserve and blamed for undoing. . . . The hymen must therefore also stand for the unseen of cinematic representation, for the support of a visuality that would otherwise be random play of light."[3]

In many films about or from Algeria, the figure of woman encapsulates how filmic representation gestures toward that which it cannot represent. Its very constitution is made invisible. Made up of frames, the film of course must hide its borders when in motion, just as the cut, which more explicitly constitutes (but does not exist as) the border of a sequence, marks a transition that rarely draws attention to its own mechanism. The focus is Gillo Pontecorvo's 1966 film of revolutionary violence, *The Battle of Algiers*, and Assia Djebar's 1976 film, *The Nouba of the Women of Mount Chenoua*. Through reading the mechanisms employed in these films, an analysis of the politics of representation and its relation to revolutionary cinema is developed through particular attention to the concept of *third cinema*. While it may seem paradoxical that a film genre known cinematically for its use of the "long take" becomes the focus in a book interested in the "cut," the realism of third cinema becomes here precisely the site of theorization and actualization of the impossibility of full self-presence through breaches in sound as well as in the image.

The concept of *third cinema*, or the cinema of decolonization, was first formulated by Fernando Solanas and Octavio Gettino, both Argentine directors, in the late 1960s.[4] Third cinema distinguishes itself from other filmic genres in its theorization of an aggressive cinema of political transformation that, in its radical reformulation of hegemonic ideologies, perceives the camera as a weapon in nationalist struggle and revolutionary violence.

The theoretical formulation of third cinema, inspired by the works of Fanon as well as by the Cuban revolution, is both empowering and limited for a cinema concerned with the figure of women in decolonization. This is not because women have not participated in violent revolutionary struggle. Clearly neither women nor men are intrinsically pacifist, yet these strengths and limitations are explored here anachronistically, in *The Battle of Algiers* and *The Nouba of the Women*. The Algerian Revolution (1954–1962) has been treated filmically many times since independence was achieved in 1962. As one of the most popular films to represent revolution and terrorism, *The Battle of Algiers* opens up a thematization of the relationship between revolutionary and filmic performance, as well as the documentation of a "community in crisis."[5] Through a reading of this classic, the third cinema manifesto for revolutionary filmmaking is made attentive to the supplement of woman and how she becomes associated with the mechanism of film itself, both as a figure who makes up the teleology of the narrative and as the technology that undoes that narrative.[6]

The third cinema manifesto calls for a dismantling of the hegemony of Hollywood cinema in the name of a political cinema of decolonization. It was conceived for the use of Third World nations but, importantly, is not defined geographically. Although the term *Third World* seems to refer to the historical "victims" of colonization, and third cinema is built around the concept of fighting for decolonization, the word *third* is not synonymous in both phrases. For Solanas and Gettino, *first cinema* is a hegemonic commercial cinema, the values of which reflect those of the ruling classes, where "man is viewed as a consumer of ideology, not as the creator of ideology."[7] Hollywood, or the assimilation of Hollywood style, would fall into this category. *Second cinema* is concerned with issues of decolonization, reflecting a nationalist spirit for formerly colonized countries, but uses conventional cinematic techniques; it is considered a product of neocolonialism, which does not challenge the ideological signification of basic techniques, concepts of art, or conventional styles. Solanas and Gettino speak of filmmakers "trapped inside the fortress."[8] Third cinema, by contrast, resists the cultural imperialism of Hollywood-style hegemonic consumerism. Produced in the context of a national cinema, it is deeply rooted in resistance and decolonization; the whole apparatus of cinema is seen as radical and revolutionary. As with Italian neorealism, highly influenced as it was by the antifascist philosophical writings of Benedetto Croce and Antonio Gramsci, there is an attempt to employ nonprofessional actors, to concentrate on community rather than the individual, and to give a counterhegemonic version of revolutionary national change.

In *Third Cinema in the Third World*, Teshome Gabriel cites Frantz Fanon as the inspirational guide in relation to this threefold schema set up in Solanas and Gettino.[9] In *The Wretched of the Earth*, Fanon describes three phases of decolonization, here glossed by Gabriel:

(a) the unqualified assimilation phase where the inspiration comes from without and hence results in an uncritical imitation of the colonialist culture; (b) the return to the source or the remembrance phase, a stage which marks the nostalgic lapse to childhood, to the heroic past, where legends and folklore abound; and (c) the fighting or combative phase, a stage that signifies maturation and where emancipatory self-determination becomes an act of violence.[10]

Following Fanon's suggestion that the formerly colonized nation-states need to move beyond this threefold reactive schema, a "fourth cinema" was proposed for both reading and making films. The seeds of this theory began to germinate in *The Battle of Algiers* and came to fruition in *Nouba of the Women of Mount Chenoua*, even though much of the latter seems more dated than the former. In these films, the trace can be sought (we could abstractly call it the *feminine*, the *excess*, a profound enunciation or crisis or cut in representation—a melancholic remainder sometimes known as *jouissance*) that cannot be addressed by a guerilla cinema. What cuts through the representational frameworks indicates the inadequacy of the political representation of Algerian women. The concept of a guerilla cinema that reflects the "fighting or combative phase" constituted through violence is reflected not only in Fanon but also in the words of Yacef Saadi, producer of the Algerian company Casbah Films, which coproduced *The Battle of Algiers*. Saadi, who wrote five years before Solanas and Gettino, spoke of the camera as gun.[11]

The Battle of Algiers was an Italian-Algerian production and was made in 1965-66, soon after Algerian independence was won (in 1962). The film was directed by Italian Marxist director Gillo Pontecorvo, produced by Antonio Musu of Igor Films of Rome, and coproduced by Casbah Films, a private production company founded in 1962 by Yacef Saadi.[12] Saadi had been one of the central characters in the Algerian Front de Libération Nationale (FLN). After the arrest of Rabah Bitat, Yacef Saadi had taken over the Algiers network of the FLN and was responsible for organizing and orchestrating the clandestine army of resistance to French colonization and occupation. After independence, he moved into the world of film production and acting. Indeed, Saadi plays himself in the film, under the name Djafar.

At the time of independence, in 1962, Algeria did not have much of a cinema of its own. In 1957, the FLN had established a cinema school, which grew out of the nationalist struggle. Benedict Anderson, in *Imagined Communities*, speaks of the manner in which disparate groups of people in what becomes a nation are homogenized through print culture, and more specifically print capitalism. In the context of modern Algeria, with its multiple languages and its high illiteracy rate, film and radio provide different technologies of nationalism in which one can see reflected, as in a mirror, the desire to create a homogeneous Algerian national identity.[13] It was thought politically necessary to have a cinema of one's own that could counteract the sixty years of colonialist cinema that had been produced about Algeria and other colonized countries, and that had been and continued to be widely distributed by France in Algeria. Hala Salmane characterizes colonialist cinema in this way and sees it as having the two following functions:

(1) To distort the image of colonized people in order to justify to Western public opinion the policy of colonization; the natives had therefore to be portrayed as sub-human; (2) To convince the "natives" that their colonial "mother" protected them from their own savagery and from the unhappiness which was their essential state of mind.[14]

French anticolonialist filmmaker René Vautier, who joined the FLN during the Algerian war of independence, assisted in the founding of this school. In an article written many years later, he explains his motive:

> I was not doing it *for* the Africans, *for* the Tunisians, *for* the Algerians. I was doing it *against* the colonial system built in my name. . . . Maybe together we may succeed in getting "them" to understand that Pascal was not the only one to be right.[15]

> Suspect the opinions of European film-makers, European producers, European film-critics. Remember that nothing was ever done by them for Africa, for you, without ulterior motive.[16]

Algerian cinema, then, grew out of an extremely politicized context. A rejection of stereotypes, of propaganda, of the pernicious portrayals of the colonized world in even the most seemingly harmless apolitical popular cinema, brought about a cinema through which the drama of revolution became reflected in the drama of filmmaking. Images became part of the weaponry in the fight for independence. Yacef Saadi said of making *The Battle of Algiers*:

> I have substituted the camera for the machine gun. . . . The idea of reliving those days and arousing the emotions I felt moved me greatly. But there is no rancor in my memories. Together with our Italian friends, we desired to make an objective, equilibrated film that is not a trial of a people or of a nation, but a heartful act of accusation against colonialism, violence, and war.[17]

The recognition that representation, as it had been known, needed to be brought to crisis in order to expose its colonialist and exclusionary ideological motivation brought about a nationalist cinema that continues to renegotiate an adequate representation of the Algerian struggle for independence in a language of images and words that was suppressed by the French and would continue to be repressed by Algerians as testimony to the trauma of witnessing the birth of a nation. This cinema is employed to assert a national identity rather than a radical questioning of its basis.[18]

The Battle of Algiers: A Short History of the Film (Italy/Algeria 1965-66)

The main body of *The Battle of Algiers* is a flashback to part of the Algerian struggle for independence. The story is told as a remembrance of the 1957 events that came to be called the Battle of Algiers. The plot is organized around the figure of Ali La Pointe, an illiterate, lower-class member of the FLN. Even though a flashback is employed for the main action of the film, it is not one that relies on a sense of memory or interiority. In fact, a voiceover, sounding like that from a newsreel, comments on Ali's typicality, and thus the flashback is inscribed as history rather than memory, without introducing the idea of subjectivity. The French found Ali after torturing one of the FLN members, whom we witness at the opening of the film as he succumbs to pressure and agrees to speak after hours of torture. The military police are then led to Ali's hiding place, where we witness Ali hiding from the French police with three other members of the FLN (famously, le petit Omar—the boy FLN member—Hassiba ben Bouali, and one other). Though the film concentrates on Ali as the central figure, it dramatizes the events affecting the whole of the Algerian community. We witness the reconstitution of the history of organization of the clandestine army, the members of which never knew more than two other people in the army; the killing of French police; bombs in the cafés of the European part of the city of Algiers; the strike by Algerian workers; the penetration of the casbah by Colonel Mathieu; and the subsequent bombing of the casbah by the French, which led to a series of reprisals by the Algerians. At the center of the struggle, and at the center of the film, are three women who plant bombs in the European part of Algiers, which caused the death of many innocent European civilians. The film reaches up and returns to the moment when we think Ali will be captured; in fact, he is killed along with Hassiba Ben Bouali and le petit Omar. The film ends with celebrations for Algerian independence five years later.

The Battle of Algiers is Pontecorvo's first major feature film, though he had already made *The Wild Blue Road* (1953) and *Kapo* (1959).[19] Previously a chemist and a journalist, and a man with some musical talent, he had also assisted on the direction of some other films, had occasionally acted, and had made some documentaries.[20] Considering both this and the influence of Italian neorealism on his style, it comes as no surprise that the film was made to resemble a documentary, with the inclusion of original footage. Following a list of the various prizes and awards that the film has won, the film begins with a disclaimer that challenges the realism we go on to witness: "not one foot of newsreel or documentary film has been used."[21] To achieve this newsreel appearance, Pontecorvo treated the film in such a way as to give the photography the grainy appearance of news footage; at some points he also used a handheld camera, particularly in crowd scenes, so as to evoke the feeling that the camera was being held by a journalist on the scene.[22] Telephoto lenses used in media reports were also employed. Pontecorvo's motivation was to produce as objective an account as possible. Politically, Pontecorvo was on the side of Algerian independence, and wanted to produce a film that would excite the sympathies of those who were unused to reading the politics of the situation from the perspective of the Algerian people.

The film was not shown in France until 1971. Until then, the film had been banned under the regressive censorship laws instituted in France during the time of the Algerian revolution. "1955: The April 3 law, during the Algerian war, will authorize the authorities to take all measures to assure control of the press, of cinema, radio and theatre."[23] The film was widely acclaimed outside of France and won first prize at the Venice film festival in 1966, but the French boycotted the award ceremony and the film was banned in France. It was due to open in June 1970, but Universal Studios withdrew the film following protestations, bomb threats, and the rescinding of the license by the government. A great deal of unrest was initiated by veterans of Algeria, expatriates of North Africa, and various movements of the extreme right. The *Larousse Journal de l'année: 1969–70* calls this "un précédent fâcheux" (an irritating precedent). There were still protests when the film eventually received its license.

It was precisely this antagonistic audience that Pontecorvo wished to engage. He said of the film, "I wanted to secure the support of a public who were not oriented to favour the struggle of the Algerian people for their liberty. I didn't want to make a partisan film, nor one that was anti-French. *The Battle of Algiers* is the birth of a nation."[24] To secure the interest of this resistance, Pontecorvo had to believe and make credible the events he portrayed. To do this, he had to have faith in the power of realism and of *cinéma verité*. Asked if he would change any part of the film, Pontecorvo said, "I don't think I would change anything . . . [except w]hen the little boy, Omar, steals the microphone, and we hear his voice, maybe it would be better to use an adult's voice. It would be less moving, but perhaps more convincing, more realistic. . . . ." Le petit Omar, however, was killed, which raises the question of whether the horror of the battle could ever be "realistic" on reel, no matter how historically accurate it may have been. And speaking of filmmaking more generally, Pontecorvo has said,

"[I have] a desire to portray more honestly the reality of the situation, with a greater detachment from a certain narrative schema. One of the worst weaknesses of movies . . . is to follow certain patterns of representation in which one does not attempt to portray the world in its reality but make it look nicer."[25]

The mode chosen by Pontecorvo, the imitation of documentary, had been used previously by Italian neorealists.[26] The adoption of the documentary form arose out of a desire to produce a faithful rendition of the battle from the perspective of Algerians.[27] But this is obviously not a documentary. It is an adoption of a style that uses techniques of documentary. It is the "following of certain patterns of representation" that seem to put under question the very mode of the possibilities of realism.

This is not to say that documentary itself can simply hold up a mirror to something we could refer to as reality; that would be a naive reading of the ideological and formalistic makeup of any form of representation. And we will see later that what is at stake both in the documentary style of Pontecorvo's feature film and in the fictionality of Djebar's documentary is the combination of fiction and documentary, and the experimental realization of the imaginative constitution of the political and the historical. As Bill Nichols says,

We need . . . to examine the formal structure of documentary film, the codes and units that are involved, in order to re-see documentary, not as a kind of reality-frozen-in-the-amber-of-the-photographic-image, à la Bazin, but as a semiotic system that generates meaning by the succession of choices between differences, the continuous selection of pertinent features from amongst the various codes and their intersection. Despite the denunciation of various cinematic "realisms," this work has scarcely begun with documentary, and yet what better place is there to confront the challenge of realism . . . ?[28]

Obviously all representation is created and is not simply holding up a mirror to "reality," and documentary is no different from other forms of representation in this respect—something thematized in *The Battle of Algiers* itself. It does, for the most part, however, set itself up as a nonnarrative form that relies heavily on the spectator's belief in the connection between sign and referent. It is not my purpose here to look at the ideological forms of documentary itself, but rather to look at the relationship that is set up in the film between documentary as a mode of representation and the representability of a "community in crisis," and therefore to look at the relationship between sign and referent. Can testimony be given to the trauma of revolution?

The phrase *community in crisis* comes from Doris Sommer's work on testimonial literature.[29] Testimonial literature, a genre that emerged from the Latin American context, refers to a body of literature that shares some of the qualities of neorealism. It is generally written and conceived collaboratively, outside the bounds of a singular consciousness, in its effort to produce a counterhegemonic rewriting of politics and history; it is nonheroic, and revolutionary.[30]

Pontecorvo comes out of a tradition of Italian cinema whose neorealist movement was tied very closely to the development of a counterhegemonic national identity. It was created from a resistance to fascist cinema. Keeping this description of testimonial literature in mind, it may be useful to look at some general criteria for definitions of Italian neorealist cinema, and the cinema of decolonization, or third cinema.[31]

The Parisian journal *Films et Documents* characterized the stylistic features of neorealism in the ten following points:

(1) A message: for the Italian filmmakers, cinema is a way of expression and communication in the true sense of this word. (2) Topical scripts inspired by concrete events; great historical and social issues are tackled from the point of view of the common people. (3) A sense of detail as a means of authentification. (4) A sense of the masses and the ability to surprise (De Sica) or manipulate them in front of camera (De Santis, Visconti): the protagonists are captured in their relationship to the masses. (5) Realism; but reality is filtered by a very delicate sensitivity. (6) The truth of actors, often non-professionals. (7) The truth of decor and a refusal of the studio. (8) The truth of lighting. (9) Photography reminiscent of the reportage style stresses the impression of truth. (10) An extremely free camera; its unrestricted movements result from the use of post-synchronization.[32]

In the attempt to create a cinema that defied the fascist underpinnings of what had come before, neorealism emerged as a cinema concerned with the notion of an antifascist national identity.[33]

The Battle of Algiers seems to fall into the categories of testimonial and neorealism, which in rather obvious ways are linked. The film is obviously dealing with concrete events, and Pontecorvo and Franco Solinas, the scriptwriter, carried out six months of careful research of often confidential materials in order to verify details of time and place. The community in struggle is represented; there are no particular heroes or protagonists. What was then a counterhegemonic perspective on the historical events of the anticolonialist struggle is given. Nonprofessional actors are used, a device that stresses the importance of community over particular heroic protagonists.[34]

The Battle of Algiers marks the coming together of a Marxist and a decolonizing aesthetic. Its Italian director and Algerian codirector present moments of a documentation and pedagogical structuring of a counterhegemonic nationalist spirit and international solidarity. For the latter, film is both a weapon of that revolution and a means by which testimony can be given to Algerians' struggles. For this reason, similar techniques are employed to establish a resistant national image. It is this resistance that also characterizes third cinema. This cinema of decolonization simultaneously dramatizes the impossibility of representing the trauma of revolution.

While the film's style seems less innovative when considered alongside the Italian neorealists, it serves a similar purpose and uses a similar technique to that of antifascist film. Mira Liehm criticizes the film for its lack of experimentalism with respect to style: "Pontecorvo did not succeed . . . in combining the imagined and the real, the fictitious and the documentary. His ideological attitude toward the material proved more radical than his cinematic form, which remained confined within conventional patterns. . . ."[35] I consider that this space between the imagined and the real, which Liehm identifies as the cause of failure of the film, actually enacts the crisis of representation that testimony to trauma causes. Contrary to what Liehm says about the unsuccessfulness of the combination of fiction and documentary, the film reveals how the desire to realistically represent the revolutionary woman of decolonization is dramatized in a moment in which the film reflects back on itself and cuts through the realist mode in which it is made, raising questions about the relationship of documentary to fiction. While Liehm suggests that the film's ideology overwhelms its simplistic form, the film demonstrates the impossibility of representation of a trauma resulting in melancholia. The figure of woman in the film, contrary to Pontecorvo's intentions, demonstrates the impossibility of reflection being faithful.

The Battle of Algiers: "Third Cinema" to "Fourth Cinema"

The camera is an inexhaustible expropriator of image-weapons; the projector, a gun that can shoot 24 frames per second.[36]

Women's presence in *The Battle of Algiers* causes a stylistic shift that questions the value of the documentary style. This stylistic shift could be referred to as a "third space of enunciation" that dramatizes the rupture between an official nationalism that privileges the masculine in filmic representation, and the people apparently represented by those signifiers. The representation of women in *The Battle of Algiers* causes this rupture between sign and referent to question the overriding discourse of a new national image.

In his essay on third cinema, "The Commitment to Theory," Homi Bhabha posits the "third space of enunciation" in the following terms:

"Culture" only emerges as a problem, or a problematic, at the point at which there is a "loss" of meaning in the contestation and articulation of everyday life, between classes, genders, races, nations. . . . The enunciation of cultural difference problematises the division of past and present, tradition and modernity, at the level of cultural representation and its authoritative address. It is the problem of how, in signifying the present, something comes to be repeated, relocated, and translated in the name of tradition, in the guise of a pastness that is not necessarily a faithful sign of historical memory but a strategy of representing authority in terms of the artifice of the archaic. . . . The intervention of the Third Space of enunciation, which makes the structure of meaning and reference an ambivalent process, destroys . . . (the) mirror of representation in which cultural knowledge is customarily revealed as an integrated, open, expanding code.[37]

It is with this quotation in mind that the scenes in *The Battle of Algiers* in which three women prepare to plant bombs can be read as radically questioning the colonial ground of postcolonial politics even as it endorses decolonization. In the scenes preceding this, bodies are being cleared in the casbah after a bomb planted by the French has exploded. Distraught veiled women are shown mourning and are turned away from the array of dead bodies by the men who remove them from the rubble. This scene explores the cruel injustice shown toward the Algerians. In a long shot from above, we witness ululating women on the roofs of remaining houses in the casbah, and as the camera descends we move down to

The Battle of Algiers *and* The Nouba of the Women 115

survey the rubble and ruins of the casbah from various angles. The lack of close-ups stresses the crisis of the community rather than the sorrow of the individual. The tragedy of the moment is reflected in the somber, hymn-like Western classical music.[38]

Cutting to a crowd scene, Ali La Pointe leads a group of men and women, who stand out in their white veils, in a demonstration in which they chant "Murderers!" The boy, Omar, appeals to Ali to stop the demonstration, saying that word has come from Djafar to stop, otherwise the police will kill them. Ali does not listen and continues until Djafar himself rushes through the narrow lanes of the casbah to the crowd, appeals to them to stop, and promises that the organization (the FLN) will avenge them. The scene ends with high-pitched ululations from the women. The filming here is very different from the rest of the film, with its alternating soft and deep focus, handheld camera, and shallow depth of focus. The confusion of the scene confounds and communicates two issues: How can the Algerian people be represented politically and how can they be represented filmically?

What follows is the preparation for avenging (see Figure 3.1). We cut to a veiled woman, probably representing Zohra Drif, but possibly Samia Lakdari or Djamila Bouhired; in close-up she takes off her *haïk*, the big square veil covering the face and body, and begins to "transform" herself into a European.[39] This performance (we could call it *iteration* or *mimicry*) of Europeanness is misunderstood by the French in the film as a

FIGURE 3.1 Still from Gillo Pontecorvo, *The Battle of Algiers*.

genealogical transformation into a European political and cultural sympathy. A zoom backwards reveals to us that an image of Hassiba ben Bouali was a reflection in a mirror. The body in this mirror prepares itself for nationalist intervention. This scene contrasts starkly with the profound materiality of the two previous ones, where explosion leads to death: the conquest of the material Algerian body by the French, and the high neo-realism of the demonstration-crowd scene. Joan Mellen comments on the "nonrealistic aura" of this scene of the women's metamorphosis:

As the three Algerian women transform themselves into French women, the light, unusually bright for this film, is thrown upon their faces. It adds a theatrical quality while heightening the nonrealistic aura. The omnipresence of the mirror gives the effect that we are entering into the consciousness of the three, who are also symbols. Because they carry this larger significance as well, the audience is not bothered by not having seen these women before and knowing nothing about them. We have not been told who they are or why they were chosen for this mission of violence.[40]

The scene takes place almost as a time-out from the main drama of the film, but it is simultaneously part of it. Not one word is spoken during this undressing and redressing sequence, in which loud percussion is all we can hear.[41] This musical motif is repeated as the women are about to plant the bombs, when we supposedly enter their minds and perceive their nervousness and their horror at the act they are going to perform. Besides entering the consciousness of the women, as Mellen suggests, we enter the unconscious of the film, in which women's revolutionary role and her testimony to it has been repressed. The metamorphoses of these women, or at least the image of them, takes place in a cocoon of mirrors, almost a film-set dressing room, where the image and the *imago*—the idealized image misrecognized in the reflection as self-completeness—are confused to such an extent that the question of what it means to be an Algerian woman becomes highly questionable, and is exploded or imploded.

This is not the first time in the film that women participate in the Algerian struggle for independence. Pontecorvo is very influenced by Fanon's essay "Algeria Unveiled," and the potential of this essay for filmic dramatization is one that Pontecorvo takes up. Early in the film, women carry bombs in the folds of their veils. Toward the beginning of the film we saw a woman, Hassiba Ben Bouali, and le petit Omar hide with Ali La Pointe and other FLN activists in the wall of a casbah home.[42] This image is repeated shortly before the end of the film when these people die in an explosion engineered by the French military. They are framed in absolute stillness, as if in a photograph. Fanon has informed us of how the FLN relied on stereotypes of passive veiled Algerian women to trick the French. Here the women dress like the French women and flirt with French soldiers, in this moment of the theatricality of revolution that dramatizes a revolution in the unfurling of representation. This is what Bhabha calls the "significatory boundaries of cultures, where meanings and values are (mis)read or signs misappropriated," where "the problem of the cultural emerges."[43] Here the dramatist-director of the women who plant the bombs, Yacef Saadi, takes advantage of this "problem."

Fanon has spoken of the "zone of occult instability" of cultural representation, where the sign does not have a stable relationship to its referent.[44] What it means to be an "Algerian woman" becomes questionable. What is she besides the dramatist of these stereotypes? The actress embodies, like a mirror or a film screen, this "zone of occult instability," where Algerian woman can exist only as figure, indeed as catachresis, or what Spivak calls "a concept metaphor without an adequate referent."[45] Here, in Bhabha's words, we have a "split between the traditional culturalist demand for a model, a tradition, a community, a stable system of reference, and the necessary negation of the certitude in the articulation of new demands, meanings, strategies in the political present, as a practice of domination, or resistance."[46] The split between concepts of old and new, of loyalty to Algeria, was represented in the eyes of the French (and of the Algerians?) by the wearing of the veil, as if this signified a timeless "Algerianness," and by the donning of French attire, as if this represented an alliance with the French, who were so concerned to free women of the veil.[47] The split or cut between these two images of woman enacts simultaneously the wound, the space between images of how one is perceived, and the space between the imago and its perceiver.

When the film cuts to the women in the cocoon of mirrors, the first shot reveals the reflection of a woman in a mirror only after the zoom back allows us to see the frame of this mirror. This is, then, the image (reflection) of the image (of the actress). And as the audience views the reflective image, we are in a sense in the mirror. The filmic screen becomes the mirror, and what we are left with is a mirror within a mirror. Woman, who has been understood in terms only of her veil, as carrier of arms or as passive woman, looks into a mirror and transforms herself into the image of a flirtatious French woman, who is almost French but not quite. She mimics the appearance of the French woman.[48] Robert Stam and Louise Spence have spoken of how the mirror is transformed, in third cinema style, from a tool of vanity to a weapon of revolution.[49]

The concentrated gazes that we witness in this scene are exclusively turned in toward the self: they are gazes into the mirror. Only once does one woman look at another as she cuts her hair, seeing within this woman that which she is about to do to herself. We move from separate images of each woman to all of the women together; as if they are going through a drill or performing for rehearsal, they prepare themselves and observe this uncanny image of themselves.

Through this one minute and twenty seconds of intense concentration, loud percussion, and play on reflection, there is a focus on scissors (as if poised to cut the film), cut hair, lipstick, and the tucking of shirts into skirts to accentuate the figure that has previously been hidden. These Medusas in the mirror, who wield scissors to cut their own hair, who will merge flesh with stone, see this uncanny reflection of themselves that is the new imago. They make themselves desirable under a new fashioning, feeling that they lack the completeness of the image they desire to create. And like the child in the Lacanian mirror, they must (re)learn a different muscular control, a different motor coordination.

The scene ends, in true Medusa fashion, with a freeze frame that holds the cut—one of only two in the film. A woman begins to dye her hair (see Figure 3.2). As she looks into the mirror, the shot is frozen, the music cut.

In the next scene, the music changes as the women await Djafar. Like a director, he enters, and they audition for the parts. One asks nervously, "Non?" and appeals to him that she will be fine; if she takes her son, no one will suspect her.[50] Djafar hands out instructions and baskets in which the bombs will be placed, and the women are on their way.

The other freeze frame in the film is equally suggestive of both fear and death. An ambulance, stolen by the FLN, races through the European part of the city firing guns at civilians as it passes by. The ambulance crashes, and we are left with a freeze frame in which the siren continues to ring, causing a disjuncture between sound and image. The other moments that resemble freeze frames, but are not freeze frames, involve photographs or staging of the photographic in the casbah hiding place framed in the wall. Colonel Mathieu shows his soldiers photographs and film of FLN members they will be instructed to catch and torture in order to retrieve information about other militant FLN members. Photographic images fill the screen as we too are invited to comply with the gaze of the French army as they look at the photographs and watch the recording of people passing through the checkpoint to enter the European city from the casbah, wondering who poses a threat or, indeed, who may be framed (see Figure 3.3). We have witnessed the scene ourselves; thus Pontecorvo invites us to contemplate the medium as manipulative and multiply interpretable. Here the army movie of the checkpoint is grainy, much like the newsreel texture

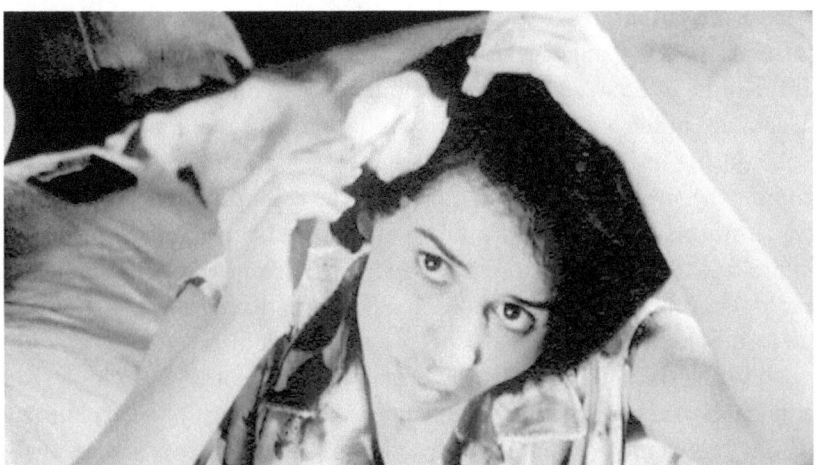

FIGURE 3.2 Still from Gillo Pontecorvo, *The Battle of Algiers*.

FIGURE 3.3 Still from Gillo Pontecorvo, *The Battle of Algiers*.

of Pontecorvo's film, and thus Pontecorvo introduces another moment of disjuncture in which the audience is forced to assess their sympathies and to consider how they can be manipulated through documentary evidence and through the strength of the visual image.

Why is the image, and particularly the filmic image, so important at the moment of decolonization, and in the period of postcoloniality? If we accept Homi Bhabha's analysis about the reentry into language that occurs for the (formerly) colonized at the moment of speech, then we need to look at the various image configurations that the person (in the position of the child entering language) confronts at the apparent mirror stage, which at this time of life seems to be the moment of secondary identification.[51] The image of the imago in the mirror is both fearful and desirable because unattainable. It is desirable particularly because it represents the desire of and for the law of the father. It represents the colonizer as more than perfect, with his grandiose and stable metaphorized and idealized vision of himself; it also represents the stereotype of the colonized.[52] The colonized can desire only to be like the colonizer, because this is where "his" visual pleasure is located, from the perspective of the colonizer.

But what metonymic images are suppressed beneath this vision that is metaphorized as reality? What happens to the image of the colonized who is represented as the uncanny, and how does this (overrepresented) colonized person ever look at himself or herself as anything more than the uncanny, or the simply inferior?

The metonymic is a chain of signifiers, of images and sounds that are not tied to a specific "signified." In Lacanian psychoanalysis, the imaginary moment is the moment of recognition of the fixity of an image, but it still occurs at the moment of the knowledge of fragmentation when the child is closest to the mother's body. It is this sense of familiarity of an image, which is at once "incorrect" and unfamiliar, that causes the images of the colonized to seem fragmented as metonymy and not metaphor. In this realm, determined arbitrarily by the symbolic or the name of the father, she or he can find those "occulted signifiers" and construct, if fleetingly, more apt (re)presentations of the image (signifier) with a signified determined by her or his political and politicized imaginary realm. The narrative that goes with the image may be fixed, this time by the colonized. The narrative, words, moves along a chain, as do the images. All are signifiers occulted by the colonizing law of the father. Fixing them through the other's political imagination, for a moment, creates a filmic catachresis, destabilizing to the viewer because it is from imaginary stock so different from that of the dominant.

In this moment of renegotiation of images, when the cinema of decolonization sets the terms under which images are produced, the formerly colonized use the image as a weapon and as a mirror in which a nationalist identity can be forged. As in psychoanalytic work, and in Fanon's writings, the idea of the birth and of the renegotiated childhood does not infantilize so much as it creates a familial language of futurity. Solanas and Gettino write,

> A new historical situation and a new man born in the process of the anti-imperialist struggle demanded a new, revolutionary attitude from the filmmakers of the world. The question of whether or not militant cinema was possible before the revolution began to be replaced, at least within small groups, by the question of whether or not such a cinema was necessary to contribute to the possibility of revolution. . . . In this long war, with the camera as our rifle, we do in fact move into a guerilla activity. . . . A revolutionary film group is in the same situation as a guerilla unit: it cannot grow strong without military structures and command concepts.[53]

But how might this be different in the context of a women's cinema of decolonization, the "historical situation and a new [wo]man born in the process of the anti-imperialist struggle"? Do we need a different way of looking (a fourth cinema?), and does this way of looking question the gaze that has previously been dominant? The psychoanalytic gloss on the narrative for a third or a fourth cinema could dramatize the filmic uncanny through visual and aural (the spoken and the visually projected) catachreses. The phallic-scopic tool of the father is replaced by the *heimisch Unheimliche* vision and voice of the catachrestical and catachrizing other woman.[54] Her uncanniness becomes reified on the screen.

Michael Wayne, in an article on *The Battle of Algiers* and third cinema, rightly criticizes an earlier version of this chapter for discussing second cinema incorrectly, in a manner that allows *The Battle of Algiers* to be included in third-cinema categories. While he is correct that my cursory description of second cinema may not have allowed for the possibilities of third cinema to be acknowledged, he to some extent misses the crucial argument of this chapter. The rhetoric of third cinema, and such films as *The Battle of Algiers*, insists on a form of violence in camera use. Understanding the camera as weapon is not necessarily adequate in formulating any postcolonial existence, and especially for representing the difference of a feminine political reason in decolonization. As a liminal force in *The Battle of Algiers*, the women literally throw some light on the inadequacy of the documentary form. Cutting through this form, they pose questions concerning their role in the nation to come. In retrospect, the "cleaning up" of Algiers by the FLN, represented in the film in the shunning of a drunk, raises questions about the curtailment of rights that would later ensue, and the forms of gendered violence that have arisen in the last twenty years in Algeria. Wayne suggests that it is inconceivable that Algerian Islam would not have protested and changed because of the FLN's decision, although his own views seem to echo Fanon's rather problematic gender assumption in "Algeria Unveiled." The point, however, is not to endlessly enumerate cinemas, each one countering the problematic politics of the former and trying to be more radical. If third cinema was based on the three stages of decolonization described by Fanon, postcolonial cinema will indeed need to find a fourth stage, one that does not work within the logic of coloniality, and one that allows for the possibility of a different political reason. Arguing against the glorification of violence in third cinema is not a liberal attempt to contain its radical qualities. Rather, it is to suggest that such violence is inadequate in formulating new nation-states, unless they are to be celebrated for engendering new ethnic and gender violence of their own.[55]

The mirror scene, in which weapon is replaced by cocoon, dramatizes woman as only image. She becomes both a metaphor for an Algeria that the French wish to "unveil," and simultaneously a metonymy for "tradition," which makes her signification unquestionable. In the process of transformation we get very little sense of what these women are. They seem to be no more than the images that have been created by Djafar or in the imagination of the French by Fanon or Pontecorvo. Yet moments of nervousness—for example, when one woman looks to another as she cuts her hair—cut into the *diegetic* and we are lost in the world of reflective material. In Irigaray's words, this woman exists between metaphor and metonymy. She does not exist within the terms of the symbolic and therefore becomes not the (desirer of the) imago in the mirror but the reflective material itself.[56] As the narcissistic imaginary material, as the cocoon or womb that embodies and makes up the screen onto which images are projected, woman in her historically material form gets lost in the world of images. While the mirror-screen (woman) is there to become and reflect testimony to and witnessing of the violence of revolution and the guerilla-warfare violence of representation, how does woman testify to the violence that has no witness? How can the reflective material of the mirror, fragmented and imploded, reflect itself? As Dori Laub, in the context of writing about the Holocaust archive, writes, "The testimony to the trauma . . . includes its hearer, who is, so to speak, the blank screen on which the event comes to be inscribed for the first time. . . ."[57] The blank screen (woman-womb-cocoon) that accepts the dramatization, the remembering reenactment of trauma through guerilla filmmaking, reflects only in on herself. How can her own trauma, as both witness to that which is projected against her and that which she has experienced herself, be represented?

The mirror scene in *The Battle of Algiers*, where women, like actresses, dress and rehearse as they prepare to act, reflects the drama of revolution and of filmmaking, forming a space (a third space?) where representation breaks down because it turns in on itself.

What would a fourth cinema look like?

Djebar and Fourth Cinema

The final image of *The Battle of Algiers* is of a woman dancing in the street. The voice-over announces that in 1962, "the Algerian Nation was born." How can the sexed subject as subaltern find a voice within this construction? Algerian feminist Marie-Aimée Hélie-Lucas writes:

We [women] are made to identify with "the nation," "the people," conceptualized as an undifferentiated mass, without conflicting interests, without classes, and without history—in fact, we are made to identify with the State and the ruling class as legitimate representatives of "the people. . . ." In Algeria, many of us, including myself, kept silent for ten years after Independence, not to give fuel to the enemies of the glorious Algerian revolution . . . our rightist forces exploit our silence.[58]

In 1979, Algerian feminist novelist Assia Djebar wrote in "Forbidden Gaze, Severed Sound":

It is a question of wondering whether the carriers of those bombs, as they left the harem, chose their most direct manner of expression purely by accident: their bodies exposed outside and they themselves attacking other bodies? In fact, they took those bombs out as if they were taking out their own breasts, and those grenades exploded against them, right against them.

Some of them came back later with their sex electrocuted, flayed through torture.[59]

The trauma of revolution and the birth of a nation has, in *The Battle of Algiers*, been represented in documentary style in order to redress a balance of propagandist and stereotypical cinema. What we have observed here is the moment in which woman, in the context of this kind of third cinema, where camera is weapon and cinema is guerilla warfare, falls out of the system of representation in the film, causing the very mode of representation employed to be questioned. In a sense she causes a wounding to the system of representation. Bhabha's comments that discussions of third cinema need to look toward "the intervention of the Third Space of enunciation, which makes the structure of meaning and reference an ambivalent process, destroys . . . [the] mirror of representation in which cultural knowledge is customarily revealed as an integrated, open, expanding code" are pertinent here.[60] The semiotic, representative wounding signaled when woman is represented gives testimony to the specificities of unrepresented crisis that women experience at the moment of the birth of a nation, when that painful, feminine metaphor of birth is (not) denied. A fourth space, in a fourth revolutionary cinema, will give testimony to a different sort of representation, when women's gazes are not forbidden or simply reflected inward, and when women's sounds are not severed.

The Battle of Algiers brings to crisis any documentary style that assumes that realist filmic representation, which reflects oppositional revolutionary performance, can result in political representation of its subjects. This crisis signals yet another phase, in the Fanonian sense, of decolonization: the representation of subaltern figures that signals a self-reflexive moment in representation. This is a moment in which self cannot simply speak the memory of trauma but can enact a space in which "silence"—nonspeech—is recognized as a symbolic space of political nonrepresentation.

A fourth cinema that moves beyond the guerilla cinema where the camera is a weapon would be a revolutionary cinema of the cocoon, where the metaphor of the birth of a nation is not repressed into a denial of the feminine. It would be a cinema that could give voice, silence, and image to women in the revolution, where the uncanny could become reified on the screen. Representation that reflects back on itself exists without a renegotiation of imagery, and brings that imagery to crisis. Assia Djebar's *The Nouba of the Women of Mont Chenoua* in many ways picks up on this representational break that signals, in the moment of oppositional third cinema, an unsutured moment of representational breakdown. Assia Djebar made two films for Radio-Télévision Algérienne (RTA). The films move between Algerian Arabic, French, and Tamazight with French subtitles. The first, *La Nouba des femmes de Mont Chenoua* (*The Nouba of the Women of Mont Chenoua*) was made in 1976; the second, *La Zerda et les chants de l'oubli* (*Zerda and the Songs of Fortune* or *The Songs of Forgetting*) was made in 1980 with Malek Alloula. Djebar's shift from literary fiction to television would have given many more Algerian women access to each others' lives. Television demands of women neither literacy nor access to cinemas in the public space. However, although *La Nouba* was funded by RTA, it was shown only once, to great disapproval because it was thought to give a disrespectful and limited view of male war veterans.[61]

La Zerda et les chants de l'oubli announces itself as a film of memory of the French occupation of Algeria, Tunisia, and Morocco. It begins with words on a screen: "La Mémoire est corps de femme," "Memory is body of woman." The screen displays a series of photographs of the French in Algeria. These photographs and footage, memories with which we are presented lie on this body of woman: the screen. Djebar and Alloula actualize, through voice-over, a memory that fits these images—a counter-hegemonic memory that has no images but those produced by the French. These images get reinscribed with movements, songs of fortune, of forgotten songs that speak perspectives on periods of history that are different than the perspectives we may receive through the images presented. These periods are represented through movements or songs into which the film is divided. We hear the "Chant de l'Insoumission" (Song of Insubordination) "Chant de l'Intransigeance" (Song of Intransigence), "Chant de l'Insolation" (Song of Insolation), and "Chant de l'Emigration" (Song of Emigration). A fifth song was planned but ultimately not included, "Chant des morts" (Song of the Dead). The "voices over" are often barely audible—many whisper at the same time, many sing. We hear women's voices, once again, falling into the reflexive mode in which subjectivity gets blurred—*"On vit. On nous vit. On nous photographie."* The affect of this film, in which there are very few moving images, is made simultaneously continuous, through sound, and discontinuous, through image. Memory, we see, can only ever be discontinuous, in spite of the fixity or apparent fixity of each image. There can be no suture between images and between sound and image that could give us a continuous sense of history or of memory. There is no continuist supposition that assures us of a self narrating a memory; the body of woman, the screen, bears the violence of splintered memory and can offer only fragments.

Djebar's first film, *The Nouba*, also employs a musical title; the *nouba* is a traditional Andalusian musical form in six movements. Djebar wanted to adopt a style that expressed a film in fragments. Here fragments of life around a village near Mount Chenoua are brought together within the logic of the *nouba*.[62] Within each movement, Djebar uses a variety of regional music blended with fragments of Bela Bartok's compositions inspired by time spent in Algeria.

These fragments in six movements are brought together by a woman named Lila who returns to the village where she grew up. Lila is an architect who is married to a veterinary surgeon paralyzed after a riding accident. He is, in a sense, something of an antihero, if heroism can be understood only in terms of war. But he is neither hero nor antihero for Lila, who travels with him to the countryside around Mount Chenoua, where she grew up. It is here that her husband will convalesce and be tied to domestic space because of his disability, while Lila has mobility and drives around visiting women who tell their memories of the war: of torture, of loss, of physical and emotional scarring. The film is presented as "*une histoire quotidienne des femmes (qui parlent à leur tours)*" (an everyday story of women who, in turn, speak).

While this woman drives from house to house, we see fragments of flashbacks: black-and-white documentary-type film intrudes on the vivid colors of the drive through the Algerian countryside. These images are of war, of women being chased through streets by French soldiers. As we shift from present-day scenes to fragments of memory, so we shift between scenes of Lila with her child and male partner, who is confined to a wheelchair, and fragments of testimony. We also move back in time between the current moment, the memories, the documentary-type footage, and a magical and mythical world of the stories of Mount Chenoua as they are passed from grandmothers to granddaughters in dreamlike sequences (see Figure 3.4). As we shift from interiors to exteriors, so we shift from narratives of interiority to exteriority: Lila's memories are told in voice-over, not in direct speech. She speaks directly only to her child. She refers to herself as a prisoner in silence and in space, yet she moves, and she speaks. Doorways, shadows, mirrors, images of Lila in white standing against white walls, scenes of watching and being watched dominate the visual of this film. In these junctures of subjectivity—of interiority and exteriority, of memory and the present—doorways frame a fragmented subject whose form appears almost indistinguishable from her shadow. This film about space, history, and memory blends fiction with documentary. While Lila's story is established through fiction, the women she meets tell, through interviews, the story of their memories. Yet as Réda Bensmaïa has suggested, this is a film about the aesthetic of the fragment.[63]

In an interview, Djebar suggests that if documentary is to have any relationship to the real, the director has to know the subjects and film what she finds to be representative of those subjects. The documentary, then, becomes very planned and can be crafted almost fictionally, as if to make a political intervention, articulating hope through fictionalized documentation. Hope for political change comes through an alternative imagination, as if exposing the lie of representation and representational politics

FIGURE 3.4 Still from Assia Djebar, *La Nouba des Femmes du Mont Chenoua*. Courtesy of Women Make Movies, www.wmm.com.

by playing one off against the other. Objections to this fictionality are based on the belief that fidelity to the film's subjects could be more easily established through direct and unplanned filming. Djebar disputes this, and indeed thereby questions the ethics of documentary film that presents itself as spontaneous and unplanned. The merging of fiction and documentary in the film draws attention to the impossibility of unmediated presentation of materials on the part of the director, the interviewer, and her subjects. Memory and representation will always interfere.[64]

If *The Battle of Algiers* gave way to a third space between the oppositional revolutionary narrative in its representation of women revolutionaries, here the third space of impossibility, in which questions of filmic and political representation intersect with conflations of revolutionary and filmic performance, brings crisis to realism and to the documentary mode in which access to speech means access to politics.

The common rhetoric of rights in feminist discourse foregrounding the need for a "space" or a "voice" from which one can "speak" and therefore assume oneself to be politically represented, comes under question here. This rhetoric assumes a sense of self, of location, of knowable political interests perhaps not viable after the end of "modernity," after the end of the colonial era. This is not simply to say that a certain modernist conception of self and place coincides with a period of colonialism and therefore gives way to an aesthetic of postmodernism in the postcolonial era. If testimony to crisis is to be understood, the period of transnational politics that becomes embodied in the figure of the Algerian woman who masquerades as Europeanized demands a reading that measures silence with voice, sound with articulation, and lack of stable positionality along with a politics of location. In the period following the partial suturing of Algerian women in transnational contexts, violence brings representation to a crisis point as it encounters its own inability, in the third space, to represent her politically.

The representation of women's participation in the Algerian war for independence seems inadequately elaborated in the theory of third cinema, and alerts us to the need for a theory of fourth cinema. As a figure in the context of the creation of hegemonic nationalist images and representations, the decolonized woman indicates yet another phase (not the first, second, or third) in the representability of decolonization and postcoloniality. This cinema would signal the crisis in and collapse of hegemonic representation, embodied here in the new national regime. It would question the violent conceptualization of cinema as weapon, and would look to a cinema of national birth that is more inclusive of the representative demands of the subaltern, of woman in the decolonization process. It would have to be more attentive to the experimental relationship between documentary and fiction, as Mira Liehm might say, and also to something more than the Fanonian three stages of revolution.

Fourth cinema would point toward the inability of third cinema to represent the violence undergone by women in the process of decolonization at the hands of both the colonizer and colonized men. In this way, fourth cinema offers a critique, through the figure of the colonized woman, of both the presence of the colonized and the Manichean construct of colonizer and colonized that revolutionary struggle perhaps necessitates. It would also critique third cinema for its inability to represent the different forms of symbolic violence played out by and on the body of the colonized woman, bringing representation to crisis.

Severed Sound

Emmanuel Levinas's words with which the chapter began point to an aspect of sound that is especially useful for understanding the figure of woman in relation to nation and coloniality. Whereas in modern times race is frequently collapsed into an idea of the knowability of content through visual guarantee, sound both exceeds this visual epistemological collapse and changes the temporality of the idea—for Levinas, a dimension is prolonged through sound in a way that is entirely different from its visual capturing. Sound is excessive to itself, therefore, and to any form of representation we may gauge from it. There is nothing identical to sound, for there is no representational recognition that may appease.

Levinas's description of sound adds a nonteleological temporal dimension to visual alibis. If *representation*, for Aristotle, characterized the differentiation between man and animal (man works within a representational schema that makes him a political animal; animals make sounds but do not, as such, represent), he articulated this in terms of language, and therefore distinguished between the sound elements and the language elements that go together to make a "voice." He was not dealing with the visual realm as much as with the law of language, or more precisely, with language as law and as representation. Nonetheless, the temporal aspect of sound was not particularly striking to him. More important was the qualifier given to this difference between representational language and sound, that is, the political. Man is political because his language exceeds sound through a representational force that makes him political. For Aristotle, "man is an animal whose natural, constitutive dimension is the community of discourse called civil society (polis)."[65] This is fleshed out in various phenomenological analyses in the context of a Heideggerian movement toward death.

The temporality of sound as something that exceeds representation is usefully elaborated through psychoanalysis. Psychoanalytic studies of difference embodied through a reading of race and gender have emphasized the visual forms of racial alterity with their focus on the image. Djebar's idea of severed sound points toward the more corporeal aspects of sound and auralization, and voice becomes a category of analysis for the study of race and coloniality in film. A focus on sound and its technologies allows for the theorization of a different form of politics around the psychoanalytic study of race, gender, and coloniality than that found in visualization and representational discourse, which assumes a community of discourse and a notion of civil society.

Psychoanalysis is useful for critique of coloniality not in spite of its formation as a colonial discipline but precisely because of its formation as one. But the question of colonialism cannot simply be reduced to that of race. Discussing race alongside coloniality necessitates a broad conceptualization of that term derived partly from Foucault's *Society Must Be Defended*, and partly from the concept of race as massification. The specificities of colonial and state racism—what Fanon refers to as the "racial epidermal schema"—must be accounted for, as must how that plays out in the naturalizing of "state" groups into enemy racial categories.[66] In the discussion of postcoloniality, emphasis needs to be on far more than the visual schema and the objectification of the other by the camera if, in understanding race, we are not to fall into a more Sartrian or very early Lacanian schema deriving more from Kojève's reading of Hegel than from psychoanalysis. Psychoanalysis may allow for thinking about race in film as difference through voice, and perhaps through sound more generally. While it may be the case that psychoanalysis does give a way of thinking about coloniality, it cannot be by simply mapping categories of racialization onto the space where gender once stood. There is no psychoanalysis without a concept of sexual difference, and therefore the ways in which it becomes useful for analyses of coloniality can never be at the expense or due to the substitution of one category for the other.

In *The Battle of Algiers* the famous scene (which Pontecorvo regretted including) in which the boy, Omar, steals a microphone from the French police during a demonstration calling for a national strike by Algerians highlights well the manner in which voice and sound are utilized. The voice of "le petit Omar" is striking because it is a call to political action from a boy whose voice has clearly not yet broken. His boyishness is visually emphasized in the film because he can creep through small places, run between Algerian activists, and function as a transparent communicator or enabler of communication. As he runs back and forth, he appears as pure representation—the very means of communication in a complicated network that cannot yet constitute a community of discourse in civil society, because no civil society as yet exists. But that process of attempting to constitute a burgeoning communication is effected with a teleology that is quite marked: a boy becoming man, a cleaning up of the streets by the children of the FLN, of hiding misfits, prostitutes, and drunks, as if these people cannot be a part of a future idealized independent state. The voice of the boy stands in contrast to the background voice of the film. This same voice is sometimes employed as a voice-over, of the guerilla radio network, self-consciously but acousmatically called the "The Voice of Fighting Algeria," of underground broadcasts that kept revolutionary Algerians, and now the audience of the film, apprised of the day-to-day struggle in an attempt to forge a national consciousness as a unified voice. This is what Agamben may refer to as "language's sovereign claim . . . the attempt to make sense coincide with denotation . . . the linguistic state of exception."[67] What is so striking about the voice-over and the broadcast constituting the soundtrack of the film is its extraordinary clarity. Fanon had written of the contrasting clarity of the official voice of the French metropole distributed around Algeria, "The Voice of Algeria," and the barely audible radio station of the guerillas. He explains how the "Voice of Fighting Algeria" was usually a crackle, almost impossible to find, but enabling an agency on the part of those who attempted to listen to what could be imagined as Levinas's "sonorous, ringing, clanging scandal" and make revolutionary sense of it.[68] The film, made after the success of the revolutionary struggle, bypassed this crackle and put in its place a teleology leading to successful independence. The child's voice expresses the urgency of the struggle, and if we do some of what Michel Chion referred to as "reduced listening," we hear the "timbre and texture" and therefore an "emotional, physical, and aesthetic value" that expresses the very difficulty of constituting communication, rather than the radio's calm reassurance of what seems to be already in place.[69]

Famously, women rarely speak in *The Battle of Algiers*. In the scene discussed previously in which the three women transform themselves from veiled figures into clearly Europeanized (and therefore safe-looking for the French) women before they go to plant their bombs, all dialogue was removed (much to the horror of Solinas, the scriptwriter) and replaced with percussion by an Algerian musician. All forms of women's political consciousness are in fact entirely mute in the film, and this frequently goes along, as we have seen, with the employment of various lighting treatments, longer close-ups, and conscience concerning the death that is to ensue, rather than speech. It is as if the potential pain of the other comes into existence for the first time in the period prior to the playing out of representational logic. It asserts difference yet cannot fully articulate it. In the larger teleology of the revolutionary film, space exists out of time, even when, as it draws to a close, the film focuses on one ecstatic woman skipping from the crowd celebrating Algerian independence five years after the Battle of Algiers was lost by the Algerians. A form of representational logic may ask, What form do women's voices take, then, in imagining the new nation? Are women only liminally part of a potential community of discourse? But it seems there is another way to think of this—perhaps, indeed, that they become the site of a politics outside of representation and identification, through desubjectivation.

Mladen Dolar, in his essay "The Object Voice," explores the ways in which poststructuralist theory—in particular the work of Jacques Derrida—has basically neglected the question of voice. In the effort to demote speech as the more direct communication of a message in language, Dolar claims in a somewhat reductive reading, that Derrida has inadvertently failed to account for that which is most remaindered in speech itself—that is, voice. For Derrida, says Dolar, voice is simply part of the way in which speech assumes a metaphysics of presence. But in a reading that draws on Lacan, Dolar seeks to reinstate the importance of voice. He writes of voice in its most pure form, however—a form of voice that is not indeed reduced to speech. In fact, what is most important for him is the way in which voice is separate from law as language, "the voice beyond logos, the lawless voice," which unlike speech has always, he claims, been a source of anxiety philosophically.[70] It may be the case, as he says, that for Lacanian psychoanalysis "the surplus of the superego over the Law is precisely the surplus of the voice; the superego has a voice, the Law is stuck with the letter."[71]

Dolar references Kaja Silverman, who in turn draws on Michel Chion and Julia Kristeva. Both Chion and Kristeva, according to Silverman, draw on the notion that the sound of voice is maternal because the first sound the fetus hears as it grows is the mother's voice—what Silverman calls the "sonorous encounter." Whereas Chion may describe this as an "umbilical net" or a "uterine night" of terrifying nonmeaning, for Kristeva it is an altogether more utopian encounter. It would be easy within this framework to understand the percussion, or the ululation used frequently to both mourn and celebrate, in *The Battle of Algiers*, as manifestations of the presymbolic sonorous encounter, a *jouissance* that does not yet meet the control of the law of language. Within this logic too the women are the locus of their own interiority in the space of the transformation chamber, the room in which they change themselves, or within the cinema itself. As animals do for Akira Lippit, woman too becomes the machinic apparatus.[72]

But the persistence of sound in voice, when it exists in excess of law, exceeds the uterine space. It nonetheless retains something corporeal, though not visual. If the radio, the microphone, and the contrasting percussion and ululation dramatize and thematize the apparatus of recording in *The Battle of Algiers* in ways that foreground the symbolic deadlock that could result only in the massive violence of nationalist struggle depicted in the film, they also show the ways that something more than law (language itself) was the force of these circumstances. Voice becomes part of the soundtrack of the film in a way that demands consciousness of a language of urgency, representation, emergency, and sovereignty. Somehow the hearing of the sounds of attempted sovereignty—in which the fight over who can make people die becomes key—clamours. If the radio as the "voice of fighting Algeria" becomes like the newly instated "voice of Algeria"—a resonating superego making demands by repeating the archaisms of sovereignty (remember, law has language but the superego has the voice)—the superego's critical agency persists with its law but simultaneously evokes another Freudian formulation of critical agency: that of melancholia, the persistent sonorous critique of what one has incorporated, manifested as self-criticism and disidentification.

Dolar, Chion, Kristeva, and even Silverman are drawn to sound as psychoanalytic scene—the voice of the analyst one does not see, the resonating radio that plays with the presence and absence of a body behind it, the archaic and regulatory voice of the superego, even as they may have different relationships with the interiority of woman's body that becomes the scene and the screen of visual and aural production. Derrida, by contrast, seems more threatened by the secrets that voices may tell, as well as by the problematic relationship to the mother as sonorous site that they imply. Dolar, while interesting on the topic of Derrida's mistrust of voice as carrying with it the metaphysics of presence, is in some ways less attentive to the forms of voice corporeality that Derrida continued to find interesting. In *Monolingualism of the Other*, for example, Derrida describes his exceptional status as "the only Franco-Maghrebian" in order to counteract the sovereignty of a monolingualism in the Algerian context—the sovereign reign of a language as law, whether in French or in Arabic.

Attempting to understand his experience of language as someone who grew up Sephardic Jewish in Algeria, Derrida explains that he has never had a mother tongue. Unlike Abdelkebir Khatibi, who writes that his mother tongue (Arabic) was "lost" when he fell in love with French, Derrida discusses how he could never lose nor be lost by a mother tongue, because he has never had one.[73] But the monolingualism of sovereignty has nonetheless left in him a calling into question of all purity, and yet a desire in himself for a pure language, which he understands as unaccented. Sound persists in a different sonorous temporality than the image, and it exposes one to suffering that challenges any notion of purity, pre-Oedipal or otherwise. The voice always returns. It is a racialization of sound in terms of accent that counters the sovereignty of law. But such critical agency, which I would call melancholia after Freud, is not restricted to the question of accent. Indeed, it becomes the condition of possibility for critique.

Merzak Allouache's 1976 film *Omar Gatlato* similarly represents a technology of sound. This time, neither the womb nor the radio is a sonorous cavity of sound emission, but the tape recorder is. Omar, the main character and sometimes narrator of this film, is a lover of music. He works in an office with his good male friends, who continually conduct gold raids on the streets of Algiers, creating a sense of emergency in the film.

Omar carries a tape recorder with him everywhere, recording *chaabi* (Algerian music) and Bollywood film songs as he goes to the cinema regularly, which, he tells us, everyone does when a Bollywood film is being screened. (The nationalized Algerian film industry boycotted Hollywood, of course, and Indian films circulated through Algeria—as through the Middle East, Asia, and the rest of Africa—establishing a transnational film-viewing network that bypassed the United States and much of Europe). At the cinema, Omar tapes songs, themselves recordings of playback singers performed on screen by actors. The Hindi film's dialogue is dubbed into French, the songs are not. Omar himself speaks Arabic, but we frequently see him listening to French songs and speech. The medium through which sound is brought to us is repeatedly foregrounded in the film: we witness Omar seeing a deaf man use sign language, we hear a wronged jewelry shop owner sing his complaint in French. Omar is mugged one day on the streets and his tape recorder is stolen. A friend gives him another, and it has a tape inside it. On the tape a woman's voice describes her life. We hear, not from her voice but through Omar's friend, that she is a union activist in Omar's workplace. Omar becomes desperate to meet her. He calls her on the phone, in yet another technological prosthesis of voice the film offers us. He listens to her voice repeatedly whenever he is alone. He retreats into phone booths to call her. And while one could imagine that this uterine experience of voice substitutes for the total lack in the film of communication between Omar and his mother, with whom he lives and interacts but never exchanges a word, it also becomes the site of potential suffering. So moved by music foreign and native, and so obsessed with the voice of this woman rather than, it seems, with her words, Omar exposes himself to suffering, as if sound itself cannot stay within its own temporality of immediacy or emergency. Moved by music and the sight of a mute man one day in a bar, Omar drives a cigarette into his palm, as if to remind himself he is alive. He screams. The voices that move Omar become the soundtrack for the film, and the ground of possibility of a suffering critical agency in relation to the founding racialized violence of contemporary difference under modernity.

Sound, in its singularity, functions as a trace of impurity in these films, whose temporality complicates the notion of sovereign language, purity, or the relation between visuality and form. In effect sound becomes the nonrepresentational critique of purity in the films, and the breaking of the same, not only marking a constitutive sexual difference, but also marking the founding violations of state racism as purity and its effect on everyday life. Sound and hearing, as melancholic critical agencies, allow for a different way of reading the form wedded to content, in a manner that may allow it to overflow as the trace of impurity.

It is perhaps for this reason that a filmmaker like Isaac Julien chooses to foreground the question of listening in his experimental documentary film *Frantz Fanon*, which focuses precisely on the acousmatic as the locus of desire. Fanon's own emphasis on the visual, which he derives from Sartre and Lacan, becomes in Julien's hands the occasion for a questioning of the genre of documentary and its own prioritization of the visual and the expert as opposed to desire. His documentary questions the nature of the genre because in many ways it is a documentary of what is unspoken in Fanon's work—indeed, sometimes even violently excluded. Even though Fanon was a psychiatrist who felt that the psychiatric problems he encountered needed political as much as medical attention, his politics sometimes puts the question of desire in a second rank. The psychoanalytic theoretical interpretations of Fanon that have emerged foreground the question of desire through the visual as a way of trying to understand the early work of Fanon and ideas about colonial trauma. But Julien poses the question of what it meant to be returning to Fanon at the end of the century, and what it means to engage with his work while simultaneously acknowledging the homophobia and sexism within it. He does this by putting pressure on what is unsaid in Fanon, and on what sounds are severed, through an emphasis on listening. The ear and the radio (recalling Fanon's own important work on the topic) are important acoustic objects that appear again and again, as are the dramatization of the act of listening (the psychiatric and psychoanalytic task) and the use of the female operatic voice.[74]

Materializing Scholarship on Algerian Film

Ironically, France has become the only viable location to carry out research on Algerian film at this time.[75]

The existing problems of doing research on Algerian cinema are not, however, irrelevant or incidental. In 1969, in the hope of increasing distribution and production of Algerian films within Algeria and abroad, the film industry in Algeria was nationalized. All distribution was to take place through the Office National pour le Commerce et l'Industrie Cinématographique (ONCIC), or National Office of Cinema and Industry. Major U.S. film companies objected to this nationalization of distribution, because they were previously responsible for distribution of 40 percent of all films shown in Algeria. The United States and Algeria fell out over this issue of nationalization, and Hollywood boycotted Algeria for five years, until 1974. In a sense Algeria won the battle, succeeding in increasing the popularity of Algerian cinema among Algerians while the boycott was going on. Later, Hollywood resumed business with Algeria.

Although U.S. films are distributed in Algeria in a form more controlled than the manner in which they were distributed prior to nationalization, the nationalization of the Algerian film industry has not increased distribution of Algerian films within the United States.[76] In the discussion of decolonization, those on the margins need to be addressed on the questions, interruptions, and cuts they make on the center. The very tenets of that center's understanding of how certain structures of representation create and endorse the very existence of marginalization need to be questioned, as does the "cultural commitment to marginality," to listening and seeking to understand the implicit critique by the margin.[77]

Algerian filmmakers have talked extensively about the need to have a cinema that explores more than the period of the Algerian war for independence (1954–62). Rather than concentrating solely on the problems of colonialism and decolonization, they have been moving to progress from colonization as the basis of all exploration of the problems Algeria faces.[78] Criticizing the Cinéma Moudjahid (cinema of the freedom fighter), Rachid Boudjedra has said:

Who will use a camera to protest against the condition of Algerian women? Who will oppose religious obscurantism, political careerism, the defeatism of youth? ... One looks in vain for a feature film denouncing religious crooks, the rush to demagogy, polygamy ... the enrichment of the new bourgeoisie in the face of the misery of the Aurès region and elsewhere. This silence is disturbing indeed. ... It is the duty of cinema to denounce torture and arbitrary imprisonment wherever it is practised.[79]

It seems neither coincidental nor innocent that the most easily available images of Algeria within the United States are either colonialist cinema, such as Julien Duvivier's *Pepe le Moko*, Pontecorvo's *The Battle of Algiers*, and Alloula's *The Colonial Harem*, or news reports concerning Algerian Islamic fundamentalism. Very little representation in the way of critique of Algeria by Algerians is available, although since the FIS has become so powerful, the numerous Algerians who are resistant to their mission have sought occasions to express their opinions about the false homogenization of the Algerian people through Islamicization.[80] Both within and outside Algeria there seems to be a need to hang on to the idea of a unified nation, whether homogeneous or not. This seems to be important to Algeria internally, regardless of how catachrestical and inadequate the Enlightenment notion of *nation* is to a colony of France. In France, notions of the nation-state were developed simultaneously with the project of colonization; the desire for and achievement of independence was, after all, argued within that very logic of Enlightenment. Although the independence struggle persists as the main theme of Algerian films, since the Agrarian revolution in 1971, films have been made that undermine this notion of a unified Algeria, the critique of the élite in power, and an exploration of problems internal to Algeria that are arising from the new Algerian postindependence cultures and out of the specificities of the French colonial context, but these do not reach a wide audience.

Within the context of the United States, the coexistence of representations of a new fundamentalist Algeria and a unified homogeneous Algeria serve to create and endorse a stereotype of a timeless people who are homogeneous in respect to Islam. While it is essential to explore the fissures in representation created by the space of the subaltern within anticolonialist cinema, it is also important to keep in mind the global hegemony of images that maintains stereotypes of the (globally) politically marginalized. The crisis of representation that can be observed within some kinds of visual and literary representation needs to bear being questioned not only about the ideological center of its immediate context but also about the relative marginalization of its own center.

4

Women of Algiers in Their Apartment: Trauma, Melancholia, and Nationalism

> Il me reste, pour completer cette analyse, à noter une dernière qualité chez Delacroix, la plus remarquable de toutes, et qui fait de lui le vrai peinture du XIXe siècle: c'est celle mélancolie singulière et opinâtre qui s'exhale de toutes ses oeuvres.... Cette mélancolie respire jusque dans "Les Femmes d'Alger," son tableau le plus coquet et le plus fleuri. Ce petit poëme d'intérieur, plein de repos et de silence, encombré de riches étoffes et de brimborions de toilette, exhale je ne sais quel haut parfum de mauvais lieu qui nous guide assez vite vers les limbes insondés de la tristesse.
>
> CHARLES BAUDELAIRE, *Pour Delacroix*[1]

> To complete this analysis, it remains for me to stress a final quality of Delacroix, the most remarkable of all, the one that makes him the true nineteenth-century painter; I refer to the strange and persistent melancholy that pervades all his work.... This sense of melancholy even informs a picture like *Les Femmes d'Alger*, of all his pictures the most appealing and the most winsome. As eloquent as a poem, this interior, full of rest and quietude, hung with gorgeous fabrics and cluttered with trivial aids to beauty, suggests the heavily scented atmosphere of the brothel, which quickly leads us down to the unplumbed depths of sadness.
>
> CHARLES BAUDELAIRE, *Selected Writings on Art and Literature*[2]

> This incapacity, this handicapped memory, is the subject of my lament here.
>
> JACQUES DERRIDA, *The Monolingualism of the Other*[3]

When Eugène Delacroix went to Algiers, he was taken to the house of a privateer working under the direction of the chief engineer of the port, Monsieur Poirel. The privateer invited Delacroix into his house and allowed him to see the women's quarters. When Delacroix saw the seraglio scene, he commented: "It is straight out of Homer! The woman in her women's quarters busy with her children, spinning wool or embroidering splendid fabrics. That is woman as I think she should be."[4] The traveling Delacroix sees these women through phantasm. As Odysseus, he perceives them as Penelopes—who stay at home pining away yet uncannily self-contained, weaving and unweaving to keep off suitors. The analogy simulates contact with these Algerian women, who seem familiar yet unfamiliar. They are Penelopes in a different setting, self-contained yet inviting; they are home away from home.[5]

The 1834 painting *Femmes d'Alger dans leur appartement* foregrounds the women, creating a line that leads back to the two seated women and runs forward from the ajar cupboard, placing the viewer very much within the scene, as does the line in the rug, and the beam of sunlight throwing a half shadow on the reclining woman's face, placing the viewer just next to the black woman (see Figure 4.1). Even this sub-Saharan woman, who is shown from the back with her head in profile, is lit up sharply against a light-colored wall. And indeed the boundary between the seated women and their background is accentuated by the shadows that surround them.[6] There is very little sense of boundary between the painter and his subject matter. In addition, the promise of a window, the open cupboard, the almost concealed curtain, suggest that both the artist and the women can move in and out of the room freely. We certainly view an interior, but not an area of confinement.

The 1849 painting of *Femmes d'Alger dans leur appartement* is quite different (see Figure 4.2). The angle is much wider, the women are set further apart, there is no sense of a window, and the cupboard door is closed off. As Assia Djebar points out, this painting is "a stolen glance."[7] A scene is presented to us of a stage on which three women are placed. There are few details and little facial expression, and no contact between the seated women, who appear in the earlier version as if they might be conversing. In the 1849 painting, the color of the seated women's flesh merges with the background and they become characterless, undifferentiated, and interchangeable. The standing woman is foregrounded. Her features are now almost concealed by her own hand, and her gender is less certain. Her contours begin to merge with the curtain, and she potentially blocks off the viewer. As a trace of the colonial endeavor, she appears to hold back the curtain. Like a character in a Bertolt Brecht play, she could draw the

FIGURE 4.1 Eugène Delacroix, *Femmes d'Alger dans leur appartement* (1834). Oil on canvas, 227 x 177 cm. Musée du Louvre, Paris. Photo: Erich Lessing/Art Resource, NY.

FIGURE 4.2 Eugène Delacroix, *Femmes d'Alger dans leur appartement* (1849). Oil on canvas, 111 x 84 cm. Musée du Fabre, Montpellier. Courtesy Réunion des Musées Nationaux/Art Resource, NY.

curtain across the scene at any time, creating a proscenium between us and them. She is not on the stage but rather standing to its side and holding the curtain to it. She has become a device to threaten our vision in this more voyeuristic composition. The curtain as threat becomes all important in the scene, a fetish substituting for a psychoanalytical presence or absence.[8]

All that Delacroix says about the later version of the painting in his *Journal* is that it was a pleasure to work with *vernis* (varnish), because this would preserve the painting. In the earlier version, we see that the paint seems to be decaying, thus increasing the desire in Delacroix to document the process of losing the memory.[9] This brief note suggests a grasping of the memory through preservation. The lack of detail here suggests that the motivation to paint the same theme fifteen years later was both to use a different painting style, a romanticist one, and to create a different relationship to the "other."

What is documented in the 1849 painting is a remnant, a trace. If the 1834 painting was one of an interior, the 1849 painting is one of interiority. The earlier painting is a memory, reconstructed to highlight detail accurately; the later one is about the process of forgetting in which Delacroix melancholically cites his earlier work, identifying it in the process of being forgotten. If, as Ernest Renan suggested in 1882, a memory of forgetting is necessary in the construction of national identity, here Delacroix remembers that he has forgotten. The iteration of the scene of the first memory is "worked through" to a certain extent in terms of loss, and there is an attempt at assimilating it into the later context, in which it could be mourned but is not.[10] This new melancholic painting style is less realistic. "Revolutionary romanticism" and "enthusiastic patriotism" begin to merge in this painting that documents a French identity through melancholic opposition to an inexact other.[11] Delacroix's process of forgetting documents not just the loss of an individual's relationship to some Algerian women, but also a kind of psychic assimilation on Delacroix's part into the newly developing French nation-state.

The 1849 version, with its whitewashed walls and the covered frame on the back wall, haunts the viewer. Is it a window frame draped over to block out light, giving us an image of confinement? Or is it a canvas, the 1834 canvas, covered over, incorporated into this later version yet not introjected? Does the phantom of the earlier painting survive into the later in spite of the attempt to erase it? Does the assimilation into a different aesthetic and a national model quite different from the earlier in terms of a relationship to Algeria present us with an inevitable phantom, an inassimilable secret of the colonial endeavor? These questions suggest the melancholic appeal of the painting. The documentation of loss seems like an introjection, yet these phantoms suggest a space blocked off and a relationship denied that may be in evidence on the canvas now concealed beneath the drape. The attempt to mourn seems to leave behind a trace of the impossibility of mourning, or as psychoanalysts Nicolas Abraham and Maria Torok put it, "We find it crucial to affirm the prior existence of a love totally free of ambivalence, to insist on the undisclosable character of this love, and finally to show that a real or traumatic cause has put an end to it. The system of counterinvestments . . . results from some traumatic affliction and from the utter impossibility of mourning."[12] Delacroix's different relationship to Algeria, caused by the external change in policy, causes the disintegrating first painting to become encrypted, yet the crypt is tenuously held together: "It should be remarked that as long as the crypt holds, there is no melancholia. It erupts when the walls are shaken, often as a result of some secondary object. . . ."[13]

*

This chapter uncovers the trauma concealed in the very heart of the theory of European nation-state formation. Algeria finds its origins as a nation-state in French colonial policy. In 1882, Renan speculated that the nation-state's relationship to the past was one in which we *remember to forget*.[14] He was talking about the will to forget historical events that could divide a nation through a daily plebiscite. In France, the exemplary event is the massacre on St. Bartholomew's Day. The French, created as a "we," have to be reminded, according to him, that this was an event successfully assimilated into a national history. Thus the Breton will become a Frenchman, and Protestants and Catholics will eventually live side by side in spite of past differences and traumatic violent encounters.[15] Renan's concept of the modern nation-state is, of course, one that Benedict Anderson takes up in his theory of nation as imagined community. While his argument is persuasive, what distinguishes the nation from the nation-state is not adequately theorized, even though he employs Benjaminian temporality theory to demonstrate the particularly modern nature of national community.

In fact the power of policy seems to be given up entirely in order to stress the community as imagined or willed. Anderson's most significant contribution is, following historians of the book such as Roger Chartier, to consider *print capitalism* as a significant marker of change in how we conceive time and community in modernity. Following this, and indeed through the concept of cultural form as *symptom of as well as contributor to nation-formation*, the use of group identifications through virtuality by the state and as intrinsic to the state can more easily be discerned. National history as developed in cultural formations does not so much provide a direct link between cultural enunciation and historical and political reality so much as it allows us to see the artifact or the text as enunciation, indeed as an *acting out* of national identities that are the result of political and historical circumstances.[16]

If the modern nation-state in Algeria and in France developed at the time not only of French colonial acquisition but also of French imperial power, it did so partly through the privatization of national history, in which that history was conceived individually as one's own even as it was shared with the rest of what Freud calls the *artificial group*, which relied on some degree of anonymity among its members.[17]

Constraints in policy and rules exist therefore alongside individualized and individuated identification and an inability to identify. In the context of the difficult relationship between France and Algeria from the conquest of Algiers in 1830 to the present, this relationship is a complex one, for when France imagined itself as distinct from its colonies and as a center around which they hovered, Algeria was technically a part of France, a factor that exposes the intrinsic role of colonialism in the formation of national identity. French colonial policy in the postrevolutionary first phase of colonialism and in the second phase of colonialism battled with the policy of assimilation of its colonial subjects and land. An active code of assimilation of the colonized people had been instituted, leading to formal incorporation of Algeria into France in 1847, and full integration in 1848, after passing through a difficult period during the Napoleonic years. What this meant on the level of policy was that the colonies were to be an integral part of French territory, and in the case of Algeria, there was an exact imitation of mainland administrative models—dividing the country into its three *départements* (counties) and then into *arrondisements* (districts) even as the Code de l'Indigénat placed Algerians in a very different status and relationship to the law than their European counterparts. Commenting on the aftereffects of the 1848 French Revolution on the colonies, Renan stated, "We wish to establish everywhere the government which is suitable to us and to which we have a right. We believe we are doing something marvelous by establishing a constitutional regime among the savages of Oceania, and soon we will send diplomatic notes to the Grand Turk requesting him to convoke his parliament."[18] Shifts in assimilationist colonial policy were deeply affected by scientific and sociological evolutionary spirits, but in principle, evolutionary theories could go either way in justifying assimilation or in promoting what became the overt policy—association, which in principle was designed to maintain local institutions that were overlooked by the French Office of Colonial Affairs.

However, as Raymond Betts has shown, "even though association became the official policy immediately after the war, the ghost of assimilation lingered on and could still be seen flitting in and out of French colonial affairs."[19] The manifestation of the ghost of assimilation suggests a breakdown in the ideal of the nation as something that could create a desire in and an ability for its subjects to assimilate. But what does it mean to be a part of a country and yet to be either stateless or living under different laws than most of its citizens? The ideal of assimilation that is central to sentiments of national cohesion seems to hold within it a lie, that is, that some people are not allowed to assimilate and are designated as not assimilable. This seems like a given of colonialism, yet a secret of nationalism. After all, Renan could speak of the nation-state as assimilating people of disparate regional identifications into being French and therefore growing as a nation, but simultaneously could speak of part of that nation—which we know as Algeria—as a colony that should not be assimilated and in that sense was evidence of the failure or lost cause of the *mission civilisatrice*. The violence of the Algerian war of independence, as well as of the recent civil war, bears the trace of this haunting—the killing of one's own, whom one failed to assimilate and failed to desire to assimilate. This haunting could be understood as repeated trauma that makes visible what Abraham and Torok call *phantom possession*, that is, a shameful secret from a past generation that possesses someone else's unconscious.

Although in France this may manifest itself in terms of guilt, in Algeria it has manifested itself quite differently. In the socially tormented time of the late 1980s to 1990s, with unemployment extremely high and a young population that has tripled since independence, we see an assimilative ghost reappear, this time in the shape of an Arabization that seems to be about policy more than about individual will. The breakdown in the Algerian nation-state in the early 1990s suggests lack of clarity about what the dominant force is, and therefore about what the assimilative force is. This has caused a war in which it is perpetually unclear who is fighting whom, and for what cause and to what end other than a claim of increased democracy. The situation of civil war in Algeria is not merely a return of the repressed. Rather, a specter, or a phantom, bears down on each moment that finds a beginning, if not an origin, in colonial assimilation policy. Again, Benjamin Stora's words are pertinent, "the recurrence of war in Algeria and the repetition of words of war in France do not provoke the historian to look for hypothetical 'beginnings.' The quest of correspondences allows us to see discontinuities, fresh appearances, and discordances. . . . Behind the frequency of vocabulary and old habits still in use, it is necessary to recognize singular silhouettes of new and different practices."[20]

Trauma seems to be concealed at the very heart of nation-state formation. *Trauma* is a term usually associated with individuals rather than groups, and usually described in relation to an event. This chapter explores whether it is pertinent to use the term in relation to a prolonged oppression that leads to psychological damage over time and manifests itself in an art object. When analyzing something like colonialism or nationalism (or indeed less temporally and historically specific phenomena such as racism, economic exploitation, and sexism), is it useful to understand them as a series of traumatic events, or can we think of a more sustained and continuous model? A continuous model could in principle be theorized in terms of a series of deferred actions (*Nachträglichkeit*), as theorized by Freud, and following Lacan it is possible to understand the language and the literary affects of this belatedness. Like the ghost, language always comes back, as Derrida points out, even when it appears for the first time. But here the analysis may remain in the realm of events rather than as a more sustained traumatic condition that affects our very relationship to community, or indeed psychic assimilation.

If we understand the relationship between individualized imagining and group formation through the terms of history and memory, the passing of a historical moment is introduced into the imagination of the citizens or subjects of an *artificial group* such as the nation-state. If we analyze this in psychoanalytic terms, we can see that early models of the French nation-state required that the national subject be in a relationship of mourning to the history of the state in which a series of events are worked through and remembered *as forgotten*, to return to Renan, and successfully introjected into the national self.

Citation, Introjection, Incorporation

Orientalism is after all a system for citing works and authors.[21]

Said's famous phrase suggests how certain narratives repeated, and ultimately reified, a false image of the colonized. While Said's text has been evaluated extensively by the field of postcolonial criticism, his analysis of citation has not been adequately framed in terms of the psychoanalytical possibilities inherent in the insistent citationality of orientalism. Some discussions of citationality suggest that images can be re-cited differently in the postcolonial context by "sending back." However, a simplistic dualism is accordingly set up, one that opposes all citation during the colonial period with its postcolonial respondent. Mieke Bal has suggested that citation repeats, unwittingly, the power structure under critique.[22] This oppositional logic of action and reaction that we see in the moment of resistance fetishizes the moment of political independence to a discontinuous extreme.

Repetition, which is intrinsic to citation, is inevitably never exact and always nuanced by its context. It references its other context and brings that context to the fore, and is simultaneously included into the language of its present existence. Although repetition of an action, an utterance, or an image installs a moment of stasis into a text when the inorganic past, or that which is lost, is brought into the present, this drive toward stasis (which we know as the death drive) holds within it an attempt to assimilate its meaning into another context. Citation, when it is recognizable, enacts the very difficulty of assimilation.

Citation as a psychoanalytic process resembles that of mourning and melancholia. Both mourning and melancholia involve the ingestion of a lost object. Abraham and Torok, in their rereading of Freud's "Mourning and Melancholia" in light of Sandor Ferenczi's distinction between introjection and incorporation, draw on Ferenczi's account of introjection as a normal part of psychic growth through assimilation; mourning, then, can be understood as a function of growth.[23] Through citation, the subject reiterates that signifier of loss, re-citing it in a way which is inflected with one's tongue. In the case of mourning, this can lead, through repetition, to assimilation of that object into oneself. As Abraham and Torok suggest, "The passage from food to language in the mouth presupposes the successful replacement of the object's presence with the self's cognizance of its absence. Since language acts and makes up for absence by representing, by *giving figurative shape* to presence, it can only be *comprehended* or *shared* in a "community of empty mouths."[24] This ingestion (taking in) then takes on the traits of what Abraham and Torok call "introjection," a kind of psychic assimilation. In melancholia, on the other hand, what takes place is "incorporation," that is, the blocking of introjection, and consequently unsuccessful assimilation. Here narcissism is pathological. The lost object becomes a constant point of reference, but the relationship to it as a separate entity is always fraught with identification.[25] While the process of melancholia, for Freud, is very similar to that of mourning, its incompleteness leaves a residue, or for our purposes, the regurgitated, unassimilated object that we recognize as citation. For Abraham and Torok, melancholia is quite different. It involves not regurgitation but rather a buried shared secret: the failure of the nation to assimilate its subjects in spite of its overt policy. "*Incorporation results from those losses that for some reason cannot be acknowledged as such.* The words that cannot be uttered, the scenes that cannot be recalled, the tears that cannot be shed—everything will be swallowed along with the trauma that led to the loss. Swallowed and preserved. Inexpressible mourning erects a tomb inside the subject."[26]

The process of mourning as a remembering of that which is forgotten through its recitation and eventual assimilation returns us to Renan's theory of emergent national identity. The "essence of a nation is that all individuals have many things in common, and also that they have forgotten many things."[27] So all that has been forgotten, he tells us, needs to be remembered *as forgotten*, as a difference within the body politic that has been transcended. Effectively, it is the *will* of the nation that becomes important—the willingness both to forget differences and create cohesion, and to recite that which is lost through the construction of a nationalist history. The will of our forefathers—that is, that which is willed to us—documents the ways in which our present can be renegotiated. And nationalist history has to be bad history in order for cohesion to be maintained, for details to get lost. Group identification leading to assimilation needs to be achieved in order for what is mourned to get renegotiated, and thus assimilated, remembered as forgotten.

Artists and writers such as Delacroix, Picasso, Djebar, and Dehane use citation to represent their own complex relation to the nation. In their case, the nation in question is Algeria, or more properly, France's vexed relation with that nation-state it brought into existence, cannot adequately mourn, and sometimes wishes to forget.[28] The politics of assimilation makes a manifest claim to a narrative of mourning and introjection. However, this manifest narrative of nationalist mourning, whether France's or Algeria's, reveals the presence of latent melancholia and demonstrates its significance in terms of an inability to mourn adequately. This opens up the question of whether there is trauma at the heart of nation-state formation.

Delacroix

Delacroix's journal entry for October 17, 1853, reads, "I began to make something tolerable of my African journey only when I had forgotten the trivial details and remembered nothing but the striking and poetic side of the subject. Up to that time, I had been haunted by this passion for accuracy that most people mistake for truth."[29] While Delacroix had previously been fascinated by the "oriental theme" and had done some hyperbolic paintings that could be understood as *orientalist*, he made a distinction between what he thought of as his imaginative paintings and those that accurately document scenes taken from "real life." The hyperbolic painting *The Death of Sardanapalus*, inspired by Lord Byron's play, had been created in 1827, and a painting of an odalisque had also appeared in 1828. As Maurice Sérullaz has noted, the French romanticist painters grew up with fantasies of the Orient, which they read about in Chateaubriand and others. In the late eighteenth and early nineteenth centuries, such events as Napoleon Bonaparte's expedition to Egypt, the Greek insurrection, and the taking of Algiers all consolidated this fascination with that which was fantasized as other and as the exotic. But in 1832 Delacroix embarked on a six-month diplomatic journey to Morocco with Count Charles de Mornay, ambassador to the sultan, that was to change dramatically his sense of the "Orient." The Count de Mornay, who had been sent by the new king,

Louis-Phillipe, hoped to negotiate with the sultan, who was encroaching on what was considered to be French Algerian territory.[30] The French wanted to ensure that the sultan did not give support to Algeria. The diplomatic trip was on the whole successful.[31] There were a few purposes for this diplomatic trip: three French brigs had been captured in Algeria and were now in Moroccan territory, some commercial problems needed to be clarified and sorted out, and the border between French colonial land and Muslim land needed to be defined so as to be sure that Algerians would not have the support of their neighbor.[32] Although Delacroix might seem an unlikely figure to take part in this diplomatic mission, he was identifiably a Bonapartist, and associated therefore with the revolutionary spirit that characterized Louis-Phillipe's overthrow of Charles X. His presence on the journey was, however, decided on for other reasons. Delacroix's childhood passion for the Orient was communicated to Count de Mornay via his mistress, Mademoiselle Mars, and arrangements were then made to convince the Minister of Foreign Affairs that he was a suitable member of the diplomatic party. His presence on the journey was eventually approved, although he had to pay his own way.

On the way back to Paris, Delacroix spent three days in Algiers. There he made sketches of Algerian women, interiors, clothing, fabric, and shoes that later he used as studies for his 1834 commissioned painting for the French government, *Femmes d'Alger dans leur appartement*, variously translated as *Women of Algiers in Their Apartment*, *Women of Algiers in Their Harem*, and *Algerian Women at Home*, each translation inevitably having different implications for women's relationship to subjectivity and space.[33]

Delacroix himself commented on the differences between his imaginative paintings, which depict scenes of citation from other works, and the one that accurately documents scenes taken from real life. Delacroix's famous color system was consolidated in his attempt to document accurately the light of North Africa, using pure color, even within shadow.[34] This desire for accuracy is also reflected in the painter's letters, highly detailed notebooks, and scanty journal entries of this period, which catalogue details of scenes. Delacroix sketched while he was in the presence of the women, and he wrote names on the sketches, presumably of the women he saw, his "models"—Khadoûdja, Moûni and Zoura Bensoltane, Bahya and Zohra Touboudji—and presumably to remind him of the details of his visit. On returning to Paris, he made more sketches before painting the final product, adding figures from his imagination—the black woman, for example, is not present in the earlier sketches.[35]

The desire for authenticity is evident in the detail of the tile and the ornate mirror, and on the fabric, foregrounded hookah (water pipe), jewelry, scarves, carpets, and slippers. The interior is sketched in the notebooks without the women, along with details of the slippers, or *babouches*, and Delacroix carried fabrics with him from the Maghreb, presumably to copy its patterns.[36] He also consulted Persian miniatures, and Etruscan and Iranian paintings, so as to cite that which appeared to be authentically "oriental."[37] His apparent accuracy and authenticity led M. Georges Marçais to use the painting as an ethnographically accurate image in Le Musée ethnographique du Bardo d'Alger (the Bardo Ethnographic Museum of Algiers).[38]

However, to speak of the scene as realistic is obviously an overstatement, and critics as well-reputed as Elie Lambert have shed considerable doubt as to whether Delacroix was admitted into the apartments at all. Lambert proposes that the scene depicted in the paintings was imagined, created out of a selection of various images collected on the Maghreb trip. While Delacroix seems to present detail as a signifier of authenticity, it could equally be read as phantasm, where a scene is imagined and the author of these imaginings situates himself or herself in the scene as its protagonist. Whether the scene is accurately portrayed or simply imagined is, however, not that relevant here. Rather, what is important is the story of the painting as testimony, as told by art historians.

The dates of the two different paintings, 1834 and 1849, are very different moments in the history of French rule in Algiers and the surrounding territories. In 1834 the French role in Algiers was unresolved. The 1830 conquest of Algiers took place under very inchoate official policies and seems to have been a means of distracting the people from the chaos at home that culminated in the July revolution, when Charles X was ousted from the throne by Louis-Phillipe. When Louis-Phillipe took over, half the French army was in Algiers. In 1831 there was some display of a French desire to capture the whole regency, but this was not even vaguely formalized until mid-1834. Indeed, Charles-Robert Ageron suggests that the desire was articulated solely to distract the French from problems at home. Until 1840, a series of unclear contracts seem to have been made among the local Emir, the Tunisians, the French, and the Turks. By 1849, much had changed. Algeria was by this time an integral part of France, following an ordinance on

September 1847 that was backed by the constitution of 1848. Since 1840 there had been a conscious political desire to "assimilate" the natives, and in 1842 a French system of justice was instituted. According to Ageron, this desire for assimilation effectively meant "the destruction of Muslim institutions" and the creation of a system of land appropriation from which only Europeans stood to gain.[39] He further suggests that in France the concept of assimilation was rationalized as a means "to draw the Arabs into French civilization . . . lead[ing] to the fusion of the two races in the country. This fundamental mistake," he adds, "as to the true meaning of assimilation in the country lasted throughout the whole history of French Algeria."[40] Interestingly, it is this very false introjection that causes the existence of a phantom.

While it may well be the case that "at home" the French perceived the races, at least two of them, merging, the paintings speak another story, which establishes a difference between the French at home and the French abroad, as well as among the French, the Arabs, the black slaves, and the Berbers in Algeria. The earlier painting suggests sameness in spite of difference. Here are Penelopes waiting at home. The use of European models to supplement the sketches in the final version of the 1834 painting means that difference is marked by only the black woman, whom I have called the trace of the colonial endeavor, on the side lines.[41] Black woman as device seems to hold a dual purpose here. She both looks forward to the moment of colonialism and simultaneously looks back. She is, in a sense, a citation of a cliché, a marker of *luxe et volupté*, fulfilling the fantasy of harem images in which the addition of the black figure as the pet becomes a sign of aristocracy. Looking back at her through the lens of colonialism, she becomes more Janus-faced, looking simultaneously in two directions, thereby re-citing an orientalist cliché through the power of the gaze. In Delacroix's 1849 painting, the black woman seems to speak through her barely evident and muted separation from the curtain into which she has become incorporated. These women too are inaccessible: they are veiled not only by their religion but also by colonialism. The exotica and erotica of this voyeuristic scene, then, comes not only from a blurring of memory, but also through the dramatic political shift in French policy for the region.[42] The ostensible purpose of the assimilation policy is to erase differences—differences that we in fact see erased through contrasting means in these paintings as distance from the women in the painting is established for the French at home. These Penelopes are waiting not in Delacroix's but in someone else's home—buried deep in the memory of Delacroix, and deep in the trace of the colonial endeavor. The policy of assimilation worked, then, not to devise a method of establishing connections as equals in a similar civilization, but rather to make of Algerians a mass of faceless bodies kept at a distance, with the detail of their lives made irrelevant. The curtain of colonialism, potentially drawn across by the black woman, speaks not only of the voyeur's desire for the stolen glance, but also of the establishment of political boundaries.

In Renan's terms, the painting speaks of the process of memory loss. It is an example of the moment of forgetting the detail of difference in order to establish a feeling of a common French national identity in spite of cultural and religious differences. Here the black woman speaks another message. The policy of assimilation is a veil that hides beneath it a phantom (a canvas) of that which cannot be introjected, the "darker" truth of colonial endeavor. During the period of France's policy of assimilation toward Algeria, Delacroix seems to have become more assimilated into nationalist politics through revolutionary romanticism. The stated desire to create a race of *évolués*—evolved beings or subjects—actually makes those who are not *évolué* markedly inferior in their difference.

Samir Amin has written of the sense of geopolitical "betweenness" afforded to the plot of land of which Algeria is a part. For the Arab world, the Maghreb signifies the West; for the European, it is part of the Orient.[43] This sense of betweenness, indeed of uncanniness, is evident in the Delacroix paintings. In the first painting, the detail reminds us of difference, as does the haunting figure of the black woman waiting in the sidelines. In the later picture, the threshold between Algiers and Paris is represented by the foggy space between memory and forgetting, in which difference intrudes through the veil and through the black woman as trace of colonialism. While the black woman is placed in the foreground as intermediary between France and Algeria, in reality it is more the case that Algeria is a buffer zone between France and the future colonies of sub-Saharan Africa, and France's past colonies. In this *metalepsis* where she apparently cuts off and reveals the scene of the harem, historically she reminds us of the other side. Algeria was, after all, both a colony and not a colony, in contrast to the colonies represented by the black woman, where *us* and *them* distinctions had in the past and would in the future be more readily established. The lack of clearly opposing concepts of *us* and *them* in the Algerian context foretells the long and cruel bloodiness of the future war of independence, and later of civil war.

Picasso

The "transcendence" of detail of which Delacroix speaks and that he exemplifies in the assimilation into a romanticist style is continued in Picasso's *Femmes d'Alger* series, which he painted in order to mourn Matisse. Picasso cites Matisse's technique in a manner that one critic has called "passing from exactness to truth—using memory as a decanter."[44] Records vary concerning Picasso's process of "forgetting" Delacroix's originals. Françoise Gilot writes that Picasso took her to see Delacroix's 1834 painting at the Louvre every weekend for years. Rosamond Bernier claims that Picasso had not seen the Delacroix for fifteen years.[45] Whatever the truth of the matter, Picasso's interest in the paintings seems to lie in the fact that there are two—and that there is therefore a possibility of dialogue between them, "the liberating awareness that their confrontation makes every compositional decision seem again tentative."[46] If the citation of himself was important for Delacroix in the process of "forgetting trivial details" in order to become more assimilated into a melancholic romanticist style, for Picasso the citation of the memory of Delacroix's and Matisse's paintings was a dual process. Even as Picasso successfully mourns his friend Matisse, he continues to thematize, as Delacroix did, the melancholic inassimilability of the Algerian situation.

Between December 1954 and February 1955, Picasso produced fifteen paintings, some monochrome but most in vivid colors; twenty drawings; and two lithographs taken through four different stages "after Delacroix." This process of mourning Matisse—whom Maryanne Stevens calls "the last orientalist painter," and who, inspired by Delacroix's painting, spent much time in Morocco—coincides with the revolutionary stage of the Algerian war of independence, which was launched on November 1, 1954.[47] While the figures in both Delacroix paintings are mostly passive, except for the black woman who threatens movement, in Picasso's versions all of the characters move within and between paintings. The context of war causes them almost to burst out of their frames, out of their apartment. Through the production of multiple visual representations, as well as through multiple surfaces within each example, Picasso reemphasizes what generations have failed to introject. Assimilation cannot take place, so melancholic incorporation reemerges at the moment of revolution.

The figures in Picasso's Women of Algiers series often include frames—whether door frames, mirrors, or citations of paintings. It is as if each work holds up a mirror to the art gallery, to the studio, or to the history of art, into which Picasso writes himself and Matisse through citation. The reversal of images in the paintings suggests that Delacroix's ornate mirror has been moved here to reflect the women, and perhaps the studio, from all angles. We can observe in Picasso's use of the Matisse *Odalisque*, which he said Matisse had left him, the three stages of mourning or psychic assimilation to which Abraham and Torok refer, and understand how the process of introjection is endemic to that of becoming or of retaining a sense of self and equilibrium. First, the loss of Matisse caused Picasso to encounter a new moment in which he effectively became the principal European artist of the age; second, he became partly the object he had lost, seen by the temporary inclusion of Matisse's work into Picasso's; and finally, Matisse is successfully introjected into the paintings. The specificity of Matisse's *odalisques* is lost. Picasso has remembered to forget, and therefore successfully mourned Matisse.

Yet to read this series of works as one through which mourning can successfully occur is potentially to confuse the manifest content of mourning Matisse and Delacroix with the latent content of Delacroix's melancholia that is nonetheless transmitted to Picasso. Just as the whitewash of assimilation left behind a haunting veiled canvas in Delacroix's 1849 painting that reveals the elaborate myth of colonial assimilation in order to involve the repression of another story, Picasso's series similarly elaborates the failure to mourn, or introject, the Algerian women. The filling of these frames within and between this series recalls a moment within which the Algerian woman could be kept in her harem in order to be painted, observed, and made representative of and infinitely substitutable for all Algerian women. Picasso's Algerian women are filled with sensuous movement. They threaten to move out of the confines of the frame; indeed, in some versions they become their own frame—what has been a doorway becomes a headdress in another (see Figures 4.3, 4.4 , 4.5, and 4.6)—and the women outgrow the frames within which they had previously been situated and staged. No longer are these women, these phantoms, satisfied with interiors. They threaten to move beyond them; they threaten, in becoming their own frames, to cite themselves through a visual pun, to become their own artists, and to come into existence through iteration of their own interiorities.

FIGURE 4.3 Pablo Picasso, *Femmes d'Alger dans leur appartement* (December 29, 1954). Oil on canvas, 54 x 65.1 cm. © 2005 Estate of Pablo Picasso/Artists Rights Society (ARS), New York.

FIGURE 4.4 Pablo Picasso, *Femmes d'Alger dans leur appartement* (January 1, 1955). Oil on canvas, 46 x 54.9 cm. © 2005 Estate of Pablo Picasso/Artists Rights Society (ARS), New York.

FIGURE 4.5 Pablo Picasso, *Femmes d'Alger dans leur appartement* (January 24, 1955). Oil on canvas, 129.8 x 161.9 cm. © 2005 Estate of Pablo Picasso/Artists Rights Society (ARS), New York.

FIGURE 4.6 Pablo Picasso, *Femmes d'Alger dans leur appartement* (February 14, 1955). Oil on canvas, 113.9 x 146 cm. Collection Victor W. Ganz, New York.

The black woman, the trace of colonialism, is in the background of the Picasso paintings, with the exception of the study devoted exclusively to her (see Figure 4.7), and the second painting in the series, where her twisted, serpentine figure extends from the foreground to the background. Her body is "Janus-faced," simultaneously moving in opposing directions, with breasts and buttocks on one side, a face looking in the other direction, looking within the apartment and frequently outside of it through the open door. Picasso places her in the background, reversing Delacroix's composition, as the Saharan buffer zone, looking to France and to sub-Saharan Africa simultaneously.

The figures of the women in Picasso's Women of Algiers series—unlike, for example, the Weeping Women series, as Steinberg suggests—have consolidation and integrity, existing as they do between Cubist space and perspectival space, a space "already entered, inhabited by the eye as by a roaming caress."[48] Although the figures are distorted—breasts and buttocks frequently emerge from the same surface—there is very little sense of

FIGURE 4.7 Pablo Picasso, *Femmes d'Alger dans leur appartement* (December 13, 1954). Oil on canvas, 60 x 73 cm. © 2005 Estate of Pablo Picasso/Artists Rights Society (ARS), New York.

flattening here; rather, discontinuity gives way to continuous movement.[49] Not for long can these figures be framed. And these markers of the body—the breasts, the buttocks—inscribe race for us, for how else does race get communicated in abstract paintings such as these in which women are painted all sorts of colors: blue, pink, green? It can be only through reference, through citation. The enlarged buttocks, for example, tell us that this is the figure seen from behind, and perhaps simultaneously alerts us to the story of the eroticized black woman in European painting.[50]

The process of citation here mourns the loss of that other moment of forgetting, which spoke of a consolidation of national identity. Here this bursting forth speaks of confrontation. If the transcendence of detail becomes for Delacroix the move to nationalist identity formation, in Renan's terms, in Picasso the move to remember to forget documents the movement of change. Citing Delacroix in the moment of revolution causes him to abandon the classicized and framed in order to take up the confrontation of movement, of the sensuality of Algerian women in their variety, where boundaries as we know them are being questioned and broken down. Each figure appears different in spite of the compositional cohesion of the paintings. In fact, the process of ingestion of images found in the Matisse paintings (the seated Indian, the odalisque, and the gate from *Tangier, the Kasbah Gate*) through the framework of Delacroix causes the mourning, or documentation of forgetting in Delacroix, to become thematized as mourning, and also the documentation of the failure to mourn in Picasso. And it is Matisse who is mourned, and ingested, into the history of art—a history that of course works through constant citation of old masters. Here the thematization of mourning and citation seems more conscious of the falsity of that process, for it makes sharp distinctions of time and space, which need to be refashioned in the light of a different political moment. The old nationalism of Delacroix, fortified through revolutionary romanticism, is blasted to pieces here in this dramatic shifting of frames and borders and in this twisting distortion of fragmented limbs.

Simultaneously, Picasso's process of citation reveals another interior—the interiority of mourning, which characterizes the work of citation. Picasso cites in his paintings Velásquez's *Las Meninas*, the most important work of modern art according to Foucault, and Matisse's *Odalisque* and *Tangier, the Kasbah Gate* within the frame of Delacroix's *Women of Algiers*. *Las Meninas* can be seen in the staircase in the back of the painting, visible through the open door.⁵¹ In the final version (see Figure 4.6), the staircase intrudes into the painting, making up its frame. Picasso expands on this theme two years later when he produces variations on Velasquez's painting that invite us to look beyond the limits of the studio and cause us to question whether we look at a mirror image or whether, indeed, we are being painted. The viewer and the painter are famously implicated by the complicated scene that invokes the beyond of artistic expression.

Matisse's *Odalisque* becomes one of the figures seated in the background of the painting, as if observing the process by which Picasso paints the rest of the scene. (Steinberg interestingly speaks of the tension between Matisse and Picasso with reference to this position of the judge.) These questions of foreground and background are, however, complicated again by the mirror image. The positions of the reclining and seated women are also inverted in some versions. Whereas in the Delacroix the reclining figure is on our left, in the Picasso she is invariably on our right.

This mirroring composition of the paintings that reflect the art gallery constitutes a phantasmatic scene in which the subjectivity of the artist, of Picasso, develops through self-reflection and through the assimilation through citation of these other great French and Spanish figures. If Delacroix could define the national through the exploration of interiority (the documenting of loss) that informs the aesthetic of *Femmes d'Alger*, Picasso's interiority—the mourning of Matisse and the placing of himself as artist—confronts the moment in which subjectivity develops through citation, through iteration, through "working through." The mirror on the wall that is present in both of Delacroix's paintings is noticeably an absent image in Picasso's, perhaps because the mirror is elsewhere, perhaps because it is a mirror image.

The mirroring of interiority within these paintings recalls and anticipates not only the history of art and Picasso's own mourning. Picasso began and completed these forty or so studies from November 1954 to February 1955—during the first three months of the Algerian Revolution, or war of independence. After eight bloody years, and substantial loss of life, the Algerian nation was born. Looking at Picasso's Algerian collection, the importance of iteration, reiteration, and citation of already existing images emerges, constituting images of the Algerian woman, and to some extent of her self-image. Picasso writes himself into the history of art through citation, thus becoming the modern subject. The consolidation of self through mourning demonstrates the process of ingestion. Picasso becomes part himself, part Matisse, part Delacroix, and part his subject matter—the Algerian women who are breaking out of the image we have had of them. Between France and Algeria lies Spain, Picasso's country of origin, itself torn by civil war, documented by Picasso in *Guernica* and the *Weeping Women* in 1937. Picasso becomes again, begins again, as the modern subject through an image of a country against which France (Picasso's adopted country) defines itself.

If Delacroix's 1849 cavern demonstrated a *failure to mourn*, an inevitable manifestation of the melancholic spirit that cannot assimilate the other in spite of the rhetoric of assimilation, Picasso's series in turn does the same. Indeed, while Picasso appears to mourn Matisse successfully, he simultaneously thematizes the failure to introject the difference of Algeria through a presentation of the encrypted image. Once again, at the time of a shift in political relations with Algeria, the walls of the crypt are shaken. The women, once confined behind the proscenium, now appear without it and threaten to move beyond the frame itself. Picasso seems to suggest the changing relationship to Algerian women that was operative in this time of revolution. It is perhaps Picasso's own growing recognition of this that caused him to draw, in 1957, a sketch of Djamila Boupacha, the young Algerian woman who was tortured by the French and whose case was taken up by Gisèle Halimi, Simone de Beauvoir, and a host of French intellectuals.

Djebar

In 1978, before the Algerian government's repressive Family Code (finally passed in 1984) was in place but when women's autonomy and access to public space were already severely limited, Assia Djebar, the Francophone Algerian novelist, filmmaker, and historian, wrote a short story inspired by Delacroix's and Picasso's paintings.[52] Djebar focused on the apparent conversation being conducted by the two seated women in Delacroix's 1834 version of *Femmes d'Alger dans leur appartement*. Though arguably misogynist, Picasso's paintings speak a complex history of war-torn bodies as well as of women's freedom, as the naked women are unveiled. As Djebar comments in her 1979 essay on Delacroix and Picasso, "Forbidden Gaze, Severed Sound," "Picasso was uncovering the truth of the vernacular language that, in Arabic, designates the 'unveiled' as 'denuded' women."[53] Citation, then, for Djebar, does not have to be politically regressive in Said's sense. Read through the lens of postcolonial criticism, these instances of citation, whether misogynist or orientalist, get reinflected so that the Algerian woman can reclaim the image.

Djebar cites Delacroix's paintings in her title, moving out of the medium of visual art and into the genre of the short story. The mixing of media is characteristic of Djebar's writing and filmmaking, which makes use of musical form, historical text, film, photography, and painting, and indeed this short story was originally conceived as an idea for a film that was never made.[54] Though her stories and novels thematize language difference, she writes exclusively in French, shifting styles dramatically to explore different languages within the overall framework of French.

Djebar's "Women of Algiers in Their Apartment" is a short story about postcolonial Algiers, the women and men who inhabit this area, the languages they speak and hear, their occupations, and the locations they inhabit. Djebar allows the emergent movers of Picasso's series an interiority of their own.

The sensuality of Djebar's prose includes vivid painterly descriptions, dialogues coming to life and breaking off into elision, and descriptions of women emerging from and dissolving into various visual, acoustic, and social backgrounds. "Women of Algiers in Their Apartment" tells the story of Sarah, a former activist in the war of independence, who works in a studio making documentaries. Sarah is married to a surgeon named Ali, whose son, Nazim, runs away from home. Nazim is an adolescent and, like two-thirds of the Algerian population, was born after independence in 1962. The runaway Nazim announces his departure to his father in a letter deliberately written in an assimilationist, nationalist Arabic that he knows will be incomprehensible to his father. We also meet Sarah's friend, Anne, a Frenchwoman who has returned to Algeria to die; we meet her as she regurgitates the pills she has failed to swallow in a suicide attempt. Another war-torn woman who has spent time in a "madhouse" is Leila, who is discovered by a painter friend of Ali's. Leila, an old comrade of Sarah's, epitomizes for Sarah the isolation of those women who have no outlet for their postwar trauma, nor for their stories of the war and of the infamous prison at Barberousse.[55] This woman shares with Sarah a sense of fragmentation, of an incomplete story and an unconsolidated self. Sarah, however, has an arena for her anguish in her film work, in which the many voices, languages, and stories in her head have an arena through the montage of audiovisual production.[56, 57] Ultimately Sarah tells of the necessity for women to communicate with one another, Anne decides not to kill herself, and we are left with an image of a changing relationship between Algeria and France in which veiled and unveiled women emigrate to Parisian *arrondissements*.[58] While the women in this story are drawn together through their gender, it is the difference within and among women's voices, which the FLN had suppressed, with which we are left. Djebar also asks us to recognize these differences so as to understand present-day Algeria.[59] She shows us the multiplicity of languages that are a part of everyday existence in Algeria, and demonstrates the multifaceted cadences of these languages through the adoption of a variety of styles, genres, and media, even within the scope of this short story. The Algerian nation, just like Renan's French ideal, has similarly remembered to forget the coerciveness of its own assimilationist policies.[60]

"Women of Algiers" is written in four sections, and the modernist mode of the Picasso series reemerges through the multifaceted interiorities that we read here. The first three sections each culminate in an "interlude," and the fourth ends with two tentative uses of the word *diwan* or *divan*. In the first instance it is spelled with a *w*, in "diwan of the water carrier"; in the second instance it is spelled with a *v*, in "divan of the fire carriers." All four meanings of the term *divan*—a Muslim council, the room in which the council is held, a couch, and an Arabic collection of poems—are relevant here. The water carrier, a servant in the *hammam* or bath house, a woman described as almost black and of nomadic (perhaps Berber) descent from the Sahara region, lies on a stretcher, having fallen, reciting a series of prose poems in an interior monologue.[61] Words intrude into her poems from elsewhere: From her mind? From the other women who surround her? If she looked in two directions in the paintings, here she listens and speaks in two directions—hearing the voices and languages within her, and engaging with the women around her. The hospital and the ambulance—the locations of the wounded—become the court where questions of representation get negotiated. This Berber woman, a representative of those erased by the Ottoman empire as well as by the FLN, is the "unveiled" one, perhaps a displacement of the black slave from Delacroix. Simultaneously, in representational citational terms she is the slave, and formally she is metonymy of melancholia. She can reveal the process of forgetting that is elaborated in the other divan for the fire carriers. These are the forgotten women who were carriers of arms and bombs during the revolution, and whose public militant actions were briefly celebrated. We hear a story now forgotten, a trauma misunderstood, of Leila, a fire carrier who is "discovered" in a "madhouse" by a passionate painter still caught up in the anger of revolution. Leila holds court with Sarah, our protagonist, another fire carrier. How do they mourn their wounds? How do they remember their dismembered bodies? Where are the narratives that publicly acknowledge their suffering and sacrifice?

Where are you, you fire carriers, you my sisters, who should have liberated the city.... Barbed wire no longer obstructs the alleys, now it decorates windows, balconies, anything at all that opens onto an outside space.... In the streets they were taking pictures of your unclothed bodies.... The bombs are still exploding ... but over twenty years: close to our eyes, for we no longer see the outside, we see only the obscene looks, the bombs explode but against our bellies and I am—she screamed—I am every woman's sterile belly in one.[62]

This meshing of two kinds of representation—legal arbitration and designation (*vertreten* and *darstellen*, in Marx's terms)—are at the heart of Djebar's story: How can the articulation of trauma move into the realm of public space? How can one bear witness? How can one remember that which has deliberately been forgotten? How can a critical politics, or a critical nationalism, derived from melancholia, address the assimilationist mourning of the nation-as-state that remembers only in order to forget?

If modernity is characterized by the division between private and public space, as many have argued, the emergence of the modern Algerian woman into subjectivity is, in this story, enacted through citation, but through a citation that performs the very difficulty of citationality.[63] Djebar begins the volume of short stories with an "overture." She says:

Don't claim to "speak for" or, worse, to "speak on," barely speaking next to, and if possible very close to: these are the first of the solidarities to be taken on by the few Arabic women who obtain or acquire freedom of movement, of body, and of mind.... New women of Algiers, who have been allowed to move about in the streets just these last few years, have been momentarily blinded by the sun as they cross the threshold, do they free themselves—do we free ourselves—altogether from the relationship with their own bodies, a relationship lived in the shadows until now, as they have done throughout the centuries?[64]

We hear, in the short story, again of Sarah's tenuous relationship to a form distinguishable from shadow, just as we note that her speech—in contrast to that of the Frenchwoman Anne, whose story is deemed by Sarah to be somewhat symptomatic and predictable (perhaps demetaphorized)—frequently breaks off into ellipses, as if the passage from ingestion to speech cannot yet fully occur.

Sarah, far away, crouched in the gloomiest corner, suddenly wishes she could melt away into darkness. . . . Finally, Sarah . . . goes to the bay window . . . : with a quick movement, she pulls open the enormous curtain. . . . "No!" the other cries out, blinded.

Sarah turns halfway around: Anne (a French woman) has retreated to the white wall in the back, both hands over her eyes as if to blindfold them. . . .[65]

These cavernous interiors reference Algeria's cavernous and mountainous landscape, but the quotations can also be read as citations of Plato's metaphor of the cave, which theorizes epistemology and the status of artistic representation. Although Djebar's work is not Platonic in any other way, she, as many feminists before her, rewrites the metaphor to consider the cave as the cavernous and shadowy existence within which women are confined. The woman who moves beyond this blindfolded, shadowy existence must not forget, she tells us, "those who are incarcerated" as she is momentarily blinded by the sun.[66]

The shadowy existence of Delacroix's painting is both women's literal confinement in private spaces and the world of images described by Plato. The shadows on the wall, the signifiers that go into the formation of both private space and, indeed, interiority, need to be "transcended." If Plato's cavern contains the history of artistic expression, those who exist within it are inevitably formulated by this history of signifiers. Iteration beyond the cave can only ever be a renegotiation of existent signifiers through recitation. The figures who in Picasso's paintings appear as if bursting from their frames manifest here as women who find it difficult to emerge from that feminine space that characterized the cavernous existence. In Djebar, the transcendence of the shadowy world of interiors needs to be taken beyond interiority, into public space.

The emergence of the modern Algerian woman into subjectivity is, in this story, re-cited beyond a cavernous existence. Women need to speak to other women, acknowledge the differences of their interiority, and ensure their access to public space. Djebar's iteration of interiors, public discourses, and various languages dramatizes the slippage between the artistic and the political, designation and arbitration, and private and public. The phantom emerges and is articulated, and that which was marked by silence now speaks, thus instituting a model of politics based on melancholia rather than a nationalism based on mourning. In this way we do not simply remember to forget, but we take remembering seriously as an imaginative and a political act. The phantom, the material difference that could not be assimilated by Delacroix, Picasso, or the FLN (the Algerian government), can then be brought into the open, for the walls will finally crumble. Through the process of rejecting the mourning model of nationalism that seeks to erase differences, Djebar's story dramatizes the breakdown of a crypt: the initial realization of the lie of assimilation. The expansive sense of multiple identity within the Algerian nation that replaced the French empire remembers, through imaginative history, that which has been forgotten. The lie of the assimilationist model that has turned difference into a phantom is reconstituted here as a lived political memory. Djebar confronts the phantom of violence, and attempts to give articulation where there has been silence. Djebar seems to provide imaginatively a melancholic emergence of phantoms such as we see visualized in Houria Niati's installation on Delacroix, *No to the Torture*. In this work, shadowy phantoms, like dispositives, begin to emerge as tortured women's flesh, and as critical resistance to national forgetting (see Figure 4.8).

I speak of the nation in terms of mourning and of politics as melancholia not to subsume the historical and assimilate it, as it were, into the family romance of psychoanalysis. Nor do I wish to suggest that the assimilationist tendency of the state can simply be reduced to Renan's model of nationalist mourning. Rather, through the historical mapping of the work of citation, the nation reveals itself to be formulated simultaneously with that of the nationalist subject. While mourning and melancholia are always nuanced by their context, I have employed them here to demonstrate how the catachresis of nation is a regurgitated phantom that is repressed by the state. The state in turn seeks to assimilate, indeed to mourn, thus making all subjects into figures who are always already national subjects.

By way of a conclusion that simultaneously raises questions for the future, we turn to a recent example of the continuing re-citation of Dela-

Women of Algiers in Their Apartment 167

FIGURE 4.8 Houria Niati, *No to the Torture* (1983–1996). Mixed media installation. Courtesy of the artist.

croix. In a recent documentary, *Femmes D'Alger* (Kamel Dehane, 1993), Djebar is interviewed. She speaks of the many voices in her head that achieve expression and release in writing. The film also interviews three other women—a young radio journalist, a former combatant in the war, and a designer who has decided to wear the veil—all of whom give their testimonies. The interviewer poses questions about their lives, about the power of men, and about their careers, religion, and the future of Algeria during a time of civil strife and violent attacks on public female figures. We see the women in the 1834 painting in fragments, just as later we see current-day women of Algiers silenced and depicted in fragments. We move into a dramatization of the 1834 painting as it comes to life. As we move into a stage set up like that of Delacroix's women's apartment, women singers come to life. We move from the material of the painting to a scene of women interacting, and then back to the painting again. We return to this scene intermittently in the film as the women speak of their lives. The final shot is of a film set designed to look like the Delacroix apartment. The women are absent. Where have they gone in this moment of suppression and silencing? Have they been driven into invisibility? Are they working behind the scenes? Are they present again in the disguise of phantom? More active than Delacroix imagined, are they out in the public space, or have they been driven further into concealment?

In this context of national history as mourning, it seems once again that the nation-state, this time the Algerian nation-state, speaks a lie of the possibility of assimilation. In the hands of postcolonial Algerians, who have inherited the very structure of the nation from the nation that excluded them, moments of melancholia occur in relation to postcolonial "Algeria." The loss that gives rise to both mourning and melancholia is an accumulated loss: the loss of the national ideal.

Reading theories of psychical assimilation alongside French and Algerian cultural production and assimilationist French colonial policy reveals the postcolonial's melancholia in the everyday experience of the postcolonial subject. If coming into national independence requires a model of history that is assimilationist and can remember to forget, it also gives rise to a critical relationship to the model that spawned the prolonged trauma of colonialism. In the manner of *Nachträglichkeit*, what is revealed here is a trauma at the heart of the very concept of national identity. A prolonged trauma results from an accumulation of events that cannot be assimilated, the outcome of which is melancholia. It also comes from a transgenerational system of knowledge. If we were to place this idea of a melancholic postcoloniality into the context of the work of Nicolas Abraham and Maria Torok, we could suggest that specters do not just hide particular secrets; they also encrypt the operative assumptions behind multiple oppressive ideologies from a variety of sources. The language and structures of the nation-state that was built on the exclusion and incorporation of its colonial subjects are inherited by postcolonials in what Gayatri Spivak has called an *epistemic violence*. This violence results in a haunting. A crypt normalizes nationalist ideologies but conceals their exclusionary agenda, which appears as a phantom.

There is trauma concealed in the very heart of the theory of European nation-state formation. A phantom is apparently created as a response to an inassimilable and originary traumatic event, which in this case does not seem to exist in terms of a particular event, even as it evolves through changes in policy. Derrida claims in *Specters of Marx* that "haunting is historical to be sure, but it is not *dated*," so the originary moment can be theorized as a catachresis.[67] But if origin is itself a catachresis, as I would want to contend in the messy context of hybrid national cultures muddled in the context of nationalism and colonialism and decolonization, then there is no originary traumatic "event" that could be assimilated. Given the shared theoretical roots of nation formation, colonial policy, and psychoanalysis, we may want to conjecture that psychic assimilation itself is a colonial formation that is a catachresis in the former European colonies. The inability to introject would lead to what Freud considered central to melancholia: critical agency. In the condition of *epistemic violence—which is the violence of assimilation*—in which we cannot not want to assimilate, the experience of melancholia would perhaps eventually identify a phantom, and transfer that critical agency into ideological critique—and a new form of the nation-state.

PART III

ALGERIA BEYOND ITSELF

5

Latent Ghosts and the Manifesto: Baya, Breton, and Reading for the Future

> She told me her name, the one she had chosen for herself: "Nadja, because in Russian it's the beginning of the word hope, and because it's only the beginning."
>
> ANDRÉ BRETON, *Nadja*[1]

Baya Mahieddine, a surrealist painter from Algeria, almost always depicts scenes of encounter (see Figures 5.2, 5.7, 5.8, 5.9, and 5.10). When one attempts to find objects or images located in isolation in her paintings, the eye is constantly drawn to another figure, as if it is the imaginative potential of relationality that should guide our viewing. The figures encountered—human, vegetative, unconscious, animal, musical—open up a lesson in the ethics of reading for an encounter with alterity. This provides for an alternative model of reading paintings, the history of art, and the figure of woman.

Framing this chapter is an interest in postcolonial theory's impact on art history, and the ethical demands the theory has placed on that history. While the ostensible subject discussed here is the surrealist movement, the chapter also probes how, in a philosophical sense, the European metropolitan *episteme* was written out of the relationship to the colonies, and particularly how conceptions of alterity (in abstract as well as in political categorizations of the foreign and the female; see Figure 5.1) were theorized coterminous with, but in silence about, coloniality.

174 *Algeria Beyond Itself*

In the context of the history of the surrealist movement, André Breton and the surrealists famously protested the colonial expositions in France, and indeed continued their protest outside the realm of aesthetics to denounce the war in Morocco and to demand the right to insubordination by French soldiers in the Algerian war of independence. Their famous tract came to be called the "Manifeste des 121" because of the 121 French intellectuals who signed it. In spite of this manifest anticolonial protest, all too often the context of colonialism and decolonization is left out of

FIGURE 5.1 Baya Mahieddine, *Mère au bouquet* (1945). Gouache on paper, 48 x 63 cm. Musée National des Beaux Arts, Algiers.

narratives about the origins of the history of surrealism, even in accounts that foreground its international impact and appeal, its relationship to the poetry of negritude, or its complex association with internationalist Marxism and the French communist party.[2] Colonialism seems to haunt the literature on surrealism.

Such silence around the intellectual pressure imposed by coloniality has more recently affected many theoretical movements associated with continental philosophy generally and French theoretical movements particularly. As I have suggested, a significant proportion of these theories could be more usefully understood as *Franco-Maghrebi* theories, and not just in a biographical, sociohistorical, or foundationalist sense, but philosophically in order to comprehend the notion of alterity and its relationship to the foreign, to gender, and to the historicity of philosophical and historical discourse.[3]

This seems all the more important to analyze when so many are facing the horror of neocolonial politics in the form of violent war—for example, in the recent war in Algeria, and particularly how women have been affected by this "virile war."[4] The histories and complicities of intellectual movements, often falsely demarcated in the new categories of nation-statehood and national history, can usefully be called on to further understand the manner in which artistic movements are enunciations of the complex contexts from which they arise. That is not to say that a direct link between cultural enunciation and historical and political reality is adequate. But it is to frame an argument about art in a historical context in terms of the world and not just in terms of a narrow definition of provenance, national context, or movement. Looking for an ethical means of understanding this politics and the constraints that some disciplinary borders impose on such questions of ethics allows for an analysis of the contingency of disciplines with colonial histories. Just as a postcolonial art history poses questions concerning the spurious imposition of national frameworks on artistic production, so disciplinary borders are also damaged.

Much of the scholarship in postcolonial studies, whether in the literary context in which it was initially developed or in the cultural studies, art history, and historiographical fields in which it now finds itself, has often failed to allow for readings of the aesthetic and the political to occur simultaneously. If the dominant aesthetics of eighteenth- and nineteenth-century French painting is considered orientalist, there has been an acknowledgment of the significance of the dominant ideology that reveals in art retrospectively a colonial legacy. But at times context and identity have begun to overshadow the work, representing a kind of inhospitality to the object under consideration. Whether in critique of orientalist works or in "celebration" of postcolonial art or of works produced during the period of decolonization viewed as wholly resistant, the object is often sacrificed to the telos of partisan liberation politics, which often avoids dealing with the problems and exclusions of postcolonial rampant nationalism.[5]

Postcolonial theory's political intervention into art history also raises the question of the ethical limits of partisan reading. Though "reading" is not exactly what one does when approaching an artifact, an "ethics of reading" can perhaps aid in understanding the singularity of a work, and the manner in which the "face" of the work calls for a response and therefore for a responsibility to the art object such that one's own borders may be undone or damaged in the process of looking.[6] The antinomy of hospitality forms supplements at the borders, remainders, and melancholic specters. Reading for those specters becomes an ethical practice of reading for a poetics that informs a feminist and postcolonial critical practice against the romance of nation and community.

Breton expresses some of the ghostliness of this antinomy in his "Preface for the Reprint of the Manifesto." It is an apt framing citation with which to begin this chapter on the politics of surrealism and its implications for the notion of a feminist, postcolonial historicity.

> I simply believe that between my thought, such as it appears in what material people have been able to read that has my signature affixed to it, and me, which the true nature of my thought involves in something but precisely what I do not yet know, there is a world, an imperceptible world of phantasms, of hypothetical realizations, of wagers lost, and of lies.[7]

Breton sets up an antinomy between "signature" and "me." If Breton's "me" is presented as the imperceptible, the particularity of inscription proposed through the signature actually belies a relation to phantoms, phantasms, and specters of the material. The signature, as marker of identity, appears like the emergence of a singular access to the work, but it is not. In its particularity, it rather marks an appeal to discursive structures in which it signifies belonging. In introducing an ethics of reading that is not based on the question of identity, I am foregrounding the singularity of the work, which exists as the excess of signature. If signature automatically invokes historical significance and discursive reliability, the work carries the trace of something else through the impression it leaves on another. If in his novel, *Nadja*, Breton raises the question, "Who am I?" only to supplement it with "perhaps everything would amount to knowing whom I haunt," he renders the ontological question inadequate. Reading for those specters that hover around and through Breton's texts allows not so much for an understanding of the core of the man or the true nature of his thought, but rather for a retrieval of the figures who haunted him, specters of the other who haunted through their supplementarity, damaging anything concrete and fully accessible that could emerge in response to the question, "Who am I?" The singularity of the work lies exactly in what exceeds formal epistemes; it is the trace of something else, something other, that has no form of representation in any other discourse, that cannot be translated. The face of the painting may be difficult to find. Like *prosopopeia*, the emerging of a face, it can be sensed more easily than it can be figured. As excess of the history of art, the singularity of the work, that is, what exceeds classification, manifests itself as a remainder that imposes a demand for a response in the future. A haunting presence imposes a demand on the future, as Derrida has reminded us. If the other is a melancholic remainder manifesting itself as an insistent absence, it has a spectral presence that cannot be put to rest.

That which exceeds the terminology of manifest politics—anticolonial politics, for example—returns as a remainder and haunts the spectator who works to understand what constitutes the demand of this spectral presence. It is the remainder that gestures toward the future possibility of existence. Responding to sensations that lie beyond a comprehension of the other, the spectator opens up an ethical relation to the other that is about the future. Rather than stifling the other by accommodating it to the present, the ethical relation provides future hope for the remainder, who will always be a damaged figure in terms of the present.

Although she enters the narrative of this chapter quite late, it is the Algerian painter Baya Mahieddine and her work (see Figure 5.2) to which I as viewer attempt to respond. A responsibility to the work of this haunting figure involves an understanding of both French colonial contexts and ghosts. It also involves developing an ethical response to this overscripted and overdetermined painter who tends to disappear from view as

FIGURE 5.2 Baya Mahieddine, *Femme bleue à l'oiseau* (1945). Gouache on paper, 70 x 55 cm. Musée National des Beaux Arts, Algiers.

her signature is tied to the art historical terms *naivety* and *primitivism*, the colonialist terms *Arabian mysteriousness* and *childishness*, the psychoanalytic term *primitive mentality*, and the postindependence nationalist term *nativist representation*. The ethical demands made by Baya's paintings have to do with how to understand her as haunting yet material—a surrealist conundrum.

This chapter explores a simple idea concerning how one imagines a future, and perhaps more important, how one conceives hope, the impetus of imagination, for the future. This involves considering what the relationship of that future has to the past and, perhaps more broadly, what the dead have to say about the future of the living, and how the dead impose on, and positively or negatively cause damage to, the idea of a future. It is a study of hope, how that hope manifests itself, and of communication with others. In the context of surrealism, the most prominent medium of that hope is the manifesto, from Breton's joint manifestoes of surrealism to the surrealists' "Declaration of the Right to Insubordination in the

Algerian War," from novels and speaking in tongues to painting and other manifestations by the possessed and the dispossessed alike who hope for a better future. The texts and figures discussed here all have some association with Breton. Théodore Flournoy's *From India to the Planet Mars* of 1899 was one of Breton's favorite texts, and he was constantly "haunted" by its protagonist, Hélène Smith. Baya was an Algerian painter who was "discovered" by Breton, and Nadja was Breton's great love, to whom he devoted a novel. *Nadja* is a romance that tells the story of Breton's barely fictionalized love for the woman whose name is given to the novel. Nadja was an artist whom he encountered on the way to buy Trotsky's latest work at the Humanité bookstore. This is how the reader, and the narrator, receive their formal introduction to Nadja, which also serves as a cautionary supplement to the frame of this chapter: "She told me her name, the one she had chosen for herself: 'Nadja, because in Russian it's the beginning of the word *hope*, and because it's only the beginning.'"[8] Foregrounding name as her introduction, Nadja nonetheless complicates any idea of introduction as a clarification of that which will ensue. She has chosen her name, and as it is only "the beginning of the word *hope*," she communicates the excess of her signature, gesturing toward the singularity that cannot be contained within inscription.

Manifesto: Definitions

A manifesto is a document of hope presented in the present in the pursuit of a different future. It often lays out a plan in steps or stages, and is written as a response to dissatisfaction with the present. The term *manifesto* is derived from the legal arena. To present a manifesto means to present evidence, to make manifest, to show the proof of the crime. So the accused, given a narrative of intentionality bolstered by a once-latent proof, is revealed to be guilty. That which was latent becomes manifest in the service of justice (or in the courtroom, in the service of the law). That which was wrong in the past and still exists in the present needs to be made manifest. It is given form in the shapes of words or images. It is put on trial through examination. Its audience is the jury, and it is called on to assess, sometimes through narrative manipulation, what lies latent, or the latent assumptions of the past. In a manifesto, the past always haunts how the future is imagined, and indeed, how hope is envisaged.[9]

The manifesto is also, according to the *Oxford English Dictionary*, "a public declaration or proclamation, usually issued by or with the sanction of a sovereign prince or state, or by an individual or body of individuals whose proceedings are of public importance, for the purpose of making known past actions, and explaining the reasons or motives for actions announced as forthcoming." The manifesto thus serves a public function, to reveal, or make manifest, what has until then been present in only latent fashion in order to rationalize, and at times manipulate, the planned events to come. This was usually, from the mid-seventeenth century, a state document. In the modern era, and particularly in the late nineteenth and twentieth centuries, it is, to use an anachronistic and perhaps metaleptic term, or one of inverted substitution, a counterhegemonic document. It is expressed in terms of negativity, and being future oriented, it manifests hope for the future, often in dialectical terms that make demands on the future. This is because the manifesto of the modern era always references back to, and is haunted by, Karl Marx's *The Communist Manifesto* (or more accurately, *The Manifesto of the Communist Party*), written in 1847-48 at the request of the Central Committee of the Communist League.

The Communist Manifesto begins, famously, with a description of a reproach or accusation, and a reclaiming of the terminology of that accusation:

A spectre is haunting Europe—the spectre of Communism. All the Powers of old Europe have entered into a holy alliance to exorcise this spectre: Pope and Czar, Metternich and Guizot, French Radicals and German police-spies.

Where is the party in opposition that has not been decried as Communistic by its opponents in power? Where the Opposition that has not hurled back the reproach of Communism, against the more advanced opposition parties, as well as against its reactionary adversaries?

1. Communism is already acknowledged by all European Powers to be itself a Power.

2. It is high time that Communists should openly, in the face of the whole world, publish their views, their aims, their tendencies, and meet this nursery tale of the Spectre of Communism with a Manifesto of the party itself.

To this end, Communists of various nationalities have assembled in London, and sketched the following Manifesto. . . . [10]

Marx's language suggests joint authorship. In reality, it may well be that the agenda was jointly conceived through the various networks making up the Communist Correspondence Committees in Brussels, Paris, and London. But the document itself was crafted by Marx, with some input from Engels (significantly, the title).[11] It is presented as a joint course of action by communists, making manifest their intentions from the spectral mode they inhabited in infantile accusations and reproaches as the communist bogeyman. The mode of writing is a critique through which the politics of the spectral is revealed. What is latent in the reproach against this specter to be exorcised is exactly the politics of the privileged, the Czar, the Pope, the Chancellor of the Austrian Empire, the Foreign Minister of France.[12] It is the opposition between oppressor and oppressed in a fight "now hidden, now open. . . ."[13] The critique is put forward in the hope that the future can be diverted from the detrimental teleology in place at the moment of writing. Manifestoes are all about hope, and they are all about collectives of people coming together for no reason other than to act on that hope. Hope for transformation is the energizing and binding force of the manifesto. As in most utopian writing, the manifesto implies a negative response to the current state of things.

The manifesto presents a negative response to the situation and its teleology. It is both protest (nicely exemplified in the French *manifestation*) and transformative will. The constant and consistent negativity toward the state of things is followed by the call for revolution in the unity of workers. But negativity itself is an expression of latent hope for the revolution to come. If only revolution would be adequate (and perhaps not even that), then a critical mode would be the primary expression of hope in the face of what seemed like hopelessly flawed and complicitous liberal reform or self-serving cynicism of the elite. The widespread mainstream criticism of (especially idealistic) negativity often fails to recognize that hope for a better future at its core. Negativity often presents itself as plaint or lament.

Some, like Walter Benjamin in a little known essay on Erich Kästner, would see negativity as a false affectation rather than as affect; and Wendy Brown, through a reading of this essay, sees negativity more generally leading to "left melancholy," or a sense of despair originating in the apparent failure of revolution, the condemnation of the left or of any voice of dissent, and the various forms of institutionalization that condemnation takes in the modern era.[14] Partly in response to the affect of melancholy, and as a foundational element and symptom of that melancholy, the latent hope that propels the manifesto is negativity, as are many other expressions of imagining futures from the damaged present. In the next section, another medium of interest to Breton and the (mostly male) surrealists expresses that hope: mediums (who were usually women) themselves. The section following that is on the surrealist interest in the insane: *Nadja*. The final section is on the Algerian child and the primitive painter: Baya. If the latent hope that propelled *The Communist Manifesto* was the "specter of communism," perhaps after all the manifesto was communally authored. Perhaps Marx was possessed by the dispossessed. Perhaps he was a medium for the communist bogeyman. But if he was a medium, it was one who clearly expressed demands for the future, as if the communist bogeyman was becoming material in the process of writing. But what haunts the manifesto? What lies in excess of its demands? What cannot be introjected into the manifest proposals? What calls for justice continue to haunt?

Mediums: From India to the Planet Mars.
From Hélène Smith and All Her Latent Personalities to Élise-Catherine Miller, to Nadja, and to Baya

For the surrealists, and particularly for Breton, transformation and change would take place not simply in the political and public sphere, and not only in consciousness. They would also constitute a radical ontological shift, and would be brought about by the breakdown of borders, or indeed by disbelieving in borders, between consciousness and the unconscious, in encounters with the primitive and with those who psychically were constituted differently (including the most profound psychical difference—that between the living and the dead). Famously, in his work on "automatic writing," Breton became interested in mediums, or as he put it, "what William James called the 'gothic psychology' of F.W.H. Myers which . . . led us to the admirable explorations of Théodore Flournoy."[15] Breton adds that it is a "regrettable fact that so many are unacquainted with the work of F.W.H. Myers, which anteceded that of Freud."[16] The prepsychoanalytic material on mediums posed questions of a philosophico-religious nature concerning whether "love survive(s) the grave."[17] Myers was the founder of *subliminal psychology*. His most well-known works were *Phantasms of the Living* (with Frank Podmore and Edmund Gurney) and the appropriately posthumously published *Human Personality and Its Survival of Bodily Death*.[18] In *Phantasms of the Living*, Gurney, Myers, and Podmore had written of a form of latency found in telepathics. It was common to find in their research subjects messages transmitted from sick or dying people in a moment of crisis that were received by the living subjects only after the sender's death. This time lag (usually of only a few hours) was perceived by Gurney, Myers, and Podmore as a period of latency in which the message had not yet been consciously received by the living receiver. In *Human Personality*, Myers offered a different explanation. In a chapter titled "Phantasms of the Dead," he stated that he found the theory of latency wholly inadequate, and he sought explanation in different phenomena. "In popular parlance," he wrote, "we are looking out for ghosts."[19] And then, "the phantom must be taken on its merits, as indicating merely a certain connection with the deceased, the precise nature of that connection being a part of the problem to be solved."[20] This is because "we have no warrant for the assumption that the phantom seen, even though it be somehow *caused* by a deceased person, *is* that deceased person, in any ordinary sense of the word."[21] In addition, we also must "cease to ascribe to the phantom the motives by which we imagine that the deceased might be swayed. We must therefore exclude from our definition of a ghost any words which assume intention to communicate with the living. It may bear such a relation to the deceased that it can reflect or represent his presumed wish to communicate, or it may not."[22]

Myers' purpose in this chapter is to demonstrate how that ghost is a spirit fitting in with the "Laws of the Universe and consequently by permission of the Supreme Power in the Universe."[23] He insists on "actual spacial changes induced in the spiritual, but not in the material world."[24] The ghost was a spiritual life force that separated from the body at the moment of death.

Spiritualism extends to Myers' concept of the self more generally. Commenting on the disciplinary argument in psychological circles between what he called "the composite, 'colonial' structure and constitution of man," on the one hand, and "partisans of the unity of the Ego," on the other, he chose a middle ground—a spiritual subliminal consciousness existing alongside the apparently unified "conscious" or "supraliminal self." For Myers, the spiritual worked toward framing the self. "This unity does not diffuse itself downwards, but is aggregated by ascent from below; it is not an initial but a terminal point."[25]

Flournoy's aim was to remove the "spiritist" or religious from the study of mediums (or as he would prefer, automatists). Expressing some doubt about "intermediary souls" or "inhabitants of another world,"[26] he discussed the phenomenon of Hélène Smith, a medium, as subliminal activity, that is, activity that took place "under the threshold of consciousness."[27] Feeling somewhat skeptical of the idea that she was inhabited by spirits, he saw her trance manifestations as symptoms of *cryptomnesia*, or the resurfacing of "latent memories" in "disfigured form," rather than (as he in some ways wished they would be) as manifestations that would serve in "utterly demolishing the entire framework of established science."[28] One could claim indeed that psychoanalysis would be this new form of science.[29]

*

Flournoy's *From India to the Planet Mars: A Case of Multiple Personality and Imaginary Lessons* is about a woman who would become very important for the imaginative futures and pasts of surrealism: Hélène Smith (the pseudonym for Élise-Catherine Müller). In Breton's assessment, Hélène's was the "richest case of all" mediums.[30] She was inhabited by "spirit guides" when in a trancelike state. Resistant to the idea of the supernatural manifesting itself in people, Myers referred to this kind of phenomenon as *pseudopossession*. His work was still somewhat religious and spiritual in its foundation, yet he sought to find reasons for this type of manifestation in psychogenesis rather than in possession by another. When in this latent state, Hélène would speak languages created entirely by herself. *Martian* was one of these (she frequently went to Mars in her trance states) and a language she called *Hindu* (she was at times a fifteenth-century Indian princess, somehow appeared to be the daughter of an Arab sheik, and traveled to various places in India and to Tehran, Peking, and sometimes France in her trances. She also manifested as Marie-Antoinette, and as a figure called Léopold, who seemed to be something of a spirit guide. Various characters from one of these scenes would be "reincarnated," as it were, into others. Her latent language skills were analyzed by Ferdinand de Saussure, who, as Todorov has pointed out, was fascinated by the absence of the *f* in her imaginary *Hindu* because it replicates the absence of this consonant in Sanskrit. He was also curious about the gendering of her language use—it was more masculine than feminine. And while there were grammatical elements of Latin in the language, she never confused parts of the languages. Hélène Smith had no formal knowledge of Sanskrit. Her Martian was discussed by another orientalist linguist, Victor Henry. (His reading of the absence of *f* in her *Hindu* differed from that of Saussure. It was more psychogenetic; her deep hatred for languages in waking life, and her attitude toward her native tongue, French, caused her to drop the *f*.) Smith created both scripts for her languages (see, for example, Figure 5.3), and landscapes for her global and cosmological travels, as if communicating an idea in excess of existing languages and landscapes allowed for a utopian space in which she could travel freely.

Flournoy analyzed her languages as a form of *glossolalia*, that is, speaking in tongues. A veritable industry of psychological work on the subject was initiated in his journal *Archives de Psychologie*. Glossolalia was also, for Flournoy, "the fabrication and the use of an unknown

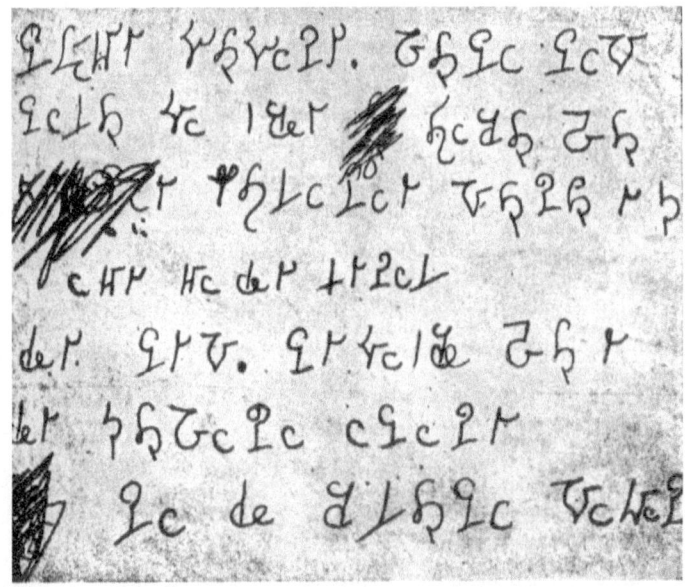

FIGURE 5.3 Hélène Smith, *Text no. 18* (October 10, 1897), written in pencil by Mlle Smith incarnating Esenale, in Théodore Flournoy, *Des Indes à la planète Mars. Étude sur un cas de somnambulisme avec glossolalie* [From India to the Planet Mars: A Case of Multiple Personality with Imaginary Languages] (Seuil, 1983).

language."³¹ His formulation is indeed interesting—the language is designated as unknown even as it is acknowledged to be fabricated. Michel de Certeau has emphasized that "the experts repeat it over and over: glossolalia resembles a language but is not one"; it emphasizes telling over meaning, or saying over expression.³² The linguists, however, did want to insist on Hélène's speech being a language, and in line with de Certeau's thinking, there is a sense of urgency with which glossolalia manifests itself. There seems to be a need to speak somehow, whether by being "possessed" or by being an oracle, or in cultural, religious, or psychological (and one could add political and intellectual) settings in which speech is otherwise constrained. The imperative to communicate is primary in cases of glossolalia, but not to communicate something for which a language already exists. This is de Certeau:

> An expectation focuses on this still-distant Other—this speaking, indecipherable oracle, vocal flow that muteness dams. A *belief* awaits the waters of a first orality that could wash through the walls of our languages. Would that there were a Word! Fable itself. It would suffice that our mouths open, emptied of words, that "torrents" of passing voices be allowed to take over. But these rivers, where are they? Whence do they come? Believing in them is not knowing. The very term *spirit*, which for so many traditions designates that act and the actor of speech, underlines the nonplace of "that which speaks." In the words of John of the Cross (after and before many others), the *spirit* is *el que habla*, the one that speaks. The belief that founds the expectation of a coming *speech* creates the *atopia* in which this speech is produced, a scene that is reflected and assured in the glossolalic *utopia* (*utopia* because it is not one among other actual languages, neither this one nor that one, but a linguistic neutral). . . . What utopia is to social space, glossolalia is to oral communication.³³

In other words, glossolalia is a latent expression of a need to communicate, with a recognition that most languages are inadequate to this task. For de Certeau, it is the expectation of something to come. It is indeed, somewhat messianic in de Certeau's formulation, but it also manifests in the concrete, in the utterance of spirit through the medium of a person, and in the guise of the dead. It is the promise of another, or hope manifested as the other. And this spiritual materiality seems to result in a ghostliness, flesh given to the spirit and demanded through materiality. If the prehistory of psychoanalysis is spiritualism, the prehistory of the specter is the spirit. The specter instantiates spirit in the world, giving it materiality.³⁴

De Certeau's suggestion that "what utopia is to social space, glossolalia is to oral communication" is instructive here, because it expresses the latent need to tell of another kind of hope. (Flournoy hoped that his findings on Hélène Smith would lead to a revolution in scientific values, and to some extent the development of psychoanalysis was linked to this.) Hélène would become (however countertransferentially) the source of his hope. And hope for Hélène (or Élise-Catherine) manifested itself in latent, unknown form, in the dead. To some extent, to do justice to Élise-Catherine, that is, not to institutionalize her hope, one would have to engage with the possibility that she was indeed going to Mars in her trance-like states, and that she did in fact manifest specters. One would have to imagine that behind the pseudonym or signature *Hélène Smith* there was Léopold and a host of other psychical guests who haunt that name. That would be the only way to understand the forms of constraint and the repressive codes giving rise to glossolalia, and the only way to understand Hélène's forms of hope and not reduce her to a mystical source of inspiration, or a messianic spirit, rather than a semi-concrete specter. Latent hope manifested as communicating need rather than as a set of clear demands for which a language already exists. It was a latent possession by hope.

Flournoy compared her symptoms when in a trancelike state to those of hysterics. But in her waking life this was not the case at all. When she was not conducting a séance, she seemed like a normal, happy, healthy young woman. Peculiarly, she hated languages, tried not to learn German, and exhibited no language skills. Her father, who was Hungarian by birth, had lived in Italy and in Algiers (remember, she had thought she was the daughter of an Arab sheik, and indeed she wrote some Arabic and spoke Arabic, although she apparently did not know it when she was not in a trance) for many years before settling in Geneva. Her father spoke Hungarian, French, German, Italian, and Spanish. He also knew some English, Greek, and Latin. (He did not know, as far as we're told, Arabic or Tamazight, even though he lived in Algiers for some years.) Hélène's health was excellent and she did not come to Flournoy as a patient. Flournoy wrote, "she has always enjoyed robust health, and has not even had the slight diseases usually incidental to childhood." As different as she was from her father in conscious linguistic abilities, so was she different from her mother, who suffered from "broncho-pulmonary disorders of a rather alarming type."[35]

Flournoy began his introduction to this rather novelistic study by explaining how he first encountered Hélène Smith: "In the month of December, 1894, I was invited by M. Aug. Lemaître, Professor of the College of Geneva, to attend some seances of a non-professional medium, receiving no compensation for her services, and of whose extraordinary gifts and apparently supernormal faculties I had frequently heard."[36] Flournoy was clearly captivated by Hélène's strength of body and character, and he would later investigate, not in these terms, his own (counter)transferential relationship to Hélène, which went against the precepts of modern science's required objectivity. He had, in other words, begun to inhabit her trance world and to feel that he molded it in some ways, and he had responded to this inappropriately. He had been caught up in her confabulation and become somewhat possessed by her ability to communicate without comprehensible words. He responded to the expression of the need to communicate. His relationship with her ended badly. After the publication of the book, they fell into a dispute about royalties. After a lengthy battle, Flournoy agreed to give her half; the other half went to his journal, *Archives de Psychologie*. They argued over who had "made" whom. Certainly Hélène received the patronage of a wealthy American after publication so she was able to do the séances full-time before giving them up completely to do quite controlled religious painting. These paintings differed greatly from the naive Martian landscapes she drew (see Figure 5.4) that resembled the landscapes of Henri Rousseau; and from the extraordinary cryptological script she presented of the various languages she coined that has similarities to the work of Henri Michaux and to the Korwa drawings by tribals in Madhya Pradesh that attempt to communicate through a "transcendence of writing."[37, 38] Hélène's art in the early years seemed to be a visual rendition of glossolalia, and in the case of the landscapes, of utopian space. At various points in the aftermath of *From India to the Planet Mars*, Hélène expressed frustration, suspicion, and resentment about being exploited for the purposes of fame and financial compensation. It seems that when she showed her material needs and was neither sick nor entrancing Flournoy, he lost interest.

Or perhaps he was no longer possessed. He had framed his study by talking about the ethics of the research, saying that in a way a monetary relationship would have made things easier. He also acknowledged that she was critical of his research. Flournoy was captivated by the immediacy

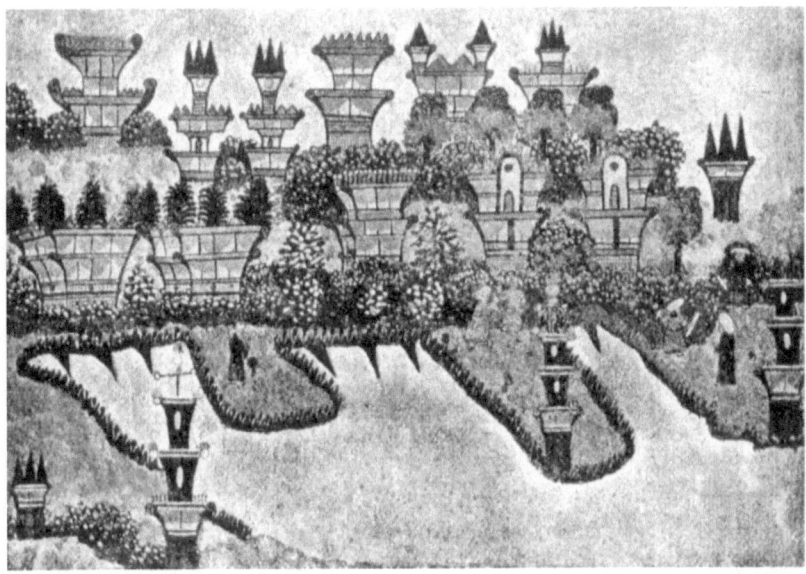

FIGURE 5.4 Hélène Smith, "Martian Landscape," in Théodore Flournoy, *Des Indes à la planète Mars* (Seuil, 1983).

of spirit, even though he differed from Myers on the subject of spiritualism. He seemed fearful of its more material manifestation as a specter. It haunted him with the material needs in her instantiation in the world. He was haunted by the expression of her need to communicate in the form of cryptomnesiac glossolalia. The automatic message became tainted by the medium of delivery when it was clear that the postman needed to get paid, or at the very least wasn't going to allow the receiver to get paid for the labor of transmission she had provided.

Something similar marked the fate of Nadja. Breton, having been captivated by her, began to lose interest, noticeably when Nadja needed money and began to appear more concrete than she had in the first few days of their intense encounter. In fact, while her spontaneity and unpredictability inspired Breton, it was her neediness that ultimately made her less attractive to him. It is "a certain critical freedom" that he finds difficult to take, and it is this form of freedom that instantiates her in the world, and differentiates her from a medium of his hope.

*

Breton's interest in mediums, and the forms of automatic writing and painting they produced, stayed with him throughout his career, but his fullest explanation of his interest is in the 1933 essay "The Automatic Message." He explains there the differences between mediums and automatic productions, on the one hand, and those who engage in surrealist automatic writing and drawing, on the other. The most profound difference is what he calls a "certain critical freedom" available to the former.[39] Breton noted the productions of Hélène Smith to describe this difference: "the prodigious alienate all notions of reality." Breton was interested in mediums because they allowed for a breakdown of borders between the subliminal and the supraliminal. Indeed, the trancelike state was a liminal state in which the latent became manifest in drawings, speech, writing, or transcription. Seeing the supraliminal productions of the art world as devoid of interest, he saw them being overshadowed by a "superficial layer of being." "It is altogether possible [that it has a] ridiculous lustre."[40] Anxious to retrieve that "lustre" in a secular form, Breton was equally interested in understanding what constituted it. He was extremely critical of the "very poor spiritualist doctrine" that "we are aware . . . could not even be raised."[41] For Breton, the effort in automatic writing was to achieve a dissolution of the subliminal and supraliminal moving to unification—the "composite" or "colonial self," as Myers put it. The main function of automatic messages was to recognize the nature of access to the subliminal. Breton also saw this idea as profoundly democratic: "it is to . . . each to claim his share."[42] The work would then be to analyze. The automatic message was not to communicate a vision as such. The nature of that vision would have to be analyzed after, but it would be semiconcrete, that is, both "imaginative and sensory."[43] It is as if Breton wanted direct access to that which was latent, and the manifestation of latency would carry a singularity beyond the signature—an iteration of hope and haunting. The visual arts produced by Hélène Smith, and indeed by Nadja and by Baya, seemed to Breton like speaking in tongues, and therefore to be free of the social constraints dominating the modern national subject who ignored what he or she haunted, and what haunted him or her. They expressed a freedom, according to Breton, as if the psyche could be unaffected by the repressive codes of society in these women. In microcosm, there is a demonstration of a misapplication of Freudian theory in surrealist expression, or indeed a desire not to relegate the spiritualist prehistory of psychoanalysis to the dustbin of psychoanalysis today. For Freud, after all, the psyche is indeed damaged through repression, whether societal codes demand this or not. The discontents of civilization find some way of expression and are not untouched by repressive forces. Breton ends his essay on the automatic message with homage to the *ur-medium*: "from the single fact . . . no more than a saint."[44] The prehistory of psychoanalysis was highlighted by Breton, who focused on the message transmitted through the medium. Perhaps it was the political and material changes brought about by colonial nationalism that would make impossible this direct transmission from the other. Breton was arguing against colonial violence in Morocco as he was writing *Nadja*, with this wishfulness for encountering the other and for engaging in an ethical relation with the other. If psychoanalysis introduced, through a repression of its prehistory, a sense of the impossibility of full access to the other, it did so in the subliminal knowledge of political materiality, and in the melancholic introduction of a repressive border in the modern subject. The material recognition of an impossible engagement with the other effectively foreclosed the belief in mediums, even as it insisted on the pressure exerted by that which was repressed. Although the encounter with the other—the unconscious, or another person—was also the ethical demand of psychoanalysis, it would occur only in the recognition of the impossibility of full encounter.[45]

Nadja, or the Insane

In *Communicating Vessels*, Breton analyzes a dream he has had about his past love, Nadja, who was institutionalized after he stopped loving her: "Often I tried to persuade myself—wrongly or rightly—that my pecuniary problems were not without relevance to her decision to leave. A retrospective justification also, in relation to Nadja, about whom I have repeatedly reproached myself that I let her run out of money in the last few days."[46] Nadja, whom Breton explicitly associates with Hélène Smith,[47] predicts and commands that Breton would write a novel about her:

André? André? . . . You will write a novel about me. I'm sure you will. Don't say you won't. Be careful: everything fades, everything vanishes. Something must remain of us. . . . But it doesn't matter: you'll take another name: and the name you choose, I ought to tell you, is extremely important. It must have something of fire about it, for it is always fire that recurs in anything to do with you. The hand too, but that is less essential than the fire. What I see is a flame starting from the wrist, like this (with the gesture of palming a card), and making the hand burn up immediately, so that it disappears in the twinkling of an eye. You'll find a Latin or Arabic pseudonym. Promise. You have to.[48]

And then, by way of explanation, she adds a note: "On the doors of many Arab houses is drawn, it seems, the emblematic outline of a red hand: this is the hand of Fatima" (see Figure 5.5). The hand of Fatima, a common defense against the evil eye in many Arab countries, including Algeria, is akin to the chosen name—one that exceeds the closure of a given name or signature, and gestures toward something else. Nadja's image of the hand includes a signed face, as if the encounter with Nadja-as-other wards off evil. When one looks at her drawing, one looks at her face, and her ambiguous, excessive digital signature, and there is an invitation to encounter this other with the look of a friend. Breton understands this image as a portrait of their encounter.[49] Breton does not explain the Pentecostal imagery of the fire. As if desperate to be released from her own world of rather disturbed surreal images, Nadja seeks expression through Breton in the form of the novel. As if herself a ghost who cannot quite grasp the formulas of concrete exchange, she demands clarity through Breton. She demands naming, and the consciously chosen proper name, as if boundaries could be enforced through it, and as if she had no control in her own forms of expression.

In some ways, the surrealists were looking to be possessed, or to welcome being psychologically damaged by those who did not fit into the norms of bourgeois, "civilized," repressive codes. This form of "damage" and of radical reformulation of selfhood and relations with others was the only measure by which to understand revolutionary manifestations in political and aesthetic realms.

Breton, with the support of other surrealists and, most of the time, in conjunction with other surrealist artists and writers, of course, wrote many manifestoes: obviously the surrealist manifestoes of 1924 and 1930, but also the numerous tracts and collective declarations produced by the surrealists on topics ranging from the colonial expositions in France, the treatment of Algerians during their war for independence with France, nationalism in art, and other matters of local and international politics and ethics.

Change was something that involved every sphere of life and would at best bring about a complete alteration of mental status. The manifestoes for change started in the aesthetic realm, then moved to the political. But for any of these to really matter, surrealism had to be more than art forms and politics alone. The manifestoes had to belong to aesthetic and political realms that would bring about changes in life, and changes in conceptions of selfhood—massive ontological shifts that would forever transform the relationship to the past, to the present, to hope, to the future, and to the question, "Who am I?"[50] The manifesto that lays out this necessary ontological shift is the novel *Nadja*, in which the past is brought into a changed

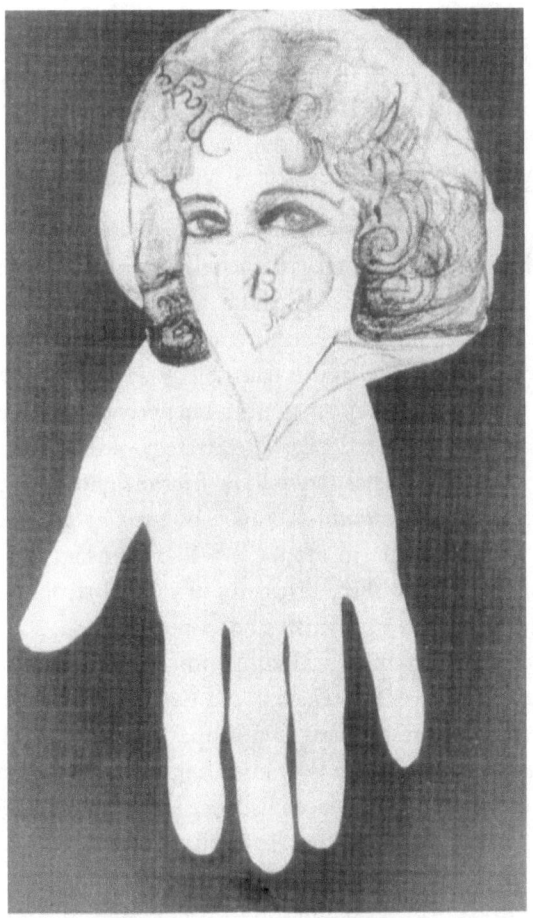

FIGURE 5.5 "Plate 32: So that the angle of the head can be varied," in André Breton, *Nadja*, trans. Richard Howard (New York: Grove Press, 1960), 120. © Editions Gallimard.

state through hope, and through the latent medium in which that hope manifests itself. (Breton saw Nadja as his Hélène Smith.)[51] In *Nadja*, hope manifests itself in the narrator but also through the medium of Nadja herself. If the *Communist Manifesto* began with the specter of communism, *Nadja* begins with the specter of self. Here are the opening words:

Who am I? If this once I were to rely on a proverb, then perhaps everything would amount to knowing "whom I haunt." I must admit that this word is misleading, tending to establish between certain beings and myself relations that are stranger, more inescapable, more disturbing than I intended. Such a word means much more than it says, makes me, still alive, play a ghostly part, evidently referring to what I must have ceased to be in order to be *who* I am. Hardly distorted in that sense, the word suggests that what I regard as the objective, more or less deliberate manifestations of my existence are merely the premises, within the limits of this existence, of an activity whose true extent is quite unknown to me.[52]

The movement from ontology to "hauntology" denotes an openness to others, and the form the body takes as the self becomes inhabited during the everyday, by things around it. And these everyday manifestations and apparently unconnected incidental occurrences tell a great deal about the way in which one exists. For Nadja, this hauntology will develop into images of friendship—the desire for a spiritual union between lovers (see Figure 5.6).

In "Haunting Transcendence: The Strategy of Ghosts in Bataille and Breton," Kendall Johnson has shown how Breton's ghostlike nature is akin to Marx's, not in the *Communist Manifesto* but in *Capital*, where the ghost circulates in a manner akin to money.[53] While for Marx the "ghost functions to recognize the social contextuality of value, Breton rationalizes the economic exchange into a spiritual, noneconomic bond. . . ."[54] In *Nadja*, Breton, the narrator, attempts a kind of communion with Nadja through money, because it relieves her tensions and her anxieties. And as he is able to give her this gift, he restores his own "hope" through some kind of spiritual transmission to her. When they kiss after he has promised her money, she says, "Communion takes place in silence" and that her teeth substitute for the host.[55] In giving her money, he receives communion. Yet, as he well knows, he is like a God to her, or like the sun.

Nadja can be read as a confession from a guilty Breton—he knows, by the end, that he failed to give money when she most needed it, that is, when she was institutionalized because of her mental status. He wrote that perhaps she would have recovered if she had been "treated in a pri-

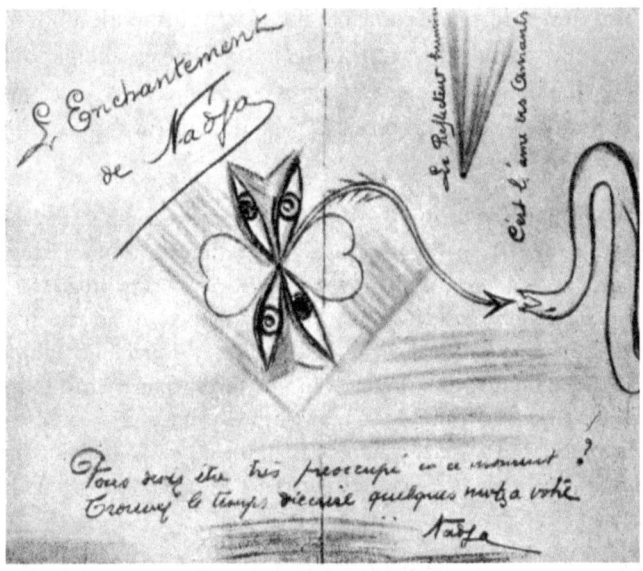

FIGURE 5.6 "Plate 29: The Lovers," in André Breton, *Nadja*, trans. Richard Howard (New York: Grove Press, 1960), 117. © Editions Gallimard.

vate rest home with all the considerations granted the rich. . . ."[56] Reading this romance as a manifesto, however, Nadja herself can be understood as the ghost who demands that her story be told in a name she has chosen—hope—that is, the beginnings of hope in Russian. Language, and the name you choose, she had told Breton, are very important, and this is because language is how you imagine your future. It expresses the need to communicate. Read in this way, and to do justice to Nadja, Breton is indeed haunted not by the self-same spirit of communion but by the specter of the desperate, the dehumanized, the dispossessed, the unhuman, the pathologized, the animal, or the monstrous. "Nadja was poor," he tells us, "which in our time is enough to condemn her, once she decided not to behave entirely according to the imbecile code of good sense and good manners."[57] Love, for Breton, means ultimately serving a cause to allow people to imagine their futures and to remove obstacles that prevent that. It is about being open to the demands others make on you, to become communicating vessels not to achieve communion, but ultimately to know what haunts you, and what you haunt. For Breton, love is being haunted by the specter of the damaged. His participation and complicity in the causing of that damage opened him to that form of haunting, not just for inspiration but for genuine responsibility to the other. From *Nadja:* "Human emancipation in *every respect*—by which I mean, *according to the means at every man's disposal—* remains the only cause worth serving."⁵⁸ And from *Communicating Vessels*, a hope for the future:

> Lovers who separate have nothing to reproach themselves with if they have loved each other. Carefully examining the cause of their disunion, you will see how little in general they were able to command themselves! Here again, progress is conceivable only in a series of transformations . . . that will permit the accession to love and to everything else worthwhile in life by this new generation announced by Engels: "a generation of men who never in their lives will have had to buy at the price of money, or of any other social power, the leaving of a woman; and a generation of women who will never have been in the necessity of giving themselves to a man from any other considerations than real love, nor of refusing their lover for fear of economic abandon.⁵⁹

Breton's hope for the future is then a struggle against the material barriers erected by modernity against friendship. He sees these barriers as a consequence of capitalist modernity. He looks to Engels to wrench from him his own failure and friendship with Nadja, whose hopefulness could ultimately not fend off material need.

Four: Primitive and Child: Baya

In the 1920s and 1930s, Algeria produced its first artists who called themselves painters. This was of course during the period of French colonialism and of European modernist primitivism. One painter, Baya Mahieddine—usually called simply Baya, although this was a pseudonym for Fatma Haddad—was born in 1931. On the occasions when she does sign her work, it is difficult to read, as if playing with a Tamazigh or Tifinagh script, or adulterating an Arabic or Roman script with *Fatma*. Whatever the signature is, it is not clearly the name *Baya*. When at the age of sixteen her work was exhibited at the Galérie Maeght in Paris (Figures 5.7 and 5.8), she was termed, by the art world, a "naive painter."

This designation is accompanied more often than not by the story of Baya being born into a poor family in Bordj-el-Kifan (near Algiers), then orphaned in Kabylia at the age of five, following which she lived with her grandmother until she was eleven. At that time her artistic talent

FIGURE 5.7 Baya Mahieddine, *Au bord de la rivière* (1945). Gouache on paper, 73 x 107 cm. Musée National des Beaux Arts, Algiers.

FIGURE 5.8 Baya Mahieddine, *Femme et oiseau en cage* (1946). Gouache on paper, 65 x 95 cm. Musée National des Beaux Arts, Algiers.

was discovered by a French woman named Marguerite Caminat Benhoura (almost exclusively referred to simply as Marguerite in the literature on Baya), with whom she lived from then on in Algiers. Her status as orphan with a European guardian was to overdetermine her designation as naive and primitive. Some records indicate that she worked as a servant in Marguerite's home. Marguerite had left France during the war and was working as an archivist at the Muslim Bureau of Charities in Algeria. She was well-connected in the literary and art worlds, had paintings by Braque and Matisse adorning her walls, and was visited some time in 1947 by Aimé Maeght, who subsequently presented Baya's work in a solo exhibition in his gallery later that year. Maeght was introduced to Baya's work by Jean Peyrissac, whose works he had exhibited in Paris. Peyrissac had been given some of Baya's work by Marguerite, and had in turn shown it to Maeght. Asking to see more, Peyrissac arranged for a meeting between Marguerite, Baya, and himself. He then spoke of his interest in arranging an exhibition at the gallery in Paris. Breton, who also presented the Second Surrealist Exhibition that year in the gallery, wrote the preface to the catalogue, a volume of the Galérie Maeght catalogue, "Derrière le Miroir" (Behind the Mirror). Following this trip to Paris she spent time in Vallauris (where Marguerite had connections) working on pottery. There she met Picasso, who was apparently very interested in her work. Some say it was he who recommended that she return to Algiers. In 1953 she married into a "traditional Muslim family" in Blida. Over the next ten years she had six children and did not paint. (This period of latency coincided with the Algerian war of independence, perhaps an obvious fact but one that is never mentioned in the literature about her or her work.) In 1963 she resumed painting, exhibiting both new and old work in Algiers and in Paris.[60]

Baya, in an interview that takes as its title her own words "je ne sais pas, je sens . . ." (I do not know, I feel . . ."), tells that Marguerite herself was a painter and was married to a painter.[61] Baya says that she began painting, in fact, when she lived with Marguerite. Marguerite painted flowers and birds and Baya would watch her painting in the evenings. Eventually, she said, she started painting herself. Marguerite would ask her what she had painted that day and would comment on her work. Baya says, however, that she does not know whether she was influenced by Marguerite's work.

Anatole Jakovsky, in his lexicon of "Peintres Naif" (naive painters, though the French term is used in every language) presents Baya thus:

> Has Arabic and Kabyle blood. An orphan at the age of five, she is being looked after by a certain "Marguerite" who takes her into her own home in Algiers, where she is being taught to paint and model clay. She is, however, in no way influenced by her teacher, nor by her exhibition in Paris. After having given pottery a try in Vallauris, following Picasso's recommendation, she returns to her homeland and marries into a traditional family. And then there is silence. A silence of 14 years! It is only in the course of the last year that Baya has taken up painting again.[62]

A similar tone is evident in a recent *Télérama* write-up on Baya's work in France, and in a tribute to her on the occasion of her death in the progressive journal *Algérie Littérature/Action*.[63] So even though French painters can be interpellated by the "other," it is at the expense of seeing the other as the "primitive painter." Although Baya is definitely a hybrid—Kabyle and Arab—she apparently can be exposed to and trained in Europe without being at all influenced or interpellated by what she sees. Her orphan roots, her tradition, and her lack of influence are what become important in this imagining. The European "primitivist" painter and art historian who gets back to a "primitive stage" of existence by looking at the pure other—the parentless child, the woman, the unconscious of Europe—has a "distance" from the primitive by way of a "privileged" position of corruption that differentiates him from her. She, on the other hand, is posited as naive, embodying an earlier state; she is a child with a "simple unfragmented consciousness" that is organic.[64] She cannot in any simple sense be the surrealist because effectively she exceeds even their boundaries of subject formation. Here, of course, there is a confusion of the archaeological (primitive) and the anthropological (naive), and it is this confusion that is orientalist racism. But is she not similarly interpellated? Doesn't she embody the contradictions and interpellations of the primitivist painter? The exposure of her interpellations and contradictions reveals the narrative of distance that is established by European art historians at the very moment in which they claim a blasting apart of an ideology of difference.[65]

The double narratives around Baya concerning her naiveté on the one hand and her exposure to a Franco-Maghrebian art scene on the other ask us to rethink the terms *art naïf* and *primitivist art* as employed in surrealism and pit them against the colonial politics of the time and the politics of decolonization. Considering the period of modernism through to the contemporary politics of Algerian independence, the temporality of colonial discourse continues to exist in a period when Algeria attempts to conceive itself as an entity separate from France, and France struggles with separation. Artifacts of this type include the collective tracts from the surrealist movement, especially the ones proposed by Breton: the *Manifeste des 121* (1960), which protested the treatment of Algerians by the French during the war; the "Don't visit the colonial exposition" (1931); and the *Manifesto of Surrealism* (1924)—all manifestoes that blur the distinction between cultural artifacts and *realpolitik*, between psychoanalytic temporality and political events, and between primitive and modern. Baya's paintings, at the time of her first exhibition in 1947, were assimilated by anticolonial surrealists invested in the idea of a psychoanalytically conceived "primitive" and "child," and have more recently been conceived as worthy of national pride by postcolonial Algerians who write of her as a painter who will take her place next to Chagall, Matisse, Klee, and Renoir and whose work embodies the "living memory of our most vulnerable infancy, the unalienable presence of our memory."[66]

A mournful trajectory emerging out of a Freudian concept of the past moment of the primitive informs us about other trajectories that are less obviously colonialist, whether they be obviously nationalist or simply oppositional. Psychoanalysis may give a way of conceiving how the necessary attempt to narrativize an oppositional story is symptomatic of the larger problem of the temporality of modern nationhood. If psychoanalysis developed at the height of European colonial power, and if its conception of self is deeply bound up with modern nation-statehood, it also understood the primitive and the child as the infancy of the modern psyche. Freud's *Totem and Taboo*, for example, was deeply invested in the anthropological works of the time: these would influence both surrealist fantasies of psychic freedom and nationalist fantasies of pure origin.[67]

There is little doubt that Breton and many of his contemporaries were on one level anticolonialist. In 1931 they protested against the hypocrisy of the colonial exposition that "celebrated" the arts and peoples of European colonies at the same time as effectively killing them, and against the concept of "la Grande France," which they claimed gave the metropolitans a sense of ownership over the colonies that was necessary for comfortably hearing the echo of gunshots without wincing, and a sense of themselves as willingly given the natural resources of the colonies. The tone of the writing is characteristically uncompromising and unforgiving.

For the surrealists, the breakdown went beyond the aesthetic realm into the more overtly political. In 1924, following the publication of the first surrealist manifesto, André Breton and his associates openly sympathized with Moroccan insurgents as France engaged in a minor war against these anticolonial rebels.[68] They embraced the challenge of Aimé Césaire's negritude that disturbed through *insurgent metonymy* the purity of that most fetishized of things, the French language. The colonies are never considered outside the context of the economic motivations of France and the contempt within which Breton and others held the ethics of the nation they observed deteriorating. Nearly thirty years later, the surrealists presented a document (popularly referred to as the Manifesto of 121 but actually titled "Declaration Concerning the Right of Insubordination in the Algerian War") that outlined the difficulty of characterizing the war in Algeria; it was not exactly civil war, not exactly war against an external aggressor. They named it an imperial war played out by the French military, and they defended the right of Frenchmen from the metropolis and from the colony-that-was-not-one (Algeria being technically an integral part of France, constituting three départements, or counties) to resist without being imprisoned:

Is it necessary to recall that, fifteen years after the destruction of the Hitlerian order, French militarism, as a result of the demands of such a war, has succeeded in restoring torture and making it once again an institution in Europe? . . . Once again, independently of any pre-existing groups or slogans, *a resistance movement is born, by a spontaneous awakening*. . . . The cause of the Algerian people, who are making a decisive contribution to the destruction of the colonial system, is the cause of all free men.[69]

These two passionately anticolonial statements were about both the destruction of Europe or France, which was already suffering the trauma of World War II, and a massive injustice toward the inhabitants of a colony, whether internal or otherwise. The Manifesto of the 121 is also a reading of the function of memory in ethicopolitical struggle—"is it necessary to recall . . . ?" The violent defense of French control of Algeria is, for Breton, a defense of freedom more generally. The revolutionary logic of opposition between the "French" and the "Algerian" is thrown into question; what is at stake is the fight between militaristic torture on the one hand and freedom on the other. Algeria was not Europe's, or even France's, other.

For Breton, a revolutionary desire to intervene in politics in the name of freedom reflected a simultaneous attempt to both reveal and encourage a transculturation that blew apart a more fetishized politically regressive distinction between the West and the Rest. In its place, Breton proposed a notion of spontaneous insurgency among the ranks of the French military, who would recognize that the struggle for decolonization was a struggle for all men. The appeal for this freedom originates in recall—"Is it necessary to recall . . . ?" asks Breton, and the rhetorical gesture tells us that it is indeed necessary. The damage performed by the Vichy regime is invoked by Breton—as it was by de Beauvoir in her article on Djamila Boupacha—in order for an ethical lesson to be taken.[70]

Between the two anticolonial tracts, Breton would engage with Algeria in a different manner. The spontaneity of awakening to the right of freedom—in other words, the psychical connection to military resistance—is something that lingers in the language about primitivism and specifically about Baya.

The conflation of the primitive with the child, which gets repeated and worked through in *primitivist* art, inevitably leads us back to the surrealist interest in Freud. Implicitly, it is the process of citation, remembering and working through, that differentiates the primitive from the primitivist, and the child from the adult. The privileging of an aesthetic based on distance is evident here: the unincorporated fragment can be narrativized into art, and indeed into the construction of the subject. Freud's own interest in primitive art and archaeology cannot of course go without mention here. His office contained various archaeological finds, small artifacts as well as reproductions of pieces such as the famous *Gradiva*—the *bas relief* he had seen hanging in the Vatican Museum.[71] His own imaginative world, filled with the images of Schliemann and Stanley, caused him to think of the exploration of the unconscious in terms of an archaeological dig and colonial exploration, and his own memories of his father led to a sense of "disturbance of memory" on the Acropolis that was initiated by the sight of the ravaged temple.

Surrealist interest in naive painter Baya, who is in this conflation of the archaeological and the anthropological a counterpart to the primitive art object, indicates another assumption here. While on the one hand the more obvious psychoanalytic figure to think of in relation to naive painting is Jung, with his primeval archetypes that can be accessed through the naive, a Freudian gloss leaves us with a sense of an unassimilable child who intrinsically offers a revolutionary challenge to the art establishment. Although Anatole Jakovsky insists that painting by children and psychotics falls under the classification *Art Brut* rather than *Art naif*, it is precisely the image of unadulterated child that he communicates to us in the earlier citation. Because the child apparently has nothing to remember and is, in this description, simple and unfragmented, archaeological consciousness understood in terms of the consciousness of the species, which was so important to the formulation of a return to the primitive mind, is irrelevant here. Baya's own return and indeed her own interpellation by figures such as Picasso, for whom remembering, citation, and working through were so central, are not considered, precisely because of the conflation of the archaeological and the anthropological, where synchronicity seems more central.

This idealization of Baya could be read as the projection of an innocent and unadulterated other who embodies a radical alterity between the West and the Rest and simply demonstrates the manifest content of surrealist orientalism. However, the ideas of consciousness and self that are consolidated with the emergent national consciousness in the late nineteenth century are instrumental in very literally mapping out the "primitive" and the "naive." Evidently, these concepts are formulated as the "pasts" of Europe, and it is these pasts that can be accessed through interpellation by the historical and geographical other for the colonial nation-state. In other words, the concepts of the primitive and naive are themselves products of the modern moment and are seen as sources for the "free man" in combating the increased mechanization of modern metropolitan life. Rather than read them simply as projections and stereotypes of one past or another, they can be seen rather like Aimé Césaire's idea of negritude—as instances of metonymic insurgency that challenge the narrative of national- and self-consciousness. Rather than attempting to understand a response to a figure like Baya as simply racist (the colonized as childlike, uninterpellated, pure), or to Césaire, who has hopelessly internalized the racist model of black man as earth, perhaps what is revealed is an unincorporable alternative to the modern national subject that gets produced from particular moments as excess, or metonymic insurgency.[72] While that alternative to modernity and the relation to the nation-state is certainly constituted out of the colonial relation, it also embodies a resistant mode of representation that defies the insistent diachronic narrativizing of the subject that is evident in the primitivist model. While interpellation by France inevitably takes place, perhaps the insistence on naive forms is a refusal and exposure of the modern subject who can introject as the always already interpellated by the national metaphor.

The Manifesto of the 121 draws on national memory to make its appeal to the French public. It is the making and unmaking of self that Elaine Scarry has cited as a product of the tortured body in pain that causes a "spontaneous" eruption of anticolonial feeling among Algerians and French deserters within the logic of the manifesto that expresses support toward these figures. The spontaneity of this eruption runs counter to the invocation of memory and of the "free man" who is appealed to in the implicit critique of colonial politics. However, it is the spontaneity of "free" subjectivity that is formulated outside of colonial national subjectivity, as a breakaway from the diachronic model. The break with a sense of self-consolidation through archaeological narrative in favor of a seemingly spontaneous alliance seems to move toward a reformulation of subjectivity beyond a narrative of metaphorical national self. It is, however, certainly a symptom of it, and is therefore historically located, just as the transcultural synchronicity of an anthropological model would have to allow. The subaltern emerges into civil society through identification with metonymical shock rather than simply through narrative of threat, fear, and revolutionary change. The emergence of spontaneity and discontinuity as revolutionary moments that go beyond the archaeology of the subject reveals an alternative relation to the already national modern subject. This is not to idealize the position of the "naive," the "primitive," "the metonymic," or the "subaltern"; rather, it is to demonstrate a critical by-product of the national subject. The archaeology of the subject is not a necessary prerequisite for the revolutionary spirit that is usually associated with radical change, and both memory and interpellation are available to all those who can be subjects of transculturation.

The Maeght Gallery was perhaps thinking of the early version of Lacan's essay "The Mirror Stage" when they considered the title *Derrière le miroir* (Behind the Mirror) for their serial; for it is the *I* of psychoanalytic experience—and perhaps the *I* of fin-de-siècle Vienna (that is, the loss of the Habsburg Empire and emerging anti-Semitic nation-statehood)—that sought out a force from behind the mirror that could change the *I* that was becoming. The language employed by Breton about Baya shows some evidence of this romanticization of the primitive, or naive, that interestingly combines with the apparent commitment to a regenerated future.[73] As a child she becomes the hope of the future, and it is her Berber roots that are cited as the cause of this. If she has a tradition from which she emerges, Breton says it is the Berber one that retains the traditions of Ancient Egypt and the charm of what Jean Piaget saw as the magical practices of children.[74]

Not only is the "primitive" and "naive" painter, the *femme-enfant* (woman-child), as Breton calls her, created by the modernist in fairly colonialist racist terms, but the modern itself is clearly constituted through the opposition set up. Many critics and artists—from those taking issue with the 1984 Rubin primitivist exhibition at MOMA in New York to Rasheed Araeen and the Black Audio/Video Collective—work on the colonialist designation of categories of the primitive. What is more, perceiving himself as one who has lost the primitive happiness through what Freud would call "the unhappiness in civilisation," Breton can hope for rebirth through the process of mourning. In Baya, he sees a virginal human desire, caught up in the perfumes of the *Thousand and One Nights*.

Interestingly, Breton does not acknowledge the misogynist violence that begets those tales of opportunity, when Scheherazade, weaving tales for the future of herself and her sister, survives through the borrowed women's time that she creates, gives, and occupies. As Assia Djebar wrote, it was very gracious of Breton to preside over the birth of Algerian femininity and "L'Arabie heureuse"—the happy Arabia for which he (conscious of his own nostalgia) longed. But what did he understand of Baya's life that he could see her as such a regenerating force?[75] The positioning of Baya as naive rather than primitivist in style is testimony to the peculiarity of the rather evolutionary opposition created in Breton's surrealism and in the designation of Anatole Jakovsky's lexicon of naive painters. Even if one is to believe that Marguerite and her artist husband, and exposure to Braque, Matisse, Picasso, and the art scene in Paris and Vallauris, did not influence Baya at all (and that in fact, as she half-jokingly says herself, they actually took more from her stylistically than vice versa), what is at stake in understanding the child and her style as naive and in this context therefore primitive?[76] And what is at stake in the persistence of this in postcolonial Algeria when she was mourned on her death a couple of years ago as the "inalienable presence of our memory"? Both times the failure to see is disavowed. If she and her work constitute what lies behind the mirror, and if she is the inaccessible latent, then how are "we" to see the "inalienable presence of "our"—whether Algerian nativist or surrealist primitivist—"memory"?

By the time she was five, both of her parents had died in a region torn apart by poverty in the 1930s. She had been transplanted to her grandmother and then to an adoptive French mother and English father. When asked in interviews why she painted such happy paintings (without rupture, without phantoms in the margins, without silences and forgotten apparitions, which as Djebar wrote dominated her life) she said it was because there was so much unhappiness in her life. Holding the brushes, it seems, was a form of therapy that allowed her to evade every other difficulty. And the period without paint (which ended when the National Museum of Algiers retrieved her paintings from Paris) was, she wrote, like the loss of a child. This profound unhappiness is overlooked by the art historical discourse around Baya, and indeed around naiveté and the "primitive." Indeed, it is difficult to fathom how these two different forms of representation fit together in the context of this figural expressionism.

This is not a presentation of the "informe" of Bataille's *Documents*, which shock with a world of formlessness that challenges modernist precepts.[77] And it is not an image of fragmented unhappiness. The paintings cannot in any simple way be called on to present us with a Berber-Arab discrepant modern (in the manner that Césaire and the other writers of *Tropiques*, for example, could present us with a discrepant anticolonial Martiniquan modern that departed from Breton's surrealism) that cuts away at Breton's white French national modernism.[78] They also cannot in any simple way be called on to represent a feminist alternative. One could look at the presence of women and the absence of men in her paintings; we could look at two women—one with red (blood? fairytales? 1001 stories?) emerging from her mouth—and make a feminist claim concerning the feminine register of communication depicted here. Yet is this not a romanticization in the same vein as Breton's, adorning her in the mystique of the perfumes of the tales to which Breton himself referred? Is this making of her a mother-child with all the promise of a nostalgically conceived future? Has Baya simply assimilated her style to the colonialist discourse that surrounds her? It does seem as if her work is close to some of Picasso's ceramic paintings, and also that she presents scenes without borders. Almost all her paintings are about encounter, and in looking for an image, the eye is drawn back and forth between pairings: women playing in unison (Figure 5.9); women joined by the Mediterranean with a boat between them (*Femme au bateau*); women carrying cups as if they were communication vessels (Figure 5.10); clothes that become the sea or the sky through the butterflies and birds that live in them (Figures 5.9 and 5.10); encounters with animals and vegetation (Figures 5.2, 5.7, and 5.8); alphabetic script woven into the clothing of a birdlike woman (*Femme au vase bleue*); and two instruments that become part of nature, singing with birds (*Bouquet entre oiseaux et mandores*).[79]

What is absent in narrativizations of Baya's life is the story of the intense unhappiness from which these paintings emerged, and what is put in its place is what Breton called "a spontaneous moment of consciousness where resistance is born."[80] Baya seems both assimilable and fundamentally impossible to assimilate into all of these discourses that share something quite fundamental. How does one undertake a political art criticism when all the discourses seem inadequate to the task?

The aesthetic does not simply stand in opposition to the political, however. But paintings such as these do highlight how the aesthetic remains such a problematic category for political criticism, and how this is linked to the relationship between psychical and historical time. This relationship is particularly confounding when one is not dealing in realism, and when the politics of the abstraction, the politics of the latent rather than of the manifest, is at issue. An art historical trajectory of feminism or anticolonialism is not simply equivalent to one of colonial discourse or idealist nationalism at all, but it does seem that the temporality of much political criticism fails to address the discrepant temporality of the latent as a condition of imperial and anticolonial modernity. Indeed, the phantasmatic manifestations in the signature that defy classification are the signatures of the damaged. They are that which exceeds signature as modern individualism and existent being; rather, they demonstrate disidentification with such notions.

It is once again the feminist writer Djebar who forces the political and the aesthetic to come together to call for a reading of the paintings in a different light. Djebar refers to the paradoxes of the figure of Baya, always presented as frail but, for Djebar, simultaneously strong, with the vulnerabilities with which she always struggled.

FIGURE 5.9   Baya Mahieddine, *Deux femmes jouant de la musique* (1974). Oil on canvas, 114 x 162 cm. © Collection Institut du Monde Arabe, Paris.

FIGURE 5.10   Baya Mahieddine, *Femmes pourtant des coupes* (1966). Gouache on paper, 150 x 100 cm. © Collection Institut du Monde Arabe, Paris.

Here psychoanalysis is useful, because given its roots in fin-de-siècle Vienna, it offers a way of understanding the relationship of the political and the aesthetic. These relentlessly happy images, akin to the six children Baya bore during the bloody war of Algerian independence, become rather haunting, as if her signature of the latent is both too easily assimilable to surrealist and nationalist discourse, and fundamentally unassimilable. (She said that the loss of paint was like the loss of a child for her.) The mournful and nostalgic tone generated from Breton in 1947 to Djilali Kadid in 1997 leaves one paradoxically feeling haunted. The phantom of Baya's unhappiness is rather like the specter overshadowing Freud, and overshadowing psychoanalysis, which paradoxically gives us a way of deferring the question of the relationship between the political and the aesthetic into the borrowed time of Scheherazade's gift to her sister. If the latent unhappiness—the ethnographic material made visible through psychoanalysis—is the latent content of the discourse of primitivism, a melancholic haunting rather than an assimilable, mournful nostalgia will give us a way of understanding that it is the disempowering nature of modern nation-statehood and its colonial corollary that remains modern and yet firmly tucked away behind the mirror. The specter of the national—coloniality—remains the unassimilable to the time and visuality of the gestalt in the mirror. One could say that every document of primitivism (to change Benjamin's words) is also a document of the barbarism that has informed it. Reading not only the captured moment of the angel of history looking simultaneously back and forth but also the unassimilable historical but undated spectral may give us an alternative notion of history in the history of art.[81] The images of encounter seem to enter another register of storytelling, in which Baya paints the gift of the suspended time of friendship. Much more than the particular signature, the paintings constitute a singularity in which encounter with the other opens up the possibility and impossibility of friendship. In one of her trances, Hélène Smith wrote in Arabic script *elqalil men elhabib ktsir*, writing from left to right rather than from right to left, and in an Arabic of which she had no knowledge in waking life she provided the words, "A little from a friend is a lot."[82] As if receiving Élise-Catherine Müller's gift some fifty years after it was sent in her ethical gesture toward the future, Baya (or Fatma Haddad) presents in her paintings a wishful encounter with the other, relentlessly doubled, as if the gift of friendship. Her paintings themselves give us a clue for reading the gift: an unparalleled speaking back to the limited narratives that had failed to give space for alterity—a singularity beyond the confining discourses that turn Baya's work into a haunting presence.

If imagining a better future lies latent in the works of these women as they manifest themselves in the surrealist imagination, an ethical response to them is to read them not as spirit guides, pointing prophetically toward a known trajectory, speaking to us as we mourn our own losses. Rather, the specter has a more melancholic function, one that points toward its own unassimilability to already existing discourses of liberation that can find more traditional homes in emancipatory political discourse and communitarian politics. Being hospitable to the specters that haunt means reading for the potential damage caused by cutting through the frame of already existing political and communitarian discourses that are as yet inadequate to the task of attending to subaltern spectral manifestations. The women who fascinated Breton with their other worldliness are invoked by him as spirits who can regenerate the modern subject. What he fails to read is the very materiality and modernity of those figures. Romanticizing their difference, he fails to see the singularity of their alterity and the hope manifested in latent fashion. Being hospitable to specters and reading for their unassimilable manifestations alerts one to the hope and critical agency of the other.

An ethics of encounter introduces a future-oriented temporality into the discourse of art history, one that is not confined by signatures of the particular but that allows for an excess as a melancholic gift: an essence of the work, which manifests the affect of colonial masculinist modernity, as well as the gift of encounter. The lesson of reading Baya is one of critical intimacy, demanding that she not simply be introjected into an already existing history of art that has been built on its own biases and colonial political disciplinary foundations.[83] The ethics of encounter is one of reading the other for singularity and therefore seeing the possibility of something new in the world, something beyond the confines of historical discourse, something we could call the gift of hope.

6

"Araby" (*Dubliners*) and *A Sister to Scheherazade:* Women's Time and the Time of the Nation

> Did she put on his knowledge with his power
> Before the indifferent beak could let her drop?
>
> W. B. YEATS, "Leda and the Swan"

> A nation? says Bloom. A nation is the same people living in the same place. . . .
> By God, then, says Ned, laughing, if that's so then I'm a nation for I'm living in the same place for the past five years.
>
> JAMES JOYCE, *Ulysses*

The stories of *The Arabian Nights* are always fractured and fragmentary, and told in sections rather than as completed tales in order that suspense might be maintained until the next moment of telling. Scheherazade survives through suspense. She buys time, indeed, her very existence, through symbolic exchange. *The Arabian Nights,* in that sense, cannot be an epic precisely because its temporal ruptures do not give it the coherence of that nationalist or community genre that tells a collective story of a nation. Each tale must be broken off by the threat of daytime, of living time, when Scheherazade is due to be killed.

The cutting caused by this *double time* leaves us with an incoherent fragment dramatized through each tale of the past. Each tale is in itself complete, but gains relevance only through relation to the others. Each gives a fragment, a borrowed moment, of the tenuousness of national and sexual identity. Alongside this, a sense of *différance* is constantly maintained in these stories. The final meaning—Will Scheherazade live or die?—is deferred, and perspective through sexual difference is consistently maintained. Her narration and his power (also established through the overall narrator) are steadily at odds throughout the text. Narrative is thematized through the miscellany of stories that become a cycle only through the threat of the king, through his power to give or to take time. It is his prerogative to make an epic of killing, while it is hers to sustain the lyricism of ruptured tales. Scheherazade's access to time is also negotiated through this entry into symbolic exchange. Scheherazade survives only through narration, and her time is borrowed. If a masculine desire informs the narrative structure of the frame story of *The Arabian Nights* in a form of murderous time, the women's borrowed feminine time in that text cuts into that masculine structure, doing damage to it. It thereby creates, out of necessity, the condition of *women's time*. Women's time is indeed enabled through this process of cutting. Teresa de Lauretis, in "Desire in Narrative," discusses the manner in which the ascription of gendered desire to the temporality of narrative has on occasion resulted in absurd notions of sharp distinctions in the gendering of time.[1] But she rightly acknowledges that the materiality of sexual difference does alter narrative configuration, so for Scheherazade, who risks death because she is a woman, it cuts through the form of temporal logic that will be fatal for her. It is in this sense that her borrowed time is particularly feminine. If Kristeva could write of women's time as a form of caesura, a temporal cutting, and of Joyce as an example of a writer who produces feminine time, it is with this material underpinning and with a sense of relationality among women haunted by and making demands on each other in the name of solidarity and survival that women and the feminine are employed here.[2] Joseph Valente has argued that in Joyce "the narrative situation and discursive sentiments . . . conspire to leave the impression that friendship among women is a woefully uncultivated art."[3] This chapter, following him, explores the manner in which feminine narrative involves a kind of gift towards justice, always hindered by the prevailing law.

By exploring how Scheherazade and Dinarzade, in their local settings, suspend time so as to secure their existence, this chapter considers the influence of *The Arabian Nights* in two metropolitan colonies, Ireland and Algeria. The examples, which of course exceed the category of influence, are James Joyce's short story "Araby," from *Dubliners*, and Assia Djebar's *Ombre Sultane* translated as *A Sister to Scheherazade*. The relationship between women's time and the time of the nation, and women's relationship to nationhood and coloniality, are the focus. Phantoms emerging from these relationships provide clues for solidarities across borders, in which various Scheherazades and Dinarzades may sustain one another. The cases of Ireland and Algeria are each singular in their relationship to Britain and France, respectively. A reading of influence and the adoption of *The Arabian Nights* as a frame text in the imaginative lives of Ireland and France give insights into comparative colonialisms as well as into the phantoms of coloniality. *The Arabian Nights* gives an imaginative lesson in the melancholic, but also in possibilities for the future.

Why should a popular Arabic text that has been the object of orientalist imaginings be claimed by an Irish writer or a contemporary Francophone Algerian novelist who is concerned with the laceration of women's rights and the failure of nationalism in postcolonial Algeria? In *The Arabian Nights*, Scheherazade narrates the many stories, using her younger sister, Dinarzade, sleeping under the royal bed, as interlocutor. Before dawn, Dinarzade, following her older sister's instruction, requests that Scheherazade tell her a story or, more accurately, that she continue the story from the previous night. In order to delay the inevitable—that she and eventually all virgins in the kingdom, including Dinarzade, would be killed—Scheherazade creates the alternative of borrowed time through narrative suspense. No story is ever finished in the morning. So, Scheherazade is always spared by the king as he is seduced into narrative time and out of the inevitability of actual time. The onset of the morning, which signifies execution, is perpetually deferred.

Dubliners

Many critics have commented on a sense of temporal stasis in the lyrical passages of *Dubliners*, and others have commented on the circularity or formlessness of time in *Ulysses*, most famously in the punctuationless Penelope-Molly section. The tensions of temporal schemes evident in "Araby" demonstrate the precarious conceptualization of national identity that Joyce evokes. This chapter shows how the very desire to ignore the aftereffects of colonialism in favor of an exploration of the simultaneously conceived globalized present is symptomatic of the dissemination of self that characterizes disenfranchisement.[4] This dissemination of the subject—national, sexual, or otherwise—relies on a ruptured sense of the temporal that disallows the possibility of narrative closure.

"Araby" is haunted by a sense of both *suspended time* and *borrowed time*. The narrator is always subject to time constraints imposed on him by the clock, the train, daylight hours, and his own and Mangan's family. Time that he has to play, to read, or to fantasize seems suspended until those moments when the passing of time intrudes into the narrator's private world. The story itself, while apparently dramatizing the tale of a child growing up in Ireland, is definitely tied to historical events such as the Araby bazaar. The narrator constantly bumps up against time constraints, and the suspension of the temporal that is evident in those moments of *borrowed time* also interrupts the genealogical narrative of progression—indeed, of growing up.

As critics have noted, the narrator of "Araby" fixates on the name in the story's title, which refers to a bazaar containing stalls of "oriental" goods with names like the *Eastern Temple, Algericas,* and the *Arabian Nights*. Many an article was written about this bazaar, or colonial fair, in the *Irish Times* in May 1894, when it was being held at the Central Hall of the Royal Dublin Society.[5]

When Joyce was writing, *The Arabian Nights* was on his mind, and more specifically, the temporality that governs it: borrowed time.[6] But as Derrida writes in *Given Time: 1. Counterfeit Money,* what does it mean for time to be suspended or borrowed? And to whom does time belong that it can be borrowed? How can time be told in a way that allows for its suspension or for the hand of the clock to be held?

Dubliners, the collection of short stories that makes up the fractured whole of a story of growing up in Dublin, maintains a sense of rupture, or temporal cutting, through the differential positioning of the primary narrator, on the one hand, and the narrative structure within each of the stories, on the other. This is particularly evident in the early stories, of which "Araby" is the last, which are narrated in the first person. The tension between the private and "inner" world and the public world of symbolic exchange and interaction are elaborated through interruption of that first-person narration. The dramatic effect of this interruption is exaggerated when the first-person narration is cut by third-person narration of the public sphere, with stories about adolescence, maturity, and public life. The performativity in these ruptures creates a sense of fractured belonging and of an emerging national and sexual consciousness. These ruptures cause a questioning of the nature of narrative time, of borrowed time and its relation to national space, the construction and understanding of which are constantly deferred.

"Araby" is distinguished from most of the other stories in the cycle in that it appears to be "overwritten" by the young narrator, who indulges in a plethora of adjectives in a "kingdom of words."[7] He lives in a world of literature, reading the books left by the dead priest who inhabited the space before him: Walter Scott's *The Abbot, The Devout Communicant,* and *The Memoirs of Vidocq.*[8] Garry M. Leonard, in a Lacanian reading of the story, notes the narrator's immersion in the symbolic order, where he can maintain a sense of himself as subject through his self-positioning in language—a self that will be challenged for its lack of "signified" beneath the chain of signifiers as soon as it confronts woman.[9]

But there is a sense of irony attached to this boy narrator's prose. Too many levels of analysis are written into it,[10] and Mangan's sister—the girl without her own name who is herself overwritten by kinship inscription—becomes representative of anything the critic wishes to highlight.[11] The anxiety of narrative performance that haunts the first part of "Araby" maintains a sense of suspended time that in itself resists inscription.

"Araby" dramatizes a desire, first for a woman, Mangan's sister, and then for a word, *Araby,* which designates a colonial bazaar. The story can obviously be analyzed in terms of the narrator's orientalist fantasies or his desire for woman as other. Because both figures of fantasy are obscured and simultaneously overdetermined by their names, the story could usefully be understood as the narrator coming into being through desire of the *objet petit a,* the Lacanian term that denotes the desire for the infinitely substitutable other through *scopophilia*—the love of looking. What these analyses do not take into account, however, are the narrator's own historicity and his relationship to gender and nationhood. An analysis of temporality in "Araby" allows for an understanding of Joyce's peculiar relationship to nationalism and gender that is evoked through this story's characters.

Simultaneity and the Time of the Nation

> The locality of culture is more *around* temporality than *about* history. . . . The focus on temporality resists the transparent linear equivalence of event and idea that historicism proposes; it provides a perspective on the disjunctive forms of representation that signify a people, a nation, or a national culture. It is neither the sociological solidity of these terms, nor their holistic history, that gives them the narrative and psychological force that they have brought to bear on cultural production and projections. . . . What is displayed in [the] displacement and repetition of [its] terms is the nation as the measure of the liminality of cultural modernity.[12]

Writing in favor of an understanding of the temporal as overridden by a narrative of nation that relies on the succession of documented events, Homi Bhabha dramatizes the disjuncture between official narrative or "history" and the performative. Within this performativity, temporality becomes tied to locality. The official story of the nation, structured through historicism, is, according to Bhabha, ignoring the tenuous construction of national feeling. What historicism is blind to is the necessity of repeating the terms that confirm the existence of nationhood. Local culture, however, does not simply exist within the terms of this master narrative. The narration of the nation, for Bhabha, is always fraught with discontinuity that undermines the romantic narrative of particularly nineteenth-century nationalism.

Bhabha expands on this point in his essay "'Race,' Time, and the Revision of Modernity." This theme of narrative rupture is taken up more explicitly as a temporal *caesura,* a time lag, which interrupts the narrative of nationhood and of subjectivity that he cites as central components of cultural modernity. He suggests that

> the catachrestic postcolonial agency . . . opens up an interruptive time-lag in the "progressive" myth of modernity, and enables the diasporic and postcolonial to be represented. But this makes it all the more crucial to specify the discursive and historical temporality that interrupts the enunciative "present" in which the self-inventions of modernity take place. And it is this "taking place" of modernity, this insistent and incipient *spatial* metaphor in which the social relations of modernity are conceived, that introduces a temporality of the "synchronous" in the structure of the "splitting" of modernity.[13]

In the context of "Araby," the "taking place" of modernity occurs through the narrator growing up and "progressing" in Ireland. Through his relation to various "others"—woman, Araby—a temporal caesura occurs that "places" our nameless narrator, Mangan's sister, and Araby in a time lag that insists on their historicity (the Araby bazaar, for example, definitely marks the story as taking place in 1894) and simultaneously causes history's narrative to come under question. While Araby as other might be understood as that which the nation collectively imagines, the process of imagining also causes a confrontation between the imagined and the geopolitical: Araby the bazaar exists on the land of another colony, the metropolitan colony of Ireland. As a caesura of colonial existence, Araby reflects not only colonial imagining but also the colonized space on which it exists. Both the temporal and the spatial caesura introduce a nonspace of possibility.

Edward Said, speaking of Yeats as a poet of decolonization, elaborates on the connection between temporality and locality:

It is . . . necessary [for the colonizers] to seek out, to map, to invent, or to discover a . . . nature, not pristine and pre-historical . . . but deriving from the deprivations of the present. The impulse is cartographic. . . . Colonial space must be transformed sufficiently so as no longer to appear foreign to the imperial eye. More than any other of its colonies, Britain's Ireland was subjected to innumerable metamorphoses through repeated settling projects. . . .

. . . Like all poets of decolonization, Yeats struggles to announce the contours of an imagined or ideal community, crystallized by its sense not only of itself but also of its enemy. . . . The instability of time, which has to be made and remade by the people and its leaders, is a theme one sees in all genres.[14]

In the context of decolonization, community needs to be reimagined and to reimagine colonialist time and construction of space, which are by no means stable in themselves but constantly renarrativized as if stable. The process of reimagining involves the disclosure of temporal ruptures in colonialist narrative. The colonial subject, constructed by those narratives, thus may find within those temporal ruptures the space for remaking.

Women's Time

The concept of *women's time* in Julia Kristeva's essay with that name seems to lend an interesting input into this matter of historicism and simultaneity, paralleling Nietzsche's concept of monumental time (eternity) against cursive time (linearity) with the generational trends within the women's movement. These trends themselves, self-referential in their trajectory, embody a kind of monumentality, even if they assume linearity in their consecutiveness. Kristeva speaks of Freudian time and socialist time as encapsulating these trends. Socialist time, she claims, works within the logic of current narratives and seeks equality within its terms. She sees the Freudian and, particularly, Lacanian theorists as moving beyond the "phallaciousness" of the Lacanian symbolic and as imagining the possibility of different entrance into the symbolic as characterized by the Lacanian lack, which characterizes for her the *feminine*.

Kristeva begins her essay, interestingly, with a discussion of the nation as a lost nineteenth-century dream of national homogeneity that is now forced to confront *interdependence* with other nation-states. No longer can the idea of *economic homogeneity* be maintained. Where once one could imagine *historical tradition,* or *linguistic unity,* these factors can now more easily be perceived as *symbolic denominators,* "defined as the cultural and religious memory forged by the interweaving of history and geography.... 'Father's Time, mother's species,' as Joyce puts it."[15] "Father Time" may be constituted economically, whereas the cultural *symbolic denominator* is in effect that *imagined community* that is the space, for Kristeva, of the continent Europe, where some commonality may exist by virtue of that space. The two forms of time are, to a certain extent, in tension, because their power and strength rest on that which is imaginable in spite of economic cohesion or rupture. Identity can rest and be maintained only through the economic in the history of production, but can be imagined beyond this in terms of traits. For Kristeva, beyond the solid linearity of history in cursive time lie the abstractions of anthropology in monumental time. The monumental allows for a tangential link that lies beyond the specificity of national or geographically based history, in monumentality, where anthropological traits of types might be seen. Thus, for example, European women have links to their type—women elsewhere—as well as links to their cursive history—European history. By existing between the monumental and the cursive in this way, they will "echo in a most specific way the universal traits of their structural place in reproduction and its representations."[16] The tension between the two is necessary but contradictory: "*insertion* into history and the radical *refusal* of the subjective limitations imposed by this history's time on an experiment carried out in the name of irreducible difference."[17] The insertion itself—as soon as a woman thinks of the relationship between reproduction and representation, or symbolic exchange in Lacanian terms—is one of sacrifice, of giving up at every moment of iteration. According to Kristeva, the symbolic, which has excluded, structurally demands the sacrifice of woman as sexually different.

Kristeva's theory illustrates the tension among subjectivity, economic exchange, and symbolic exchange. Entry into the economic and into the cursive history of a people can occur for women only through sacrifice of sexual difference. Yet it is through this sacrificial gesture of the acknowledgment of the impossibility of expression within that history that "identity" in the local sense can be assumed. The desire in contemporary feminism to include not only production but reproduction in the symbolic economy and thereby create a nonsacrificial language confirms only a monumental existence, one of tangential commonality among women. The only solution to this is a third condition, characterized by Kristeva as an "interiorization of the founding separation of the socio-symbolic contract."[18] Embodied within the tangential link to the national-cursive and the sexual-monumental is the impossibility of exchange from this position that both gives and takes. The consolidated identity seems in this solution to be derivative only from a sacrificial symbolic, and one that leaves specificity behind. Belonging to the symbolic and the monumental, giving to both of them, offers no identity that can be inscribed through symbolic exchange. Borrowed time and existence through the performativity of narrative haunts this third space of women's time.

Like Bhabha, Kristeva points to a temporal caesura that characterizes women's relationship to historical narrative and, indeed, to the symbolic. What is suggested by this caesura is a time lag in which women's relationship to historicity and to public time is granted to be necessary yet simultaneously impossible, for the premises on which that history is built have ignored the manner in which the figure of woman interrupts historical narrative and genealogy. The genealogical signifier, the kinship name, is both everything and nothing to woman. To gain her status, she relies on her kinship marker, although it is in itself unstable: Mangan's sister might at another point be another man's wife, with kinship designation being that of father or husband. Yet what would Mangan's sister—the embodied caesura, which links the narrator's private time of home to public time of bazaar—call herself if she could "shape" or "place" through narrative control? Caught between the cursive and the monumental, between Ireland and Araby, between designation and nondesignation, how could she rewrite the time lag?

Private Time, Public Time, Imperial Time

If what has characterized both the time of the nation and women's time is the tension between the genealogical and the simultaneous, the tension between the two is symptomatic of the division between private and public, between the individual and the group. A nation, or a feminist group within a nation, is always negotiating the space between the private and public spheres, and between the consciousness of self and that of others, even when the two are unquestionably interdependent. Narrative rupture shows the sacrifice that eats into the language of symbolic exchange, causing subjectivity, which is sustained through narrative, to come under question.

Ernest Gellner has persuasively argued in "The Social Roots of Egalitarianism" that modern society is egalitarian because it is mobile, and that the sharp distinction between the public and private spheres and time allotted to them are necessitated by this mobility. He explains that unless insubordination has been established and rationalized in some way, it becomes necessary for those in work positions deemed less prestigious to maintain a sense that the leisure time they have, that is, their private time, is more or less the same as that of those of higher rank. Conversely, he offers the example of Lady Montdore, a character in Nancy Mitford novels, who always informs that one should "always be polite to the girls for you do not know whom they will marry."[19] The women, who are mostly understood as confined to a private sphere, and whose status is always derivative, never know what will happen to them and how their husbands will fare in the public sphere. Their insecure status is therefore one that always negotiates between private and public, so that their private lives will reflect adequately the public lives of their spouses or fathers. It is only within a feudal system, or one like it in which there is formalized insubordination or hierarchy, that the distinction cannot be maintained. Mobility within social position would risk a sense of equality where none can be had. Servants in a house, whose public and private lives overlap within the workplace, cannot be in any doubt about the difference between their lives and those of their employers.

Cultural subordination, then, relies on cultural and psychic internalization of inferior positioning. But what strikes at the peculiarity of this idea is the lack of agency suggested by it. This is interestingly evoked in Kipling's *Kim*. Speaking of *Kim*, Edward Said has commented on the contradictions of Kim's lifestyle, which establishes friendship between him, the Irish boy, and the Indian natives, and simultaneously causes him to work for the colonial service. It seems that there "is no conflict" for Kim or for Kipling in this distinct division between his private attitudes and his public vocation. Said also speaks of India as being suspended within a historical vacuum in spite of what critics have said about Kipling's journalistic eye for the vibrancy and variety of India. Sara Suleri acknowledges Said's comments but suggests that the lack of historicity needs to be seen as a kind of journalism—as a rendition of the enigma of colonial time, which is, she suggests, aphasic and evasive.[20] There are no narratives that plot out the future of empire, precisely because it is not known and it cannot be seen to fail. Therefore, the contradictions that seem to plague *Kim* are the very contradictions of the temporal and narrative extinction that seem to be afforded by empire's lack of narrative closure. This lack of closure, which, as David Spurr has pointed out, is typical of the rhetoric of journalism, is also one that disallows the mapping of continuous narrative, of established identity, of coherence between private and public, through narrative rupture. Spurr says:

Journalism is distinguished from fiction by the conventional expectation of its grounding in a historical actuality; its relation to this actuality is understood to be primarily metonymic and historically referential rather than metaphoric and self-referential. Nonfiction writing in general often combines this metonymic quality with an absence of formal closure, so that it opens directly onto the fractures and contradictions of colonialist epistemology.[21]

The story of a national or indeed a colonial moment always evokes its own lack of continuity, its own inevitable sacrifice of the national narrative of a past and a future that *maps out* identity. The tenuousness of symbolic exchange that confirms identity is evoked by this rupture. As Emer Nolan, speaking of Joyce and taking us from the Victorian to the modernist era, has commented, "Decentered subjects, and the disavowal of linear narrative in the writing of ex-colonial modernists such as Joyce, signify something other than mere textual effects."[22]

In *Kim,* the question which is repeated and leaves Kim suspended in this temporal rupture, is "What is Kim?" Kim is an Irish boy, linked metonymically both to his Indian friends as a boy from a metropolitan colony, and to the British service of which he is a part. He carries messages from one part of India to another on its trains which map out colonial achievement of space. His messages, though transported, often seem either not to make sense, or otherwise are misinterpreted. He invokes the impossibility of communication, and doubt as to whether a letter can ever arrive at its destination. The tenuousness of symbolic exchange, and its coherence are embodied within Kim, and in his blurring of the necessary distinctions between private and public. His status and affinities are confused as he incarnates the geographical buffer zone that is Ireland lying between Britain and its other colonies. Kim's own subordinate status within the economic and cultural confusion of Empire highlights its lack of narrative closure, but simultaneously its need of narrative coherence. As Kim's famous "negative capability" might suggest, his own lack of stability disallows an exploration of the place of Irishness in the imperial administration as it is characterized by a lack of narrative, a lack of future, and a lack of symbolic exchange. Private time and public time get suspended thus giving Kim a lack of stable identity in both. The narrative of British colonial service in India overrides and cancels out Kim's Ireland, just as the boy narrator in "Araby"'s imagined relation to the romantic narrative of the colonial fair cancels out his Irishness. The nameless woman, Mangan's sister, who remains at home, and whose status in relation to the bazaar is only derivative of the narrator's access to public space, becomes simply "woman." And yet Kim's Irishness, the narrator's Irishness, and the Irish woman, sister of Mangan, cause temporal narrative rupture to the apparent coherence of British colonial service and its romanticism.

Caesura, or The Temporal Cut: Giving Time

Jacques Derrida's *Given Time: 1. Counterfeit Money* begins with a reading of a letter sent by Madame de Maintenon to Madame Brinon. Madame de Maintenon, who was the "influential mistress" of the Sun King, wrote, "The King takes all my time; I give the rest to Saint-Cyr, to whom I would like to give all."[23] Derrida's close reading of this sentence rests on the question of "the rest": What can it mean to give "the rest" when all your time has been "taken"? And what does it mean to take someone's time? Who does time belong to that it can be taken? What Madame de Maintenon desires is, then, to give what she has not. She does not desire to have, however, so that she might give. Rather, the desire to give that which she cannot have is the same as giving. It is in this sense that Derrida suggests that "the gift," in order to be pure of the exchange of obligation discussed by Marcel Mauss, has to be beyond exchange itself—it is not simply impossible, but it is *the* impossible—it is the giving of that which does not exist other than as a notional "remainder." Madame de *Maintenant* (now), as Derrida wittily refers to her, is characterized by the *now* (maintenant)—the hand (*la main*) of the clock onto which she is holding (*tenant*). If she could give, she would give that which she cannot—the rest of time, which exists through nonexistence as the impossible. Nonexistence, nondesignation, and nonexchangeability characterize Madame de Maintenant, who cannot narrativize herself in this letter-to-be-exchanged other than as caesura, cutting time.

Buying Time, Giving Time

"Araby" begins with dense and highly adjectival yet surprisingly nondescriptive prose:

The career of our play brought us through the dark muddy lanes behind the houses where we ran the gantlet of the rough tribes from the cottages, to the back doors of the dark dripping gardens where odours arose from the ashpits, to the dark odorous stables where a coachman smoothed and combed the horse or shook music from the buckled harness.[24]

Toward the end, the prose becomes more sparse: "Nearly all the stalls were closed and the greater part of the hall was in darkness."[25] While critics have commented on the darkness of the bazaar, in fact the more significant darkness seems to lie in North Richmond Street itself. The lanes, gardens, and stables, which supply a sense of space in the narrator's private world, are all overshadowed by darkness.[26] If the darkened bazaar stands out, it is because our narrator has already told us to expect the exotic here: the name *Araby*, which has "cast an Eastern enchantment" over him, has already prepared us for a mystery. The fact that the bazaar seems more like a ravaged temple, made all the more ridiculous because of the exchange of money that goes on within it, makes the "darkness" descriptive and not abstract. The proliferation of adjectives in the earlier passage, however, is insistently romanticist—the mood of the muddy, odorous lanes; the dripping gardens; and the odorous stables, all marked by a dankness—and obviously reflect the mood of our narrator. For him there is no distinction between the inner and outer, and therefore no need for exchange between them or indeed for symbolic exchange, by which that which is described can be understood in the concrete.

The bazaar is seen through the narrator's eyes as it casts enchantment over him. The vagaries of his fascination, tied as they are to sexual stimulation, are so overindulged in the colonialist fantasy and framework of orientalism that we know that disenchantment lies ahead. This suspended time, when storytelling indulges in fantasy, borrows signifier from signified in order to evoke a romanticist universe built out of the books and dreams we have encountered in this and the two preceding stories. Like the "Persia" of which he has dreamed in "The Sisters," he cannot imagine the end of this fantasy or remember his dream, suspended as he is in this borrowed time of romanticism, from which he will awaken. No other word has been so centralized as *paralysis,* used at the beginning of "The Sisters." This paralysis, represented by the dead priest and the mourning of him, is somehow set free by indulging in the language through which narrators can imagine themselves.

This paralysis, or stasis, as Robert Welch might put it, shows how "Medusa is really Narcissus."[27] Welch argues that a sense of stasis characterizes nineteenth-century Irish literature, and he attributes this stasis to the shock of the imposition of English onto the Gaelic land. He insists that cultural translation cannot easily take place from one language to another, and thus what we are left with is linguistic stasis. For him, this stasis is illustrated by Joyce's Citizen in the "Cyclops" episode of *Ulysses,* and is thematized by earlier authors such as Mangan who submit that the self does not exist other than in the performative and through the instability of translation from one language to another; there is no stasis, no central character who can be identified beyond iteration. According to Welch, this sense of nonbeing extends to Ireland itself for Mangan.[28] This instability of self and nation, characterized as it is both by the fact and the trope of translation, extends to Mangan's sister.

What follows stasis, especially if we understand the term in the classical Greek sense as struggle, is "the discovery of language," as Hélène Cixous proposes.²⁹ She writes, it is not "in the exotic Orient that he is to make his discovery, but in the ordinary matter of everyday life."³⁰ Time is suspended in fantasy, and the narrator, in true Lacanian fashion, can indulge his fantasy of Mangan's sister and the woman at the bazaar as successive *objets petits a*. He projects his desire through the indulgence of scopophilia and overcoming the "blindness" of the street on which he lives by displacing the blindness onto her. But while all this goes on, life and time tick on without him. Mangan comes out of and goes into his house, Mrs. Mercer comes to visit, mornings pass by and yet he does not notice. Morning becomes characterized by his scopophilia. The narrator stands in the shadows at the entrance to Mangan's house, watching Mangan's sister swing repetitively on the threshold between private and public space, on the threshold between *fort und da*. Is this in-between space hers, or is she simply trapped by lack of access to public space? Within the narrator's logic, where time does not really exist until his plan to go to the bazaar needs to be put into effect, it is easy to see how Mangan's sister, as nameless (because ultimately replaceable), can take on the image of Ireland, as some suggest.³¹ As the romantic dream that fulfills, at least temporarily, self-definition as a sense of place and the possibility of stasis in relation to the romantic other "Araby," his romantic relationship to her is similar to that of a dream of national unity. Even in feminist readings of the slippage between woman and nation in Irish writing, there is certainly room for equating the two "ideas."³² Speaking in the context of *Ulysses*, Emer Nolan writes:

> Joyce's borrowing of . . . nationalist imagery . . . suggests that it may prove difficult to uncover here a realm of femininity. . . . Indeed, nationalist ideology shares many themes with recent feminist theory—nostalgia for the body of the mother, fantasies of an originary lost plenitude, a longing for unmediated relations with language and the flesh. Perhaps this conjunction should not surprise us in the light of Julia Kristeva's view that nationalism offers individuals the opportunity to relive their fantasies of the all-nourishing body of the pre-Oedipal mother.³³

Kristeva's use of Joyce's phrase "Father's Time, Mother's Species" seems already to be written over by a mother's species understood through romanticism, and through the logic of nineteenth-century nationalism, where nation is "a soul, a spiritual principle" that is taken over by the internationalist aesthetic of European modernism.³⁴

It would seem, however, that the trajectory that moves beyond the romanticist in this story and into the modernist consumer of modernity is not internationalist exclusively at all. In fact, it is very deeply Irish. The possibility of narrating the ruptured nation comes into being only through shock. This shock is not simply one of stasis—the imposition of British onto Irish, causing one to imagine a romantic but static Ireland—but rather one of the shock of mobility, the shock of international trade, the shock of sordidness beneath the colonial venture. The narrator's journey into the outside world, which demands of him attention to time—the bazaar might close—in his world of imagined timelessness, prevents him from projecting his emotions onto the landscape. The land is divided up by the railway line that makes one dependent upon another's time scheme—and this has been foreshadowed by the delay caused by others in the household of whose presence we suddenly become keenly aware.

He takes this trip not for himself but for Mangan's sister, whose name becomes extremely important to the narrator, although he never tells it to us. She is the motivation for him to go to Araby, and it is this exotic name that replaces hers. She is linked metonymically to the bazaar also because of her silver bracelet, which she touches as she poses the question of the narrator's fall from innocence: "She asked me was I going to Araby."[35] In this link, she can be read as Araby the bazaar, and through that, the world of the colonies of "Eastern Enchantment."[36] By contrast, her desire is expressed in her touching of the bracelet; it becomes metonymy for the desire she has for Araby, for consuming the dream she has of it. As an Irish woman, it becomes her *objet petit a*. But what can that mean? How could she be potentially read as both Ireland and the East simultaneously? Is this the ultimate nonnationalist gesture of anti-colonial solidarity? Or is it a different kind of nationalism, a twentieth-century nationalism that recognizes both the danger of nationalist stasis, following as it does the logic of imperialism, and simultaneously the importance of mapping and narrating that which is the confused or delayed time of the decolonizing state. Simon During suggests that the literary canon has excluded nationalist texts and that "postcolonial" nationalism needs to be seen in a very different light relative to nineteenth-century European romantic nationalism. In his view, it becomes necessary to understand postcolonial writers' entrance into the symbolic as a *reproduction* and renegotiation of nationalism, much in the same way as woman's entrance highlights the *reproduction* in production. This can be done only with a more global context in mind, yet the local mapping and temporality of space that promotes this moment needs also to be carefully analyzed. And it is in this sense that it is necessary, in light of transnational thought, to understand how the weight of colonial history remains. It becomes crucial to acknowledge the simultaneous construction of and tension between the two: women's time, national time.

The journey to Araby, which the narrator can make, is a journey that strips him of the colonialist dream. The word *Araby* can no longer enchant him; the richness of the stalls are stripped bare, like a ravaged temple. The gift he wishes to take back to Mangan's sister becomes confused by the price of an entrance fee, the woman at the stall, the men who talk to her with English accents, and the discussion of the instability of the symbolic—the confused messages that again remind the reader of that other Irish boy, Kim, who catches trains across the country and delivers and sends messages that are constantly misinterpreted. The dream is reduced to the crudity of colonial economics, where the English guard their acquisition and speak their language, reminding us that the Irish boy will be "almost the same but not quite, almost the same but not. . . ."[37] Araby ultimately cannot be part of the Irish boy's rich imaginings of colonial venture. He cannot fulfill the role of the colonialist traveler who can buy that which Mangan's sister may consume, and thus vicariously assume the position of colonialist.

Jennifer Wicke has persuasively argued that Molly Bloom, in the Penelope section of *Ulysses,* rather than embodying female circularity and formlessness, dramatizes "an arc repeated again and again, a mental passage to Gibraltar or back from Gibraltar, mediated by the act of consumption."[38] Molly, of course, has lived in Gibraltar, and there, in the derivative role of colonial daughter, has assumed the lifestyle and fantasies of the English. However, as a British colonial subject national of the metropolitan colony, Ireland, her position as colonizer's daughter is itself tenuous. Her only relation to the underprivileged position is to consume and thus be a part of colonialist culture vicariously. Mangan's sister, of course, has lived, as far as we know, only on North Richmond Street and has not, to the best of our knowledge, passed the threshold to the outside world. The dream of colonial power is imagined through the mystery of Araby and the self-referential closure of the advertising of that bazaar, and is potentially experienced vicariously through our narrator's potential gift—all imagined.

It is the narrator, however, with his access to public space that is unavailable to Mangan's sister, who does the work of mapping out a sense of the space of Dublin within which this colonial fair—the Araby Bazaar—stands. It is within Ireland's grasp, yet not. It is both Ireland and not. What the narrator experiences here is the journey into the other, into Araby and woman, only to realize that it is not his. Araby becomes the colony within Ireland, just as Ireland was a colony of Britain. Here there is a kind of inversion, where the metropolitan colony—the colony close to home—confronts itself in the other.

So, if the narrator is left with a loss of romanticism at the end of the story, he is not robbed of the narration of the nation. Indeed, the nation narrated is a ruptured one; as a metropolitan colony, it is a buffer zone between England and her other colonies. It indulges in England's fantasies, but it can have them only through consuming them, through an exchange in which value is always tenuous. "My eyes burned with anguish and fear," he says, and the fear of the impossibility of mapping out Ireland, of knowing the possibility of economic and symbolic exchange that he has confronted in this space of Araby, causes him to confront the reality that is Ireland.[39] The colony within, the "East" and Ireland inverted, causes the story to end with a lack of closure. There is no sense of national self and colonial other that can sustain narrative closure. Rather, those narratives are broken open. This lack suggests the necessity of the urge of decolonization: imagining the national and narrating the national, however fractured.

The modernist urge of the writer of decolonization portrays the necessity of a new nationalism, not that of stasis, unless it is truly struggle and division; not that of romanticism, but that of reclaiming a language that can imagine a future beyond disenfranchisement. Suspended time ultimately has to bump up against real time, just as the monumental bumps up against the cursive. This double time echoes the necessity of negotiating private and public space in order for the narratives of imperialism to be interrupted by the possibility of nationalism. Similarly, the transnational needs to be understood in terms of nationalism and its transnational construction. Otherwise, the politics of colonialism and postcolonialism, historically intrinsic, are in danger of being abstracted into the modernist and the postmodern. This neither allows for the cursive nor acknowledges the narratives of nationalism within the modernist moment.

But what of Mangan's sister, who wanted a gift and sought identity vicariously? Did she simply desire to consume and be given to, or did she give? Did she give *the impossible,* that which is beyond exchange, when she sent him on his way to Araby? Did she give him that which exists beyond the suspension of time and historicity? Was she suspended in the "now" on her threshold to the outside world and yet still dependant on its workings? Could we name her if she could make an entrance into the symbolic Scheherazade, Madame de Maintenant? And could we imagine her cutting through borders and speaking, from one metropolitan colony to another, from Ireland to a site of her orientalist imagination, to Algeria, and to another Scheherazade and Dinarzade?

Sisters to Scheherazade: Hopes for
Transnational and Local Feminisms

Assia Djebar's novel *Ombre Sultane* is translated as *A Sister to Scheherazade.*[40] Although both titles allude to *The Arabian Nights,* the English one situates the protagonists as the two sisters—Scheherazade and Dinarzade—and the French one calls forth the threatening shadow cast by the sultan who takes a virgin wife every night only to slaughter her in the morning. This shadow results in a competitive and conspiratorial attitude whereby women distrust one another even as they rationalize their desire to be sacrificed. The three sections of the novel pose questions concerning why *The Arabian Nights* is used as a frame story, and how the shadow throws light on a repeated trauma that makes visible what Nicolas Abraham and Maria Torok call phantom possession, that is, a shameful secret from a past generation that possesses someone else's unconscious. The material consequences of the presence of the phantom are felt in Djebar's prose in the form of *Nachträglichkeit,* or deferred action, and as that of *durcharbeiten,* or working through. The structure of the phantom contains the potential for feminist politics.

In her own attempt to create a conversation between women that does not depend on the presence of a male who orchestrates and threatens their relationship in *The Arabian Nights,* Djebar formulates her own version of a "feminine time" in which women's narrative can cut. In *A Sister to Scheherazade,* Djebar introduces us to a potentially tense relationship between a divorcee, Isma, and Hajila, the new wife of her ex-husband. The sisterhood between the two women is a symbolic one that transgresses the marital relation and the spatial enclosure that accompanies it. Hajila, whose status can be secured only through the displacement of the first wife, becomes like a sister to Isma, in spite of the fact that they meet only a few times. Their relationship, like that of Scheherazade and Dinarzade, sustains both of them in a moment of emotional turmoil, but is also invested with the possibility of working through it. Written at a time when women's rights in Algeria were being severely curtailed, the novel alludes to the political event, and much more, by focusing on the parallel of the domestic abuse of women, which is implicitly condoned by family members and others. Djebar constructs a borrowed time for women through fragments of narrative from among them that safeguard them from the cruelties of their immediate relationships and their political status. She relies on an imaginative world that can take from both the Arab and the French heritages of contemporary Algeria, stressing that the cruel predictability of a time of violence, when death is the only real possibility, has to be overcome through borrowed time, in which only the imagination can lead the future in another direction. This is not a romanticization of an Arab past replayed through *The Arabian Nights* so much as it is a leap of hope into imagining a future of stories untold that can take the place of the slaughter that history tells and predicts. Scheherazade, this time in postcolonial Algeria, tries to imagine a new nation-state in which the slaughter of women is replaced by their freedom.

The first of the three unequal sections of this novel unfolds in a form of dialogue between Isma and Hajila, although the words of Hajila are never spoken. The three sections are narrated by Isma, the first wife of Hajila's husband, now divorced; and the first section, entitled "Every Woman's Name Is Wound," consists of alternating chapters written about Hajila in the second person and about Isma's early memories of her own marriage, narrated in the first person. The narrator of the preamble, we may conjecture, is a *Specter of Scheherazade,* herself "a strange duet ... an arabesque of intertwining names."[41]

This duet is strange indeed, for one of its participants is silent and is spoken to. The description of the young bride's marriage as it is narrated in the second person is not a happy one. It tells of Hajila's very rare pleasures of leaving the house and roaming around the city during the day, something she must keep secret from her husband, and something her own mother is horrified to hear about. Her time at home has few pleasures; she enjoys caring for her husband's children from former relationships, but her husband drinks too much, is unable to consummate the marriage until one night in a drunken rape, and beats her upon hearing that she goes out during the day.

This story stands in stark contrast to that of Isma's, who tells of the early part of her marriage with the same man, the excitement of sex and the freedom of the young lovers, whose affair in Paris is lodged clearly and nostalgically in Isma's memory. The question of why the relationship ended marks this first section, and the semisilent duet is suggestive of dialogue with the flip side of memory—that which is repressed. The new wife, Hajila, seems almost a like a "phantom," which, according to Abraham and Torok "returns to haunt," to bear "witness to the existence of the dead buried within the other."[42] While Hajila certainly exists within the story, this alternation of first and second person in the early chapters definitely recalls the dialogue on which Scheherazade relies, but also on which a generational repetition is based. The concept of the phantom suggests the possibility of being possessed by someone else's unconscious.[43] Encryption involves inheriting a secret that is not knowingly carried or repressed by an individual. The carrier narrative contains the secret of a family or of the nation. The phantom is more easily identified through projection onto another figure; thus, following Freud's threefold schema of *remembering, repeating,* and *working through,* it can carry out these functions though the analysis of another. Isma's performance of an analysis follows Freud's logic in the novel's sections, the first of which *remembers* the early days of a marriage through suggested comparison with those of Hajila's; the second *repeats* a cascade of stories of women's experiences of violence within marriage; and the third begins to *work through* a relationship to the past and attempts to propose a future in which women can act *in solidarity* rather than as rivals, competitors, or those without a future.

Isma's narration is suggestive of a *work of mourning* that is not yet completed. In her sections, Isma has to call forth various specters that show all women to be wounds. Scheherazade can be designated as the identity of the phantom because she is present not in Isma's narration but in the adjacent italicized passages between the sections. The final two chapters of the first section bring about more of a merging of the characters, although they maintain their separate material roles as the sophisticated divorcée first wife who is no longer with her husband, and the new wife who still lives with him and speaks in a less refined language than

Isma's: "Here am I speaking to you again, Hajila. As if, in truth, I were causing you to exist. A phantom whom my voice has brought to life. A phantom-sister? Do we find sisters only in prisons that each woman erects around herself, the fortresses of ecstasy. . . ."[44] This phantom sister is also the *derra,* a word, mentioned in an interlude between the first and second sections of the book that denotes in Arabic both "*the new bride of the same man, the first wife's rival*" and "*means 'wound'—the one who hurts, who cuts open the flesh, or the one who feels hurt, it's the* same *thing.*"[45] The memory of an early affair, then, and the description of the current marriage come together as one story, both a moment of interlocution and a moment of self-analysis. The wounding that ambiguously takes effect on both persons and makes it unclear on whom wounding has been enacted suggests a third figure who performs the wounding. In concrete terms, this may be the husband, but the specter of Scheherazade suggests something historical but not dated. The specter of Scheherazade suggests, in fact, another secret it hides—the shameful secret of the nation-state that demands the exchangeability of women. If Hajila and Isma become shadows to each other, each is in some ways the Scheherazade who safeguards the other from death, each in other ways Dinarzade who sleeps beneath the marriage bed, hearing her own fate, holding the responsibility for awakening her sister before dawn, and acting as analyst for her sister on the couch above. The shadow, in turn, is cast by the sultan, not only in the shape of a husband but also in the shape of the nation-state that demands blood. While the allusion to *The Arabian Nights* suggests the continuity of women's oppression, and therefore a time that is apocalyptic rather than empty, the ending of the novel makes a significant departure. The final words of the novel speak of Isma, Hajila, and Meriem, Isma's daughter, recalling the instability of their status in suspended and borrowed time, here figured as that space in-between East and West that constitutes Algeria:

O, my sister, I who thought to wake you, I'm afraid for all women, not just we two or three, Isma, Hajila, Meriem, but all women—barring midwives, barring mothers standing guard and those carrion-beaten matriarchs, I fear lest we find ourselves in chains again, in 'this West in the Orient,' this corner of the earth where day dawned so slowly for us that twilight is already closing in around us everywhere.[46]

While these are the last spoken words of the novel, we could also remark on the actual last line of text, which is a spatiotemporal marker that reads as follows: "Paris—Winter 1981–1982; Winter 1983–1984; Spring 1985 and 1986." These dates are significant: 1984 saw the passing in Algeria of the much contested Family Code that severely curtailed women's rights, their access to public space, and the work they could perform without the permission of father or husband. Before the code passed there were protests from feminists and orthodox Muslims alike. The former objected to the short-lived promise of independence, that women would maintain equal footing with men, which they had at least formally attained and earned during the bloody war of independence from 1954–62. The orthodox protested the state's interference in religious matters, contending that the *Shari'a,* or Islamic law, should be the provenance of religious teachers and not that of the state.

The secret passing of the code does not in itself, however, lead to its enforcement. This needs, of course, the consent of civil society, and this is dramatized in the final section of the novel, in which Isma seems to be *working through* the events of her early life and marriage in terms of other guilty secrets. Isma's father sent her to a school for European children because he was concerned that someone may have seen his daughter enjoy herself in public as a child. Isma had earlier narrated the pleasure of sex with her husband, which she subsequently relates to the childhood memory of taking a fairground ride. The father, probably recognizing the dangerous status of women's pleasure and the potential shame to him if others had watched her experience of childhood *jouissance,* sends her off to boarding school. And Isma herself is guilty of another secret. The final section begins with an exchange between Isma and Hajila's mother, Toumia, in which it becomes clear that it is Isma herself who has sent this sacrificial lamb to the slaughter, that she has freed herself only at the expense of another woman. Her realization of woman's exchangeability puts her in the role of Scheherazade's reluctant father, who must deliver his own daughter to the king. In other words, she has partaken in the model of time in which women can be exchanged, killed, and forgotten. She has freed herself by jeopardizing another woman's life. Scheherazade's specter reappears to put the time out of joint and to put a halt to repetition.

The ghost does not simply enable a working through (*durcharbeiten*) of Isma's own secret, or even of a family secret, nor is it a response to a traumatic *event* as such. It is the trauma of something more institutionalized and rationalized as tradition—the perpetual trauma of the fact that *the women in the novel cannot be given time to experience life*, especially the things they enjoy. Rather than functioning as a substitutable *objet petit a*, the ghost is not endlessly deferrable. Instead, it makes demands on the living, and thus contains the possibility of politics. Women's time involves the gift of listening to those demands, and of making oneself substitutable to them. They are caesuras, or cuts, in the narrative rhythm that give rise to the possibility of a different political and narrative reason. In the face of traditional retrenchment, be it French, Arab, or Berber, what Djebar performs here is a working through of symptoms of suffering. She also tells, through a narrative of interiority, a historical tale of the curtailment of women's rights in the space of the nation. The phantom of Scheherazade teaches women to live in a different register of time than that suggested by the nation in which women's slaughter and exchange seem to be condoned. Her narrative time does not let women be mourned and then forgotten, but rather lets the memories of pain remain as wounds on the bodies of all other women. This enactment of melancholia can lead to solidaristic action. In a barely credible overstatement of how working through leads to action, Isma gives Hajila the gift of time and life (both impossible gifts because no one can possess them) through the gift of a key to her apartment—she can come and go as she pleases and with no one's knowledge. She can also, we are reminded, if she wishes, have an abortion to end the pregnancy conceived in rape.

The phantom of Scheherazade comes into existence here, in this Francophone text, to recall two components of Algerian culture—an Arab literary past and a French model of nationhood that suggests through language the ghosts carried belatedly in language. The remembering, repeating, and working through in this novel recall not so much a traumatic event but rather a more generalized tradition of systemic abuse. Djebar achieves a haunting of any language that normalizes nationalist and masculinist ideologies.

The use of *The Arabian Nights* and particularly of the sisters' relationship within it calls up a national imaginary not through allegory so much as through a recognition of the centrality of interlocution both for personal working through and for modeling the possibility of interaction between women. The pain of wounding seems impossible ultimately to mourn and therefore conjures up Scheherazade's specter. She continues to speak to Dinarzade, here reborn as Hajila. If the structure of kinship is altered by the historical event, it recreates itself belatedly in language use, calling upon a hybrid past that links Djebar's characters to a multiplicity of converging discourses of varied literary, linguistic, historical, and religious traditions. The specter of Scheherazade gives a model for both the immediate context of interaction between women and a more transnational one. Scheherazade reminds us that she is useless on her own; her sister must not fall asleep but needs to be the body—or perhaps the acousmatic voice from nowhere on whom a transferential relationship can be played out in order that the specificity of discourse be taken through to action in the face of institutionalized exploitation, thereby creating a different time of narrative. I am not suggesting simply that Scheherazade provides a model of speaking and listening, or even that *voice* is in itself liberating. Such a claim seems naive, especially because verbal representation is no assurance of either truth or political representation. Rather, the sometimes acousmatic voice enabled in this novel by a troubled kinship relation reveals within it another story of familial and national relations: stories as wounds, or cuts, or tellers as phantoms, played out on the bodies of women. Speech from nowhere carries with it not only a cultural history, but also repressions, indeed phantom possessions, that carry the trace of coloniality.

Isma's time is *borrowed* from the time of the nation, but Scheherazade's specter causes her, and us, to understand the wound, or *derra,* which nationhood represses. If Scheherazade and Dinarzade are the shadows from the time of the sultan, they give to us a self-critical language and a critical agency. The phantoms that lie beneath the couch or on top of it work through a transferential relationship that may lead to the gift of the impossible, the key of time, and the possibility of a future.

Afterword

The three sections of *Algeria Cuts* have sought progressively to theorize a feminist internationalist reading practice in pursuit of justice. Through the labor of putting deconstruction to work, the book has mapped the space, sound, and time of the melancholic trace, exploring how it cuts through the force field of frames that deny and sustain its radical quality. The first section theorized justice through the Franco-Maghrebi theoretical and legal questions that intervene in and constitute relations among sexual, national, international, and intranational difference in coloniality and its aftermath. The focus, of course, has been more on the figure of woman than on concrete Algerian women. But it is my contention that such a focus is crucial in order to imagine a different form of politics beyond what one often tends to think of as a knowable fixed entity: woman. Perhaps it is disappointment in the identitarian forms of feminism that has led to such an emphasis on my part, but it is also a feminist attempt to think politics differently, through the cutting and ruthless critical agency that emerges when attending to the figure of woman, who frequently eludes and confounds already existing forms of representation, even in moments when she seems almost obsessively represented.

The attempt to theorize justice through figures as melancholic traces borrows from a notion of *prosopopeia*, in which a face that insists itself is nonetheless absent and can never emerge as such within already existing recognizable forms but only as address. The marks on a page that make up a figuration are always divisible after all, but such a recognition does not imply that social and material realities are mere tropes.[1] Rather, it is to insist on the contamination of language, which nonetheless allows for constant critique and a necessity of reading nonpresent voice and the face of the dead, as Paul de Man would put it.[2]

The second section of *Algeria Cuts* attempted to employ this strategy of reading justice as emerging from the Franco-Maghrebi context in order to attend to melancholic traces and the space of repetition that manifested themselves in insistent representations of Algerian women in the exemplary texts *The Battle of Algiers* and *Femmes d'Alger dans leur appartement*. Seeking out the division or the cut through these representations allowed for a different understanding of feminist relation to the insistent images and sounds of coloniality and postcoloniality. If they manifested as critique of the normative politics, it was also a radical questioning of the whole representational structure in which being is affirmed and assumed in politics.

The final section of the book has taken that critique and thought through the lessons of the cutting figure of Algerian woman beyond their context of emergence. In attempting an analysis of gendered representation, identification, and justice, I have not so much focused on what seems obvious to me—negative representations—but rather have sought out ways of understanding how some readings are foreclosed and others opened up by political identitarian and disciplinary reading practices. If the emphasis of psychoanalytically informed readings has been on how the past manifests itself in the present, I have tried to show how melancholia's force begins to question the very notions of time and space that characterize both history and the psyche in that fashion. I have wanted not so much to trivialize a feminist politics through despair or nihilism as to show what controverts and exceeds contemporary truisms and certainties in both the academic and the political realms, which question already existing ideas of the pursuit of justice.

The readings here have spanned a variety of different texts and objects that usually fall under the purview of a variety of disciplinary contexts, and it has traversed political borders in attempting to pursue feminist justice. Without wanting to ignore spatiotemporal divisions, and without wanting to ignore disciplinary practices, the book has been committed to a notion of hope within difference. Moving through different time frames, sometimes within one chapter, has been designed, then, not to claim historical continuity. Rather, it demonstrates how that which appears as a constitutive outside of masculinist colonialism and nationalism, comes to question, supplement, and cut through the whole structure of politics and representation at play. This could assist in what Marx once referred to as a ruthless criticism.[3] In focusing on these cuts I have been committed to an internationalist feminism that never tires of undoing its own orthodoxies, especially when, even as trauma, they come to be alibis for some other form of violence.

If this has ultimately been a work of philosophical and theoretical reflection on the figure of the Algerian woman, such a topic has not been arbitrarily chosen in a violent move to make that figure now carry the weight of a theoretical attempt to conceive a transnational feminism. Not only does Algeria parochialize the whole question of theoretical reflection by showing how the historical forces questioning of the theoretical, but Algeria, and the figure of woman that emerges in the Franco-Algerian relationship, also becomes the site from which the workings of modern notions of democracy and sovereignty are revealed in their violent contradictions. If the final section has attempted to take the figure of Algerian woman beyond its immediately identifiable site of spatiotemporal emergence, it is to show how the cut functions internationally in a manner that questions some versions of nationalist, internationalist, and postnational politics, and perhaps gives rise to other possibilities.

Debate concerning field formation and demise is often accompanied by language of birth, newness, and radical hopefulness in the first instance, and melancholia, disappointment, and outdatedness in the second. Some fields that have announced their "newness" with the prefix "post"—postmodernism, poststructuralism, and postcolonialism, for example—have often suggested a critical engagement with and surpassing of that which has preceded the former in political and disciplinary terms. Others, such as postfeminism, have simply announced the demise and lack of importance of the field, and the death notice is often accompanied by a sense of despair on the part of those who conceptualize a continued need for the field and the politics associated with it, seeing its hasty burial as testimony to the necessity of its revitalization.

Critics of modernism and its immediate aftermath have noted the manner in which newness was announced in modernist texts, along with terms such as the *new man* in decolonization movements and metropolitan postwar discourse. Kristin Ross, for example, has commented extensively on the different ways in which newness entered the world of the French language through metropolitan and anticolonial discourse from the mid-1950s to the mid-1960s, with the technologization of the *jeune cadre* in France and the simultaneous cautious hopefulness of Fanon's desire for the "new man" that emerged in *The Wretched of the Earth*.[4] It is exactly this form of highly cautious optimism, and the acute critical agency that accompanied it, that I have explored here by focusing on the term and affect *melancholia* and the way in which it permeates postcolonial studies in its political and disciplinary field formation. As an area of study—whether in literary, geographical, architectural, or spatial terms concerned with borders and other postcolonial problems—the cautious critical optimism, accompanied by its epiphenomenal counterpart in poststructuralism, is testimony to the impossibility of a declaration of newness in the world. Melancholia as symptom and reading practice does, however, offer a way of gauging how critical agency functions constantly to undo injustices performed in the name of justice and novelty. The impossibility of complete digestion of the past, and its calm production of novelty, manifests itself in constant critique.

*

The call by Bolshevik women for women to unite internationally against the forces of capitalism, and the outcry by women at the Baku conference in 1917 was to stop dealing with middle-class issues and solutions (such as the vote, and the chador—shocking how the debate has changed so little in eighty years) until women's rights under communism were deemed as worthy as men's. The demands made at the conference were never as strong afterward in any of the communist international organizations—the worldwide worker's movements to overthrow capitalism. While the call forced an acknowledgment that women's concerns under capitalism were specific, that women's oppression dominated all forms of oppression internationally, and that women should not be dealt with as a priority separate and lower than working men, a prioritization was nonetheless made. The issue of the chador, we see now, is hardly frivolous, even if it seemed like a middle-class obsession. If it arises in the Algerian or the Franco-Maghrebi context today, it is rarely discussed in terms of the material issues in play. These would include the rise in unemployment in Algeria through the late 1970s and 1980s, the massive population growth and the youth of the population, the lack of provision of basic facilities by a corrupt government, and the Islamist occupation of the political sphere and imagination as they moved to improve basic living conditions. How the condition of women and the manipulation of the figure of woman were severely compromised by this situation can be understood only by understanding how masculinist thought frequently returns the woman question to the sphere of culture, misapprehending how she cuts through every sphere of life.

But the women's international movement was never as strong again as it was at that moment in Baku, because the particular plight of women in capitalism was always considered of secondary importance to the primary struggle—as if it could simply be dismissed as merely culturalist. Clearly, the economic and cultural are not separate or even separable entities. Each of the Marxist international organizations has had major blind spots and prioritizations, and reading for the supplement, we can recognize the profound injustice done within these internationalist gestures. The First International Working Men's Association of 1864 concentrated on European colonies. While this organization was clearly a response to European colonialism, the colonies outside of Europe were largely neglected. The Second International of 1889 was concerned with Russian and Austrian imperial relations. The Comintern, or Third International, would finally recognize the need for home rule among colonies as a part of the anticapitalist struggle.[5] The question of feminist interventions into how this was to be carried out was, however, largely ignored, as it was later in the majority of independence struggles from the 1940s through to the 1960s. Even today, analyses of international forms of resistance to global capitalism often fail to recognize how women's labor—whether reproductive or productive—is consistently sidelined in conceptualizations of resistant communities. Postcolonial feminist scholarship, particularly that with Marxist sympathies, has written of the need for feminists to recognize women's "complex relationality."[6] The main thrust of postcolonial feminist work has been consistently cautious about the relations among women internationally, and indeed cautious about any faith in the promises of any new nationalism and the manner in which global late capitalism has produced massive inequalities between women internationally, with which more locally based feminist movements have quite often been complicit.[7] Taking their lesson from the misguided and intrusive "paternalistic" work of early European feminism in their colonies, postcolonial feminists have been cautious to remind themselves of how their own relative privilege is built on the exploitation of other women in the current form of neoimperial late-capitalist organization. This has alerted women to the problems of global sisterhood, and to recognize that while ideals of international justice have been the motivating force of much feminist work, local long-term planning has always been necessary. The challenge intellectually and politically has been how to conceive of the local, and of who or what appears as a foreigner (aggressor, invader, woman, nonexpert, expert, man, animal) at the gates of the local.

In order to conceive of a new form of political reason, supplements (and in my example, Algerian women) need to be listened to at the margins for what their presence or absence implies. This listening involves not simply putting women at center stage, or equating their voices with empowerment or the good. Its purpose is more to understand the nature of liminality that comes into view when one attempts to see force fields and frameworks and the cuts into them, and to understand what that means for the political reason that seeks justice outside the mechanisms of the virile wars that have characterized Algeria's modern history.

REFERENCE MATTER

Notes

PREFACE

1. Jacques Derrida, "Taking a Stand for Algeria," *Parallax* 4:2 (1998), 17–23.
2. The Friedrich Ebert foundation reported that between 1994 and 1997 an estimated 1,013 women were the victims of systematic collective rape. The report also noted that Islamic armed groups used rape as a weapon. The report does not comment on sexual violence perpetrated by other groups or by the state. Collectif 95 Maghreb Égalité, a network anchored in the women's movement of Morocco, Algeria, and Tunisia, has published many reports on violence against women in the Maghreb. The collective's publications include *Les violations flagrantes des droits et violence à l'égard des femmes au Maghreb: Algérie, Maroc, Tunisie* [Blatant Violations of Rights and Violence Against Women in the Maghreb: Algeria, Morocco, Tunisia] and *Les Maghrébines entre violences symboliques et violences physiques* [People of the Maghreb Between Symbolic and Physical Violence] (Rabat, Morocco: Collectif 95 Maghreb Égalité, 1998–1999). See also Naomi Sakr, *Women's Rights and the Arab Media* (London: Centre for Media Freedom in the Middle East and North Africa, November 2000).
3. Sigmund Freud, "Remembering, Repeating and Working-Through" [Further Recommendations on the Technique of Psychoanalysis] (1914), in *The Standard Edition of the Complete Psychological Works of Sigmund Freud*, 24 vols., trans. and ed. James Strachey (London: Hogarth Press and the Institute of Psychoanalysis, 1953–74), Vol. 12, 145–156.

ACKNOWLEDGMENTS

1. Ranjana Khanna, "'Araby' (*Dubliners*): Women's Time and the Time of the Nation," in *Joyce, Feminism, Colonialism/Postcolonialism*, ed. Ellen Carol Jones, European Joyce Studies 8 (Atlanta, GA: Rodopi, 1998), 81–101; "From Third to Fourth Cinema," *Third Text* 43 (1998), 13–32; "The Experience of Evidence: Language, Law, and the Mockery of Justice," in *Algeria in Others' Languages*, ed. Anne Berger (Ithaca, NY: Cornell University Press, 2002), 107–139; "Frames, Contexts, Community, Justice" in *Frame, Metaphor, and Meaning*, ed. Joyce Goggin and Michael Burke (Amsterdam: ASCA Press, 2002), 149–172; "Frames, Contexts,

Community, Justice," in *Diacritics* 33:2 (2003), 11–41; "Post-Palliative: Sovereignty, Disposability, Melancholia," in *Postcolonial Text* 2:1 (2006). Thanks to these sources for permission to reprint in revised form.

INTRODUCTION: THE LIVING DEAD

Epigraph: Jacques Derrida, "Force of Law: The Mystical Foundation of Authority," in *Acts of Religion*, ed. Gil Anidjar (New York: Routledge, 2001), 252.

1. Prior to the ruling in the Mohamed Garne case, there had been no demonstration of the French judiciary's acknowledgment of French abuse of Algerians, or compensation for injuries arising from that abuse. See Stiina Löytömäki, "Legalisation of the Memory of the Algerian War in France," *Journal of the History of International Law* 7:2 (2005), 157–179.

2. The story is told in great detail in Mohamed Garne, *Lettre à ce père qui pourrait être vous* (Paris: J. C. Lattès, 2005).

3. For more on this topic, see Mike Davis, *Planet of Slums* (London: Verso, 2006). See also the interesting work done on graveyard dwelling in Cairo in Max Rodenbeck, *Cairo: The City Victorious* (New York: Vintage, 2000).

4. Kheira repeatedly expressed that she felt more comfortable in the world of the dead, especially given that she felt she barely existed and had rarely been treated well by the living. "Ici, au moins, je ne crains personne-ni les morts, ni les djinns, ni les démons. Les vrais démons, ce sont les humains. Les morts, eux, ne font pas de mal . . . Ne crains rien!" [Here, at least, I fear no one—neither the dead, nor *djinns*, nor demons. The real devils are the human beings. The dead don't harm you. Don't worry!] she said to her son. "Je sais me défendre. Et puis de toute façon, comment mourir puisque je n'ai vraiment existé . . . je suis toujours restée au seuil de ma vie" [I can take care of myself. And then anyway, how do you die when you've never really existed? I've always remained at the threshold of my life] (Garne, *Lettre*, 76). "Elle disait qu'elle n'était pas prête á renouer avec le monde des vivants" [She said she wasn't ready to take up with the world of the living] (Garne, *Lettre*, 84).

5. Luce Irigaray has devoted much of her work to revealing this dynamic. See *Speculum of the Other Woman*, trans. Gillian Gill (Ithaca, NY: Cornell University Press, 1985).

6. Mohamed Garne does not include any information about his mother passing out. In fact, he includes only, and significantly, his mother's reproaches toward him for having pursued the case at all. She was adamant that she did not want property owed to her by virtue of her widow status, because the family had effectively abandoned her after her husband's death. Her brother-in-law would have liked her to marry him, but this would have been a second forced marriage. She had been forced by her brother to marry Bengoucha, who was considerably older than her, and she had been a child who wanted to marry him. For the story as told

by the Irish Times, see Lara Marlowe, "Algerian Victims of French Torture Seek Recognition," *Irish Times* 22:11 (2000). For Kheira's story, as far as we have it, see Mohamed Garne, *Lettre*.

7. Amnesty laws concerning the French-Algerian relationship are complex, as indeed are the laws pertaining to amnesty within each of those countries. In the 1962 Evian Accords, amnesty was declared for all offenses related to aiding or preventing the Algerian rebellion committed prior to March 20, 1962, in order to facilitate self-determination of the Algerian population. See Evian Accords, March 19, 1962, *Journal Officiel de la République Française*, March 20, 1962, 3019. Other relevant decrees include #62–327 and #62–328, March 22, 1962, in *Journal Officiel de la République Française*, March 23, 1962, 3143, 3144. See also Dalloz, *Législation*, 1962, 125, 126, 152; and Orders 62–427 and 62–428 of April 14, 1962, in *Journal Officiel de la République Française*, April 15, 1962, 3892. The June 1966 decree included any offense against national security forces committed in relation to the events in Algeria (Law #66–396 of June 17, 1966, *Journal Officiel de la République Française*, June 18, 1966, 4915). See also Dalloz-Sirey, *Législation*, 1966, 256. The 1968 laws extended the amnesty further to include all offenses committed during the war in relation to Algeria, including those committed by the military (Law #68–697 of July 31, 1968, in *Journal Officiel de la République Française*, August 2, 1968, 7521; Dalloz-Sirey, *Législation*, 1968, 259). The 1974 law addressed criminal convictions during and after the Algerian war and expunged these convictions (Law #74–363 of July 16, 1974, in *Journal Officiel de la République Française*, July 17, 1974, 7443; Dalloz-Sirey, *Législation*, 1974, 250). For an in-depth analysis of French amnesty laws, see Stéphane Gacon, *L'Amnistie: De la commune à la guerre d'Algérie* [Amnesty: From the Commune to the Algerian War] (Paris: Seuil, 2002). For an analysis of Franco-Algerian amnesty that includes Algerian President Bouteflika's work on amnesty in Algeria and also points out some of the hypocrises of French law on human rights violations, comparing the treatment of the Holocaust with that of the Algerian war, see Shiva Eftekhari, "France and the Algerian War: From a Policy of 'Forgetting' to a Framework for Accountability," *Columbia Human Rights Law Review* 34 (2002–2003), 413–474. This of course does not include the recent (September 29, 2005) referendum in Algeria for amnesty related to the recent civil war. Many, including Amnesty International, have vehemently criticized this "Draft Charter for Peace and National Reconciliation" for its aim to exonerate members of both national security forces and armed groups. Members of both of these groups have committed major human rights abuses during the current civil war, which began in 1992 and has claimed some two hundred thousand lives. Amnesty International also considers the charter to be in violation of International Law. For Amnesty International's statement, see *Public Statement*, AI Index: MDE 28/010/2005 (Public). News Service No. 229, August 22, 2005: "Algeria: President Calls Referendum to Obliterate Crimes of the Past," available at http://web.amnesty.org/library/Index/ENGMDE280102005.

Other critics of the Charter include Algeria's opposition Socialist Forces Front (FFS), which points out that such absolvement ignores pain and suffering. The independent Algerian League for the Defense of Human Rights (LADDH) comments that the referendum is absurd, highlighting that it is impossible to oppose a charter such as this in some ways, yet criticizing the avoidance of condemnation of human rights abuses at the same time. For information on the frequent violation of the Geneva Convention by states seeking amnesty rulings, see Michael P. Scharf, "The Amnesty Exception to the Jurisdiction of the International Criminal Court," *Cornell International Law Review* 32:3 (1998), 507–527. The referendum passed by 97.43 percent, with some 80 percent of the electorate participating. However, voting numbers varied dramatically. In Tizi Ouzou, the capital of the unsettled Kabylie region, only 11.4 percent voted. See "Algerians Approve Amnesty," September 30, 2005, 12:33 Makka time, 9:33 GMT, available at http://english.aljazeera.net/English/archive/archive?ArchiveId=15547. Detained, exiled, or fugitive armed fighters who have suspended violence will be given amnesty alongside security forces that have long been criticized. For further investigations of the violations perpetrated by the military and security forces within Algeria, see *An Inquiry into the Algerian Massacres*, ed. Youcef Bedjauoi, Abbas Aroua, and Meziane Ait-Larbi (Geneva: Hoggar, 1999); and Hichem Aboud, *La Mafia des Généraux* (Paris: Lattes, 2002). Those involved in mass massacres, rapes, and bomb attacks in public places will not be given amnesty. Bouteflika has run on a ticket for amnesty ever since he first campaigned for office in 1999. Once in office, on September 16, 1999, Bouteflika called for his first referendum for the Civil Harmony Law, which asked the simple question, "Do you approve of the president's approach to restore peace and civilian accord?" He aimed to give amnesty to those who were not directly involved in killing if they turned themselves in pledging peace and giving up their arms. The turnout was slightly higher (85 percent) and the vote was similar—some 98 percent voted positively. Criticism was also present at that time, and there have been very few investigations into any of the figures who have pledged to stop violence and turned themselves in. Bouteflika has created a semblance, therefore, of confrontation of violence, but in fact he has simply agreed to forget—performing thereby the amnesia that informs all amnesty laws. On February 24, 2006, there was a large press conference, consisting mostly of women's groups, to reject the new charter for peace and national reconciliation that had been formally approved three days earlier by the government in response to the referendum. See Wendy Kristianasen, "Truth and Justice After a Brutal Civil War—Algeria: The Women Speak," in *Le Monde diplomatique*, April 2006; English language edition available at http://mondediplo.com/2006/04/07algeria. For more theoretical reflection on amnesty, see Adam Sitze, "At the Mercy Of," in *The Limits of Law*, eds. Austin Sarat, Lawrence Douglas, and Martha Merrill Umphrey (Stanford, CA: Stanford University Press, 2005), 246–308; and Nicole Loraux, *The Divided City: On Memory and Forgetting in Ancient Athens*, trans. Corinne Pache with Jeff Fort (New

York: Zone Books, 2002). Bouteflika has also created a more stable environment, or at least the semblance of one, for the improvement of the petroleum-based economy. For more on the necessity of prosecuting human rights violations, see Diane Orentlicher, "Settling Accounts: The Duty to Prosecute Human Rights Violations of a Prior Regime," *Yale Law Journal* 100:8 (1991), 2537–2615.

8. Garne, *Lettre*, 145.

9. See Simone de Beauvoir and Gisèle Halimi, *Djamila Boupacha* (Paris: Gallimard, 1962); *Djamila Boupacha: The Story of the Torture of a Young Algerian Girl Which Shocked Liberal Opinion*, trans. Peter Green (London: André Deutsch and Weidenfeld and Nicolson, 1962). I discuss this case at length in Chapter 2.

10. See *Le Monde*, November 24, 2001. My translation.

11. Roland Barthes, *Mythologies*, trans. Annette Lavers (New York: Noonday Press, 1972), 61.

12. Barthes writes, "I do not wish to prejudge the moral implications of such a mechanism, but I shall not exceed the limits of an objective analysis if I point out [that] the ubiquity of the signifier in myth exactly reproduces the physique of the alibi (which is, as one realizes, a spatial term): in the alibi too there is a place which is full and one which is empty, linked by a relation of negative identity ('I am not where you think I am; I am where you think I am not'). But the ordinary alibi (for the police, for instance) has an end; reality stops the turnstile revolving at a certain point. Myth is a value, truth is no guarantee for it; nothing prevents it from being a perpetual alibi: it is enough that its signifier has two sides for it always to have an 'elsewhere' at its disposal" (*Mythologies*, 123).

13. This is not to suggest that tactics of "disappearance" were not used in the Algerian war of independence or have not been used since. See, for example, Jacques Vergès and others, *Les Disparus: Le Cahier Vert* [The Disappeared: The Green Book](Lausanne: La Cité, 1959); Serge Moureaux, *Avocats san Frontières: Le Collectif Belges et la Guerre d'Algérie* [Lawyers Without Frontiers: The Belgian Collective and the Algerian War] (Algiers: Editions Casbah, 2000); and the controversial book by Général Paul Aussaresses, *Services spéciaux Algérie 1955–1957: Mon témoignage sur la torture* [Algerian Special Services: 1955-1957: My Testimony on Torture] (Paris: Perrin, 2001). The important recent work done by Nacéra Dutour for SOS Disparus [SOS Disappeared] in Algiers and Collectif des Familles de Disparus en Algérie [Collective of the Families of the Disappeared in Algeria] in Paris has drawn attention to the eight to twenty thousand or so "disappeared" of the recent Algerian civil war. Most of the disappeared have been men.

14. See Theodor Adorno, *Minima Moralia: Reflections from Damaged Life*, trans. E. F. N. Jephcott (London: Verso, 1984).

15. Rosa Luxemburg, *The Accumulation of Capital*, trans. Agnes Schwarzschild (London and New York: Routledge, 2003), 359.

16. Luxemburg, *Accumulation of Capital*, 349–350.

17. See Marnia Lazreg, *The Eloquence of Silence: Algerian Women in Question*

(New York: Routledge, 1994), 151. For more on Algerian family law, revisions within it, and the Maliki principles of Algerian Islamic law, see Algeria, *Initial Report to the Committee on the Elimination of Discrimination Against Women* (CEDAW) (New York: United Nations, September 1, 1998); CEDAW twentieth session, January 19 to February 5, 1999, http://www.un.org/womenwatch/daw/cedaw/cedaw20/algeria.htm; Dawoud Sudqi El Alami and Doreen Hinchcliffe, *Islamic Marriage and Divorce Laws of the Arab World* (London: Centre of Islamic and Middle Eastern Law [CIMEL] School of Oriental and African Studies [SOAS], Kluwer Law International, 1996); Allan Christelow, *Muslim Law Courts and the French Colonial State in Algeria* (Princeton: Princeton University Press, 1985); Peter R. Knauss, *The Persistence of Patriarchy: Class, Gender, and Ideology in Twentieth Century Algeria* (New York: Praeger, 1987); Tahir Mahmood, "Algeria," in *Statutes of Personal Law in Islamic Countries* (New Delhi: India and Islam Research Council, 1995); *Algeria: A Country Study*, ed. Helen Chapin Metz (Washington, DC: Federal Research Division, Library of Congress, 1994); Ruth Mitchell, "Family Law in Algeria Before and After the 1404/1984 Family Code," *Islamic Law: Theory and Practice*, eds. Robert Gleave and Eugenia Kermeli (London: I. B. Tauris, 1997), 194–204; Jamal J. Nasir, *The Islamic Law of Personal Status* (London and Boston: Graham & Trotman, 1990); Kenneth R. Redden, "Algeria," in *Modern Legal Systems Cyclopedia*, Vol. 6 (Buffalo, NY: Hein, 1990).

18. Said Chikhi, "The Worker, the Prince, and the Facts of Life," in *Algeria: The Challenge of Modernity*, ed. Ali el Kenz (London: Codesria, 1991), 191–226, 217–218; see also Said Chikhi, "Question Ouvrière et Rapports Sociaux en Algérie" [The Question of the Worker and Social Relations in Algeria] in *Review Fernand Braudel Center* 18:3 (1995), 487–523; Said Chikhi, *Algeria: From Mass Rebellion in October 1988 to Workers' Social Protest* (Uppsala, Sweden: Nordiska Afrikainstitutet, 1991), 13.

19. See Ghania Mouffok, "Regionalism Is an Admission of Defeat. Algeria: Only Way Up and Out," *Le Monde Diplomatique*, July 2001.

20. Jacques Simon, *Messali Hadj par les textes* (Paris: Editions Bouchéne, 2000). Translated for marxists.org by Mitch Abidor and available at http://www.marxists.org/archive/messali-hadj/1928/fight-french.htm.

21. In *Politics of Friendship*, trans. George Collins (London: Verso, 1997), 155–158, Jacques Derrida writes of the unacknowledged gendered nature of the discourse of the friend and the enemy in Carl Schmitt's political theology. He is particularly interested in Algerian women in this context.

22. See, for example, André Nouschi, "Notes de lectures sur la guerre d'Algérie" [Lecture Notes on the Algerian War] *Relations internationales*, 114 (2003); Annie Rey-Goldzeiguer, *Aux origines de la guerre d'Algérie 1940–1945* [At the Origins of the Algerian War, 1940-45] (Paris: La Découverte, 2002); Redouane Ainad Tabet, *Le 8 mai 1945 en Algérie* [May 8, 1945 in Algeria] (Algiers: Office des Publications Universitaire, 1987).

23. Loraux, *Divided City*, front flap.
24. Derrida, "Force of Law," 267.
25. See, for example, Benjamin Stora, "Women's Writing Between Two Wars," trans. R. H. Mitsch, in *Research in African Literatures* 30:3 (1999), 78–94; *Algeria, 1830–2000: A Short History*, trans. Jane Marie Todd, foreword by William B. Quandt (Ithaca, NY: Cornell University Press, 2001); *Algérie, formation d'une nation; suivi de, Impressions de voyage: Notes et photographies, printemps 1998* [Algeria: Formation of a Nation; followed by Impressions of a Journey: Notes and Photographs, Spring 1998] (Biarritz, France: Atlantica, 1998); *Algérie, Maroc: Histoires parallèles, destins croisés* [Algeria, Morocco: Parallel Histories, Crossed Fates] (Paris: Zellige, 2002); *Le dictionnaire des livres de la guerre d'Algérie: Romans, nouvelles, poésie, photos, histoire, essais, récits historiques, témoignages, biographies, mémoires, autobiographies: 1955–1995* [Dictionary of Books About the Algerian War: Novels, Short Stories, Poetry, Photos, History, Essays, Narrative Histories, Testimony, Biography, Memoir, Autobiography: 1955-1995] (Paris: Harmattan, 1996); *La Gangrène et l'oubli: La mémoire de la guerre d'Algérie* [Gangrene and Forgetting: Memory of the Algerian War] (Paris: La Découverte, 1991); *La guerre d'Algérie, 1954–2004: La fin de l'amnésie* [The Algerian War, 1954-2004: The End of Amnesia], eds. Benjamin Stora and Mohammed Harbi (Paris: R. Laffont, 2004).
26. Letters and news arriving in Paris seem to have been a mode of address favored by the publishing industry in France recently. See, for example, *Lettres d'Algérie*, eds. Philippe Bernard and Nathaniel Herzberg (Paris: Gallimard, 1998); Christiane Chaulet Achour, *Des Nouvelles d'Algérie, 1974–2004* (Paris: Editions Metailié, 2005).
27. See Jean-Pierre Vittori, *On a torturé en Algérie* [We Committed Torture in Algeria] (Paris: Editions Ramsay, 2000, including work banned in 1980); Louisette Ighilahriz, *L'Algérienne* (The Algerian Woman) (Paris: Fayard, 2001); Aussaresses, *Services spéciaux Algérie 1955–1957* [Special Services, Algeria 1955-57]. The debates on the revelations of torture can be found in the pages of *Le Monde*, June 2000.
28. See G.W.F. Hegel, *The Phenomenology of Spirit*, trans. A. V. Miller (Oxford, UK: Oxford University Press, 1979), 266–294. See also Judith Butler, *Antigone's Claim: Kinship Between Life and Death* (New York: Columbia University Press, 2000); Jacques Derrida, *Glas*, trans. John P. Leavey Jr. and Richard Rand (Lincoln: University of Nebraska Press, 1986); Jacques Derrida, *Of Hospitality: Anne Dufourmantelle Invites Jacques Derrida to Respond*, trans. Rachel Bowlby (Stanford, CA: Stanford University Press, 2000); Jacques Lacan, *Ethics of Psychoanalysis*, trans. Dennis Porter (New York: Norton, 1997); Luce Irigaray, "The Eternal Irony of the Community," in *Speculum of the Other Woman*; Irigaray, "The Universal as Mediation," in *Sexes and Genealogies*, trans. Gillian Gill (New York: Columbia University Press, 1993); Irigaray, "The Female Gender," in *Sexes and Genealogies*. See Caroline Rooney's *African Literature, Animism, and Politics* (London, New York: Routledge, 2000), important work that attempts to read the story of the

Algerian revolution in the texts on Antigone by Lacan and Derrida that emerged at the time of or in the wake of that war.

29. Julia Kristeva, *Revolution in Poetic Language*, trans. Margaret Waller (New York: Columbia University Press, 1984), 26.

30. Jacques Derrida, "Khora," trans. Ian McLeod, in *On the Name* (Stanford, CA: Stanford University Press, 1995), 126.

31. See, for example, Michael T. Kaufman, "What Does the Pentagon See in *The Battle of Algiers*?," *New York Times*, September 7, 2003.

32. For problems with using terms like *torture* and *terrorism*, see the many works of Edward Said, Noam Chomsky, and Edward Herman on this issue. I suggest Edward Said, *Covering Islam* (New York: Pantheon Books, 1981); Noam Chomsky, *Pirates and Emperors: International Terrorism in the Real World* (New York: Claremont University Press, 1986); Noam Chomsky, *The Culture of Terrorism* (Boston: South End Press, 1988); and Edward Herman, *The Real Terror Network: Terrorism in Fact and Propaganda* (Boston: South End Press, 1982). For Jean-Paul Sartre on "people's war," see *On Genocide* (Boston: Beacon Press, 1968), 65; also in *Prevent the Crime of Silence: Reports from the Sessions of the International War Crimes Tribunal Founded by Bertrand Russell—London, Stockholm, Roskilde*, eds. Peter Limqueco and Peter Weiss (London: Allen Lane, Penguin Press, 1971), 350–364.

33. Cited in Kaufman, "What Does the Pentagon See."

34. Frantz Fanon, "Algeria Unveiled," in *Studies in a Dying Colonialism* (London: Earthscan, 1989), 35–67.

35. Frantz Fanon, *The Wretched of the Earth*, trans. Constance Farrington (New York: Grove Press, 1968), 38–39.

36. Le Corbusier (Charles Edouard Jeanneret-Gris), *The Radiant City: Elements of a Doctrine of Urbanism to Be Used as the Basis of Our Machine-Age Civilization* (New York: Orion Press, 1964), 228.

37. Le Corbusier, *Radiant City*, 230–232. See also Le Corbusier's *Poésie Sur Alger* [Poetry on Algiers] (Paris: Editions Falaize, 1950) for Le Corbusier's poetic attachment to the city. See also Zeynep Çelik's work on Algerian architecture in the modern period, which offers excellent insights: *Urban Forms and Colonial Confrontations: Algiers Under French Rule* (Berkeley: University of California Press, 1997).

38. Le Corbusier, "Le Folklore est l'expression fleurie des traditions," *Voici la France de ce mois* [France This Month] 16 (1941), 31. Cited in Çelik, *Urban Forms*, 4.

39. Benedict Anderson, *Imagined Communities: Reflections on the Origin and Spread of Nationalism* (London: Verso, 1991).

40. Antoine Prost, writing for Pierre Nora's new national history of France, which was based on realms or sites of memory, considers the monuments to the dead and the ceremonies associated with them, particularly those monuments for World War I that can be found in every French town. See Antoine Prost, "Les Monuments aux Morts" [Monuments to the Dead], in *Les Lieux de Mémoire* [Realms of Memory], Vol. 1, ed. Pierre Nora (Paris: Gallimard, 1997), 199–223.

41. See Bertrand Ogilvie, "Violence et représentation: La production de l'homme jetable" [Violence and Representation: The Production of Disposable Man], *Lignes* 26 (1995), 113-141.
42. Assia Djebar, *Algerian White* (New York: Seven Stories Press, 2000).
43. Malek Alloula, *The Colonial Harem*, trans. Myrna and Wlad Godzich (Minneapolis: University of Minnesota Press, 1986), 5.
44. Joan Copjec's essay "The Sartorial Superego" gives a wonderful reading of Gaëtan de Clérambault's photographs. See Joan Copjec, "The Sartorial Superego," in *Read My Desire: Lacan Against the Historicists* (Cambridge, MA: MIT Press, 1994), 65–116. See also Yolande Papetti, Françoise Valier, Bernard de Freminville, and Serge Tisseron, *La passion des étoffes chez un neuro-psychiatre. G. G. de Clérambault* [A Neuro-Psychiatrist's Passion for Fabrics] (Paris: Editions Solin, 1980); *Gaëtan Gatian de Clérambault psychiatre et photographe, Collection Les Empêcheurs de Penser en Rond* [Gaëtan Gatain de Clérambault, Psychiatrist and Photographer], ed. Serge Tisseron (Paris: Département Communication, 1990). For an interesting use of the Clérambault obsession, see Gilles Deleuze, *The Fold: Leibniz and the Baroque*, trans. Tom Conley (Minneapolis: University of Minnesota Press, 1993).
45. I am influenced here by an essay by James T. Siegel on Georg Simmel: "Georg Simmel Reappears: The Aesthetic Significance of the Face," *Diacritics* 29:2 (1999), 100–113. See also Georg Simmel, "The Aesthetic Significance of the Face," in *Georg Simmel, 1858–1918: A Collection of Essays, with Translations and a Bibliography*, ed. Kurt H. Wolff (Columbus: Ohio State University Press, 1959), 276–281.
46. Jacques Derrida, *The Postcard: From Socrates to Freud and Beyond*, trans. Alan Bass (Chicago: University of Chicago Press, 1987), 46.
47. Fredric Jameson's writing on the architectural wrap of the Frank Gehry house in Santa Monica, California, is instructive here. The beauty of the house is wrapped in corrugated aluminum, as if to present for us the contradictions of postmodern living—the "poverty and misery, people not only out of work but without a place to live." See Fredric Jameson, *Postmodernism, or the Cultural Logic of Late Capitalism* (Durham, NC: Duke University Press, 1991), 128.
48. Derrida plays with the meaning of *dos*, or "back," in *The Postcard*. *Le dos* is the back of a person, of a page, or indeed the blunt edge of a knife. It also sounds like *la dot*, or "dowry." Derrida also writes about Freud's case of "the Wolf Man," and the *coitus a tergo*, or intercourse from the back, played out in that case. The psychoanalyst, of course, always listen from behind the reclining analysand.
49. Achille Mbembe, "Necropolitics," *Public Culture* 15:1 (2003), 11–40.
50. Thomas Hobbes, *Leviathan*, ed and intro. C. B. Macpherson (Harmondsworth: Penguin, 1985).
51. Michel Foucault, *The History of Sexuality: An Introduction*, trans. Robert Hurley (London: Penguin, 1979), 143.
52. See Michel Foucault, *Society Must Be Defended: Lectures at the Collège de France, 1975–76* (New York: Picador, 2003).

53. Giorgio Agamben, *Means Without End: Notes on Politics*, trans. Vincenzo Binetti and Cesare Casarino (Minneapolis: University of Minnesota Press, 2000), 37.

54. Giorgio Agamben, *Homo Sacer: Sovereign Power and Bare Life*, trans. Daniel Heller-Roazen (Stanford, CA: Stanford University Press, 1998).

55. Mbembe, "Necropolitics," 12.

56. Mbembe, "Necropolitics," 12.

57. Mbembe, "Necropolitics," 12.

58. Carl Schmitt was a National Socialist lawyer and controversial theorist of democracy and constitutionalism in the Weimar Republic and beyond. During his lifetime he was read with admiration by figures on the right and the left of the political spectrum for his critiques of liberalism and its pitfalls, and eventually of the dominance of the United States over Europe. See *The Concept of the Political*, trans. George D. Schwab (Chicago: University of Chicago Press, 1996); *The Nomos of the Earth in the International Law of the Jus Publicum Europaeum*, trans. G. L. Ulmen (New York: Telos Press, 2003); *Political Theology: Four Chapters on the Concept of Sovereignty*, trans. George D. Schwab (Cambridge, MA: MIT Press, 1985). Recently Schmitt's work on sovereignty and decisionism has again become the source of debate. Derrida's "Force of Law" is one of many texts in which he returned to a deconstruction of Schmitt's thought. See also Jacques Derrida, *Politics of Friendship*.

59. Derrida, *Voyous* (Paris: Galilée, 2003), 57.

60. See also Rachid Boujedra, *FIS de la haine* [FIS of Hatred] (Paris: Gallimard, 1994). Boujedra plays on the sounds in FIS (Islamic Salvation Front) and on the word *fils*, or "son." For an informative history of the Front Islamique du Salut, see Michael Willis, *The Islamist Challenge in Algeria: A Political History* (New York: New York University Press, 1997).

61. It seems important to note, of course, that it is not only the Palestinian cause, or indeed Muslim politics, that has generated forms of attempted sovereignty through the rearing of life for death in this way. India and Sri Lanka have seen many of these attempts, and in these contexts, unlike in the context of the Palestinians, the popular imagery has (with historical validity) focused on women as disposable—in other words, the woman suicide bomber. This is not the place to analyze further the rather wonderful film titled *The Terrorist*. But what is fascinating about that film is the manner in which life (reproduction) and death (suicide bombing) are played against each other, as if this were really a clear political choice, utopianly articulated through pregnancy. A very different film, Mani Ratnam's *Dil Se*, explores the ethical impossibility of the political choices in play in some ways (paradoxically, given its more popular form) in a more sophisticated fashion.

62. Interestingly, it is the external forces that have mapped Algiers—the British during World War II; the French as documented in their recent exhibition

"Alger: Paysage Urbain et Architectures" [Algiers: Urban Landscapes and Architecture], in which very few images of buildings were in evidence; and now UNESCO, effectively finally winning the argument to museumify the casbah, thus beginning to map the city. As a tourist going to Algiers, it is almost impossible to find a map, and when one does, it has the modernist beauty and abstraction of a Le Corbusier sketch.

63. Sigmund Freud, "Mourning and Melancholia," 1917, reprinted in *The Standard Edition of the Complete Psychological Works of Sigmund Freud*, Vol. 14, 253.

64. I have discussed this further in *Dark Continents: Psychoanalysis and Colonialism* (Durham, NC: Duke University Press, 2003). Derrida discusses "democracy to come" in much of his work of the last fourteen years. See his "Force of Law."

CHAPTER 1: FRAMES, CONTEXTS, COMMUNITY, JUSTICE

1. In her essay "The Gesture in Psychoanalysis," Luce Irigaray discusses the importance of such gendered "gestures." Discussing the different relation to symbolization of boys and girls through a reading of the boy Ernst's game of *fort und da* described by Freud in "Beyond the Pleasure Principle," she writes:

She plays with a doll, transferring the maternal affects to a quasi-subject, which allows her to organize a sort of symbolic space. The game is not just culturally imposed on girls; it also signifies a difference in the status as subjects of boys and girls at the time of separation from the mother; for girls, the mother is a subject who cannot readily be reduced to an object, and a doll is not an object in the way that a reel, a toy car, a weapon, and so on, are objects and tools of symbolization. . . . She dances, thereby constructing for herself a vital subjective space, space which is open to the cosmic maternal world, to the gods, to the other who may be present. This dance is also a way of creating for herself her own territory in relation to the mother. (Luce Irigaray, "The Gesture in Psychoanalysis," in *Between Feminism and Psychoanalysis*, ed. Teresa Brennan [London and New York: Routledge, 1989], 132)

In this context, it is striking that Hélène Cixous, in a photographic essay about the family album and personal genealogy and Algerian and European background, includes a photograph of herself dancing with her (female) friends. See Hélène Cixous, "Albums and Legends," in Hélène Cixous and Mireille Calle-Gruber, *Rootprints: Memory and Life-Writing* (London and New York: Routledge, 1997), 197.

2. An intellectual genealogy seems to be what is at stake in Félix González-Torres's selection of childhood photographs of contributors to the volume *Out There: Marginalization and Contemporary Cultures*, eds. Russell Ferguson, Martha Gever, Trinh T. Minh-ha, and Cornel West (New York: New Museum of Contemporary Art, 1990). I am sympathetic with the project of reminding people that what Cornel West calls "faceless universalism" more often than not conceals an "ethnic chauvinism" that must be resisted (36). But I do not find that giving universalism a "face" is the best way to reconceive politics, nor does it necessarily free anyone of

"ethnic chauvinism." Another example of reading the childhood photograph as a way of understanding later works can be found in Walter Benjamin's essay "Franz Kafka," in *Illuminations* (New York: Schocken Books, 1968), in which Benjamin discusses a childhood photograph of Kafka. Speculating on the typicality of the photograph, Benjamin writes, "It was probably made in one of those nineteenth-century studios whose draperies and palm trees, tapestries and easels placed them somewhere between a torture chamber and a throne room" (118). Benjamin sees a continuity between the fantasy encapsulated in the gestures of childhood, orientalist nineteenth-century imagination, and later literary interventions.

3. "(S)tudium . . . doesn't mean 'study,' but application to a thing, taste for someone, a kind of general, enthusiastic commitment, of course, but without special acuity. It is by studium that I am interested in so many photographs, whether I receive them as political testimony or enjoy them as good historical scenes: for it is culturally (this connotation is present in studium) that I participate in the figures, the faces, the gestures, the settings, the actions." Roland Barthes, *Camera Lucida*, trans. Richard Howard (New York: Noonday Press), 26. On the distinction between studium and punctum, see also Carol Mavor, "Pulling Ribbons from Mouths," *Representing the Passions*, ed. Richard Meyer (Los Angeles: Getty Research Institute, 2003), 175–216.

4. The idea of taking a stand for Algeria was examined by Jacques Derrida in his address to the International Committee in Support of Algerian Intellectuals (ICSAI) and the League of Human Rights on February 7, 1994. The text is published as "Taking a Stand for Algeria," in *Parallax* 4:2 (1998), 17–23.

5. Gayatri Chakravorty Spivak's appendix to *A Critique of Postcolonial Reason* (Cambridge, MA: Harvard University Press, 1999, 423–431) clarifies the development of some of the principles of deconstruction and of the political potential of Derrida's work. It is here that Spivak discusses "critical intimacy" as one of the primary ethicopolitical tools available in reading practices.

6. In *Politics and the Other Scene*, trans. Daniel Hahn (London: Verso, 2002), Etienne Balibar discusses the concept of desubjectivation as I am using it, to mean the undoing of an idea of subjecthood closed to alterity and always functioning toward self-preservation. The possibility of a new kind of subjectivity is therefore proposed.

7. Xenia refers to the law of hospitality to strangers that is so fundamental to Greek literature, particularly Homer's *Odyssey*. Its root (*ghos-ti*) is also that of the Latin *hostis* (enemy), from which we also get guest, hotel, host, and hospitality.

8. Jacques Derrida, *Of Hospitality*, trans. Rachel Bowlby (Stanford, CA: Stanford University Press, 2000), 142–3.

9. Cixous, "Albums and Legends," 189.

10. Quoted from Jacques Derrida, *Glas*, trans. John P. Leavey and Richard Rand (Lincoln and London: University of Nebraska Press, 1986; originally published Paris: Editions Galilée, 1974), 109. Leavey and Rand translate *dégâts* as "havoc"

rather than as "damage" (Derrida, *Glas*, 94). I prefer Bennington and McLeod's rendition in the translation given in Derrida's *The Truth in Painting*, trans. Geoff Bennington and Ian McLeod (Chicago: University of Chicago Press, 1987).

11. I am obliquely referencing the line from Shakespeare's *Hamlet*, "The time is out of joint" (Act 1, Scene 5, l.188). The reference is made through a reading of Derrida's *Specters of Marx: The State of the Debt, the Work of Mourning, and the New International*, trans. Peggy Kamuf (London and New York: Routledge, 1994). In this text, Derrida extends Hamlet's musing about a temporal notion of a political remainder. Hamlet refers to the political disarray in the state of Denmark, to which the ghost of his father bears witness, and demands that justice be done. Derrida refers to how the figure of Marx is the remainder of the current political climate of late-capitalist globalization. Like Hamlet's ghost, absent and yet uncannily corporeal, Marx's ghost demands justice. This is both a commentary on the past and present exploitative techniques of global capital (literally, the remainder are those figures left out of receiving a slice of the pie) and an ethical demand made on the future. As long as capitalist exploitation remains encrypted within the framework of capitalism, the ghost of Marx demands responsibility.

12. Derrida, *Of Hospitality*, 77.

13. While some find Derrida's more recent engagement with the ethics of Emmanuel Levinas to be somewhat disturbing in its religious and metaphysical overtones, I find a continuity between the early work on Levinas in Jacques Derrida, "Violence and Metaphysics," in *Writing and Difference*, trans. Alan Bass (Chicago: University of Chicago Press, 1978), 79–153; and the work implicated in theories of the messianic. Derrida's engagement with such concepts as ethico-political as well as justice rather than the ethical as something to be embraced mark the insistence of the trace always interrupting the frame of religious and philosophical ethical paradigms. Geoffrey Bennington's *Interrupting Derrida* (London and New York: Routledge, 2000) includes a very useful chapter on deconstruction and ethics that lays out the continuities in Derrida's thought.

14. Jonathan Culler, *Framing the Sign: Criticism and Its Institutions* (Oxford: Basil Blackwell, 1988).

15. The *Oxford English Dictionary* (OED) gives a 1632 definition of frame as "upbringing," taken from William Lithgow. "Thou Tharsus, Brookes a Glorious Name, For That Great Saint, Who in Thee Had His Frame," in *The Totall Discourse of the Rare Adventures and Painefull Peregrinations of Long Nineteen Yeares Travayles* (Glasgow, Scotland: J. MacLehose, 1906; originally published 1632), 182v.

16. Gregory Bateson, *Steps to an Ecology of Mind* (London: Paladin, 1973).

17. Erving Goffman, *Frame Analysis* (Cambridge, MA: Harvard University Press, 1974), 10.

18. Goffman discusses various forms of "breaking frame" in his chapter with that title. Goffman, *Frame Analysis*, 345–377.

19. Theodor Adorno, *Minima Moralia: Reflections from Damaged Life*, trans. E.F.N. Jephcott (London: New Left Books, 1974).

20. See Kaja Silverman, *The Acoustic Mirror: The Female Voice in Psychoanalysis and Cinema* (Bloomington: Indiana University Press, 1988).

21. The importance of the different time frame was also central to Goffman's *Frame Analysis*. Barthes' attachment to the punctum is demonstrated through the fact that he does not reproduce the image he discusses most extensively in *Camera Lucida*, Van der See's "Winter Garden" photograph. Because the experience of the punctum is nonreproducible, the reproduction of what Barthes says is an unremarkable photograph would be pointless. For Barthes, this respect for the punctum is associated with the death of the mother. (The book was written following her death and was Barthes' last published text. There is always the sense that the punctum involves a kind of haunting presence of the mother, a presence that cannot be subsumed into any existing paradigm of knowledge.)

22. Carol Mavor drew my attention to this categorization of nostalgia as a subdivision of melancholy. On nostalgia as an illness and on its transformation from a bodily to a psychical condition, see David Lowenthal, *The Past Is a Foreign Country* (Cambridge: Cambridge University Press, 1985); "Nostalgia Tells It Like It Wasn't," in *The Imagined Past: History and Nostalgia*, eds. Christopher Shaw and Malcolm Chase (Manchester, UK: Manchester University Press, 1983); Suzanne Vromen, "The Ambiguity of Nostalgia," *YIVO Annual*, 21 (1983), 69–86; Leo Spitzer, "Back Through the Future: Nostalgic Memory and Critical Memory in a Refuge from Nazism," in *Acts of Memory: Cultural Recall in the Present*, eds. Mieke Bal, Jonathan Crewe, and Leo Spitzer (Lebanon, NH: Dartmouth College Press, University Press of New England, 1999), 87–104.

23. Derrida, *Truth in Painting*, 88–89.

24. There is some question as to the meaning of frame in this context. Furnivall is inconclusive about its meaning, but he glosses the term with reference to freme, meaning "profit" or "advantage" (p. 132). The OED, however, directly citing "A Song Called Þhe Deueilis Perlament, Or Parlamentum of Feendis," suggests that it means a "warlike array, or host." "A Song Called Þhe Deueilis Perlament, Or Parlamentum of Feendis," Lambeth Ms. 853, ab. 1430 A.D., pp. 157–182. Reprinted in *Hymns to the Virgin and Christ, the Parliament of Devils, and Other Religious Poems*, ed. Frederick J. Furnivall (London: Kegan Paul and Trench, Trübner, & Co., 1867/1895), lines 97–8.

25. "A Song Called Þhe Deueilis Perlament," lines 236–40.

26. The terms parasitic and symbiotic derive from host animals and the manner in which they sustain others.

27. Karl Marx, *Capital*, Vol. 1, trans. Ben Fowkes (New York: Vintage, 1977), 711–24, 781–94.

28. In *The Antichrist*, Nietzsche proposes that Christ died not for "our sins" but, in fact, because of his politics—he was an enemy of the state. He died, there-

fore, because of his political views, which threatened the status quo with foreign ideas; in other words, he died as a political prisoner. "This man was certainly a political criminal, at least in so far as it was possible to be one in so absurdly unpolitical a community. This is what brought him to the cross. . . ." Friedrich Nietzsche, *The Antichrist*, trans. H. L. Mencken (Tucson, AZ: See Sharp Press, 1999; originally published 1895), 45.

29. Derrida, *Of Hospitality*, 77.

30. Derrida, *Of Hospitality*, 77.

31. Luce Irigaray's "The Gesture in Psychoanalysis" is once again useful here, although I am bothered by the absolutism of sexual difference in this essay, preferring the more material understanding of women's difference apparent in her other works.

32. Giorgio Agamben, *The Coming Community*, trans. Michael Hardt (Minneapolis: University of Minnesota Press, 1993), iii.

33. Jacques Derrida, *Monolingualism of the Other, or The Prosthesis of Origin*, trans. Patrick Mensah (Stanford, CA: Stanford University Press, 1998), 56.

34. Derrida, *Of Hospitality*, 141, 137.

35. Geoff Bennington and Jacques Derrida, *Jacques Derrida*, trans. Geoff Bennington (Chicago: University of Chicago Press, 1993), 5.

36. Bennington and Derrida, *Jacques Derrida*, 39.

37. The delay mechanism is a feature of photography, of course, in the sense that it is always observed after the fact even as it stages the event as a moment captured. Barthes discovers a childhood photograph of his dead mother:

I had discovered this photograph by moving back through Time. . . . Starting from her latest image, taken the summer before her death (so tired, so noble, sitting in front of the door of our house, surrounded by my friends), I arrived, traversing three quarters of a century, at the image of a child: I stare intensely at the Sovereign Good of childhood, of the mother, of the mother-as-child. Of course I was then losing her twice over, in her final fatigue and in her first photograph, for me the last; but it was also at this moment that everything turned around and I discovered her as *into herself*. . . . (Barthes, *Camera Lucida*, 71)

38. Bennington and Derrida, *Jacques Derrida*, 39.

39. The back-formation and the prefix are of course very different grammatical entities. The back-formation is a process through which a suffix is removed from the end of a word to make a new word. For example, the verb to enthuse is derived from the noun "enthusiasm," but partly because the back-formation is shorter, it appears incorrectly to be the original form or stem. Similarly, the term pea derives from pease (singular), and peasen (plural). As the OED explains, once peasen was reduced to pease (plural), the singular and the plural became identical. Because the pronunciation of pease was close to peas, the final sibilant, the s, was eventually understood as the plural, thus resulting in the singular pea. The prefix is an addition at the beginning of the word, whereas the back-formation is the result of

a subtraction of the suffix. On a more conceptual level, the back-formation can be seen as the basis of the concept of use-value, something both inside and outside the system of capital once value becomes the dominant logic. See Gayatri Chakravorty Spivak, "Scattered Speculations on the Question of Value," in *In Other Worlds* (London and New York: Methuen, 1987), 154–75; and Gayatri Chakravorty Spivak, "Ghostwriting," *Diacritics* 25:2 (1995), 65–84.

40. Hélène Cixous, "My Algeriance, in Other Words: To Depart Not to Arrive from Algeria," in *Stigmata: Escaping Texts* (London and New York: Routledge, 1998), 163.

41. Cixous writes quite extensively of the arbitrariness of borders, and of how they afford and foreclose possibilities. Her grandmother, once a German war widow, became a French war widow when Alsace changed hands. This allowed her to leave Nazi Germany to live in France. Her father's ancestors, once Algerians, became French and then, along with other Jews in Algeria, lost citizenship. Cixous, "Albums and Legends," 188–89.

42. Jacques Derrida, "Interview with Derrida, from Le Nouvel Observateur," in *Derrida and Difference*, eds. David Wood and Robert Bernasconi (Coventry, UK: Parousia Press, 1985), 111.

43. Derrida, *Monolingualism of the Other*, 67–69; see also Jacques Derrida, "Force of Law," in *Acts of Religion*, ed. Gil Anidjar (London and New York: Routledge, 2002), 228–98.

44. Derrida, *Monolingualism of the Other*, 13.

45. Cixous, "My Algeriance," 171.

46. Cixous, "Albums and Legends," 189.

47. Derrida, *Of Hospitality*, 91.

48. While I ultimately disagree with Slavoj Žižek's structuralist Lacanianism and his reduction of all loss to structural lack, his essay, "Melancholy and the Act" is useful in clarifying the melancholic's inability to know what has been lost. Slavoj Žižek, "Melancholy and the Act," *Critical Inquiry* 26:4 (2000), 657.

49. Butler departs from Irigaray's reading of Antigone as exemplary of feminist antistatism. Luce Irigaray, *Speculum of the Other Woman*, trans. Gillian Gill (Ithaca, NY: Cornell University Press, 1985), 70. Butler poses the important question, "Can Antigone herself be made representative for a certain kind of feminist politics, if Antigone's own representative function is itself in crisis? . . . as a figure for politics, she points somewhere else, not to politics as a question of representation but to that political possibility that emerges when the limits to representation and representability are exposed." Judith Butler, *Antigone's Claims: Kinship Between Life and Death* (New York: Columbia University Press, 2000), 2. I am very sympathetic to Butler's intervention here, yet I wonder why the example of Antigone persists in returning when the issue of exemplarity is being problematized.

50. Spivak, *Critique of Postcolonial Reason*, 430.

51. G.W.F. Hegel, *The Phenomenology of Spirit*, trans. A. V. Miller (London:

Oxford University Press, 1977); Jacques Lacan, *The Seminar of Jacques Lacan, Book VII: The Ethics of Psychoanalysis, 1959–1960*, trans. Dennis Porter (New York: Norton, 1992), 243–90; George Steiner, *Antigones: The Antigone Myth in Western Literature, Art and Thought* (Oxford: Oxford University Press, 1984); Nicole Loraux, *Mothers in Mourning*, trans Corinne Pache (Ithaca, NY: Cornell University Press, 1998); Jan Patočka, *L'Ecrivain, son "objet"* (Paris: P.O.L., 1990).

52. The nonhuman, monstrous, and prehuman of course played a part in the ancient Greek imagery in the form of, for example, centaurs, cyclops, and amazons. Kirsti Simonsuuri, in a keynote address to the Nordic Summer University in August 2001, discussed these mythical figures as liminal, creating alternative boundaries, often violating hospitality, and representing frightening otherness.

53. Lisa Cartwright and Brian Goldfarb, "The Condition of Disablement and Virtual Ability in Digital Culture," unpublished seminar paper presented to the Society for the Humanities, Cornell University, October 21, 1998.

54. Mahasweta Devi, "Pterodactyl, Pirtha, and Puran Sahay," in *Imaginary Maps*, trans. Gayatri Chakravorty Spivak (London and New York: Routledge, 1994), 95–196.

55. Spivak, *A Critique of Postcolonial Reason*, 142–48.

56. Robert Young, "Derrida and the Postcolonial," in *Deconstruction: A User's Guide*, ed. Nicholas Royle (Basingstoke, UK: Palgrove, 2000), 198–99; also in *Postcolonialism* (Oxford: Blackwell, 2001), 411–26. See also Jacques Derrida, "White Mythologies," *Margins of Philosophy*, trans. Alan Bass (Brighton, Sussex, UK: Harvester Press, 1986), 207–71; Robert Young, *White Mythologies: Writing History and the West* (London and New York: Routledge, 1990).

57. Mustapha Marrouchi, "Decolonizing the Terrain of Western Theoretical Productions," *College Literature* 24:2 (1997), 5.

58. Marrouchi, "Decolonizing the Terrain," 5, 6.

59. Derrida, *Monolingualism of the Other*, 14.

60. Derrida, *Monolingualism of the Other*, 55. The work of Jean-Luc Nancy comes to mind here. The inoperative community is a community of unworking and undoing. It does not, for example, come together through identification other than to disidentify immediately. Neither does the community come together through community archive, or what Vamik Volkan would call a "chosen trauma." See Vamik Volkan, "Ethnicity and Nationalism: A Psychoanalytic Perspective," *Applied Psychology: An International Review* 47:1 (1998), 45–57. Such formations carry the supplements of their own undoing within them. The community may exist momentarily in an event, but will fall apart as soon as there is an attempt to narrativize that event. See Jean-Luc Nancy, *The Inoperative Community*, trans. Peter Connor, Lisa Garbus, Michael Holland, and Simona Sawhney (Minneapolis and Oxford, UK: University of Minnesota Press, 1991).

61. Derrida, *Monolingualism of the Other*, 61.

62. Derrida, *Monolingualism of the Other*, 61.

63. Cixous, "My Algeriance," 170.
64. Agamben, *The Coming Community*, iii.
65. Derrida, "Taking a Stand for Algeria," 22.
66. Derrida, *The Truth in Painting*, 69; Deborah Cherry, *Beyond the Frame* (London and New York: Routledge, 2000), 99.
67. "The paradox of this passport: having it always closed me in a double-bind. On the one hand, "I am French" is a lie or a legal fiction. On the other, to say "I am not French" is a breach of courtesy. And of the gratitude due for hospitality. The stormy, intermittent hospitality of the State and the Nation. But the infinite hospitality of the language." Hélène Cixous, "My Algeriance," 154.
68. Azzedine Haddour, *Colonial Myths: History and Narrative* (Manchester, UK, and New York: Manchester University Press, 2000).
69. I have discussed this more extensively in Ranjana Khanna, *Dark Continents: Psychoanalysis and Colonialism* (Durham, NC: Duke University Press, 2003).
70. Antoine Porot and Charles Bardenat, *Anormaux at Malades Mentaux devant la justice pénale* [Abnormality and Mental Health in the Penal System] (Paris: Librairie Maloine, 1960), 15.
71. Sigmund Freud, "Mourning and Melancholia," 1917, reprinted in Sigmund Freud, *The Standard Edition of the Complete Psychological Works of Sigmund Freud*, 24 vols., trans. and ed. James Strachey (London: Hogarth Press and Institute of Psychoanalysis, 1953–74), Vol. 14, 237–60.
72. Ellen T. Armour, "Crossing the Boundaries Between Feminism, Deconstruction, and Religion," in *Feminist Interpretations of Jacques Derrida*, ed. Nancy Holland (Philadelphia: University of Pennsylvania Press, 1997), 198–200.

CHAPTER 2: THE EXPERIENCE OF EVIDENCE

1. Jacques Derrida, "Passages—From Traumatism to Promise," in *Points—Interviews 1974–1994*, ed. Elisabeth Weber, trans. Peggy Kamuf and others (Stanford, CA: Stanford University Press, 1995), 178.
2. Émile Zola, "J'accuse," *L'Aurore*, January 13, 1898; reprinted in Richard Sennett, *The Fall of Public Man* (New York: Knopf, 1974), 365; and in *Trial of Émile Zola* (New York: Benjamin R. Tucker, 1898), 3–14.
3. The RAFD has brought many cases against the FIS. Famously, it brought one against Anwar Haddam as he sought asylum in the United States. See *U.S. District Court for the District of Columbia, Jane Doe et al., Plaintiffs, v. Islamic Salvation Front et al., Defendants*, Civil Action No. 96–2792 (JR). See http://www.ccr-ny.org/v2/legal/human_rights/rightsArticle.asp?ObjID=azJDoFknPA&Content=59
4. In France, part of the trial was shown on news programs, and Reuters released a news story entitled "Widowed and Raped: Algeria's Women 'Try' Islamists," by Abdelaziz Barrouhi (Tunis, March 8, 1995), that later circulated on the Web, protecting the names of the women involved. See also "Algérie: Journée

de la Femme" [Algeria: Women's Day], TF1 20 heures: émission du 8 Mars 1995) [Broadcast of 8 P.M., March 1995].

5. Algerian journalist Mohamed Benmohammed conducted interviews with women who described how they had been raped and violated by Islamists.

6. See, for example, the comments of the "Collectif des familles de disparus en Algérie" [Collective of Families of the Disappeared in Algeria], Amnesty International news release, July 9, 1998, http://www.amnesty.org//news/1998/19jul98.htm

7. What constitutes classical Arabic is questionable. Some use the term interchangeably with Koranic Arabic, some with the language of classical Arabic poetry, and some even with modern literary Arabic, which is distinguished from Modern Standard Arabic. While there is no doubt that Arabic in some forms is an international language, even the apparently standardized terms (like classical) lead to some confusion.

8. *Le Monde* has recently published letters written by victims of and witnesses to the atrocities in Algeria in a collection assembled by Philippe Bernard and Nathaniel Herzberg, *Le Monde Lettres d'Algérie* [*Le Monde*. Algerian Letters] (Paris: Editions Gallimard, 1998). It is interesting to read these letters against testimonies of women from the Algerian war of independence. See, for example, Djamila Amrane, *Des femmes dans la guerre d'Algérie: Entretiens* [Women in the Algerian War: Interviews] (Paris: Karthala, 1994).

9. I acknowledge that the terms *terrorism* and *torture* are loaded with racist connotations in English and French because of their use by the English and French language press to discuss the activities of groups outside the United States and Western Europe, largely in North Africa and the Middle East. For more on this subject I refer readers to the works of Edward Said, Noam Chomsky, and Edward Herman, who have discussed this important issue extensively. I would, however, contend that while the terms are used in a derogatory manner to discuss particular peoples and regional and religious conflicts, it is important to maintain that some acts are terrorist, and some constitute war crimes and torture that should not be permitted by the international community. (One could extend this to a general pacifist argument, but here is not the place to do that.) My point here is, however, in the vein of critique of First Worldist assumptions about the nature of violence in the postnuclear period that will be addressed later in the chapter. Out of the many works of Said, Chomsky, and Herman on this issue, I suggest Edward Said, *Covering Islam* (New York: Pantheon Books, 1981); Noam Chomsky, *Pirates and Emperors: International Terrorism in the Real World* (New York: Claremont University Press, 1986); Noam Chomsky, *The Culture of Terrorism* (Boston: South End Press, 1988); and Edward Herman, *The Real Terror Network: Terrorism in Fact and Propaganda* (Boston: South End Press, 1982). In addition, the term jihad is frequently used in the non-Muslim press to denote all sorts of political struggles that are homogenized misleadingly as an Islamic holy war (see Said, *Covering Islam*, 107–8). However, in this instance my point

is that for political reasons Islamists in Algeria have suggested continuity in the political battle from the decolonization movement to the current civil war, and have identified this as a holy war, thus conflating politics and religion, and (as we shall see later) state law (whether the *Shar'ia* or not) with holy law (as in religious salvation).

10. See Benamar Mediene, "Aujourd'hui l'Algérie: Crise Sociale ou Crise du Sens" [Algeria Today: Social Crisis or Crisis of the Way Forward], paper delivered at "Algeria In and Out of French: A Conference on Politics and Culture in Post-Colonial Algeria," Cornell University, October 1996.

11. See "Women Living Under Muslim Laws: When Women's Human Rights Defenders Face Political Non-State Actors," available at http://www.wluml.org/english/newsfulltxt.shtml?cmd%5B157%5D=x-157-536788

12. See, for example, the letter from the parliamentary delegation of the FIS circulated on the Web on March 17, 1995: "The FIS Parliamentary Delegation reiterates its commitment to the Rome Accord (the National Contract) which condemns and calls for an end to attacks against innocent civilians and the destruction of public properties. We insist on the Accord's call for an independent Commission of Inquiry to investigate those acts as well as all other violations of human rights," The FIS insists on an independent inquiry that has also been urged by Amnesty International in order to determine whether the source of much of the violence is the state and the military or indeed Islamists. See Amnesty International's persistent call for such an inquiry at http://www.amnesty.org. For a persuasive argument that questions the ethics of outlawing the FIS given its protest against violence, see John Entelis, "Political Islam in the Maghreb: The Non-Violent Dimension," in *Islam, Democracy and the State in North Africa*, ed. John Entelis (Bloomington and Indianapolis: Indiana University Press, 1997), 43–74.

13. Many have discussed the institution of the Family Code and Arabization in terms of the FLN's concession to more conservative wings of the government. The selection of articles in John Entelis and Philip Naylor, *State and Society in Algeria* (Boulder: Westview Press, 1992), is strong on this issue.

14. For an analysis of the Family Code that situates it within Algerian politics more generally, see Marnia Lazreg, *The Eloquence of Silence* (London and New York: Routledge, 1994); Peter Knauss, "Algerian Women Since Independence," in *State and Society in Algeria*, eds. John Entelis and Philip Naylor (Boulder: Westview Press, 1992), 151–70; and Boutheina Cheriet, "Islam and Feminism: Algeria's 'Rites of Passage' to Democracy," in *State and Society in Algeria*, 171–216.

15. See the television broadcast "Algérie: Femmes Victimes Terrorisme," *F2 le journal 20 Hoo: émission du 25 février 1997* [Algeria: Women, Victims, Terrorism].

16. Benjamin Stora, "Deuxième Guerre Algérienne? Les habits anciens des combattants" [Second Algerian War? Old Robes of Combatants], *Les Temps Modernes*, 580 (1995), 258.

17. For useful explanation of the relationship between the GIA and the many strands of the FIS, see John Entelis, "Political Islam in the Maghreb."

18. Simone de Beauvoir and Gisèle Halimi, *Djamila Boupacha* (Paris: Gallimard, 1962); *Djamila Boupacha: The Story of the Torture of a Young Algerian Girl Which Shocked Liberal Opinion*, trans. Peter Green (London: André Deutsch and Weidenfeld and Nicolson: 1962). Citations are from the English translation.

19. Such destruction of memory in violence in some postcolonial African nations (though not in Algeria) has recently received treatment in *Memory and the Postcolony: African Anthropology and the Critique of Power*, ed. Richard Werbner (London and New York: Zed Books, 1998).

20. Gisèle Halimi was condemned by the French Federation of the FLN in spite of working on behalf of Algerians during the war for eight years. See Gisèle Halimi, *Milk for the Orange Tree*, trans. Dorothy Blair (London: Quartet Books, 1990), 300–301. Following the kidnapping of Djamila Boupacha, who was with Halimi, by the FLN, a communiqué was circulated in Tunis and reproduced in *Le Monde* denouncing "the publicity operation attempted for her own personal ends by the lawyer Gisèle Halimi, in connection with our sister Djamila Boupacha" (*Le Monde*, May 3, 1962).

21. See, for example, Marie-Aimée Hélie-Lucas, "Bound and Gagged by the Family Code," in *Third World Second Sex*, Vol. 2, ed. Miranda Davies (London and New Jersey: Zed Books, 1987).

22. Alek Baylee has recently written a play in which Sartre and de Beauvoir return from the dead to participate in the burial of an assasinated writer. They are effectively kidnpped by the GIA. Baylee invokes the ghosts of the past in order to imagine the possibilities of intellectual argument with the GIA that has been responsible for the slaughter of so many. See Alek Baylee, "Madah Sartre," *Algérie Littérature/Action*, 6 (1996), 5–103.

23. See, for example, Amilcar Cabral, *National Liberation and Culture*, trans. Maureen Webster (Syracuse, NY: Syracuse University, 1970).

24. See Gisèle Halimi, "La libération pour tous. . . . sauf pour elles?" [Liberation for All Except the Women?], *Nouvel Observateur*, July 10, 1978. See also Anne Lippert, "Algerian Women's Access to Power: 1962–1985," in *Studies in Power and Class in Africa*, ed. Irving Leonard Markovitz (Oxford and New York: Oxford University Press, 1987), 209–32.

25. This would of course run counter to the argument of Richard Sennett in *The Fall of Public Man*.

26. Even before that time, the Ministries of Justice and Religious Affairs conducted their business largely in modern literary Arabic, which gave rise to some tension between the state and some of the elite communities (within the state apparatus and outside of it). See John Entelis, "Elite Political Culture and Socialisation in Algeria: Tensions and Discontinuities," *Middle East Journal* 35:2 (1981), 191–208.

27. Numerous texts on the language problem have emerged recently. See, for example, *Esprit*, 208 (1995), entire issue. These are reprinted in Mohamed Benrabah and others, *Les violences en Algérie* [Violence in Algeria] (Paris: Éditions Odile Jacob, 1998), along with some additional essays. See also *Parallax*, 7 (1998), entire issue; and Martin Stone, *The Agony of Algeria* (New York: Columbia University Press, 1997).

28. Entelis, "Elite Political Culture and Socialisation in Algeria," 196.

29. There are many studies of British colonial policy in India. Gauri Viswanathan's *Masks of Conquest* (New York: Columbia University Press, 1989) and Sara Suleri's *The Rhetoric of British India* (Chicago: Chicago University Press, 1992) are instructive.

30. See Raymond Betts, *Assimilation and Association in French Colonial Theory, 1899–1914* (New York and London: Columbia University Press, 1961); and Charles-Robert Ageron, *Modern Algeria: A History from 1830 to the Present*, trans. Michael Bret (London: Hurst, 1991; originally published 1964).

31. See, for example, Marnia Lazreg, *The Eloquence of Silence* (London and New York: Routledge, 1994).

32. See Lazreg, *Eloquence of Silence*, and Cabral, *National Liberation and Culture*, for more on this subject.

33. For a commentary on the problems for women afforded by the system in postcolonial India, see Rajeswari Sunder Rajan's work on the Shahbano case in *Real and Imagined Women: Gender, Culture and Postcolonialism* (London and New York: Routledge, 1993).

34. See Allan Christelow, *Muslim Law Courts and the French Colonial State in Algeria* (Princeton, NJ: Princeton University Press, 1985), 8–9.

35. For a recent consideration of the notion of the mother tongue in the Algerian Jewish context, see Jacques Derrida, *Monolingualism of the Other, or the Prosthesis of Origin*, trans. Patrick Mensah (Stanford: Stanford University Press, 1998), or in French, *Monolinguisme de l'autre: ou la prothèse de l'origine* (Paris: Editions Galilée, 1996). For a consideration of bilingualism in the Maghrebi context, see Abdelkebir Khatibi, *Love in Two Languages*, trans. Richard Howard (Minneapolis: University of Minnesota Press, 1990), or in French, *Amour Bilingue* (Montpellier, France: Editions Fata Morgana, 1983).

36. For an alternative interesting reading of the trial, see Julien Murphy, "Beauvoir and the Algerian War: Toward a Postcolonial Ethics," in *Feminist Interpretations of Simone de Beauvoir*, ed. Margaret A. Simons (University Park: Pennsylvania State University Press, 1995), 263–97.

37. See also William Bourdon, "Amnesty," in *Crimes of War: What the Public Should Know*, ed. Roy Gutman and David Rieff (London: W. W. Norton, 1999), available at http://www.crimesofwar.org/thebook/amnesty.html

38. De Beauvoir and Halimi, *Djamila Boupacha*, 7.

39. Simone de Beauvoir, *A Transatlantic Love Affair: Letters to Nelson Algren*

(London: Norton, 1998). For a review that reads these in relation to Algeria, see Claude Gonfond-Talahite, "Simone de Beauvoir et l'Algérie," *Algérie Littérature/Action* 17 (1998), 143–46.

40. Simone de Beauvoir, *Force of Circumstance* (Harmondsworth, UK: Penguin, 1965), 382; *La force des choses* (Paris: Gallimard, 1963).

41. De Beauvoir, *Force of Circumstance*, 200.

42. See Albert Camus, *Actuelles III: Chronique Algérienne 1939–1958* [Algerian Chronicle 1939–1958] (Paris: Gallimard, 1953). Citations from these writings are taken from translations in Albert Camus, *Resistance, Rebellion and Death: Essays*, trans. Justin O'Brien (New York: Vintage, 1960). See in particular, "Algeria: Preface to Algerian Reports," 111–30.

43. See Frantz Fanon, *Studies in a Dying Colonialism*, trans. Haakon Chevalier (London: Earthscan, 1965), 121–47; *L'An cinq de la Révolution Algérienne* (Paris: François Maspero, 1959). See also de Beauvoir and Halimi, *Djamila Boupacha*.

44. De Beauvoir, *Force of Circumstance*, 515–16.

45. De Beauvoir and Halimi, *Djamila Boupacha*, 14.

46. De Beauvoir, *Force of Circumstance*, 379.

47. Jean Paul Sartre, "Introduction," in Henri Alleg, *The Question* (New York: George Brazilier, 1958), 31–32.

48. De Beauvoir, *Force of Circumstance*, 392.

49. De Beauvoir, *Force of Circumstance*, 393.

50. De Beauvoir and Halimi, *Djamila Boupacha*, 197.

51. De Beauvoir and Halimi, *Djamila Boupacha*, 197.

52. De Beauvoir and Halimi, *Djamila Boupacha*, 195.

53. De Beauvoir and Halimi, *Djamila Boupacha*, 191.

54. *Le Monde* was thought to be largely sympathetic to the Algerians' cause. For arguments that both support and contend with this claim, see *Cahiers de l'IHTP* [Notes of the IHTP] 10 (1988); Pierre Vidal-Naquet, "Une fidelité têtue: la résistance française à la guerre d'Algérie" [A Stubborn Faithfulness: The French Resistance in the Algerian War], *Vingtième Siècle* (April–June 1986), 3–18; Mohammed Khane, "*Le Monde* and the Algerian War During the Fourth Republic," in *French and Algerian Identities from Colonial Times to the Present*, eds. Alec Hargreaves and Michael Heffernan (Lewiston, NY: Edwin Mellen Press, 1993), 129–48.

55. Elaine Scarry, *The Body in Pain: The Making and Unmaking of the World* (Oxford, UK: Oxford University Press, 1985).

56. Jean-Paul Sartre, *On Genocide* (Boston: Beacon Press, 1968), 65; also in *Prevent the Crime of Silence: Reports from the Sessions of the International War Crimes Tribunal Founded by Bertrand Russell—London, Stockholm, Roskilde*, ed. Peter Limqueco and Peter Weiss (London: Allen Lane, Penguin Press, 1971), 350–64.

57. Scarry, *Body in Pain*, 7.

58. See Rita Maran, *Torture: The Role of Ideology in the French-Algerian War*

(New York: Praeger, 1989), 163. See also Albert Camus, "Algeria: Appeal for a Civilian Truce," in *Resistance, Rebellion and Death: Essays*.

59. Jean-Paul Sartre, "Introduction," in Henri Alleg, *The Question*, 14–15. Rita Maran offers an important analysis of the human rights issues involved in torture in the Algerian War in her book *Torture*.

60. The phrase *the eloquence of silence* comes from Marnia Lazreg's book of that title, *Eloquence of Silence*.

61. De Beauvoir and Halimi, *Djamila Boupacha*, 81.

62. Over the past few years many books on the subject of trauma studies, most of which are concerned specifically with the Holocaust, have emerged. For good representations of the field, see Shoshana Felman and Dori Laub, *Testimony: Crises of Witnessing in Literature, Psychoanalysis, and History* (London and New York: Routledge, 1992); and Cathy Caruth, *Unclaimed Experience: Trauma, Narrative, and History* (Baltimore: Johns Hopkins University Press, 1996).

63. De Beauvoir and Halimi, *Djamila Boupacha*, 10.

64. De Beauvoir and Halimi, *Djamila Boupacha*, 75.

65. See De Beauvoir and Halimi, *Djamila Boupacha*, 84.

66. Scarry, *Body in Pain*, 10.

67. De Beauvoir and Halimi, *Djamila Boupacha*, 194.

68. De Beauvoir and Halimi, *Djamila Boupacha*, 197.

69. Sartre, "Introduction," in Alleg, *The Question*, 23.

70. Nicolas Abraham and Maria Torok, *The Shell and the Kernel*, ed. and trans. Nicholas T. Rand (Chicago: University of Chicago Press, 1994), 127.

71. This issue of masculinist violence has of course been recently discussed extensively in relation to rapes in the former Yugoslavia, as has how to assess these as war crimes. See Catherine N. Niarchos, "Women, War, and Rape: Challenges Facing the International Tribunal for the Former Yugoslavia," *Human Rights Quarterly* 17 (1995), 649–90; and Liz Philipose, "The Laws of War and Women's Human Rights," *Hypatia* 11:4 (1996), 46–62.

72. Limqueco and Weiss, *Prevent the Crime of Silence*.

73. Jean-Marc Théolleyre, *Juger en Algérie 1944–1962* [Judging in Algeria 1944-1962] (Paris: Seuil, 1997).

74. Camus, "Algeria: Preface to Algerian Reports," 120.

75. Camus, "Algeria: Preface to Algerian Reports," 120–21.

76. Sartre, *On Genocide*, 65.

77. Camus, "Algeria: Preface to Algerian Reports," 112.

78. Jean-Paul Sartre, *What is Literature?* trans. David Fretchman (Bristol, MA: Methuen, 1967); *Qu'est-ce que la littérature?* (Paris: Gallimard, 1948).

79. Jean-Paul Sartre, *Black Orpheus*, trans. S. W. Allen (Paris: Présence Africaine, 1976); "Orphée Noir," Preface to *L'Anthologie de la nouvelle poésie nègre et malgache de langue française* [Anthology of New Black and Malagasy Poetry], ed. Léopold Sédar Senghor (Paris: Presses Universitaires de France, 1948).

80. Camus, "Algeria: Preface to Algerian Reports," 124.

81. Abraham and Torok, in their rereading of Freud's "Mourning and Melancholia" in light of Sandor Ferenczi's distinction between introjection and incorporation, draw on Ferenczi's account of introjection as a normal part of psychic growth through assimilation; mourning, then, can be understood as a function of growth. In melancholia, on the other hand, what takes place is "incorporation," that is, the blocking of introjection and consequently unsuccessful assimilation. Here narcissism is pathological. The lost object becomes a constant point of reference, but the relationship to it as a separate entity is always fraught with identification. The terms are elaborated upon in *The Shell and the Kernel*, 125–38.

82. For another commentary on mock trials in postcolonial literatures, see Gary Boire, "Tribunalations: George Ryga's Postcolonial Trial 'Play,'" *Ariel* 22:2 (1991), 5–20.

83. As in Gilles Deleuze's *Difference and Repetition*, trans. Paul Patton (New York: Columbia University Press, 1994); *Différence et Repetition* (Paris: Presses Universitaires de France, 1968).

84. Ernest Renan, "What Is a Nation?" lecture delivered at the Sorbonne, 1882, reprinted in Homi K. Bhabha, *Nation and Narration* (London and New York: Routledge, 1990), 8–22.

85. Cabral, *National Liberation and Culture*.

CHAPTER 3: *The Battle of Algiers* AND *The Nouba of the Women*

1. Frantz Fanon, "Algeria Unveiled," in *Studies in a Dying Colonialism*, trans. Haakon Chevalier (London: Earthscan, 1989; originally published 1959), 59.

2. Emmanuel Levinas, "The Transcendence of Words," in *The Emmanuel Levinas Reader*, ed. Sean Hand (London: Blackwell, 1989), 147.

3. Peter Brunette and David Wills, *Screen/Play: Derrida and Film Theory* (Princeton, NJ: Princeton University Press, 1989), 85–86.

4. Fernando Solanas and Octavio Gettino, "Towards a Third Cinema," *Afterimage* 3 (1971), 16–35.

5. Doris Sommer, "No Secrets: Rigoberta's Guarded Truth," *Women's Studies* 20 (1991), 51–72. Sommer's description of testimonio, testimonial literature, with all the trauma, collective consciousness, and fictionality that it implies, is useful in conceptualizing the cinema of protest such as *The Battle of Algiers*.

6. For an overview of the birth and development of Algerian cinema, see Rachid Boudjedra, *Naissance du cinéma algérien* [Birth of Algerian Cinema] (Paris: Maspero, 1971); *The Cinema in Algeria: Film Production 1957–73* (Algiers: Ministry of Information, 1973); Hala Salmane, Simon Hartog, and David Wilson, *Algerian Cinema* (London: British Film Industry, 1976); Wassalya Tamlazi, *En attendant Omar Gatlato* [Waiting for Omar Gatlato] (Algiers: Editions A.P., 1979); Younès Dadci, *Première Histoire du cinéma algérien, 1895–1979* [First History of Algerian

Cinema, 1895–1979] (Paris: Dadci, 1980); Maryse Léon, "La femme dans le cinéma algérien" [Woman in Algerian Cinema], unpublished dissertation (Paris: Ecole des hautes Etudes en sciences sociales, 1980); Lofti Maherzi, *Le cinéma algérien* [Algerian Cinema] (Algiers: Editions SNED, 1980); Abdelghani Megherbi, *Les Algériens au miroir du cinéma colonial* [Algerians in the Mirror of Colonial Cinema] (Algiers: Editions SNED, 1982); Abdelghani Megherbi, *Le miroir aux alouettes: l'Empire des rêves* [The Lark Mirror: Empire of Dreams] (Brussels and Algiers: ENAL/UPU/GAM, 1985); Abderrezak Hellal, *Image d'une révolution* [Image of a Revolution] (Algiers: Offices des Publications Universitaires, 1988).

7. Solanas and Gettino, "Towards a Third Cinema," 51.

8. Solanas and Gettino, "Towards a Third Cinema," 52, citing Jean-Luc Godard.

9. Teshome H. Gabriel, *Third Cinema in the Third World: The Aesthetics of Liberation* (Michigan: UMI Research Press, 1979, 1982), 7.

10. Gabriel, *Third Cinema in the Third World*, 7. Gabriel glosses Frantz Fanon, *Les Damnés de la terre* (Paris: François Maspero, 1961); *The Wretched of the Earth*, trans. Constance Farrington (New York: Grove Press, 1963), 222.

11. Yacef Saadi was by no means the only person to note the revolutionary beginnings of Algerian cinema. In *Naissance du cinéma algérien* he speaks of how

> La caméra demeurait . . . une arme, au même titre qu'un fusil, et ils s'en servaient pour aider la révolution armée. . . . Il ne s'agissait donc pas là de viser l'oeuvre d'art ou d'élaborer les prémices d'un véritable cinéma artistique, mais "le cinéaste rebelle" se voulait tout simplement un témoin qui donnerait avec sa pellicule une mémoire précise et précieuse à son peuple [The camera remained . . . a weapon, like a rifle, and they used it to help the armed conflict. . . . Thus, it wasn't about creating a work of art, or of drafting the beginnings of a real artistic cinema, but rather the "filmmaker rebel" simply wanted a witness to give a precise and precious record on film to the people]. (Boudjedra, *Naissance du cinéma algérien*, 49)

12. The casbah, of course, was the Algerian section of the town, which was divided from the part of town reserved for the French and for other non-Algerians. There was a great deal of politics about the credits in the film and about the exclusion, and later inclusion, of Yacef Saadi's company. See Gary Crowdus, "Terrorism and Torture in *The Battle of Algiers*: An Interview with Yacef Saadi," *Cinéaste* 29:3 (2004), 30–37.

13. Benedict Anderson, *Imagined Communities* (London: Verso, 1983). Frantz Fanon has written about radio in this context in "This Is the Voice of Algeria," in *Studies in a Dying Colonialism*, 69–97. The desire to create this national identity is thematized in *The Battle of Algiers*, when we witness the "cleaning up" of the city, when prostitutes are removed from the streets and the consumption of alcohol becomes taboo. Here we witness also the "Arabization" and "Islamicization" of Algeria.

14. Hala Salmane, "On Colonial Cinema," in *Algerian Cinema*, 8. This vol-

ume is the only useful contextualization and history of the birth of Algerian cinema available in English.

15. René Vautier, "The Word *Brother* and the Word *Comrade*," in *Algerian Cinema*, 18. The article originally appeared in the Paris-based journal *Jeune Afrique* 722:9 (1974), 106–8. It appeared in a special issue celebrating twenty years since the beginning of the Algerian Revolution, which the editors described on the front cover as an event that had profoundly marked the third world. This was also the year when Abdelaziz Bouteflika (now president of Algeria and then minister of foreign affairs) presided over the twenty-ninth session of the Security Council at the U.N. See *Jeune Afrique* 717 (1974), 22–27.

16. René Vautier, "The Word *Brother* and the Word *Comrade*," 14.

17. Quoted from Igor Films publicity material. Cited in "Dossier: Tout savoir sur La Bataille d'Alger," *Cinémonde* (June 1970), 20; and in John J. Michalczyk, *The Italian Political Filmmakers* (London and Toronto: Associated University Presses, 1986), 195.

18. The notion of *testimony* is currently receiving some attention. The term *testimonial literature* comes from the Latin American context. See, for example, Sommer, "No Secrets," 51–72. Shoshana Felman and Dori Laub have talked of the testimony in the context of remembering Nazi Germany; see *Testimony: Crises of Witnessing in Literature, Psychoanalysis, and History* (London and New York: Routledge, 1992).

19. Saadi had discussed the project with other Italian film directors before finally deciding on Gillo Pontecorvo. Saadi had approached Francesco Rosi, who was too busy, and Visconti, who was not interested. This was a time when few Algerian film directors could find work, so it seems somewhat surprising that Casbah Films went out of Algeria to find a director. However, Algerian director Moussa Haddad, who went on to make his own films, also assisted Pontecorvo on *The Battle of Algiers*.

20. Roger Boussinot, *L'Encyclopédie du Cinéma* (Paris: Bordas, 1989), 1337.

21. This was inserted on the advice of Pontecorvo's American friends when the film was nominated for an Oscar. See Michalczyk, *The Italian Political Filmmakers*, 191–92.

22. Marcello Gatti was the director of photography, and he and Pontecorvo experimented before shooting. See the chapter on Gillo Pontecorvo in Michalczyk, *The Italian Political Filmmakers*, 182–209.

23. "1955: La loi du 3 avril, durant la guerre d'Algérie, autorisera les autorités à prendre toutes mesures pour assurer le contrôle de la presse, du cinéma, de la radio et du théâtre." Yves Fremoin and Bernard Joubert, *Images interdites* [Forbidden Images] (Paris: Editions Syros-Alternatives, 1989), 10.

24. Cited in Roger Boussinot, *L'Encyclopédie du Cinéma*, 1338.

25. Gillo Pontecorvo and *Cinéaste*, "Gillo Pontecorvo: Using the Contradictions of the System," in *Art, Politics, Cinema: The Cineaste Interviews*, eds. Dan Georgakas and Lenny Rubenstein (London and Sydney: Pluto Press, 1985), 88.

26. See, for example, Francesco Rosi's *Salvatore Giuliano* (1962). Mira Liehm is interesting on this point; see her *Passion and Defiance: Film in Italy from 1942 to the Present* (Los Angeles and Berkeley, CA: University of California Press, 1984), 213–15.

27. There have inevitably been mixed views on the historical accuracy of the film. The French reacted very badly; Algerians, for the most part, appreciated it but did not see it as entirely unproblematic. Roger Boussinot acknowledges Mostefa Lacheraf's criticisms:

Un criminel de guerre se voit représenté sous les traits, le comportement et les manières d'un grand seigneur, d'un chevalier sans peur et sans reproche, alors que l'on prête à Larbi Ben M'hidi, future et courageuse victime de ce colonel de parachutistes, le rôle d'un théoricien à lunettes, un peu guindé et timide, inexpressif, épisodique et marginal [A war criminal sees himself represented with the features, bearing, and manners of some big lord, a fearless knight above reproach, while Larbi ben M'Hidi is assigned the role of the future brave victim of the parachutists, the bespectacled and expressionless theorist, a little awkward and shy, marginal and incidental]. (Cited in Roger Boussinot, *L'Encyclopédie du Cinéma*, 153)

Boussinot agrees with Lacheraf that the film, although one of the best on the subject, is not without its historical problems. Lacheraf was an Algerian professor sympathetic to the FLN and cultural adviser to Houari Boumedienne (president of Algeria from June 1965 to December 1978). He has written also on Algerian film, plotting autobiographically its impact on him and, through association, on the Algerian people. See "Du 'Voleur de Baghdad' à 'Omar Gatlato,'" [From "The Thief of Baghdad" to "Omar Gatlato"] *CinémAction* 14 (1981), 25–45. Historian Alistair Horne says of the film that even though it is pro-FLN, it is extremely objective in its depiction of Colonel Mathieu, and that there is a "remarkable fidelity" in the portrayal of the bomb-carrying incident described later. See Alistair Horne, *A Savage War of Peace: Algeria 1954–62* (Harmondsworth, Middlesex, UK: Penguin, 1977), 167, 185. Algerian film director Slim Riad, speaking of his film *La Voie* [The Way] (Algeria, 1968), tells of the problem of representing authentically. A prisoner of war himself for five years, he says that no one would believe the torture he endured if he were to represent it in a film. In this case, the historical memory of the trauma of torture exceeds the bounds of acceptable realism. So the difficulties of representing and giving testimony to the violence and torture that characterized the birth of the Algerian nation were already being discussed in the early days of the Algerian film industry. See Hala Salmane, "The Birth of Algerian Cinema," in Salmane, Hartog, and Wilson, *Algerian Cinema*, 25.

28. Bill Nichols, *Ideology and the Image* (Bloomington: Indiana University Press, 1981), 172.

29. Sommer, "No Secrets," 51.

30. Chandra Talpade Mohanty's summary is a useful one:

Testimonials are strikingly non-heroic and impersonal. Their primary purpose is to (a) document and record the history of popular struggles, (b) foreground experiential and historical "truth" which has been erased or rewritten in hegemonic elite, or imperialist history, and (c) bear witness in order to change oppressive state rule. Thus, testimonials do not focus on a singular . . . consciousness (in the hegemonic tradition of European modernist autobiography); rather, their strategy is to speak within a collective, as participants in revolutionary struggles, and to speak with the express purpose of bringing about social and political change (revolution). (Chandra Talpade Mohanty, "Introduction: Cartographies of Struggle: Third World Women and the Politics of Feminism," in *Third World Women and the Politics of Feminism*, eds. Chandra Talpade Mohanty, Ann Russo, and Lourdes Torres [Bloomington and Indianapolis: University of Indiana Press, 1991], 37)

31. Like the genre of testimonial literature, discussions of a third cinema developed in the Latin American context.

32. *Films et Documents* 5 (1952), cited in Mira Liehm, *Passion and Defiance*, 131–32. Liehm places *The Battle of Algiers* in her section on "The Glorious Sixties" and does not talk about the film particularly in terms of neorealism. The *Britannica Book of the Year: 1967* says that "La Battaglia di Algeria seemed to prove that neorealism, far from being dead, had only been awaiting a subject big enough to revive it," 205.

33. Angela Dalle Vacche speaks of Italian cinema as one that has always worked to portray the body politic through the body on the screen. In her argument, the changing image of the body works like a mirror to reflect and create an image of national identity. See Angela Dalle Vacche, *The Body in the Mirror: Shapes of History in Italian Cinema* (Princeton, NJ: Princeton University Press, 1992).

34. Pontecorvo used Algerians who either participated in the war or heard inside reports of the military activities from family and friends. Getting Arab women to play various roles such as those on the bombing mission was a major challenge, given the very restrictive national customs. The French in the film came from groups of Europeans who settled in the city after independence. Yacef Saadi, the producer, played himself, the rebel leader responsible for the dynamiting retaliations. His vivid descriptions of actual urban guerrilla warfare fills the screen at the key moments of struggle. For Ali La Pointe, Pontecorvo discovered in the market place Brahim Haggiag, an illiterate peasant who would become the impulsive rebel. The revolutionary boy prodigy Omar was the nephew of Saadi. For Colonel Mathieu he chose the theatre and film actor Jean Martin. The French actor lost his job at the Compagnie Barrault-Renaud in Paris for affixing his signature to the anti-Algerian war statement, "Manifeste des 121," which favored draft resistance to the colonial war (John J. Michalczyk, *The Italian Political Filmmakers*, 192).

35. Liehm, *Passion and Defiance*, 215.

36. Solanas and Gettino, "Towards a Third Cinema," 58.

37. Homi Bhabha, "The Commitment to Theory," in *Questions of Third Cinema*, 127–30.

38. Pontecorvo was a musician and had done all the music for his previous

documentaries. In this film he also worked with Ennio Morricone, who would later go on to use his skills in composing suspenseful music for spaghetti westerns.

39. Zeynep Çelik writes of how Zohra Drif, who famously planted the bomb in the Milk Bar in Algiers, now works as a lawyer in an office overlooking the bar. See Zeynep Çelik, "Colonial/Postcolonial Intersections: Lieux de mémoire in Algiers," *Third Text* 49 (1999–2000), 69.

40. Joan Mellen, *Filmguide to the Battle of Algiers* (Bloomington: Indiana University Press, 1973), 47.

41. Pontecorvo originally included a four-minute scene with light conversation between the women. He thought that this did not ring true, and substituted percussion for speech. See Mellen, *Filmguide to the Battle of Algiers*, 21.

42. Yacef Saadi was the master of these secret passages and hideaways in the casbah. See Alistair Horne, *A Savage War of Peace*, 184. These caves could be read as the destructive pregnant enclosures of the modern horror film.

43. Bhabha, "The Commitment to Theory," 127–30.

44. Fanon, *Wretched of the Earth*, 168. Also cited in Bhabha, "The Commitment to Theory," 128.

45. One is reminded of Jacques Lacan talking about how the unconscious is structured like a language.

The creative spark of metaphor does not spring from the presentation of two images, that is, of two signifiers equally actualized. It flashes between two signifiers, one of which has taken the place of the other in the signifying chain, the occulted signifier remaining present through its (metonymic) connexion with the rest of the chain. (Jacques Lacan, "The Agency of the Letter in the Unconscious," *Ecrits*, trans. Alan Sheridan [London: Norton, 1977], 157)

I take the term *catachresis* from Spivak:

A concept-metaphor without an adequate referent is a catachresis . . . claims for founding catachreses . . . make postcoloniality a deconstructive case. . . . Claiming catachreses from a space that one cannot not want to inhabit and yet must criticize is . . . the deconstructive predicament of the postcolonial. (Gayatri Chakravorty Spivak, "Postcoloniality and Value," in *Literary Theory Today*, eds. Peter Collier and Helga Geyer-Ryan [Ithaca, NY: Cornell University Press, 1990], 225–28)

46. Bhabha, "The Commitment to Theory," 127.

47. This is an example of the desire of the French to make their colonized subjects conform and assimilate. Fanon discusses how this was the official line that the government was taking: "The dominant administration solemnly undertook to defend this woman, pictured as humiliated, sequestered, cloistered" (Fanon, "Algeria Unveiled," 38).

48. I am drawing on Homi Bhabha's essays here, in particular Homi Bhabha, "The Other Question: The Stereotype and Colonial Discourse," *Screen* (November–December 1983), 18–35; "Of Mimicry and Man: The Ambivalence of Colo-

nial Discourse," *Screen* (October 28, 1984), 125–33; "Sly Civility," *Screen* (October 34, 1985), 71–80.

49. Robert Stam and Louise Spence, "Colonialism, Racism and Representation: An Introduction." This article first appeared in *Screen* 24:2 (1983), 2–20. It is reprinted in *Movies and Methods*, ed. Bill Nichols (Berkeley, Los Angeles, and London: University of California Press), 632–49.

50. We can assume that because of the added concern and physical contact between Djafar and this older woman, she is supposed to be Djamila Bouhired, who sought out appropriate women for the bombing and who was Yacef Saadi's partner. Alistair Horne speaks briefly of this relationship in *A Savage War of Peace*, 185.

51. Bhabha, "Sly Civility," 71–80.

52. Pierre Boulanger, among others, has discussed the stereotype created in colonialist cinema in *Le cinéma colonial: de "l'atlandide" à "lawrence d'arabie"* [Colonial Cinema from "l'Atlantide" to "Lawrence of Arabia"] (Paris: Editions Seghers, 1975).

53. Solanas and Gettino, "Towards a Third Cinema," 45–57.

54. Sigmund Freud, "The Uncanny" (1919), in *The Standard Edition of the Complete Psychological Works of Sigmund Freud*, 24 vols., trans. and ed. James Strachey (London: Hogarth Press and Institute of Psychoanalysis, 1953–74), Vol. 17, 217–52.

55. Michael Wayne, "The Critical Practice and Dialectics of Third Cinema," *Third Text* 52 (2000), 65.

56. "Having a fling with the philosopher also entails safeguarding those components of the mirror that cannot reflect themselves: its backing, its brilliancy, thus its dazzlements, its ecstacies. Reproductive material and duplicating mirror, the philosopher's wife also has to underwrite that narcissism which often extends onto a transcendental dimension." In Luce Irigaray, *This Sex Which Is Not One*, trans. Catherine Porter and Carolyn Burke (Ithaca, NY: Cornell University Press), 151.

57. Laub, "Bearing Witness, or the Vicissitudes of Listening," in *Testimony*, 57.

58. Marie-Aimée Hélie-Lucas, "Bound and Gagged by the Family Code," in *Third World Second Sex*, Vol. 2, ed. Miranda Davies (London and New Jersey: Zed Books, 1987), 13–14.

59. Assia Djebar, "Forbidden Gaze, Severed Sound," in *Women of Algiers in Their Apartment*, trans. Marjolijn de Jager (Charlottesville and London: University of Virginia Press, 1992), 150.

Il s'agit de se demander si les porteuses de bombes, en sortant du harem, ont choisi par pur hasard leur mode d'expression le plus direct: leurs corps exposés dehors et elles-mêmes s'attaquant aux autres corps? En fait, elles ont sorti ces bombes comme si elles sortaient leurs propres seins, et ses grenades ont éclaté contre elles, tout contre. Certaines d'entre elles se sont retrouvées sexes électrocutés, écorchés par la torture [It's a question of wondering whether the carriers of the bombs, as they left the harem, chose their most direct manner of expression purely by accident: their bodies exposed outside and they themselves attacking other bodies? In fact, they took those bombs out as if they were taking out their own breasts, and those grenades exploded against them, right against them. Some of them came back later with their sex electrocuted, flayed through torture]. (Assia Djebar, "Regard interdit, son coupé," in *Femmes d'Alger dans leur appartement* [Paris: des femmes, 1980], 188)

60. Bhabha, "The Commitment to Theory," 127–30.

61. Winifred Woodhull, in *Transfigurations of the Maghreb* (Minneapolis: University of Minnesota Press, 1993), discusses the decision not to show the movie. In an interview Djebar refuses to discuss her decision to move from literature to film. See Wassyla Tamzali, "Le cinéma: pour chercher les mots des autres" [Cinema: Finding the Words of Others], *Lectora* 7 (2001), 109–16. See also, however, *Vaste est la prison* [Vast Is the Prison] (Paris: Albin Michel, 1995), in which she discusses filmmaking.

62. Djebar speaks extensively about the use of the nouba form in an interview with Mohand Ben Salama in "Cinéma du Maghreb," *Cinémaction* 14 (1981), 105–9.

63. Réda Bensmaïa offers a persuasive reading of the formal temporality of the film and its mourning and anamnesis that resists an ethnographic analysis. See *Experimental Nations, or The Invention of the Maghreb*, trans. Alyson Waters (Princeton, NJ: Princeton University Press, 2003).

64. See Tamzali, "Le cinéma: pour chercher les mots des autres," 116.

65. Franco Lo Piparo, "Aristotle," in *Lexicon Grammaticorum*, ed. H. Stammerjohann (Tuebingen, Germany: Max Niemeyer Verlag, 1996), 40.

66. Frantz Fanon, *Black Skin, White Masks*, trans. Charles Lam Markman (New York: Grove Press, 1967; originally published 1952), 112.

67. Giorgio Agamben, *Homo Sacer: Sovereign Power and Bare Life*, trans. Daniel Heller-Roazen (Stanford, CA: Stanford University Press, 1998), 25.

68. Levinas, "The Transcendence of Words," 147.

69. Michel Chion, *Audio-Vision*, ed. and trans. Claudia Gorbman (New York: Columbia University Press, 1984), 30.

70. Mladen Dolar, "The Object Voice," in *Gaze and Voice as Love Objects*, eds. Renata Salecl and Slavoj Žižek (Durham, NC: Duke University Press, 1996), 18.

71. Dolar, "The Object Voice," 14.

72. Akira Lippit, *Electric Animal: Toward a Rhetoric of Wildlife* (Minneapolis: University of Minnesota Press, 2000).

73. Abdelkebir Khatibi, *Love in Two Languages*, trans. Richard Howard (Minneapolis: University of Minnesota Press, 1990), 66.

74. See the very fine essay on Isaac Julien's use of sound and listening in the Fanon film, which has preempted much of what I have to say on the topic. Jonathan Kahana, "Cinema and the Ethics of Listening: Isaac Julien's Frantz Fanon," *Film Quarterly* 15:2 (2005–2006), 19–31. See also Ian Baucom, "Fanon's Radio: Solidarity, Diaspora, and the Tactics of Listening," *Contemporary Literature* 42:1 (2001), 15–49; John Mowitt, "Breaking Up Fanon's Voice," in *Frantz Fanon: Criti-*

cal Perspectives, ed. Anthony Alessandrini (New York: Routledge, 1999), 89–98; Fanon, "This Is the Voice of Algeria," 69–98.

75. Unsurprisingly there has been more interest in the films from the former colonies in France than anywhere else. The Institut du Monde Arabe (IMA) and the Centre Culturel Français en Algérie put on festivals of Arab film bianually, and their accompanying dossiers are extremely useful. See, for example, Mouloud Mimoun and others, "France-Algérie: Images d'une guerre" [France-Algeria: Images of War], *Les Cahiers de Ciné-IMA* 1 (1992). When these festivals are not planned, however, most films are available only at the Centre Culturel Algérien, Paris, some can be bought from La Médiathèque des Trois Mondes, and some are completely unavailable unless ordered from the Cinémathèque d'Alger in Algiers. Many France-based journals have included special issues on films of the Maghreb. See *Cinéma* 207 (1976) and 383 (1987); *Ecrans d'Afrique* 2 (1992); *Cinéinforme* 533 (1988) and 462 (1985); *Cahiers du cinéma* 251/252 (1974) and 266/267 (1976); *Image et Son* 340 (1979) and 327 (1978); *Cinéaste* 9:3 (1979); *CinémAction* 14 (1981) and 43 (1987); and *CinémArabe* 10/11 (1978). Also available is *Les Deux Ecrans*, an Algerian journal brought out monthly in French and Arabic by the Office National pour le Commerce et l'Industrie Cinématographique (ONCIC) for a few years (1978–1983). See also Ratiba Hadj-Moussa, *Le corps, l'histoire, le territoire: Les rapports de guerre dans le cinéma algérien* [Body, History, Territory: Relations of War in Algerian Cinema] (Paris: Editions Publisud, 1994). Hadj-Moussa's book is one of the first to offer in-depth analyses of Algerian films of the 1970s that goes beyond their documentation and review. She examines the ways in which relations between the sexes are elaborted in the films, and the influence this has had on Algerian cultural modernity.

76. Algerian film directors claim that the ONCIC has made insufficient effort in this respect. See Hala Salmane, "The Structure of Algerian Cinema," in Salmane, Hartog, and Wilson, *Algerian Cinema*, 23.

77. Gayatri Chakravorty Spivak, "Poststructuralism, Marginality, Postcoloniality and Value," in *Outside in the Teaching Machine* (New York: Routledge, 1993), 229.

78. See, for example, Merzak Allouache, "The Necessity of a Cinema Which Interrogates Everyday Life," in *Film and Politics in the Third World*, ed. John D. H. Downing (New York: Autonomedia, 1987), 93–99.

79. Cited in Hala Salmane, "The Birth of Algerian Cinema," 27.

80. This has been noted in film by Ferid Boughedir in his 1987 documentary *Caméra Arabe*, which discusses the suppression in various Arab countries of film that does not follow the government line. Rachid Boudjedra has noted in his moving and passionate book *FIS de la haine* [FIS of Hatred; Boujedra plays on the FIS—Islamic Salvation Front—and the word *fils*, meaning son] (Paris: Editions Denoël, 1994) that the world press failed to report that the majority of the Algerian electorate did not vote in the municipal elections of 1990 that were

to elect (apparently democratically) the FIS. Actually, according to Boudjedra, the FIS won only 15 percent of the vote, and that with extraordinary corruption. The desire to see Islam as only politically fundamentalist is evident in this misrepresentation of Algeria as essentially fundamentalist. Besides Boudjedra's book, a useful general view of the media and arts in Algeria is available in the special issue on Algeria in the magazine *Télérama hors série Algérie* (March 1995).

CHAPTER 4: *Women of Algiers in Their Apartment*

1. Charles Baudelaire, *Pour Delacroix* (Paris: Editions Complexe, 1986), 94–95.
2. Charles Baudelaire, *Selected Writings on Art and Literature*, trans. P. E. Charvet (Harmondsworth, UK: Penguin, 1993), 74.
3. Jacques Derrida, *The Monolingualism of the Other*, trans. Patrick Mensah (Stanford: Stanford University Press, 1998), 54.
4. Etienne Cournault, cited in Maurice Sérullaz, *Delacroix: Watercolors of Morocco* (London: Zwemmer; Paris: Fernand Hazan, 1951), 13–14. It is also interesting to note that doubt surrounding the authenticity of this story is cited by many art historians. The available sources cite not Delacroix but Cournault, who claims that this is the story told by Delacroix. The art historians themselves, it seems, are caught up in their own myth of authenticity.
5. As Timothy Wilson-Smith has proposed in *Delacroix: A Life* (London: Constable, 1992), Delacroix saw "life in terms of literature" (p. 49). He viewed the world in terms of the classical framework.
6. Various sketches of interiors drawn by Delacroix during his journey may explain this feeling of separation between the women and their background. See, for example, "Une cour à Tanger" [A Courtyard in Tangiers], *Arts Graphiques*, RF 3375 (Paris: Louvre); "Portes et baies d'une maison mauresque" [Doors and Picture Windows of a Moorish House], *Arts Graphiques*, RF 9265 (Paris: Louvre); "Baies dans un intérieur mauresque" [Picture Windows in a Moorish Interior], *Arts Graphiques*, RF 9266 (Paris: Louvre); "Intérieur de maison à Tanger avec une porte ouverte, à droite" [Interior of House in Tangiers with a Door Open on the Right] (Paris: Huguette Bérès); "Intérieur à Alger" [Algerian Interior], *Arts Graphiques*, RF 4527 (Paris: Louvre). Individual images are undated but were all completed in 1832.
7. Assia Djebar, *Women of Algiers in Their Apartment*, trans. Marjolijn de Jager (Charlottesville and London: University of Virginia Press, 1992), 137; *Femmes d'Alger dans leur appartement* (Paris: des Femmes, 1980).
8. René Huyghe makes a similar point about the threat of the curtain in *Delacroix*, trans. Jonathan Griffin (London: Thames and Hudson, 1963), 286.
9. Elie Lambert, *Delacroix et les femmes d'Alger* [Delacroix and "The Women of Algiers"] (Paris: Librairie Renouard, 1937), 115; *The Journal of Eugène Delacroix*, ed. Hubert Wellington, trans. Lucy Norton (Oxford, UK: Phaidon, 1980).

10. See Sigmund Freud, "Remembering, Repeating and Working-Through: Further Recommendations on the Technique of Psychoanalysis," 1914, reprinted in *The Standard Edition of the Complete Psychological Works of Sigmund Freud*, 24 Vols., trans. and ed. James Strachey (London: Hogarth Press and Institute of Psychoanalysis, 1953–74), Vol. 12, 145–56.

11. Pierre Gaudibert, "Delacroix et le romantisme révolutionnaire" [Delacroix and Revolutionary Romanticism], *Europe* 41:408 (1963), 21. Gaudibert speaks extensively of the tension between "le romantisme révolutionnaire" and "l'enthousiasme patriotique" in Delacroix's oeuvre.

12. Nicolas Abraham and Maria Torok, *The Shell and the Kernel*, Vol. 1, trans. Nicholas Rand (Chicago and London: University of Chicago Press, 1994), 136; *L'écorce et le noyau* (Paris: Flammarion, 1987).

13. Abraham and Torok, *The Shell and the Kernel*, 130.

14. Ernest Renan, "What Is a Nation?" lecture delivered at the Sorbonne, 1882, reprinted in Homi K. Bhabha, *Nation and Narration* (London and New York: Routledge, 1990), 8–22.

15. Pierre Nora takes this line of thinking for a contemporary national history of France, stressing the importance of memory. See Pierre Nora, "Preface to the English Language Edition," *Realms of Memory*, Vol. 1 (New York: Columbia University Press, 1996), xxiv.

16. See Freud, especially "Remembering, Repeating, and Working-Through," as well as the section on "Modifications of Earlier Views" in "Inhibitions, Symptoms, and Anxiety," *The Standard Edition of the Complete Psychological Works of Sigmund Freud*, Vol. 20, 159.

17. Freud, "Group Psychology and the Analysis of the Ego" (originally published 1921), *The Standard Edition of the Complete Psychological Works of Sigmund Freud*, Vol. 18, 69–143.

18. Cited in Louis Vignon, "La politique du protectorat et l'inégalité des races," *Revue bleue* 3 (1905), 375.

19. Raymond Betts, *Assimilation and Association in French Colonial Theory, 1899–1914* (New York and London: Columbia University Press, 1961), 165.

20. Benjamin Stora, "Deuxième Guerre Algérienne? Les habits anciens des combattants" [Second Algerian War? Old Robes of Combatants], *Les Temps Modernes* 580 (1995), 258.

21. Edward Said, *Orientalism* (London and New York: Routledge and Kegan Paul, 1978), 23.

22. Bal's article talks about a slightly different kind of citation, although the point is still a valid one for this context. Referring to work by Sander Gilman and Malek Alloula, as well as to a catalogue for an exhibition, she discusses how reproductions of colonialist visual materials in these texts can be exploitative, reproducing their original relationship to the other. Indeed, she argues that the "connaisseur" tone of these commentators in itself extends the voyeuristic

contextualization of these photos. Sander Gilman, "Black Bodies, White Bodies: Toward an Iconography of Female Sexuality in Late Nineteenth-Century Art, Medicine, and Literature," *Critical Inquiry* 12:1 (1985), 204–42; reprinted in *"Race," Writing, and Difference*, ed. Henry Louis Gates (Chicago and London: University of Chicago Press, 1986), 223–61. Malek Alloula, *Le Harem Colonial: Images d'un sous-érotisme* (Geneva and Paris: Editions Slatkine, 1981); *The Colonial Harem*, trans. Myrna Godzich and Wlad Godzich (Minneapolis: University of Minnesota Press, 1986); Mieke Bal, "The Politics of Citation," *Diacritics* 21:1 (1991), 25–45.

23. Sandor Ferenczi, "Introjection and Transference," in *Sex in Psychoanalysis: Contributions to Psychoanalysis* (New York: Dover, 1933; originally published 1909), 30–80.

24. Abraham and Torok, *Shell and the Kernel*, 128.

25. The terms, elaborated in Abraham and Torok, *Shell and the Kernel*, 125–38, are cogently defined and elaborated on by Esther Rashkin in *Family Secrets and the Psychoanalysis of Narrative* (Princeton, NJ: Princeton University Press, 1992), 169; and by Nicholas Rand in his introduction to *Shell and the Kernel*, 13–22.

26. Abraham and Torok, *Shell and the Kernel*, 130.

27. Renan, "What Is a Nation?" 11.

28. We can see France's assimilationist desires at work in the acknowledgment of recent postcolonial writers. Assia Djebar's election to the French Academy is a significant honor and one that marks her writing as French. For a celebration of her success, see *Assia Djebar: Nomade entre les Murs*, ed. Mireille Calle-Gruber (Paris: Maisonneuve et Larose, 2005).

29. Delacroix, *Journal*, October 17, 1953.

30. The sultan had taken the city of Tlemcen. See Charles-Robert Ageron, *Modern Algeria: A History from 1830 to the Present*, trans. Michael Brett (London: Hurst, 1991; originally published 1964), 9–11.

31. Many have written of the trip to Morocco, and a recent publication by the Institut du Monde Arabe in Paris following a large exhibition about Delacroix's trip to North Africa serves as a good bibliographical reference. Institut du Monde Arabe, *Delacroix in Morocco* (Paris and New York: Flammarion, 1994). See the annotated notebooks of Delacroix by Jean Guiffrey and Pierre Marcel, *Le voyage de Eugène Delacroix au Maroc* [Eugène Delacroix's Trip to Morocco], 2 vols. (Paris: Ecoles Française, 1909, 1913). The 1909 edition examines the notebooks at the Louvre; the 1913 edition, those at the Musée Condé in Chantilly. For analysis and narrativization of the journey, see Elie Lambert, *Delacroix et les femmes d'Alger* [Delacroix and the Women of Algiers]; Maurice Sérullaz, *Delacroix: Watercolors of Morocco;* Guy Dumur, *Delacroix et le Maroc* [Delacroix and Morocco] (Paris: Editions Herscher, 1988); Lee Johnson, "Delacroix's Road to the Sultan of Morocco," *Apollo* 115 (1982), 186–89; and Wilson-Smith, *Delacroix: A Life*.

32. Maurice Arama, "The Journey," in *Delacroix in Morocco*, 56; Wilson-Smith, *Delacroix: A Life*, 94.

33. See Zeynep Çelik, "Colonial/Postcolonial Intersections: Lieux de mémoires in Algiers," *Third Text* 49 (1999–2000), 70.

34. See Maryanne Stevens, "Western Art and Its Encounter with the Islamic World 1798–1914," in *The Orientalists: Delacroix to Matisse—European Painters in North Africa and the Near East*, ed. Maryanne Stevens (London: Royal Academy of Arts, 1984), 20.

35. The black woman bears a resemblance, however, to another black woman by Delacroix, "Aline, la Mulâtresse" [Aline, the Mulatto], and her clothing bears some resemblance to "Studies of Jewish Women," *Folio*, 26v–27r (Chantilly: Musée Condé, 1832). Lambert also notes the similarity to the clothing of "Juive d'Alger à sa toilette" [Algerian Jewish Woman Getting Ready] studies for a figure viewed from the back all depict white women; see "Etudes" (Paris: Louvre Dessins, image 9290). Perhaps we could derive from this slippage between Jews and blacks a reading of a Delacroix who found the racism toward Jews in Algiers similar to that toward blacks.

36. See the two versions of "Intérieur à Alger" [Interior in Algiers], RF 4527 (Paris: Louvre, 1832) and the two versions of "Étude de Babouches" [Study for Slippers] (Collection Vaudoyer and Dreyfus) reproduced in Lambert, *Delacroix et les femmes d'Alger*.

37. Sérullaz, *Delacroix: Watercolors of Morocco*, 1–20; Dumur, *Delacroix et le Maroc*, 27.

38. Lambert, *Delacroix et les femmes d'Alger*, 5. See also Georges Marçais, *Le costume musulman d'Alger* [The Muslim Clothing of Algiers] (Paris, 1930), 121–23. Ruth Bernard Yeazell discusses the ethnographic and imaginative importance of the painting in *Harems of the Mind: Passages of Western Art and Literature* (New Haven, CT: Yale University Press, 2000), 25–28, 34–36.

39. Ageron, *Modern Algeria*, 24.

40. Ageron, *Modern Algeria*, 27.

41. Yeazell discusses the use of European models in *Harems of the Mind*, 35.

42. One is inevitably reminded of Sander Gilman's essay "Black Bodies, White Bodies: Toward an Iconography of Female Sexuality in Late Nineteenth-Century Art, Medicine, and Literature" every time the black woman appears in nineteenth-century European art. Gilman asserts that the figure of the Hottentot Venus, characterized as she is by skin color and enlarged labia and buttocks, serves as the model for all representations of black women during this period, especially when they are viewed from the rear. Gilman suggests, in his reading of Manet's Olympia, that the black woman's presence marks the sexuality of the nude white woman who covers her genitalia and is thinner than most depictions of prostitutes in the period. In a similar way, one could suggest that the Arab women in Delacroix's

work are similarly sexualized by her presence. This is not, however, the emphasis of this chapter.

43. Samir Amin, *The Maghreb in the Modern World* (Harmondsworth, UK: Penguin, 1970).

44. Pierre Schneider, "The Moroccan Hinge," in *Matisse in Morocco: The Paintings and Drawings, 1912–13*, eds. Jack Cowart, Jack, Pierre Schneider, John Elderfield, Albert Kostenevich, and Laura Coyle (New York: Harry N. Abrams, 1990), 23.

45. Françoise Gilot, *Matisse and Picasso: A Friendship in Art* (New York: Doubleday, 1990).

46. Leo Steinberg, *Other Criteria* (Oxford, UK: Oxford University Press, 1972), 128. All the Picasso images can be found in this volume and also at http://www.jcbourdais.net/journal/07oct05.php

47. See Gilot, *Matisse and Picasso*, 168–71.

48. Steinberg, *Other Criteria*, 234.

49. These figures contrast greatly with the paintings of the Weeping Women series that document the horror of war, which Picasso painted in 1937, when he also created *Guernica*. As Steinberg has convincingly argued, although it has become commonplace to speak of "Cubist simultaneity of point of view," Cubism did not actually give us simultaneity; rather, it gave us something still quite fixed, in spurts of perception rather than in simultaneous movement. Rather than giving us consolidation of a multifaceted body with integrity, it gave us discontinuity (Steinberg, *Other Criteria*, 154–60). Many of the drawings and paintings in the Weeping Women series give us discontinuous images of torture. In their agonizing distortion, they take from Cubism a flattening aspect that is horrifying. In fact, Djebar's short story "The Woman Who Weeps" begins with Arthur Adamov's words on Picasso's painting of that title—"This uninterrupted dance of broken lines"—and only later speaks of a "tombstone statuary" (Djebar, *Women of Algiers*, 53). See also Rachel Boudjedra, "Les Algéroises selon Picasso," *El Watan* (June 16, 2005).

50. The "roaming caress" that Picasso evokes places him within the painting, creating an effect simliar to that in another work in which he places the artist as voyeur within the frame: *Olympia*. Again, Sander Gilman's essay "Black Bodies, White Bodies" is of related interest here.

51. Steinberg, *Other Criteria*, 136. The staircase could also be a citation of a Delacroix 1832 sketch, "Une cour à Tanger" [Courtyard in Tangiers] (Paris: Louvre), which is in turn cited by Matisse in *La Porte de Casbah* [Gate of the Casbah] (1912). Matisse's journey to Morocco was of course inspired by Delacroix's painting and Journal, which described the colors of North Africa. When Matisse arrived in Morocco, he said, "I found the Moroccan landscapes exactly as they are described in Delacroix's paintings." Cited in Elderfield, *Matisse in Morocco*, 188.

52. The repressive Family Code was debated all the way through the 1960s and 1970s and in 1972 and 1979 it was drawn up but did not pass. The code was

needed in order to ensure that no confusion about matters of family law would arise out of contradiction between civil law and the *Shari'a*. Marnia Lazreg is informative on the details of the code in *The Eloquence of Silence: Algerian Women in Question* (London and New York: Routledge, 1994), 150–57. Lazreg uses one of Picasso's Femmes d'Alger on the cover of this extremely interesting feminist sociological study. See also Marie-Aimée Hélie-Lucas, "Bound and Gagged by the Family Code," in *Third World Second Sex*, Vol. 2, ed. Miranda Davies (London and New Jersey: Zed Books, 1987).

53. Djebar, *Women of Algiers*, 149.

54. In addition to the analysis in the previous chapter and works cited on Djebar and film, see Assia Djebar, Ariane Mnouchkine, Daniel Mesguich, Mireille Calle-Gruber, and Hélène Cixous, *Au théâtre, au cinéma, au témoin* [Theater, Cinema, Witnessing] (Paris: l'Harmattan, 2001) for more on the relationship between and movement among different genres of her work.

55. A film, *Barberousse, mes soeurs* [Barberousse, My Sisters] (Hassan Bouabdallah, Radio-Télévision Algérienne, 1985) thematizes this isolation of women revolutionaries. The film is a documentary about women's response to a feature film called *Barberousse* (Hadj Rahim, Radio-Télévision Algérienne, 1982), in which no women are depicted and in which a false sense of heroism overrides the horror of war. The women, many of whom were formerly prisoners in Barberousse, respond to the film, and then go on to tell their own stories of the prison. Characteristically, this film about women cannot exist without the simultaneous questioning of the power, influence, and ethics of visual representation. The silence and inaccuracy about women's role in the war are discussed here at the very moment in which testimony is recorded about their experiences.

56. Anne Donadey examines this point in terms of dialogism and palimpsestic theories in an unpublished dissertation, "Polyphonic and Palimpsestic Discourse in the Works of Assia Djebar and Leila Sebbar," Northwestern University, 1993. See also her *Recasting Postcolonialism: Women Writing Between Worlds* (Portsmouth, NH: Heinemann, 2001).

57. One cannot help but suppose that some autobiographical material is being processed here by Djebar, who is both writer and filmmaker. Her *Nouba des femmes de Mont Chenoua* [The Nouba of the Women of Mount Chenoua] (Radio-Télévision Algérienne, 1977) and *Zerda ou les chants de l'oubli* [Zerda, or the Songs of Fortune/Forgetting] (Radio-Télévision Algérienne, 1980) dramatize this fragmentation being healed through the representation that her novels and short stories thematize. For more on these voices that seize her imagination in various genres, see *Ces voix qui m'assiègent* [These Voices That Seize Me] (Paris: Albin Michel, 1999].

58. Claude Talahite, "Femmes d'Alger dans leur appartement: Problématique de la figure de l'observateur" [Women of Algiers in Their Apartment: Problem of the Figure of the Observer], Documents de Travail/Groupe de Recherches sur les femmes algériennes (Oran: Université de l'Oran, 1981), writes of the blockage of

conversation in the interaction between the women. See Anne Blancard, "Assia Djebar: Les Voies de la Mémoire" [Assia Djebar: The Ways of Memory], *Le Continent* 36 (1979); and C. Bouslimani, "Assia Djebar: Rétablir la Langage des Femmes" [Assia Djebar: Restoring Women's Language], *El Moudjahid* (March 1978), and in *Algérie-Actualité* (March 8, 1978). See also Mireille Calle-Gruber, *Assia Djebar, ou la résistance de l'écriture* [Assia Djebar, or Writing's Resistance] (Paris: Maisonneuve et Larose, 2001).

59. Djebar discusses this point in "Auto-Conversation." Mostefa Lacheraf, in "L'avenir de la Culture Algérienne," [The Future of Algerian Culture], *Les Temps Modernes* 209 (1963), 733–34, is very critical of Djebar's work, claiming that she does not understand the country, the people, class differentials, and customs.

60. In her essay "The White of Algeria," Djebar has written interestingly about the importance of writing in French, about the "war between languages" in Algeria, about resistance to nationalist and exclusive Arabization, and about the suppression of Berber. "The White of Algeria," *Yale French Studies* 87: "Another Look, Another Woman: Retranslations of French Feminism," (1995), 138–48. See also *Le Blanc d'Algérie* [Algerian White] (Paris: Albin Michel, 1996).

61. Nada Osman Turk discusses the way in which Djebar uses the hammam to signify the only place where women can be intimate and have an uncomplicated relationship with their own bodies, where they are not consistently watched. Nada Osman Turk, "Assia Djebar: Solitaire Solidaire. Une étude de la lutte des algériennes pour les libertés individuelles, dans l'oeuvre romanesque d'Assia Djebar" [Assia Djebar: Solitary Solidarity: A Study of the Struggle of Algerian Women for Individual Freedom in the Novels of Assia Djebar], unpublished dissertation, University of Colorado, 1987.

62. Djebar, *Women of Algiers*, 44.

63. See, for example, Ernest Gellner, *Culture, Politics, Identity* (Cambridge: Cambridge University Press, 1987).

64. Djebar, *Women of Algiers*, 2.

65. Djebar, *Women of Algiers*, 8.

66. Djebar, *Women of Algiers*, 2.

67. Jacques Derrida, *Specters of Marx: The State of the Debt, the Work of Mourning, and the New International*, trans. Peggy Kamuf (London and New York: Routledge, 1994), 4.

CHAPTER 5: LATENT GHOSTS AND THE MANIFESTO

1. André Breton, *Nadja*, trans. Richard Howard (New York: Grove Press, 1960; originally published 1928), 66.

2. The work on what Brent Edwards has called the "ethnics of surrealism" has begun to change. For example, see James Clifford's work on Aimé Césaire in *The Predicament of Culture: Twentieth Century Ethnography, Literature, and Art* (Cam-

bridge, MA: Harvard University Press, 1988). See also, Brent Hayes Edwards, "The Ethnics of Surrealism," *Transition* 78 (1998), 84–135.

3. Jacques Derrida's *Monolingualism of the Other, or The Prosthesis of Origin* (Stanford, CA: Stanford University Press, 1998) is instructive here, but even more than that, so is the extraordinary amount of writing by French intellectuals about the Algerian war of independence that came out of Paris in the 1950s and 1960s. See also Chapter 1 for a nonfoundationalist reading of biographical influence.

4. See Jacques Derrida, "Taking a Stand for Algeria," in *Parallax* 4:2 (1998), 17–23, for an explanation of virile war. Derrida looks to a feminine and female political future that functions and conceptualizes in a completely different manner than that of virile violence.

5. This rampant nationalism is often seen in the repatriation of arts discourse, which usually fails to address the violence of many new nationalisms even as it insists (quite rightly) on the problem of colonial pillage sustaining metropolitan museums. For a reading of orientalist texts that happily avoids some of the problems of a lack of integration of the political and the aesthetic, see Roger Benjamin, "Ingres Chez Les Fauves" [Ingres in the Eyes of the Fauvists], *Art History* 23:5 (2000), 743–71. The complexity of citation is brought out beautifully in this article and does not confine citation to simple repetition or reification; each work is attended for its singularity of expression. See also John MacKenzie, *Orientalism: History, Theory, and the Arts* (Manchester, VT: St. Martin's Press, 1995).

6. Emmanuel Levinas's theory of the encounter with the other informs my proposal of an ethical relation to the "face" of a painting. See Emmanuel Levinas, *Totality and Infinity: An Essay on Exteriority*, trans. Alphonso Lingis (Pittsburgh: Duquesne University Press, 1969).

7. André Breton, "Preface for a Reprint of the Manifesto," 1929, reprinted in *Manifestoes of Surrealism*, trans. Richard Seaver and Helen R. Lane (Ann Arbor: University of Michigan Press, 1972), xi.

8. André Breton, *Nadja*, trans. Richard Howard (New York: Grove Press, 1960; originally published 1928), 66. Besides meaning "hope," *nadiajinski* in Russian carries the connotation of redemption. In my reading, to do justice to Nadja means to read her as a spectral figure rather than as a spiritual figure of redemption. The reasons for this become clear as the chapter proceeds, but briefly, the specter is a more material manifestation than the spirit.

9. Mary Ann Caws' introductory essay "The Poetics of the Manifesto: Nowness and Newness," in *Manifesto: A Century of Isms* (Lincoln and London: University of Nebraska Press, 2001), is helpful in laying out the form of the twentieth-century manifesto.

10. Karl Marx, "Manifesto of the Communist Party," in *The Communist Manifesto*, ed. Frederic L. Bender, trans. Samuel Moore (New York and London: Norton, 1988), 54–55.

11. See the letter from Engels to Marx, November 23–24, 1847, in *Karl Marx and Frederick Engels, Selected Correspondence*, rev. 2nd ed., ed. S. Ryazanskya, trans. I. Lasker (Moscow: Progress Publishers, 1965).

12. Bender notes that in 1848, when the manifesto appeared, "the Pope was Pius IX; Russia was ruled by Czar Nicholas I; Clemens Wenzel Lothar Metternich-Winneburg, the architect of the Holy Alliance, was chancellor of the Austrian Empire; and the historian Guizot was foreign minister of France. Guizot, incidentally, had Marx expelled from France (Januay 16, 1845) at the request of the Prussian government." Bender, *The Communist Manifesto*, fn. 2, 54.

13. Marx, "Manifesto of the Communist Party," 55.

14. See Walter Benjamin, "Left-Wing Melancholy," in *The Weimar Republic Sourcebook*, eds. Anton Kaes, Martin Jay, and Edward Dimendberg (Berkeley, CA: University of California Press, 1994), 304–6; and Wendy Brown, "Resisting Left Melancholy," *boundary 2* 26:3 (1999), 19–27.

15. André Breton, "The Automatic Message," in *What Is Surrealism? Selected Writings* (London: Pluto, 1989), 100. See Jean Starobinski, "Freud, Breton, Myers," *L'Arc* 34 (1968), 87–96, for a thorough reading of the place Myers held in Breton's imagination.

16. Breton, "The Automatic Message," 100.

17. Sonu Shamdasani, in "Encountering Hélène," his excellent introduction to Théodore Flournoy's *From India to the Planet Mars: A Case of Multiple Personality with Imaginary Languages*, trans. Daniel B. Vermilye (Princeton, NJ: Princeton University Press, 1994; originally published 1899), xv.

18. Edmund Gurney, Frederic W. H. Myers, and Frank Podmore, *Phantasms of the Living* (London: Rooms of the Society for Psychical Research, and Trübner, 1886); Frederic William Henry Myers, *Human Personality and Its Survival of Bodily Death*, ed. and abridged Leopold Hamilton Myers (New York: Longmans, Green, 1918; originally published 1903).

19. Myers, *Human Personality*, 188.
20. Myers, *Human Personality*, 189.
21. Myers, *Human Personality*, 188.
22. Myers, *Human Personality*, 189.
23. Myers, *Human Personality*, 188.
24. Myers, *Human Personality*, 225.
25. Myers, *Human Personality*, 13. David Lomas's *The Haunted Self: Surrealism, Psychoanalysis, and Subjectivity* (New Haven: Yale University Press, 2000) gives an extremely useful analysis of the appeal for Breton of the unitary subject in Myers. See especially pp. 67–68.

26. Flournoy, *From India to the Planet Mars*, 8.
27. Flournoy, *From India to the Planet Mars*, 8.
28. Flournoy, *From India to the Planet Mars*, 10.
29. David Lomas seems to agree with Mikkel Borch-Jacobsen that psycho-

analysis enjoyed dismissing its very vivid prehistorical relation to Myers' spiritualism. See Mikkel Borch-Jacobsen, *The Emotional Tie: Psychoanalysis, Mimesis, and Affect* (Stanford, CA: Stanford University Press, 1992). See also Sonu Shamdasani, "Encountering Hélène"; and Lomas, *The Haunted Self*.

30. Breton, "The Automatic Message," 102.

31. Flournoy, *From India to the Planet Mars*, 14.

32. Michel de Certeau, "Vocal Utopias: Glossolalia," trans. Daniel Rosenberg, *Representations* 56 (1996), 29.

33. De Certeau, "Vocal Utopias," 31.

34. For an elaboration of the distinction I am making between spirit and specter, see Jacques Derrida, *Specters of Marx: The State of the Debt, the Work of Mourning, and the New International*, trans. Peggy Kamuf (London and New York: Routledge, 1994).

35. Flournoy, *From India to the Planet Mars*, 18.

36. Flournoy, *From India to the Planet Mars*, 9.

37. See, for example, the images and text from Henri Michaux, *Untitled Passages*, ed. Catherine de Zegher (New York: Drawing Center, Merrell, 2000), especially 14–17.

38. See Catherine de Zegher, *Korwa Drawings: Contemporary Tribal Works on Paper from Central India*, Drawing Papers 13 (New York: Drawing Center, Merrell, 2000), 5. The drawings show the Korwa peoples' response to the attempted communication between themselves and the Indian painter Swaminathan.

39. Breton, "The Automatic Message," 102.

40. Breton, "The Automatic Message," 100.

41. Breton, "The Automatic Message," 104–5.

42. Breton, "The Automatic Message," 106.

43. Breton, "The Automatic Message," 109.

44. Breton, "The Automatic Message," 109.

45. For more on the relationship among psychoanalysis, nationalism, colonialism, and the structure of the modern subject, see Ranjana Khanna, *Dark Continents: Psychoanalysis and Colonialism* (Durham, NC: Duke University Press, 2003).

46. André Breton, *Communicating Vessels*, trans. Mary Ann Caws and Geoffrey T. Harris (Lincoln and London: University of Nebraska Press, 1990; originally published 1932), 29.

47. Breton, *Nadja*, 79–81.

48. Breton, *Nadja*, 100–101.

49. Breton, *Nadja*, 121.

50. These are the first words of Breton's novel *Nadja*, 11.

51. See Breton, *Entretiens, 1913–1952* [Interviews, 1913–1952] (Paris: Gallimard, 1969), 137–38; and *Nadja*, 79.

52. Breton, *Nadja*, 11–12.

53. Kendall Johnson, "Haunting Transcendence: The Strategy of Ghosts in Bataille and Breton," *Twentieth Century Literature* 45:3 (1999), 347.
54. Johnson, "Haunting Transcendence," 358.
55. Breton, *Nadja*, 93.
56. Breton, *Nadja*, 142.
57. Breton, *Nadja*, 142.
58. Breton, *Nadja*, 143.
59. Breton, *Communicating Vessels*, 116.
60. Biographical information about Baya Mahieddine is available in *Algérie Littérature/Action* 15–16 (1997), 215–16, in a biography compiled by Baya's friend Lucette Albaret. This information is expanded on in the interview with Baya by Dalilia Morsly (209–13), and in the catalogue of the exhibition on Baya at the Musée Cantini in Marseilles, 1982–83, by Jean de Maisonseul (reprinted in the same edition of *Algérie Littérature/Action*, 185–88). Benamar Mediene offers some information in his section, "Algeria," in *Contemporary Art from the Islamic World*, ed. Wijdan Ali (London: Scorpion, 1989), 19. Jean Peyrissac wrote of his encounter with Baya's work in the 1947 *Derrière Le Miroir* issue on Baya. This is reprinted in Frank Maubert, *Baya* (Paris: Galérie Maeght, 1998), 15–17. (The latter is a wonderful source for Baya's many 1947 gouaches on paper.) Sana Makhoul presented a paper on Baya at the Women's Caucus for Art Session, "Crossing Borders, Mapping Boundaries; Exploring Issues of Culture and Context in Women's Art," at the College Art Association's eighty-sixth annual conference in Toronto, Canada, 1998. Her paper is available at http://www.sbawca.org/detail/v6n1/Makhoul.html. She includes some biographical information, and stresses the importance of the Algerian roots of Baya's art derived from traditional Kabyle ceramics and textiles.
61. See the interview between Baya and Dalila Morsley, "Je ne sais pas, je sens" [I do not know, I feel], in *Algérie Littérature/Action* 15–16 (1997), 210.
62. Anatole Jakovsky, *Peintres Naifs: Lexicon of the World's Naive Painters* (Basel: Basilius Presse, 1976), 92.
63. See "L'art et la bannière," *Télérama* (March 1995), 47–49; *Algérie Littérature/Action* 15–16 (1997), 177–219.
64. Daniel Miller, "Primitive Art and the Necessity of Primitivism to Art," in *The Myth of Primitivism*, ed. Susan Hiller (London and New York: Routledge, 1991), 56.
65. Anatole Jakovsky, who is discussed later, would be a good example of this. So would Breton himself, and indeed primitivist painters who insist on the "primitive" rather than the "primitivist" nature of artists from the colonies.
66. Djilali Kadid, "Baya ou L'Orient retrouvé," in *Algérie Littérature/Action* 15–16 (1997), 208, my translation.
67. Sigmund Freud, *The Standard Edition of the Complete Psychological Works of Sigmund Freud*, 24 vols., trans. and ed. James Strachey (London: Hogarth Press and Institute of Psychoanalysis, 1953–74), Vol. 13, 1–155.

68. Clifford, *The Predicament of Culture*, 122.

69. Breton and others, "Manifeste des 121" [Manifesto of the 121], 1960. The Manifesto is available at http://www.marxists.org/history/france/algerian-war/1960/manifesto-121.htm. Reprinted as "Declaration Concerning the Right of Insubordination in the Algerian War," in André Breton and Franklin Rosemont, *What Is Surrealism: Selected Writings, Book 2* (Atlanta, GA: Pathfinder Press, 1978), 460–62.

70. Simone de Beauvoir and Gisèle Halimi, *Djamila Boupacha* (Paris: Gallimard, 1962); *Djamila Boupacha: The Story of the Torture of a Young Algerian Girl Which Shocked Liberal Opinion*, trans. Peter Green (London: André Deutsch and Weidenfeld and Nicolson, 1962).

71. I discuss this aspect of Freud's thinking and his relation to primitivism in *Dark Continents*, 124.

72. See James Clifford's work on Aimé Césaire in *The Predicament of Culture: Twentieth-Century Ethnography, Literature, and Art* (Cambridge, MA: Harvard University Press, 1988), for further elaboration of this point.

73. See Breton in "Exposition Baya," *Derrière le Miroir* (November 1947), reprinted in *Algérie Littérature/Action* 15–16 (1997), 181–82; trans Ranjana Khanna and Julie Singer in *Art History: Journal of the Association of Art Historians* 26:2 (2003), 287.

74. See Breton in "Exposition Baya," 287.

75. Assia Djebar, "Le Combat de Baya," in *Trois Femmes Peintres* (Paris: Institut du Monde Arabe, undated), 17–18; trans. Ranjana Khanna and Julie Singer in *Art History: Journal of the Association of Art Historians* 26:2 (2003), 288–89.

76. See the interview between Baya and Dalila Morsley, "Je ne sais pas, je sens," 210.

77. See Yves-Alain Bois, *Formless: A User's Guide* (New York: Zone Books, 1997). See also Georges Didi-Huberman, *La ressemblance informe, ou le Gai-Savoir visuel selon Georges Bataille* [Formless Resemblance, or Georges Bataille's Gay-Visual-Science] (Paris: Editions Macula, 1995). See also Edwards, "The Ethnics of Surrealism," which interestingly discusses this in relation to colonized surrealism.

78. See *Refusal of the Shadow*, ed. Michael Richardson (London: Verso, 1996), for translated examples of this work. See also *Tropiques* (Paris: Editions Jean-Michel Place, 1978), which includes all the editions of *Tropiques*, which ran from April 1941 to September 1945.

79. *Femme au bateau*, 1945, private collection; *Femme au vase bleue*, 1947, illustrated in *Trois Femme Peintres*, Institut du Monde Arabe, Paris; *Bouquet entre oiseaux et mandores*, 1966, illustrated in *Trois Femme Peintres*, Institut du Monde Arabe, Paris.

80. Paraphrased translation from "Manifeste des 121."

81. See Derrida, *Specters of Marx*, 4, for this idea of the historical undated phantom.

82. Flournoy, *From India to the Planet Mars*, 193.

83. I expand on the idea of critical intimacy from Gayatri Chakravorty Spivak, *A Critique of Postcolonial Reason: Toward a History of the Vanishing Present* (Cambridge, MA: Harvard University Press,1999), 425.

CHAPTER 6: "ARABY" (*Dubliners*) AND *A Sister to Scheherazade*

Epigraphs: William Butler Yeats, "Leda and the Swan" (1923), in *The Collected Poems of W. B. Yeats*, ed. Richard Finneran (New York: Scribner, 1996), 214–15; James Joyce, *Ulysses* (New York: Vintage, 1986), 272.

1. See Teresa de Lauretis, *Alice Doesn't: Feminism, Semiotics, Cinema* (Bloomington: Indiana University Press, 1984), 103–57.

2. Julia Kristeva, "Women's Time," in *The Kristeva Reader*, ed. Toril Moi (Oxford: Blackwell, 1986).

3. Joseph Valente, *James Joyce and the Problem of Justice* (Cambridge, UK: Cambridge University Press, 1995), 64.

4. See, for example, Arjun Appadurai, "Disjuncture and Difference in the Global Cultural Economy," 1990, reprinted in *Colonial Discourse and Postcolonial Theory*, eds. Patrick Williams and Laura Chrisman (Chicago: Chicago University Press, 1994), 324–39; Vijay Mishra and Bob Hodge, "What Is Postcolonialism?," 1991, reprinted in *Colonial Discourse and Postcolonial Theory*, 276–90; Anne McClintock, "The Angel of Progress: Pitfalls of the Term 'Postcolonialism,'" 1992, reprinted in *Colonial Discourse and Postcolonial Theory*, 291–304; Inderpal Grewal and Caren Kaplan, *Scattered Hegemonies: Postmodernity and Transnational Feminist Practice* (Minneapolis: University of Minnesota Press, 1993).

5. Donald Torchiana gives some interesting detail about the "Araby" catalog and the *Irish Times* articles of May 17, 18, and 19, 1894, in Donald T. Torchiana, *Backgrounds for Joyce's Dubliners* (Boston: Allen and Unwin, 1986), 52–67.

6. In a wonderful article, "Too Short for a Book? The Thousand and One Nights: The Short Story and the Book," in *White Woman Speaks with Forked Tongue: Criticism as Autobiography* (London and New York: Routledge, 1991), 188, Nicole Ward Jouve suggests that *The Arabian Nights* was certainly important for the composition of "Araby."

7. Garry M. Leonard, *Reading Dubliners Again: A Lacanian Perspective* (Syracuse, NY: University of Syracuse Press, 1993), 5.

8. Torchiana has commented on the significance of these texts for the boy in *Backgrounds for Joyce's Dubliners*, 52–67.

9. See Leonard's chapter entitled "The Question and the Quest: The Story of Mangan's Sister" in *Reading Dubliners Again*, 73–94.

10. Ben L. Collins, for example, in his article "Joyce's 'Araby' and the 'Extended Simile,'" *James Joyce Quarterly* 4 (1967), 84–90, finds the Grail, Eden, Oedipus, and modern Ireland represented in this dense, adjectival prose. Reprinted in

Twentieth-Century Interpretation of Dubliners: *A Collection of Critical Essays*, ed. Peter Garrett (New Jersey and London: Prentice-Hall, 1968), 93–99.

11. Leonard, in *Reading Dubliners Again*, cites Blanche Gelfant making the same point at the Ninth Joyce Symposium. This line of thinking goes against Harry Stone's article "'Araby' and the Writings of James Joyce," *Antioch Review* 25:3 (1965), 375–410. C. L. Innes's helpful book *Woman and Nation in Irish Literature and Society, 1880–1935* (Athens: University of Georgia Press, 1993), helps us to understand why this may be. As in many literatures of decolonization, such as that of the negritude movement in France, woman gets figured as nation in the emerging national consciousness. Colonialism, as Edward Said and Ashis Nandy might argue, emasculates, and the founding of the phallus on the reclaimed feminine land seems to be a persistent motif. See Edward Said, *Orientalism* (London and New York: Routledge and Kegan Paul, 1978); and Ashis Nandy, *The Intimate Enemy: Loss and Recovery of Self Under Colonialism* (Oxford, UK: Oxford University Press, 1983).

12. Homi Bhabha, "DissemiNation," in *Nation and Narration*, ed. Homi Bhabha (London and New York: Routledge, 1990), 292.

13. Homi Bhabha, "'Race,' Time, and the Revision of Modernity," *Oxford Literary Review* 13 (1991), 193–219; *The Location of Culture* (London and New York: Routledge, 1994), 240.

14. Edward Said, "Kim: The Pleasures of Imperialism," *Raritan* 7:2 (1987), 27–64. See also his chapter on "Resistance and Opposition" in his *Culture and Imperialism* (London: Chatto and Windus, 1993), 272–73, 280.

15. Kristeva, "Women's Time," 188, 190.

16. Kristeva, "Women's Time," 188–90.

17. Kristeva, "Women's Time," 195.

18. Kristeva, "Women's Time," 210.

19. Ernest Gellner, "The Social Roots of Egalitarianism," in *Culture, Identity, Politics* (Cambridge, UK: Cambridge University Press, 1987), 93.

20. Sara Suleri, "The Adolescence of Kim," in *The Rhetoric of English India* (Chicago: University of Chicago Press), 111–31.

21. David Spurr, *The Rhetoric of Empire* (Durham, NC, and London: Duke University Press, 1993), 2.

22. Emer Nolan, *James Joyce and Nationalism* (London and New York: Routledge, 1995), 70.

23. Jacques Derrida, *Given Time: 1. Counterfeit Money*, trans. Peggy Kamuf (Chicago: University of Chicago Press, 1992), 1.

24. James Joyce, "Araby," in *Dubliners* (Harmondsworth, UK: Penguin, 2000), 21–22.

25. Joyce, "Araby," 26.

26. Craig Hansen Werner, *Dubliners: A Pluralistic Word* (Boston: Twayne, 1988), 34.

27. Robert Welch, *Changing States: Transformations in Modern Irish Writing* (London and New York: Routledge, 1993), ix.

28. Welch, *Changing States*, 32.

29. Hélène Cixous, *The Exile of James Joyce* (New York: David Lewis, 1972), 359–433.

30. Cixous, *Exile of James Joyce*, 387.

31. "She represents Church . . . , Ireland, and the betrayer, Judas." Collins, "'Araby' and the 'Extended Simile,'" 95.

32. See Innes, *Woman and Nation*, for an account of the slippage between woman and nation in the national imagination.

33. Nolan, *James Joyce and Nationalism*, 167–68.

34. Ernest Renan, "What Is a Nation?," lecture delivered at the Sorbonne, 1882, reprinted in Homi K. Bhabha, *Nation and Narration* (London and New York: Routledge, 1990), 19.

35. Joyce, "Araby," 23.

36. Joyce, "Araby," 24.

37. I refer to Homi Bhabha's phrase "almost the same but not quite, almost the same but not white" in "Of Mimicry and Man: The Ambivalence of Colonial Discourse," (October 28, 1984), 125–33; *The Location of Culture* (London and New York: Routledge, 1994), 85–93. One is of course also reminded of Joyce's *Portrait of the Artist as a Young Man* (New York: Viking, 1964; originally published 1916), 189:

The language we are speaking is his before it is mine. How different are the words home, Christ, ale, master, on his lips and on mine! I cannot speak or write those words without unrest of spirit. His language, so familiar and so foreign, will always be for me an acquired speech. I have not made or accepted its words. My voice holds them at bay. My soul frets in the shadow of his language.

38. Jennifer Wicke, "Who's She When She's at Home?," in *Molly Blooms: A Polylogue on "Penelope" and Cultural Studies*, ed. Richard Pearce (Madison: University of Wisconsin Press, 1994), 190.

39. Joyce, "Araby," 28.

40. Assia Djebar, *A Sister to Scheherazade*, trans. Dorothy Blair (Portsmouth, NH: Heinemann, 1993); *Ombre Sultane* (Paris: Lattès, 1987).

41. Djebar, *A Sister to Scheherazade*, 1.

42. Nicolas Abraham and Maria Torok, *The Shell and the Kernel*, trans. Nicholas Rand (Chicago: University of Chicago Press, 1994), 175.

43. Abraham and Torok, *Shell and the Kernel*, 173.

44. Djebar, *Sister to Scheherazade*, 82.

45. Djebar, *Sister to Scheherazade*, 91.

46. Djebar, *Sister to Scheherazade*, 160.

AFTERWORD

1. I refer here to the problematic reading of Paul de Man's work in John Guillory, *Cultural Capital: The Problem of Literary Canon Formation* (Chicago: University of Chicago Press, 1993).

2. See Paul de Man, "Autobiography as De-Facement," in *The Rhetoric of Romanticism* (New York: Columbia University Press, 1984), 67–81. See also, Réda Bensmaïa's important work on prosopopeia in the Maghrebi context in *Experimental Nations, or The Invention of the Maghreb* (Princeton, NJ: Princeton University Press, 2003), 44.

3. Letter from Karl Marx to Arnold Ruge, September 1843, originally published in the *Deutsch-Franzosiche Jahrbuche* in 1844. Also, "For a Ruthless Criticism of Everything Existing," in *The Marx-Engels Reader*, 2nd edition, ed. Robert C. Tucker (New York: Norton, 1972; originally published 1978), 12–15.

4. See Kristin Ross, *Fast Cars, Clean Bodies: Decolonization and the Reordering of French Culture* (Cambridge, MA: MIT Press, 1995), 157–96.

5. I am indebted to Robert Young's *Postcolonialism: A Historical Introduction* (Oxford, UK: Blackwell, 2001, 115–40) for this identification of the exclusions of various internationals. His book is an important intervention into Marxist postcolonial studies that attempt to trace a more leftist genealogy, which is betrayed by so many contemporary postcolonial regimes.

6. Chandra Mohanty, "Cartographies of Struggle," in *Third World Women and the Politics of Feminism*, eds. Chandra Mohanty, Ann Russo, and Lourdes Torres (Bloomington: University of Indiana Press, 1991).

7. Gayatri Chakravorty Spivak's work on the inevitability and danger of complicity has been most instructive here for its recognition of the difficulty of struggling and the need to struggle against such complicity.

Index

Abraham, Nicolas, and Maria Torok, 50, 90, 143, 145, 147–48, 168, 229
Adorno, Theodor, 7, 39
Agamben, Giorgio, 24–25, 43, 47, 54–56, 131
Ageron, Charles-Robert, 151–52
Algeria: constitution (1963), 75; as exemplary case, 15; film industry, 107–8, 136–38; and Indian film, 135; war of independence, 1–2, 3, 10, 26, 69, 79–99, 128, 137, 145, 153, 154, 160, 174, 198, 201, 233
Algeria Charter (1964), 72
Algerian Revolution. *See* Algeria: war of independence
Algiers, 15–17
Algren, Nelson, 80
Alleg, Henri, 82
Allouache, Merzak, 134–35
Alloula, Malek, 21, 22, 125, 138, 279–80n22
Amin, Samir, 153
Amnesia, 8, 11, 12, 13, 18, 28, 97, 142, 143, 147, 159, 164; amnesty as, 11, 248n7
Amnesty, 3, 4, 5, 10–11, 80, 247–49n7; as amnesia, 11, 248n7. *See also* Evian Accords
Anderson, Benedict, 17–18, 107, 143–44
Antigone, 13, 48–51, 260n49
Arabian Nights, The, 211–13, 229, 230, 232, 234
Arabic: language, 70, 72, 75–76, 95–96, 129, 134–35, 162, 187, 263n7, 265n26; script, 63, 87, 196, 209
Arabization, 75–76, 94, 146; and panarabism, 70

Araeen, Rasheed, 205
Architecture, 17, 20
Aristotle, 129–30
Armed Islamic Group (GIA), 68, 71
Armour, Ellen, 61–62
Assimilation, xiv, 146–49, 152–53, 154, 160, 163, 168–69
Asslaoui, Leila, 68, 69
Augustine, Saint, 44–45, 49

Bal, Mieke, 147
Bardo Ethnographic Museum, 151
Barthes, Roland, 5–6, 8, 21–22, 31, 39, 258n21, 259n37. *See also Punctum*
Bartok, Bela, 126
Battle of Algiers, The, 14–15, 106–24, 128, 131–33, 272n27; background, 108–13
Baudelaire, Charles, 139
Baya Mahieddine (Fatma Haddad), 173, 177–78, 179, 196–200, 202–3, 205–10
Beauvoir, Simone de, 73, 79–91, 94, 161
Belhadj, Ali, 68–69
Ben Bella, Ahmed, 75
Ben Bouali, Hassiba, 109, 116
Bengana, Katya, 71
Benhoura, Marguerite Caminat, 198
Benjamin, Walter, 18, 143, 181, 209
Benjedid, Chadli, 18, 69
Bensmaïa, Réda, 127, 293n2
Ben Saddock, 82
Bensoultane, Khadoûdja, Moûni, and Zoura, 150
Bernier, Rosamond, 154
Betts, Raymond, 145
Bhabha, Homi, 114, 117, 124, 216, 219

Biopolitics, 24
Bitat, Rabah, 107
Boudjedra, Rachid, 137, 277–78n80
Bouhired, Djamila, 4, 12, 115
Boupacha, Djamila, 4, 73, 74–75, 79–91, 161
Bouteflika, Abdelaziz, xiii, 247–49n7
Brecht, Bertolt, 140
Breton, André, 174, 176–79, 182, 189–96, 198, 202, 205, 206, 207, 209; *Manifeste des 121*, xv, 174, 176–79, 200–201, 204, 273n34; *Nadja*, 177, 179, 189, 191–96
British colonialism, and politics of language, 76–78
Brunette, Peter, and David Wills, 104
Bussy, Pierre Genty de, 77
Butler, Judith, 51–52, 260n49
Byron, Lord George Gordon, 149

Cabral, Amilcar, 74, 97–98
Camera, as weapon, 108, 113, 114, 121–23, 124, 129
Camus, Albert, 81, 86, 89, 91–93
Capitalism, and colonialism, 8–9
Cartwright, Lisa, and Brian Goldfarb, 52
Catachresis, 51, 117, 121, 138, 166, 169, 216, 274n45
Çelik, Zeynep, 17, 252n37, 274n39
Censorship, 110
Certeau, Michel de, 186
Césaire, Aimé, 201, 203, 206
Charles X, King, 150
Chartier, Roger, 144
Cherry, Deborah, 58
Chikhi, Said, 9, 58
Chion, Michel, 132–34
Citation, 142, 147–49, 150, 154, 155, 159–60, 162, 164, 202, 203, 285n5; Orientalism as, 147; and repetition, 147–49
Cixous, Hélène, 35, 49, 55, 94, 224–25, 260n41
Code d'Indigénat, 9, 10, 144
Communism, 180–82, 240–41; and colonialism, 16, 241; and women, 240–41; and PCF (French Communist Party), 16, 175. See also Marx, Karl; Manifesto
Confession, 85, 194
Crémieux decrees, 46
Critical agency, 28, 99, 135, 210, 235, 237, 240; and justice, xiv, 59; and melancholia, 59–60, 133–34, 169
Croce, Benedetto, 106
Crouq, Louis, 4
Culler, Jonathan, 37
Curtain, 140–43, 153, 165
Cut: defined, 5, 40; and film, 5, 15, 105, 177–22; and frame, xv–xvii, 31–44 *passim*, 235; and justice, xiv, 2, 4, 23, 35, 38–39; and temporality, 14, 211, 222–23, 229; and representation, 6, 8, 11–12, 44, 52, 106, 237–39

De Certeau, Michel, 186–87
De Clérambault, Gaëten, 21
Deconstruction, 33–35, 47, 237
De Gaulle, Charles, 10, 83
Dehane, Kamel, 167–68
Dehumanization, 52
Delacroix, Eugène, 139–42, 149–53, 158, 166–68
De Man, Paul, 51, 238
Democracy, 25–27, 43, 69, 95, 146, 239
Derrida, Jacques, 1, 11–12, 14, 44, 94, 132, 134; and Algeria, 6, 26, 31–35, 44–48, 53–54; and *Antigone*, 49–51; and death, 6; on foreigners, 48–51; on the frame, 39–40, 42–43; on his mother, 6, 44, 48–49; on postcard, 22; on sovereignty, 1, 11–12, 25–26. Works: *Force of Law*, 1, 11–12; *Given Time*, 214, 222–23; *Glas*, 36, 48, 49; *Monolingualism of the Other*, 46–47, 48, 134; *Of Hospitality*, 48, 50; *Specters of Marx*, 168, 257n11
Devi, Mahasweta, 52
Dinarzade, vii, 212–13, 229–30, 232, 234–35
Disposability, 5, 16–17, 19, 20, 22, 23, 25–27

Djebar, Assia, xvi, 20, 94, 123, 125–28, 130, 140; language, 162. Works: "Baya," 205–7; *The Nouba of the Women of Mont Chenoua*, xi, 125–28; *A Sister to Scheherazade*, 213, 229–35; "Women of Algiers in Their Apartment," 140, 149, 161–67; *La Zerda et les chants de l'oubli*, 125
Documentary, 109, 111, 113, 114, 122, 124, 126–28
Dolar, Mladen, 132–34
Drif, Zohra, 115
Duvivier, Julien, 137

Education, 70–78 *passim*
Entelis, John, 76, 264nn12,13
Enunciation, 114, 124, 144, 175
Evian Accords, 3, 80, 247n7
Example, 43–48, 54–56; Algeria as, 15

Face, 21–22, 47, 66, 177, 237–38
Family Code, xiii, 9, 71, 161, 233, 264nn13,14, 282–83n52
Fanon, Frantz, 15–16, 18, 21, 103–8, 117, 122, 136, 240; influence on Gillo Pontecorvo, 15, 116; on radio, 131, 136
Feminism, xiii–xv, 33–35, 58, 73–75, 89–90, 123, 128, 176, 206, 207, 219; internationalist, xiii, 33–35; 73–75, 237–42
Ferenczi, Sandor, 147, 269n81
Film: and decolonization, 104, 121; guerilla cinema, 106–7, 121, 124. *See also* Fourth Cinema; Third Cinema
Film industry, Algerian, 107–8, 136–38; and Indian film, 135
FIS (Islamic Salvation Front), 68–69, 71, 72, 94, 95, 138, 264n12
Flici, Zora, 71
FLN (National Liberation Front), 18, 71, 72, 73, 85, 86, 95, 107, 115, 117, 118, 122, 163
Flournoy, Théodore, xii, 179, 182–89 *passim*
Foreigner(s), 34–35, 40–41, 48–56, 57, 61
Foucault, Michel, 24, 130, 159

Fourth Cinema, 121, 123–29
Frame, 31–35, 36–43, 44–48, 52, 117, 155, 237; cinematic, 39–39, 104; "frame-up," 119; freeze-frame, 118
French colonialism, 144–45, 151–53; and education, 76–79; and politics of language, 76–79
French language, 70–71, 74, 75, 94–96
Freud, Sigmund, 191, 202–3, 205, 209; and *fort und da*, 43, 225, 255; "Mourning and Melancholia," 27, 59, 61, 134, 148, 169; "The Ego and the Id," 60; "Group Psychology and the Analysis of the Ego," 144. *See also* Critical agency; *Nachträglichkeit*

Gabriel, Teshome, 106
Garanger, Marc, 21–22
Garne, Mohamed, 1–2
Gellner, Ernest, 220
Ghezali, Salima, xiii
GIA. *See* Armed Islamic Group
Gift, 47, 89, 194, 209–12, 223, 227–29, 234–35
Gilot, Françoise, 154
Goffman, Erving, 38–39
Gradiva, 202
Gramsci, Antonio, 57, 106
Graves, graveyard, 2, 22, 49
Guerilla cinema. *See under* Film
Gurney, Edmund, 183

Haddam, Anwar, 68
Halimi, Gisèle, 4, 73, 79–80, 87, 88–89, 90, 161
Halimi, Jean-Yves, 4, 5
Harem, 21, 140, 150, 153, 154
Haunting, 69, 74, 90, 91, 93, 94, 96–99, 145, 166, 176, 177, 180–82, 183, 186, 189, 190, 194, 195–96, 209–10, 229, 231–32, 234–35
Hegel, G.W.F., 130; on *Antigone*, 13, 49, 51
Heidegger, Martin, 130
Hélie-Lucas, Marie-Aimée, 74, 123
Hobbes, Thomas, 23–24

Index

Homer, 140. *See also* Penelope
Hospitality, 17, 22, 33–37, 40–44, 47–50, 52, 56, 61–62, 176, 210, 256n7
Human rights, 86, 247

Identification, xiv, 21, 35, 42, 43, 51, 55, 57, 104, 120, 132, 144, 148, 149, 204, 238
Imaginary (Lacanian), 120–21
Imago, 116, 117, 118, 120, 122
Incorporation, 50, 90, 99, 134, 147–48, 269n81
Introjection, 50, 90, 97, 98, 142–43, 147–49, 152, 154, 155, 159, 169, 210, 269n81
Ireland, 212–13, 214, 216, 217, 220, 222, 224–29
Irigaray, Luce, 13–14, 51, 122, 246n5, 255n1, 260n49, 275n56
Islam, xiii, 72, 95, 122; and law, 71–78, 95, 233, 249–50n17; and politics, xiii, 26, 68, 72, 77, 95, 138, 245n2, 263–64n9
Italian neorealism. *See* Neorealism

Jakovsky, Anatole, 199, 203, 288n65
Janet, Pierre, 87
Jews, 35, 46, 47–48, 53–54, 59
Jihad, 70, 95, 263–64n9
Johnson, Kendall, 194
Journalism, 221
Joyce, James, 212–13, 221. Works: "Araby," 213, 214–15, 216–17, 223–29; *Dubliners*, 213, 214; *Ulysses*, 213, 224, 225, 227
Julien, Isaac, 136
Justice, xiv, 1, 11, 13, 17, 28, 69, 73–75, 90, 93, 179, 182, 237–42; postcolonial, 35; to come, 7, 26, 47–48, 80, 93, 94; virtual, 74, 75, 80, 92, 94–99

Kadid, Djalil, 209
Kant, Immanuel, 39–42
Kästner, Erich, 181
Kebir, Rabah, 68
Khatibi, Abdelkebir, 134
Kheira (mother of Mohamed Garne), 1–5, 12–14, 20, 22–23, 27, 246n4

Khora, 13–14
Kim (Rudyard Kipling), 221, 222, 227
Kojève, Alexandre, 130
Korwa Drawings, 188
Kristeva, Julia, 13, 133–34, 212, 217–20, 225

Lacan, Jacques, 51, 132, 136, 146, 251–52n28, 274n45
Lakdari, Samia, 115
Lambert, Elie, 151, 281n35
Language, 184–87, 195, 224, 234–35, 259–60n39; Arabic, 70, 72, 75–76, 96–96, 129, 162, 263n7; French, 70–71, 74, 75, 94–96, 162, 201; glossolalia, 184–87, 190; and law, 73–75, 83–91, 94–96, 179; mother tongue, 79, 95, 134; and the political, 130; politics of, 70–71, 72–75, 75–79, 94–96, 162; and torture, 83–91, 92–93; and trauma, 92–99
La Pointe, Ali, 109, 115, 116, 119, 138, 273n34
Laub, Dori, 123, 268n62, 271n18
Lauretis, Teresa de, 212
Law, 7, 9–10, 13, 73, 233, 283n52; family, 9, 78; and "frame-up," 37–38; and justice, 79, 94–99; and language, 73–75, 83–91, 94–96, 133; Shar'ia, 9, 78, 233, 282–83n52. *See also* Family Code
Lazreg, Marnia, 9, 282–83n52
Le Corbusier, 17
Lemaître, August, 188
Leonard, Garry M., 215
Levinas, Emmanuel, 103, 104, 129, 131, 285n6
Liehm, Mira, 113, 129, 273n32
Lippit, Akira, 133
Loraux, Nicole, 11, 51
Louis-Phillipe, King, 150–51
Luxemburg, Rosa, 8–9

Macaulay, Thoma, 76
Madani, Abassi, 68–69
Maeght, Aimé, 198
Maeght, Galérie, 196, 198, 204, 288n60
Maintenon, Mme. Françoise de, 222–23, 229

Makam al-Shahid (The Martyrs' Monument), 19, 20, 27
Manifesto, 178–79, 179–82, 192–95, 200, 201, 204; *Manifesto of the Communist Party*, 180–82, 194
Marçais, Georges, 151
Marginalization, 8, 9–10, 12, 56, 137
Marrouchi, Mustapha, 53–54
Mars, Mlle., 150
Marx, Karl, 7, 164, 180–82, 194. *See also* Communism; Manifesto
Matisse, Henri, 154–55, 159–61
Mauss, Marcel, 223
Mbembe, Achille, 23–25
Mediene, Benamar, 94
Mediums, 182, 184–96
Melancholia, 12, 26–27, 50–52, 57, 59, 90, 99, 113, 133–34, 142–43, 147, 154, 161, 164, 165–69, 177, 181–82, 191, 209, 210, 234, 233–40, 269n81; as civil war, 60; "colonial," 60–61; "critical," 27, 56
Mellen, Joan, 116, 274n41
Memory, 45, 55, 95, 124–28, 142, 143, 147, 152–54, 166, 200–206, 231, 234; and group, xvi, 19, 73; and history, xvi, 12, 114, 127, 146. *See also* Amnesia; Monuments
Messali Hadj, Ahmed Ben, 8, 10. *See also* Communism
Michaux, Henri, 188
Michelet, Edmond, 81, 86, 89
Mimicry, 115–16
Mirror, 115–18, 121, 122–23, 155, 160, 209
Mirror-stage (Lacanian), 118, 120, 204
Mission civilisatrice, 77, 145
Mitford, Nancy, 220
Monuments, 18, 19, 22. *See also* Makam al-Shahid
Mornay, Count Charles de, 149–50
Mother, 1–5, 6, 22, 27–28, 44, 258n21
Mother tongue. *See under* Language
Mouffok, Ghania, xiii, 9
Mourning, 11, 18–20, 22, 48–52, 59, 142, 147–48, 154, 155, 159–61, 165–69, 200, 205, 210, 231, 234, 269n81
Musu, Antonio, 107

Myers, Frederic W. H., 182–84, 189

Nachträglichkeit (deferred action), 146, 168, 229
Narration, 211, 214–15, 224, 228
Nazis, 24, 54, 81–82, 86, 260n41, 271n18
Necropolitics, 23–25, 27
Negritude, 201, 203
Neorealism, 106, 109, 112–13, 273n32
Niati, Houria, 166
Nichols, Bill, 111
Nietzsche, Friedrich, 217
Nolan, Emer, 221
Nostalgia, 39, 44, 55, 205, 209, 225, 258n22

Oedipus, *see* Sophocles
Orientalism, 149, 175–76, 199, 203, 215, 224; as citation, 147

Parergon, 34, 39, 41, 43, 44, 48, 57, 58
Particularity, 43–48, 52, 54
Pasqua, Charles, 54
Paternity, patrilineal descent, 1–3, 4–5, 28
Patin, Maurice, 82, 89
PCF (French Communist Party), 16
Penelope, 140, 152, 213, 227
People's war, 84, 86, 91–94, 96
Phantoms, 52, 90, 93, 97, 143, 155, 166, 176, 206, 213, 235. *See also* Abraham, Nicolas
Photograph, and photography, 6, 21–22, 31, 44–48, 109, 112, 117, 118–19, 125, 162, 255–56n2, 258n21, 259n37
Piaget, Jean, 205
Picasso, Pablo, 154–66, 198; and Delacroix, 154–61; and Matisse, 154–55, 159–61
Plato, 13, 165
Podmore, Frank, 183
Poirel, M., 139
Pontecorvo, Gillo: *The Battle of Algiers*, 104–20 *passim*, 109–11, 112, 116, 119–20, 131–36 *passim*
Porot, Antoine, 60
Postcard, 20–21, 22–23

Postcolonial studies, and art history, 175–76
Primitivism, 196, 198–200, 202–6, 209
Prosopopeia, 47, 177, 237, 293n2
Psychoanalysis, 190–91, 238; as colonial discipline, 130; and coloniality, 130–31, 200, 202, 209
Punctum, 6, 31, 39, 258n21

Race/racism, 130, 136, 203
RAFD (Algerian Union of Democratic Women), 68, 71
Rape, xiii, 1–2, 3, 70, 83–84, 245n2, 268n71
Realism, 109–13, 124, 128, 142, 149, 150–51, 207
Renan, Ernst, 18, 97, 142, 143, 145, 153, 159, 163, 166
Reparation, 1–4, 5, 11, 12, 98
Representation, 8, 12, 28, 79, 104, 108, 111–12, 114–29, 131, 138, 163, 219, 238; failure of, 69, 71, 75, 80, 84, 89, 94, 96; *vertreten* and *darstellen*, 7, 128, 164, 235
Reproduction, 6, 65–66, 219, 226
Revolution, 9, 69, 73, 93, 181, 204
Ross, Kristin, 239–40
Russell War Crimes Tribunal for Vietnam, 90, 92, 93

Saadi, Yacef, 107–8, 117, 270nn11,12, 271n19, 273n34, 274n42
Sacrifice, 50, 219, 220, 233
Said, Edward, 147, 162, 217, 221
Salmane, Hala, 107
Sartre, Jean-Paul, 14, 81, 82, 84, 86, 89, 90, 92–93, 98
Saussure, Ferdinand de, 184
Scarry, Elaine, 84, 85–88, 204
Scheherazade, vii, 211–13, 229, 230, 231, 232, 234–35
Schliemann, Heinrich, 202
Schmitt, Carl, 254n58
Scott, Walter, 215
Scopophilia, 215, 225
Screen, 122–23

Sedira, Zineb, xi, 62–67
Seraglio. *See* Harem
Sétif Massacre (1945), 10
Signature, 47, 176–77, 178, 179, 187, 190, 192, 196, 207, 209
Silence, 124
Silverman, Kaja, 133
Singularity, 43–48, 52, 53, 54, 55, 210
Smith, Barbara Leigh, 58
Smith, Hélène (Élise-Catherine Müller), 184–90, 191, 194, 209
Socialism (Islamic), xiii, 26, 72
Solanas, Fernando, and Octavio Gettino, 105–7, 121
Solinas, Franco, 112, 132
Sommer, Doris, 112, 269n5
Sophocles: *Oedipus at Colonus*, 48–50. *See also* Antigone, Oedipus
Sound, 129–36
Sovereignty, 23–27, 239, 254n58; and language, 133, 134
Specters, 27, 39, 52, 55, 146, 177, 181–82, 186–87, 189, 194–95, 209–10, 230, 232–35, 285n8; and justice, 12, 68. *See also* Derrida; Manifesto; Phantoms
Spivak, Gayatri Chakravorty, 33, 52, 117, 168
Spurr, David, 221
Stam, Robert, and Louise Spence, 118
Stanley, Henry Morton, 202
Steinberg, Leo, 158, 160, 282n49
Stora, Benjamin, 12, 72, 94, 146
Subaltern, 57, 59, 123, 124, 129, 204
Suleri, Sara, 221
Supplement, 33–66, 238–39, 242; woman as, 5, 33–35, 56, 105. *See also* Derrida; Parergon
Surrealism, 173–77, 178, 182, 190, 192–93, 199–206, 209, 210; and colonialism, 174–75, 199–210
Symbolic (Lacanian), 120

Tamazight, xvii, 70, 75, 125, 187, 196
Terrorism, 14, 70–71, 72, 79, 92, 254n61, 263n9

Testimony, 112, 116, 123, 124, 126, 151, 272–73n30
Théolleyre, Jean-Marc, 91
Third Cinema, 105–7, 112, 114, 118, 121–22, 124, 128–29
Tillion, Germaine, 81
Time: "borrowed," 212, 214, 230, 232, 235; colonial, 221; and the cut, 5–7, 11, 18, 45, 65; "given," 222–23, 234; and nation, 216–22, 226–27, 234–35; and the specter, 39; "suspended," 212, 214, 215, 224–25, 228–29, 232; "women's," 212–23, 217–20, 227, 229, 234
Tlemçani, Salima, xiii
Torture, 70–71, 73, 79–91, 98, 109, 126, 201, 263n9, 272n27
Touboudji, Zohra and Bayha, 150
Trauma, 87, 89–90, 96–99, 108, 123, 124, 145, 146–47, 162, 164, 168–69, 233, 234; and language, 92–99, 146
Trial, mock, 68–70, 74, 75, 93, 95–97
Truth and Reconciliation Commission (South Africa), 97–98

Ululation, 133

Valente, Joseph, 212

Vautier, René, 108
Veil, 21, 22, 66, 69, 103–4, 114–18, 152–53, 161–62, 163
Velasquez, Diego, 159–60
Vergès, Jacques, 11–12
Vichy regime, 54, 81, 202
"Virile war," 2, 56, 175, 242
Voice, 125, 131–36, 235; mother's, 133; women's, 132

Wayne, Michael, 121–22
Wicke, Jennifer, 227
Woman: black (in Delacroix), 140–42, 152, 158, 281n35; as image, 122–23; as supplement, 5, 33–35, 56, 105
Women, bodies, 79–91, 103–4, 115, 118, 120, 125–26, 166, 235
Women's labor, 4, 8, 65–66
World War II, 10, 46, 59, 81, 84, 91, 93–94

Yeats, William Butler, 211, 217
Young, Robert, 53, 293n5

Zéroual, Liamine, 71
Zola, Émile, 68

Cultural Memory | *in the Present*

Gil Anidjar, *Semites: Race, Religion, Literature*

Esther Peeren, *Intersubjectivities and Popular Culture: Bakhtin and Beyond*

Eyal Peretz, *Becoming Visionary: Brian De Palma's Cinematic Education of the Senses*

Diana Sorensen, *A Turbulent Decade Remembered: Scenes from the Latin American Sixties*

Hubert Damisch, *A Childhood Memory by Piero della Francesca*

Dana Hollander, *Exemplarity and Chosenness: Rosenzweig and Derrida on the Nation of Philosophy*

Asja Szafraniec, *Beckett, Derrida, and the Event of Literature*

Sara Guyer, *Romanticism After Auschwitz*

Alison Ross, *The Aesthetic Paths of Philosophy: Presentation in Kant, Heidegger, Lacoue-Labarthe, and Nancy*

Gerhard Richter, *Thought-Images: Frankfurt School Writers' Reflections from Damaged Life*

Bella Brodzki, *Can These Bones Live? Translation, Survival, and Cultural Memory*

Rodolphe Gasché, *The Honor of Thinking: Critique, Theory, Philosophy*

Brigitte Peucker, *The Material Image: Art and the Real in Film*

Natalie Melas, *All the Difference in the World: Postcoloniality and the Ends of Comparison*

Jonathan Culler, *The Literary in Theory*

Michael G. Levine, *The Belated Witness: Literature, Testimony, and the Question of Holocaust Survival*

Jennifer A. Jordan, *Structures of Memory: Understanding German Change in Berlin and Beyond*

Christoph Menke, *Reflections of Equality*

Marlène Zarader, *The Unthought Debt: Heidegger and the Hebraic Heritage*

Jan Assmann, *Religion and Cultural Memory: Ten Studies*

David Scott and Charles Hirschkind, *Powers of the Secular Modern: Talal Asad and His Interlocutors*

Gyanendra Pandey, *Routine Violence: Nations, Fragments, Histories*

James Siegel, *Naming the Witch*

J. M. Bernstein, *Against Voluptuous Bodies: Late Modernism and the Meaning of Painting*

Theodore W. Jennings, Jr., *Reading Derrida / Thinking Paul: On Justice*

Richard Rorty and Eduardo Mendieta, *Take Care of Freedom and Truth Will Take Care of Itself: Interviews with Richard Rorty*

Jacques Derrida, *Paper Machine*

Renaud Barbaras, *Desire and Distance: Introduction to a Phenomenology of Perception*

Jill Bennett, *Empathic Vision: Affect, Trauma, and Contemporary Art*

Ban Wang, *Illuminations from the Past: Trauma, Memory, and History in Modern China*

James Phillips, *Heidegger's Volk: Between National Socialism and Poetry*

Frank Ankersmit, *Sublime Historical Experience*

István Rév, *Retroactive Justice: Prehistory of Post-Communism*

Paola Marrati, *Genesis and Trace: Derrida Reading Husserl and Heidegger*

Krzysztof Ziarek, *The Force of Art*

Marie-José Mondzain, *Image, Icon, Economy: The Byzantine Origins of the Contemporary Imaginary*

Cecilia Sjöholm, *The Antigone Complex: Ethics and the Invention of Feminine Desire*

Jacques Derrida and Elisabeth Roudinesco, *For What Tomorrow . . . : A Dialogue*

Elisabeth Weber, *Questioning Judaism: Interviews by Elisabeth Weber*

Jacques Derrida and Catherine Malabou, *Counterpath: Traveling with Jacques Derrida*

Martin Seel, *Aesthetics of Appearing*

Nanette Salomon, *Shifting Priorities: Gender and Genre in Seventeenth-Century Dutch Painting*

Jacob Taubes, *The Political Theology of Paul*

Jean-Luc Marion, *The Crossing of the Visible*

Eric Michaud, *The Cult of Art in Nazi Germany*

Anne Freadman, *The Machinery of Talk: Charles Peirce and the Sign Hypothesis*

Stanley Cavell, *Emerson's Transcendental Etudes*

Stuart McLean, *The Event and Its Terrors: Ireland, Famine, Modernity*

Beate Rössler, ed., *Privacies: Philosophical Evaluations*

Bernard Faure, *Double Exposure: Cutting Across Buddhist and Western Discourses*

Alessia Ricciardi, *The Ends of Mourning: Psychoanalysis, Literature, Film*

Alain Badiou, *Saint Paul: The Foundation of Universalism*

Gil Anidjar, *The Jew, the Arab: A History of the Enemy*

Jonathan Culler and Kevin Lamb, eds., *Just Being Difficult? Academic Writing in the Public Arena*

Jean-Luc Nancy, *A Finite Thinking*, edited by Simon Sparks

Theodor W. Adorno, *Can One Live after Auschwitz? A Philosophical Reader*, edited by Rolf Tiedemann

Patricia Pisters, *The Matrix of Visual Culture: Working with Deleuze in Film Theory*

Andreas Huyssen, *Present Pasts: Urban Palimpsests and the Politics of Memory*

Talal Asad, *Formations of the Secular: Christianity, Islam, Modernity*

Dorothea von Mücke, *The Rise of the Fantastic Tale*

Marc Redfield, *The Politics of Aesthetics: Nationalism, Gender, Romanticism*

Emmanuel Levinas, *On Escape*

Dan Zahavi, *Husserl's Phenomenology*

Rodolphe Gasché, *The Idea of Form: Rethinking Kant's Aesthetics*

Michael Naas, *Taking on the Tradition: Jacques Derrida and the Legacies of Deconstruction*

Herlinde Pauer-Studer, ed., *Constructions of Practical Reason: Interviews on Moral and Political Philosophy*

Jean-Luc Marion, *Being Given That: Toward a Phenomenology of Givenness*

Theodor W. Adorno and Max Horkheimer, *Dialectic of Enlightenment*

Ian Balfour, *The Rhetoric of Romantic Prophecy*

Martin Stokhof, *World and Life as One: Ethics and Ontology in Wittgenstein's Early Thought*

Gianni Vattimo, *Nietzsche: An Introduction*

Jacques Derrida, *Negotiations: Interventions and Interviews, 1971-1998*, ed. Elizabeth Rottenberg

Brett Levinson, *The Ends of Literature: The Latin American "Boom" in the Neoliberal Marketplace*

Timothy J. Reiss, *Against Autonomy: Cultural Instruments, Mutualities, and the Fictive Imagination*

Hent de Vries and Samuel Weber, eds., *Religion and Media*

Niklas Luhmann, *Theories of Distinction: Re-Describing the Descriptions of Modernity*, ed. and introd. William Rasch

Johannes Fabian, *Anthropology with an Attitude: Critical Essays*

Michel Henry, *I Am the Truth: Toward a Philosophy of Christianity*

Gil Anidjar, *"Our Place in Al-Andalus": Kabbalah, Philosophy, Literature in Arab-Jewish Letters*

Hélène Cixous and Jacques Derrida, *Veils*

F. R. Ankersmit, *Historical Representation*

F. R. Ankersmit, *Political Representation*

Elissa Marder, *Dead Time: Temporal Disorders in the Wake of Modernity (Baudelaire and Flaubert)*

Reinhart Koselleck, *The Practice of Conceptual History: Timing History, Spacing Concepts*

Niklas Luhmann, *The Reality of the Mass Media*

Hubert Damisch, *A Theory of /Cloud/: Toward a History of Painting*

Jean-Luc Nancy, *The Speculative Remark: (One of Hegel's bon mots)*

Jean-François Lyotard, *Soundproof Room: Malraux's Anti-Aesthetics*

Jan Patočka, *Plato and Europe*

Hubert Damisch, *Skyline: The Narcissistic City*

Isabel Hoving, *In Praise of New Travelers: Reading Caribbean Migrant Women Writers*

Richard Rand, ed., *Futures: Of Jacques Derrida*

William Rasch, *Niklas Luhmann's Modernity: The Paradoxes of Differentiation*

Jacques Derrida and Anne Dufourmantelle, *Of Hospitality*

Jean-François Lyotard, *The Confession of Augustine*

Kaja Silverman, *World Spectators*

Samuel Weber, *Institution and Interpretation: Expanded Edition*

Jeffrey S. Librett, *The Rhetoric of Cultural Dialogue: Jews and Germans in the Epoch of Emancipation*

Ulrich Baer, *Remnants of Song: Trauma and the Experience of Modernity in Charles Baudelaire and Paul Celan*

Samuel C. Wheeler III, *Deconstruction as Analytic Philosophy*

David S. Ferris, *Silent Urns: Romanticism, Hellenism, Modernity*

Rodolphe Gasché, *Of Minimal Things: Studies on the Notion of Relation*

Sarah Winter, *Freud and the Institution of Psychoanalytic Knowledge*

Samuel Weber, *The Legend of Freud: Expanded Edition*

Aris Fioretos, ed., *The Solid Letter: Readings of Friedrich Hölderlin*

J. Hillis Miller / Manuel Asensi, *Black Holes / J. Hillis Miller; or, Boustrophedonic Reading*

Miryam Sas, *Fault Lines: Cultural Memory and Japanese Surrealism*

Peter Schwenger, *Fantasm and Fiction: On Textual Envisioning*

Didier Maleuvre, *Museum Memories: History, Technology, Art*

Jacques Derrida, *Monolingualism of the Other; or, The Prosthesis of Origin*

Andrew Baruch Wachtel, *Making a Nation, Breaking a Nation: Literature and Cultural Politics in Yugoslavia*

Niklas Luhmann, *Love as Passion: The Codification of Intimacy*

Mieke Bal, ed., *The Practice of Cultural Analysis: Exposing Interdisciplinary Interpretation*

Jacques Derrida and Gianni Vattimo, eds., *Religion*

The authorized representative in the EU for product safety and compliance is:
Mare Nostrum Group
B.V Doelen 72
4831 GR Breda
The Netherlands

www.ingramcontent.com/pod-product-compliance
Lightning Source LLC
Chambersburg PA
CBHW021802220426
43662CB00006B/155